# "MAKING HOME"

*We [the gods] have not taken away any of your original integrity because no one can do that. But we have badly distorted one part of your reality. Since we journey so far, we are great warriors, and we are very male. You are meant to Make Home and live in harmony with all species on Earth. To resonate with Gaia, you need to be very female. We have forced you to be too warlike, too compulsive, too focused in linear space and time, too fearful. Now these incompatible tendencies are exploding your cells. Luckily your genetic matrix also has stellar contributions, and now this stellar-cellular matrix must awaken. You must interact with other dimensions to heal.*

**Also by Barbara Hand Clow**

*Chiron: Rainbow Bridge Between the Inner and Outer Planets* (1987)

*Liquid Light of Sex: Understanding Your Key Life Passages* (1991)

THE MIND CHRONICLES TRILOGY:

*Eye of the Centaur: A Visionary Guide into Past Lives* (1986)

*Heart of the Christos: Starseeding from the Pleiades* (1989)

*Signet of Atlantis: War in Heaven Bypass* (1992)

# THE PLEIADIAN AGENDA

## A New Cosmology for the Age of Light

Introduced by Brian Swimme

### Barbara Hand Clow

BEAR & COMPANY
PUBLISHING
ROCHESTER, VERMONT

Bear & Company
One Park Street
Rochester, Vermont 05767
www.InnerTraditions.com

Bear & Company is a division of Inner Traditions International

**Library of Congress Cataloging-in-Publication Data**

Clow, Barbara Hand, 1943–
    The Pleiadian agenda : a new cosmology for the age of light /
Barbara Hand Clow.
        p.  cm.
    Includes bibliographical references.
    ISBN 1-879181-30-4
    1. Pleiades—Miscellanea.  2. Spiritual life.  3. Cosmology—Miscellanea.
I. Title
BF1999.C593    1996
133.9'—dc20
                                                                    95-35401
                                                                       CIP


Printed in the United States

12  11  10  9  8  7


Cover design: © 1995 by Lightbourne Images
Interior page design and typography: Melinda Belter
Text illustrations: Melinda Belter
Author photograph: Malcolm MacKinnon
Editing: Gerry Clow, Sonya Moore, and John Kaminski

# Contents

ACKNOWLEDGMENTS — xi

FOREWORD — xiii

PREFACE — xix

CHAPTER ONE: THE COSMIC PARTY — 3
  *Invitations to the Cosmic Party—5*
  *The Story of the Photon Band and the Galactic Night*
    *and the Alchemy of Nine Dimensions—26*

CHAPTER TWO: THE PHOTON BAND — 41
  *The Photon Band and the Process of Transmutation—41*
  *The Photon Band, the Mayan Calendar, and the Pleiades—46*
  *Snake Medicine and the Mayan Calendar—50*
  *Elementals and the Telluric Realm—51*
  *Feelings and the Pleiadians—53*
  *The Danger of Beliefs and Groups—55*
  *Healing and Orgasms During the Photonic Activation—57*
  *The Galactic Information Highway and the Sirians—61*
  *Making Home—63*
  *Your Sacred Altar and Your Ka—69*

CHAPTER THREE: ALCHEMY OF NINE DIMENSIONS — 77
  *Finding Your Monad—81*
  *Abraham and Uranium—84*
  *Relations Between the Anunnaki and Sirians—90*
  *Anubis and Your Bodies—96*
  *Higher-Dimensional View of Radiation—97*
  *Enoch and Radiation—102*
  *Comet Shoemaker-Levy Hits Jupiter, July 1994—104*

CHAPTER FOUR: THE LIZARDS AND THE ROMAN CHURCH — 105
  *King Lizard Speaks about Kundalini—106*
  *Doctor Lizard and God—114*
  *Satya and the Cosmic Restart Button—120*
  *Meditations from Satya for Opening Dimensional Portals—130*

CHAPTER FIVE: THE STORY OF GODDESS ALCHEMY                    135
    *Satya and Female Alchemy—135*
    *The Moon Speaks—136*
    *How to Manifest the Physical Reality that You Desire:*
        *Lunar Manifestation Technique—140*
    *Satya and the Awakening in the Blood—147*
    *Creating Realities from the Future—153*
    *A Deeper Exploration of Blood Codes—154*
    *Christ and the Activation of the Plant Realm—157*
    *The Multidimensional Explosion—161*

CHAPTER SIX: LUCIFER'S DILEMMA AND THE POWER OF ANU          169
    *Sixth-Dimensional Light Geometry—169*
    *Lucifer and the Anunnaki Diversion—172*
    *Anu, The Great Sumerian God—177*
    *Satya and the Chosen People—190*
    *Isaiah and the Egyptian Temple of the Reptiles—191*
    *Khem, the Reptilian Temple of the Nile Delta—193*

CHAPTER SEVEN: ALCYONE LIBRARY AND TZOLK'IN—KEEPER OF TIME   203
    *Reading the Mind of the Sun—207*
    *Satya Takes You into the Alcyone Library—211*
    *The Nine-Dimensional Lenses of the Illuminated World—213*
    *Photons as Popcorn Popping in the Pleiades and Gaia—222*
    *Anubis Tells the Real Story of Christ—224*
    *Tzolk'in Weaves the Story of Time—229*

APPENDIX A: *Astrological Transits, 1972 to the End of the*
    *Mayan Great Calendar, December 21, 2012 A.D.*          247

APPENDIX B: *The Timing of the Solar System's Entry into the Photon Band*   255

APPENDIX C: *Galactic Precipitation: Metonic Cycle of the Fifth World*      261

APPENDIX D: *The Sirius Star System and the Ancient Records of Orion*       271

NOTES                                                        281

GLOSSARY                                                     293

INDEX                                                        299

ABOUT THE AUTHOR                                             305

# *Illustrations*

FIGURE 1: PHOTON BAND AND PRECESSION OF THE EQUINOXES     27

FIGURE 2: THE SIX POLARITIES     29

FIGURE 3: 7D GALACTIC PHOTON BANDS     31

FIGURE 4: THE ALCYONE SPIRAL     33

FIGURE 5: THE SOLAR SYSTEM ENTERING THE PHOTON BAND     37

FIGURE 6: ANUBIS GUARDS THE GALACTIC NIGHT     39

FIGURE 7: THE 13/20 *AHAU CAN*     51

FIGURE 8: THE GALACTIC BRIDGE     68

FIGURE 9: THE HUMAN CHAKRAS     71

FIGURE 10: THE CANOPY OF LIGHT     73

FIGURE 11: THE EIGHT-POINTED STAR—NIBIRU     122

FIGURE 12: VERTICAL AXIS     163

FIGURE 13: THE ALCYONE LIBRARY     212

FIGURE 14: THE GREAT STORY OF TIME     228

FIGURE 15: GALACTIC PRECIPITATION     262

*To Gerry Clow*

# Acknowledgments

This book would never have been written without the incredible support given to me by Gerry Clow. Gerry was the main editor on this book, and his extraordinary skill and dedication is what made it possible to express such a broad and difficult range of material.

Thank you, Brian Swimme, for introducing this book. As we transit from the heliocentric mind to the galactic mind, you have always been with me during this radical shift in consciousness.

I channeled this book to Gerry Clow, John Kaminski, and Audrey Peterson. Thank you, John, for transcribing the tapes and assisting with editing, and for being on guard for any untruths or misplaced emphases. Audrey, thank you for your openness, your love, and your vision of the light, and I thank the three of you for being willing to go on another wild ride with the Pleiadians!

I would like to thank the people who helped me the most to clarify my Pleiadian voice. They are Barbara Marciniak, Ken Carey, Lyssa Royal, Wendy Munro, Tom Cratsley, and Tobi and Teri Weiss of Power Places Tours. Thank you Jeanne Scoville and filmmaker David Drewry, for your unfailing ability to see the importance of this work in time to film it in Egypt in 1994.

I would like to thank the people who have helped me understand the Mayan Great Calendar. They are Hunbatz Men, Alberto Ruz Buenfil, José and Lloydine Argüelles, Tony Shearer, John Major Jenkins, Terence McKenna, Stephen McFadden, Hugh Harleston, and José Diaz-Bolio.

I would like to thank all the Bears for supporting me on this project. I am deeply grateful to Mindy Belter for her excellent design and illustrations, Sonya Moore for her careful proofing, Lightbourne Images for an exquisite cover design, and Malcolm MacKinnon for a great photo.

Thank you Carol White, Audrey Peterson, and Nicki Scully for helping me see the elementals; Dawn Erhart Wingard for keeping me in my body while I was working too hard; and Barbara Morgan for the gardens. I might not have always been so clear about the equality of animals, insects, rocks, humans, and stars without the truthful gentleness of my four children, Tom, Matthew, Christopher, and Elizabeth; thank you for sharing Earth with me.

# *Foreword*

## *Entering The Universe*

BARBARA HAND CLOW'S NEW BOOK, *THE PLEIADIAN AGENDA,* CAN BEST BE approached by seeing it within the traditional cosmological task of learning how to "enter the universe." For most modern people, this may seem to be a strange task, even an entirely trivial one. After all, where is the universe but all around us? So what could be easier than entering it? But, in fact, this challenge of entering the universe is an ancient one indeed. And we humans in particular are challenged in a way unique as a species because we do not rely solely on our genetic inheritance. Other animals are spared all this. At least in most situations, the instructions for how to behave are right there at hand.

We have an entirely different challenge. We've amassed storehouses of information concerning the universe and how it operates, and all of this is to be drawn upon to learn how to act intelligently in the universe.

*To enter the universe* simply means learning the ways of the wider world and how a person is to relate to all this. The first humans felt this to be a deep and pressing challenge. Possibly for as long as 300,000 years, and certainly for at least 40,000 years, humans gathered in the night and pondered the ways of the universe in order to find their way through the Great World. No matter what continent humans lived on, no matter what culture, no matter what era, they gathered in the night—around the fire of the African plains, in the caves of the Eurasian forests, under the brilliant night sky of the Australian land mass, in the long houses of North America—and there they told the sacred stories of the universe, and of what it takes to live a noble human life.

I say that every culture did this, but that of course is not exactly true. For we contemporary humans do not. Modern humanity seems to be the first culture to break with this primordial tradition of celebrating the mysteries of the universe. What can it mean that we have abandoned something that's worked for 300,000 years?

Modern industrial society does it differently. Questions of ultimate meaning are dealt with not in caves or on the open plains, but in the churches, mosques, and temples. Here each weekend billions of humans gather to reflect on their relationship with the divine. In all these millions of weekly religious ceremonies, so essential to the health and spirituality of humanity as a whole, one will find a diversity of religious celebrations, but one rarely finds any serious contemplation of *the universe,* where by "universe" I mean simply the universe of stars and topsoil and amphibians and mammals and insects and rivers and wetlands.

Thus we have the contemporary impasse: contemporary religions have come to focus primarily on the relationships of humans with each other and with the divine, and have pushed aside the ancient questions of how to enter the universe; whereas science, on the other hand, even though it does focus on the universe, teaches a universe that has no sacred meaning or destiny, and avoids speaking of the essential role of humans in the universe.

Now we come to Barbara Hand Clow's latest book. From beginning to end she is concerned with the universe as a sacred realm, a universe of matter and energy and information but also a universe filled with spiritual beings. And hers is a universe with a sacred destiny. As well, and again from beginning to end, Clow is focused on the role that humans have to play in this cosmic drama. She writes that she will help each one of us "remember how to swim in the stars." She promises that she will help us "activate our cosmic selves." In exact opposition to the nihilistic postmodern temper that haunts most modern universities, she speaks of the central role humans, and Earth as a whole, have to play, for she writes, ". . . you are the bodies for all [cosmic] dimensions as Earth enters the Age of Aquarius."

Nor does she commit the besetting sin of even the best of classical western philosophy which extols the human while denigrating the entire nonhuman world. For Clow, all life is sacred, and every species plays a vital role. In a beautiful phrase she writes that "animals are the source for the star wisdom of humans." And not just our close kin, the mammals. In her vision, the reptiles too have a special power that we must respect, as when she writes that "we reptiles who remain in Earth are the ones who hold this incredible [Gaian] intelligence. We hold this knowledge right within our physical bodies."

Before we proceed further, we need to stop and ask a very simple question: If our young were initiated in the universe via such a cosmology, one that held the universe to be sacred, one that showed to the human a vast and cosmic role, one that adored animals and other forms of life, would our children be condemned to grow up and destroy Earth, as so many of us have done?

If we are ever to fashion a culture grounded in a living cosmology, we need to know why visions such as Clow's are inevitably going to be dismissed by the "World Management Team."

Humanity lost speculative cosmology five centuries ago when the new scientific enterprise destroyed medieval humanity's common understanding of the universe. In 1543, Nicolaus Copernicus, an obscure Polish astronomer, announced that it was the Sun, not Earth, that was the center of the world. Of course, we now accept this as true, but we need to remember that the entire culture was based on the assumption that Earth was the center. And one result of this transformation was to cast all speculative cosmological works, works similar to the one you find in your hands, to cast them all into the trash bin. Let me explain how this happened.

Copernicus, more than most anyone, was aware of how dangerous his research was. As a canon of the Church, he refused to publish his findings until he was on his death bed. And what he feared would happen indeed did take place: the scientific content of his research was accepted, and the cosmological orientation of the entire medieval world was slowly but decisively rejected. The modern world, based on a split between science and religion, had its beginning here. Henceforth, religion would be increasingly viewed as a repository of truths concerning the behavior necessary to get to heaven; science, on the other hand, would come to be understood as a method for discovering the truth about the physical universe, a universe no longer considered to be filled with spiritual realities, but composed entirely of crass matter.

What we need to appreciate here is that Copernicus's discovery of the truth concerning Earth's motion around the Sun also put humans at odds with *how truth is apprehended.* For maybe a hundred thousand years, humans held that Earth was in the center of the universe. Those earlier humans would have been deeply confused by any suggestion that the Sun resided at the center, and that Earth was spinning around it.

For the naive or pre-Copernican mind, the Sun is this hot thing up in the sky that travels around Earth every day. We can't tell how big it is but it couldn't be that big, because you can block it out entirely with just your thumb. Earth is, in contrast, the whole world! It's a place of great oceans and tidal waves and vast mountain ranges and frightening hurricanes! Of blizzards and avalanches!

The greatness of Copernicus is that with his book he provided a process by which the most advanced thinkers of Europe could come to grasp this new, subtle, and amazing truth: the Sun resides in the center of the solar system while Earth and Mars and Jupiter and all the planets circle around it. But the unfortunate consequence was to convince us that our feelings, and our intuitions, were not to be trusted. Henceforth all such work relying largely on these modes of knowing—and certainly these are the primary modes in Clow's *Pleiadian Agenda*—were to be regarded as senseless, stupid, worthless, and a waste of time.

How then is one to approach speculative visionary work, especially this work in hand? I think there are three basic approaches:

First would be that of modern mainstream science, which would regard all discussion based on astrology or galactic attunement as worthless. This approach would characterize most scientists today.

The second approach would be to regard such a work as literally and scientifically true, in much the same way that some people regard the Bible as literally and scientifically true. This approach, perhaps even more popular that the first, has the unfortunate defect of putting its adherents at odds with science, which is our culture's most powerful consensual approach to the truth.

The third approach, one hinted at by the text itself, is to think of the work as belonging to the realm of poetry. In order to understand how poetic vision can be true, but true in a way distinct from the truth of science, I would like to offer the following both as an explanation, and as an image, for *The Pleiadian Agenda* as a whole:

Imagine that moment when Beethoven was first playing his "Ode to Joy" in an empty room. But the room was not so empty if we consider all lifeforms, in particular the single-celled prokaryotes that were, let's imagine, floating in the room's air. Undoubtedly—if we can grant a single-celled organism the slightest drop of sentience—such prokaryotes were unable to appreciate the music that was filling the room. But what if, out of the billions of these creatures, just one of them was a genius? What if, instead of simply allowing the musical vibrations to flutter through her unnoticed, she awoke to the presence of something vast?

Surely what she would experience would be only the most miserable cipher of the full reality of Beethoven's music, but isn't it conceivable that she would be jolted by the strange sense that she was suddenly pervaded by the magnificence far beyond the usual activities of her day?

If a human has the sensitivity to respond to an intelligence sweeping through the Milky Way Galaxy—an intelligence that has organized three hundred billion stars for ten billion years, an intelligence whose form and functioning lies outside anything yet articulated by the careful, empirical techniques of modern astronomy—one can imagine such a human would have to create a wild, poetic imagery. If the neocortex or some other region of the central nervous system has been set ablaze by a vast cybernetic or galactic mind, one would expect to hear not the careful and safe statements of yesterday's truth, but the wild and speculative visions of Barbara Hand Clow in *The Pleiadian Agenda*.

Brian Swimme, Ph.D.
August 1995

*Brian Swimme is a cosmologist and a gravitational physicist at the California Institute of Integral Studies. He is the author of* The Universe is a Green Dragon *and coauthor, with Thomas Berry, of* The Universe Story.

# Preface

## Reality Splitting

THE BOOK YOU HAVE IN YOUR HANDS WILL BE MORE COMPREHENSIBLE IF you have an understanding of how the Pleiadians have been communicating with humans. Many indigenous people of Earth have claimed Pleiadian origins, and then in the 1970s Billy Meier of Switzerland reported direct contact with Pleiadian ships and individuals. In the 1980s, Ken Carey published *Starseed Transmissions,* a remarkably clear and inspiring breakthrough of Pleiadian intelligence; Lyssa Royal and myself were experiencing direct transmissions; Barbara Marciniak suddenly opened a very potent channel of Pleiadian thought in 1988; and many other channels were reporting similar veins of teaching coming from this star system. *The Pleiadian Agenda* comes primarily through Satya of Alcyone, a very forceful Pleiadian wisdom figure who is closely identified with the Goddess.

When the Pleiadians first began to impulse me as an adult in 1984, I heard their transmissions for months in Morse Code! Gradually their voices clarified, but the next thing I experienced was a great deal of confusion about the way they discuss Earth sciences, human behavior, and spiritual evolution. To put it simply, what they were saying about us was like trying to decode light going through a kaleidoscope; their view of us is multifaceted and geometrically interrelated and it can be difficult to translate. In the late 1980s, their complex point of view seemed jumbled and confused to me, but I kept on transmitting their perspective because what they had to say was more fascinating than anything I was hearing on Earth. I have to admit, this was not an easy time for me. It was often very psychologically complex because the more I got to know the Pleiadians, the more I realized that their voice was actually my own inner child voice; these wisdom teachings coming in stronger and more clearly were forcing me to remember my true and nonimprinted natal self. As I saw that, I began to remember myself all the way back to when I was four months old, when a whirlwind swished the curtain next to my crib and the beautiful small blue beings came to visit me. As hard as it was, I knew I was finally totally integrating this presence, and then Satya began speaking to me in 1992. As a result of her appearance, I wrote *The Pleiadian Agenda* in anticipation of a *reality splitting* that the Pleiadians say is coming in 1998. Satya has a very clear voice, as you will see, and so, it's time for Satya to just speak with you.

"I am Satya, director of a large group of Pleiadians. I am the keeper of the records of Alcyone, the central Pleiadian library, and by developing a direct conduit through herself to you, Barbara Hand Clow has also improved her own communications skills. Therefore, this book offers a wide range of Pleiadian entities and groups who all have a great big agenda about getting certain information to you—*The Pleiadian Agenda.* The Pleiadians are very anxious to reach you, and so they pack themselves into your thoughts and rush through your portals. John Kaminski attended the channelings when *The Pleiadian Agenda* was coming in during 1994 and 1995, and he commented, 'The Pleiadians are kind of like bees. You see them around so often that eventually they've built something you hadn't noticed them building.' Now the beehive would like to address you as a group."

"Actually, we Pleiadians have built quite a nest, and when we inhabit our vehicle's body, she feels a special kind of excitement that is just like a buzzing hive of bees. She has learned to recognize this frequency and use it as a *tool,* and if you want to know how she did it, read her trilogy, *The Mind Chronicles.* She has discovered through much experience that her own perceptual range has been greatly increased by working with us, and now she can *see* the nature of the coming reality split. To choose to participate in the newly evolved world, you will need to understand and consciously work with the nine-dimensional vertical axis described in this book. During her own personal training phase, she became dedicated to opening our records for you. She discovered that our wisdom improves your lives, answers your deep questions, intensifies your feelings, sharpens your minds, and leads you to selecting evolution instead of devolution. *The Pleiadian Agenda* is finally complete, and we would like to offer you our Pleiadian reflections as a group on what Barbara Hand Clow has managed to glean from us.

"You may wonder, what is a cosmology? According to Earth astronomers, a cosmology studies the nature of the origin, structure, and space-time relationships of the universe. Well, we Pleiadians will go much far-ther. To us, a cosmology is a story of existence in time that awakens your cellular memory. What is cellular memory? Cellular memory is the memory of all that has ever occurred in the universe that is encoded right in the cells in your body. You already know about this *New Cosmology for the Age of Light,* and all you need now is to hear the story told again.

"Why would you want to remember your story again? Of course, it might be creative and fun—and it is—but the real reason for telling the story now is so you can make a choice about which reality you will inhabit when your world splits into two paths in 1998. We can see the movies of these two worlds playing in the cells of your bodies. Since we believe that each one of you deserves total choice, we have come into your reality to describe these two paths to you. People, you would be amazed if you knew how difficult it is for us to come so far to spend so much time with you. After all, we have lovely homes of white marble in a land of greenery and exquisite clear water and air. Our children are beautiful and love us, and our animals enjoy our presence. We have come all this distance and time because if you do not have a choice, then you have no free will, and then the essential basis of the universe—freedom of consciousness—ends. If that ended, no one would choose existence any more, and all motion would cease. Of course, you cannot imagine that, but we have contem-plated exactly that apocalypse and played it out, and it is an unacceptable probable reality, which you could walk into if you remain asleep. Seems easier to just roust you out of bed! We can assure you of one thing; the nest we've made is big enough and and we buzz loudly enough so that every one of you will be able to make a clear choice. As we peer into the two worlds that will be Earth during the Age of Aquarius, it is easy to describe and discuss the qualities of each one.

"In one reality—Zombie Land—there you are staring into your tele-vision in a trance with your brain being filled with images of news and sto-ries that are not real. What's *real* is something going on in the now while you are there. We see you playing with virtual reality with your brain impulsing the machine to create any image that stimulates your urges to possess things or have sex. As you look at the images, you get stimulated to go shopping or have sex or eat. You put your food in a microwave which vibrates its essence into matter that fits your taste receptors, and you eat it as your body settles down for a few hours. The individuals in your house as well as those you socialize with all fit the latest fashion fads—they are the perfect outgrowth of what *you* want to look at, yet you feel absolutely nothing about any one of them. If asked to describe their facial features, you would not be able to. You have no interaction with politics or world affairs because such things only exist only in the television. You rarely travel because you think it's dangerous, and if you do travel, you move from one isolated hotel to another into rooms with televisions that are better than the one at home because they have the sex channel. You don't have to react to or change anything or anyone. As for thinking, the computer does all that for you, since it has more left-brain neuronal capacity than any human can have. You have no way of knowing whether the data it contains describes anything real, since you do not go out and study real things and observe your own reactions. As for your soul, your desire for freedom of choice has so atrophied that you are convinced you have one lifetime, and you are in the middle of it now. Each one of your days is another opportunity to satisfy as many desires as possible while you experience absolutely no stress. You are a Zombie that will be in your body only as long as you are useful to somebody who is in control, while the expenses you incur make a profit for somebody. Who is in control? The World Management Team—powerful forces in banking, media, government, and business—who are exposed in this book.

"Before we describe the other potential path, we will tell you how the Zombies were created, since the technology they've embodied is the same technology that evolved beings either totally reject or use differently. Technology can be a means or an end, and the reality splitting will emerge out of which is chosen. We have alluded to four different technologies in the paragraph above—television, microwave ovens, artificial light, and computers. There are other ones impulsing you in one direction or another, but we Pleiadians feel that these are the four that are triggering the unseen and unknown dimensions so thoroughly described in this book. We will even say that this book had to be written now just to help you realize what is happening to you as a result of your technology; The Pleiadian Agenda is a manual on how to walk out of technological Zombie Land. These are the technologies that are accelerating you into the critical leap—multidimensional merge-and-purge. We will tell you one thing for sure: get conscious about these things or you will be or already are one of the Zombies.

"What is technology? To many of you, technology makes fun gadgets that save you time and work, and your main consideration is whether you can pay for them or not. To us Pleiadians, ideally, technologies are devices you invent that are an outward manifestation of some unknown power within yourselves; you invent them to find a way to make your own inner power comprehensible. In your interaction with a technology, you are activating and identifying something inside yourself, yet you appear to be almost totally unconscious about what you're doing! We enjoy watching you identify your inner powers, but we wish you understood the difference between true creativity and technology. If you really saw how true creativity enhances nature and how technology always stresses nature, then you would not overuse technology, and you would ban some technological devices, such as television, once you identified the inner power it had activated. A few of you *do* discover the initial thought pattern that activates the power within as well as the technology outside. These ones are your geniuses who also have the ability to bypass materialization and just work with the process via thought, as well as invent more things. More and more of you are figuring this out with some guidance from us. For example, the television cathode ray technology stimulated inner visual cortex receptors, and you remembered how to do inner visualization as a process to open cellular memory. This means you can become telepathic, now that you know how to create images in your brains that can be transmitted. Virtual reality goes one step farther because it can create from the images in your head.

"Why are we here to guide some of you? On the Pleiades, our inner or magical shamanic powers are brought out of us when we are children, and we do not need to materialize gadgets to activate them. As it once was in all indigenous cultures on Earth, the lives of each one of us are as complex as the individual's body/mind who sits at the controls of Starship Enterprise. However, if you visited us, we would look like a small Maya village in the Yucatan or Chiapas.

"Before we describe the evolved world in detail, we will describe the inner and outer processes inherent in the four technologies that are vibrating you to implosion.

Television teaches you that everything you see is actually perceptual because you know you are looking at a screen that makes images out of dots and not at a tree or live person. So, what is that image? It is a transmitted idea, and that is all anything is! From a shamanic perspective, if you can activate how images actually manifest in your brain, then you realize that an outer image that manifests is actually an inner idea. What?!? Your cat only appears when your inner image draws it to you; everything that comes before you is created by your mind; and once you really get this, you will finally be diligent about what is "on your mind." Humans with indigenous consciousness observe very carefully what is, or is not, in their minds.

"The microwave teaches you that everything is vibration, everything is made out of waveforms. Before it, you needed fire to activate the energy in food, but now you can warm it by bombarding it with a section of the wave spectrum that vibrates faster than 3D. We Pleiadians have to confess that we've been having some good laughs about you and your microwaves because it is a direct teacher about unseen portions of the light spectrum. In the book, you'll discover that photons are in the microwave range, not the range of solar light, and you have invented the microwave in order to realize that you can be "cooked" by wave frequencies, if you are not aware and stay in them too long. Have you ever left anything in your microwave too long? Then, as the book teaches, you will be in the Photon Band full time beginning in 1998, and how do you keep from getting cooked? We Pleiadians have a surprise for you; the Sun is the antidote to increased photon light.

"Artificial light is the technology that has significantly impacted your reality that you understand better because you've lived with it longer. Imagine the world over a hundred years ago when you had to work to create all light. The most important thing to grasp is that all of you thought of darkness as a great all-encompassing force, and all you could do was light up a little part of it when there was no solar, lunar, or star light. To you, the dark was all-encompassing, it actually was the dominant reality, and you loved light when you had it. With artificial light, you began to imagine that you could know your inner self as you watched the new light making everything visible, and so you started exploring your subconscious. In your world, you are in the Galactic Night for much more time than you are in the Photon Band, and the creation of artificial light has caused you to have the courage to explore dark space. Today, it's hard to remember the days before artificial light, but before the new light, you believed that gigantic parts of reality were unknowable. You think you've discovered during the last hundred years that all things are knowable, and in the short run you got a swelled head. You have a lot of facts, but you are getting bored.

"You invented the computer to store and access all the facts, and it actually does that. More importantly, it gives you feedback on how your brain functions. Many of you are unconscious about how this technology is actually mutating your brains, but not our vehicle. She began working with computers soon after they were available because they speed up and simplify the huge data bank that astrologers must use in practice. Many of you who are working with computers are accessing an increasingly complex data bank; the data itself is speeding up, and this data merge increases your perceptual velocity. This book is the direct result of that speedup; the multidimensional merge-and-purge is being potently impulsed by computer activation. Your brains are freeing themselves as data banks, and they are mutating into data processors; that is exactly the training you need for accessing and manipulating the nine-dimensional vertical axis being taught in this book. For example, the seventh dimension of *The Pleiadian Agenda* model is the galactic informational highways of light, the photon bands. You are moving into the localized photon band that spirals out of Alcyone to your Sun. You are moving into this galactic informational highway of light, and you have the capacity to be aware of this process because of working with computers and the Internet.

"Many of you have noticed that the World Management Team is always trying to control your reality and use you as material for its agendas. The world of the Zombies is a totally controlled world. However, unlike being in prison or working on the assembly line, or being stuck in a bad marriage, all *you* have to do with the television is turn it off! Store the microwave—because it is needed for travel in space—and go back to cooking your food with real fire and heat. Turn most of your lights off, and use the power of the computer only as a tool to synchronize huge and complex data banks instead of having it use you. We wonder, why would you consider using the computer for reading books? Reading a book all by yourself in a peaceful room is the only time you get to really think about what *you* think about things. Never let that freedom go! Our libraries and homes are filled with books, and the only material objects most Pleiadians have are books, cooking utensils, and arts and crafts. It is our fond hope that this book will help many of you never become Zombies in the first place, and it is our even fonder hope that this book will impulse you to activate your own powers and walk back into the numinous world of live essences—Gaia.

How can this particular book help you? As we've said, 104,000 years ago we Pleiadians went through the acceleration that you are experiencing now, and we've learned to use technology with great respect. We have little need for it because our magical/shamanic brain powers are so developed. For example, we have one big computer that has the data we actually need (we threw out 99% of all the old facts), and anybody can access the data by holding a coded crystal and *remembering.* A few of us, such as astrologers or directors of complex groups, use the computer to merge huge data banks to reveal new insights between things. We wouldn't use microwaves to cook food if you begged us; we use light sparingly because the darkness is soothing and we like to see the stars; and, as for television, it is just too boring, and we discovered that it reduces intelligence and destroys the immune system. Most importantly, we do not have a World Managament Team that controls us and destroys nature.

"As you will discover reading *The Pleiadian Agenda,* the World Management Team in your world is directed by the Anunnaki of the planet Nibiru. Many of you already intuit this. They were involved in your evolution, and they know how to control you; however, nothing can really control you if you consciously utilize your magical/shamanic powers! *You can only be controlled if you think you are a victim; if you believe somebody can do something to you.* We ask you, what *can* anybody do to you? So what if somebody kills you? You just return again. What amuses us the most about Zombie Land is that all you have to do is turn the devices off and return to your world. Remember, we are speaking to those of you who are free to sit and read this book, and we know at least some of you are thinking, 'What about the atrocities that are going on in places like Bosnia and Rwanda?' Well, we ask you, since we are not in bodies on Earth, what do you know about Bosnia or Rwanda? Is there anything we say in this that is not really true for *you?* As we read you, your heads are filled with images that come out of the television and newspapers of the World Management Team. Literally *all* of your responses to human suffering are being utilized as a method to manipulate your feelings by somebody who wants you to react to it for some reason. You are being impulsed to feel afraid, sad, helpless, bruised, desperate, and raw, and the more you respond to things you have no part of, the more you ignore things that need to be taken care right in front of your noses. These dramas are set up to distract you from seeing the new reality that is building and getting ready to split off from Zombie Land: Even the Zombies will wake up eventually, too, but how long do you really want to keep on being so slow? We Pleiadians also say to you, if you are one of the compassionate humans who will be going to the Bosnias or Rwandas of your world, go for it! We admire you, we will travel along inside you to see what is going on ourselves; otherwise, it is lethal for any of you to give any thought to any reality transmitted to you via television—*tell-a-vision.* Get your own vision! .

"People! Pay attention! Many multidimensional beings such as angels, Pleiadians, Sirians, Christ, Andromedans, Enoch, Abraham, and Mary Magdalene are moving in and out of your bodies! You are living in a time when they express themselves right within you. The point of seeing saucers and spaceships was to open you up, for you to realize that beings from other worlds are in your realm all around you. They *are* you, and you are *being them,* unless you are a zombie. Remember, the new reality coming is an exquisite green planet with communty celebrations going on at sacred sites during solstices, equinoxes, and key lunar times. Remember, you created television to activate *telepathy;* telephones to learn how to *transduce energies;* and airplanes *to remind you that you can fly* and that distances are relative to speed. In this new world, you are telepathic and you are seers. You enhance the natural forces—nature—of your planet instead of clutter it with artifical things, and your computers are library tools that free you from cluttering your heads with facts.

This computer is called *Interweb* and not Internet, and you are drawn to it for connection and activation of the multidimensional merge-and-purge of the Age of Light.

Barbara Hand Clow
July 1995

# THE
# PLEIADIAN
# AGENDA

# 1

## THE COSMIC PARTY

I AM SATYA, KEEPER OF THE LIBRARY ON ALCYONE, THE CENTRAL STAR OF the Pleiades. I am here to help you decode the central intelligence of your planet, to prepare you for the Cosmic Party that begins on winter solstice, December 21, 2012. I will activate my Pleiadian cellular memory as you activate your own cellular memory banks. I am here to experience the memories of your origins with you. Coded holograms in your bodies— galactic morphogenetic fields easily visible to me right now—have been hidden from your eyes because light precipitation from higher dimensions has been almost totally blocked by a great Net over your realm. This light precipitation brings information from all dimensions in the universe. We Pleiadians observed this Net, consisting of juicy archetypal forces, as it was being thrown around your planet at Zero Point, the exact moment between 1 B.C. and 1 A.D. This was the time when Christ came to Earth, so discovering the real story of what happened at Zero Point will be your access to the multidimensional consciousness of Christ. Now this Net is binding you tighter and tighter, and many of you have decided to penetrate its empty spaces and explode it open. I, Satya, want you to realize that you have drawn the Pleiadians to your planet by your desire for more light, which is intelligence.

We Pleiadians have responded to your signals by participating in your evolution during the last 26,000 years. This has been possible because your Sun is actually the eighth star of a spiral sourced from Alcyone of the Pleiades. Now the time has arrived for you to remember your stellar identity. The great cow gods and goddesses have been preparing you to swim through the spaces within the interlocking strings of the Net. You are to be like illuminated fish swimming out of the Age of Pisces into galactic synchronization with all the other stars of the Pleiades. The time since Zero Point will be transformed into a gossamer web of photonic light that will open your inmost heart to the exquisite liquid essence of the Pleiadian love vibration.

I am here to help you recall your Pleiadian heritage and to open the Alcyone Library to reveal the massive record banks of your own stellar intelligence. Every 26,000 years, your solar system moves into the Photon Band as the Earth precesses into Aquarius. This is when I always return. I am the knowledge of the library, and if you find yourselves resisting me, this is simply the Net confusing you, anesthetizing you. You are ready to graduate from a history of fear into a future of love, and if you want your diplomas, you must now stretch your minds right out of your skulls!

In the Pleiades, Earth's Age of Aquarius is known to be the Age of Light of Gaia, the time when the third star out of the Alcyone spiral—Maya—along with the eighth star—your Sun—move into the Photon Band together. In your legends, this is the story of the return of the twin. Alcyone always remains in the Photon Band because it is the progenitor of one of many Milky Way stellar spirals. Van Gogh, one of many incarnated Pleiadians during this grand cycle, was imprisoned because he painted stars as spirals. As a Pleiadian, he was naturally free and creative; yet he felt totally trapped in linear space and time, and this terrified him. Now your scientists are seeing that some stars do form spirals of light in empty space. Van Gogh could actually see this spiral form of stars, which is a faculty of multidimensional sight. It's time for van Gogh and all the great artists who have excited you by enabling you to see beyond your realm to be freed from prison! Yes, a renaissance is happening on Earth once again. If you doubt this, observe the children of Earth. Study van Gogh's star paintings, for they will help you see how your own Sun is actually part of the Pleiades.

Alcyone always basks in the Photon Band, which emanates from the Galactic Center. Its constant location in the Band activates its spiral light. Now is the time of the sacred twinning, when Maya and the Sun move into that Band, impelled by the writhing stellar light of the Alcyone spiral. Imagine the Galactic Center itself as a spinning gravitational nucleus, and see Alcyone and many other stars existing in beautiful galactic beams of Light—photon bands. To be simple about these concepts for now, this is the time when the Maya return to Earth and catalyze Earth's intelligence for the whole Milky Way Galaxy. You already know something is coming because it is all recorded in the Mayan Great Calendar, which is also

26,000 years long, just like the precession cycle and the orbit of your solar system around Alcyone. Maya researcher Linda Schele discovered in 1992 that the "Crocodile Tree," an ancient creation symbol of the Maya in their sacred book, the *Popul Vuh,* is the crossing point of the ecliptic with the Band of the Milky Way. [1] Then Maya researcher John Major Jenkins discovered that there will be an extremely close conjunction of the winter solstice Sun with that crossing point on December 21, 2012, the end of the Mayan Calendar. This conjunction has been approaching for thousands and thousands of years; now many researchers are realizing the whole Calendar is based on star maps. According to Jenkins, the fall equinox Sun conjoined the Sacred Tree around 4400 B.C., when Earth precessed into the Age of Taurus, the previous "fixed age." [2] The ages of Taurus (bull), Leo (lion), Scorpio (scorpion), and Aquarius (man) are the fixed ages, and these are the ages when new agendas are set in place to then work out for 6400 years. The ellipse on the cover of this book with the symbols for the four fixed ages shows these times in relationship to the Photon Band, and the Sun is visible on the ellipse ready to move into Aquarius. I, Satya, am bringing this book in through my vehicle, who is an astrologer, because it is incredible that the ancient Maya invented a Calendar that ends with this winter solstice/Sun conjunction! The synchronicities between the precession cycle, the Mayan Calendar, and the Alcyone spiral are mind-boggling; furthermore according to our libraries, Maya, third star of my spiral, moves into the Photon Band with your solar system when Earth enters the Age of Aquarius. Obviously these dates really mean something. For example, how in the face of 500 years of genocide could the Maya daykeepers of Guatemala still be keeping the daily calendars of the last Great Cycle, which began in 3114 B.C., unless they knew about this star map. These daykeepers have not lost the day count in 5000 years! Why is this so important to them? I can tell you because your Sun and Maya are part of my system: At the end of the Mayan Calendar in 2012 A.D., Alcyone, Maya, and your solar system all merge in the Photon Band, and this will synchronize you with the Galactic Center. Then, the Cosmic Party begins! Everybody who is in body on Earth is hereby invited.

## Invitations to the Cosmic Party

I will be frank with you. It will not be easy to get into this Party. As with any culminating social experience, you must make it your goal. You will have to prepare yourself for it, and you must begin by figuring out all the steps to this goal through the end of time. To accomplish that, you must have a model. To have a model for what will happen from now until December 21, 2012, you must gradually integrate the astrology of stellar orbits and cycles. The astrologers and Maya researchers will continue to keep you updated about key times. *There is no need to become a daykeeper or astrologer yourself. Just meditate during solstices, equinoxes, and new and full moons.*

My beloved Maya colleagues, who are all astrologer daykeepers as we Pleiadians are, have always told my vehicle, Barbara Hand Clow, that you humans are lazy. After teaching you for ten years, she has shown us that cycles, orbits, and star patterns are very difficult for you. However, attuning to these cyclical patterns is very exciting and creative, and it tends to activate your cosmic self. Astrology is simply the "logic of the stars," and it is also cosmic Pleiadian and Maya science for recovering the story of your origins. Linda Schele comments about the *Popul Vuh*, "The gods wrote all of these actions in the sky so that every human, commoner and king alike, could read them and affirm the truth of the myth."[3] Throughout *The Pleiadian Agenda*, I will describe cosmic models in detail, as well as diagram them for you. For now it is enough just to realize that when your solar system moves into the Photon Band as Earth precesses into Aquarius at the end of the Mayan Great Calendar, the biology of Earth awakens and goes through a new stage of evolution triggered by our Pleiadian love vibration.

This cycle began around 24,000 B.C., when you became *homo sapiens*, and wasn't that a great job of triggering you? Have you seen the exquisite wonder of Paleolithic cave art? Have you seen how awesome animals were in the eyes of your ancient ancestors? Now after 20,000 years, you have become self-reflective, and we are here as you remember us, existing deep in your cellular memory. We are in your blood. Our light pulses your heartbeats. You need no pacemakers.

In this supernal dawning of the Age of Aquarius, I, Satya, have returned to collect the galactic intelligence you gathered while your solar system journeyed through the Galactic Night since 8800 B.C. I am here to receive these gifts of your knowledge in exchange for your information. If you will just follow your own fascinations, together we will penetrate this constricting Net until you are finally free.

Think of this last cycle for a moment: Would any of you like to go back to being cavepeople? No, and now you have grown very tired of being stuck in the Net. Last time around, you got sick of gnawing raw leg bones in cold caves, and this time you're sick of McDonald's and "Whoppertunities."

I will help each one of you remember how to swim in the stars while you also ply your own planetary waters. I am able because I have lived with you and listened well to you for a long time. This will be your choice, a choice to be made after you read my story.

I will give you one guarantee as you begin: I will not bore you. We Pleiadians have noticed that you enjoy stories, and so in these pages you will encounter Lucifer, Enoch, Abraham, Anu, Mary Magdalene, Isaiah, Doctor Lizard and King Lizard, and even your Moon and planets, as well as your Sun and other stars. Since I would like as many of you as possible to be able to enjoy this grand tale, I have a few words for the skeptics. It is perfectly fine to think of this material as just an archetypal drama emerging out of what you call your collective unconscious. But once you could see Earth as a tiny blue dot in space, then you discovered you needed to explore the cosmic collective conscious, which is much vaster than your "un"-conscious.

The stage is now set for the drama in our library on Alcyone, where there is a temple with a circle of nine white Ionic columns surrounding a crystalline model of Earth. Your vitality is our heartbeat. And as you enter the Photon Band with Maya, an alliance has been forming between the Pleiadians and the Sirians, and this alliance is creating all kinds of new possibilities. From 1992 through 1994, my vehicle worked on this alliance in Egypt. In 1994, Sirian channel Wendy Munro of Australia worked with her in the Great Pyramid and many other temples in Egypt.[4] The Sirians are assisting the Pleiadians to help you find ways to tear down the Net that is enveloping your planet. The first stage occurred when Wendy and Barbara worked with the spirit crocodiles of Kom Ombo, Egypt. You so easily judge these magnificent beings, calling them nasty lizards, yet you fail to look at your own slimy, carnivorous selves. Lizards will be great activators of blocks in your consciousness that have formed the Net and reptilian forces will cause you to examine your own inner darkness. That is probably why the Mayas saw the star pattern where the Milky Way crosses the ecliptic as the "Crocodile Tree."

Speaking of the alliance between the Sirians and Pleiadians, we Pleiadians are sisters to these great male intelligences of Sirius, and as is natural with the female vibration, we are the ones who begin the mating dance. I, Satya, was activated to this new level within my vehicle as she struck the opening chord between Alcyone and the central star of Sirius while deep within the Great Pyramid during a series of ceremonies. Thus began the mating dance of Sirius and the Pleiades. The Sirians are the designers of the Temple of Light, and I am a Pleiadian goddess who activates energy in that temple. Since you are always so well entertained by the tales of Earth's sacred prostitutes, you will not be bored. So, if astrology is too much for you, perhaps you are one of many who will be opened by means of sacred sex.

Our library opened in your minds in 1992 as we recalibrated Earth with Sirius, the star that has been preparing you for this opening since August 1972. The electromagnetic field of Earth was so heightened in the summer of 1972 that many scientists reported later that they feared your planet might explode or undergo a polar shift.[5] Sirius holds the 6D geometrical light body of Earth in form. The ancient Egyptians came from Sirius to teach temple technology to you just so you could learn about sacred geometry. Just as the Maya time records are opening now, so is Sirian spatial knowledge, and I will tell you all about that opening. Gaia is opening her body like a lusty woman as the Sirians and Pleiadians choreograph the dance of Earth's indigenous peoples, who still remember this ancient knowledge. This triggered a geomantic activation of planetary telluric powers, so your planet was very unstable in 1972. In August 1972, the Sirians generated a great stabilization beam out of the stellar computer below the Great Pyramid at Giza, and directed it right into the Sun. This caused a green healing spiral to shoot out of the Sun, awakening solar initiates into remembering their Pleiadian origins.[6]

Who are these indigenous peoples? Forget all this arguing about "Who is an Indian?" and notice that many indigenous peoples are Sun worshippers who remember they are part of the Pleiades. When I address you as "people" or "peoples", this is a sign of great respect because I only do that when I feel you are ready to remember your stellar source. I only address you that way when I feel in your vibration that you are really hearing me.

Who are the Sirians? They are magnificent feline gods from Sirius who built the Great Pyramid and Sphinx to hold open the geometric portals of the stars while your solar system is travelling in the Photon Band. They first built the Great Pyramid in 10,800 B.C., and then rebuilt it in 2450 B.C., casing it with white limestone and installing a Sirian seer staring out to Orion.[7] This seer has held your Sirian cellular memories in the Earth records until you activated the planetary telluric field during Harmonic Convergence, a time of worldwide meditation in August 1987. The awakening of planetary sacred sites relinked your planet with the Galactic Center. You have been traveling in the Galactic Night since 8800 B.C., and playing out duality as you always have. Now the seeds sown by the light activation that began in 2450 B.C.—when the Great Pyramid was realigned to Orion—are beginning to flower.

As you enter Aquarius, the women as daughters of Earth will be the first players on the stage as Pleiadian storytellers. This has already begun. We Pleiadians do not express ourselves via sexual gender, but we are the guardians of the Goddess and we have a very feminine vibration. As we speak of "woman," we speak of Gaia in each one of you. Your male and female selves are both goddess and god, and as Earth has witnessed an overabundance of male energy, we Pleiadians are here to help all of you awaken the Goddess within.

During this most recent journey through the Galactic Night, you became highly self-reflective and your brains are getting very activated. You've developed yourselves magnificently so that you would be ready to challenge forces that control your reality at the Cosmic Party. We Pleiadians like to refer to these forces as the World Management Team, first named through channel Barbara Marciniak,[8] and as far as I, Satya, can ascertain as I read your vibrations, these forces are directed on Earth by the Anunnaki, the Nephilim of the Bible, which means in Hebrew, "gods who came down to Earth."[9] These Anunnaki/Nephilim are the ones who established the extensive and deeply ingrained management system—the Net—at Zero Point. For a gilded and engraved Party invitation, you still have time to challenge your inner belief systems about these great gods. Nobody with residual "God" poison gets an invitation to the Cosmic Party in 2012. To exorcise these lords, you must integrate the stellar intelligence of Gaia. Gaia does not resonate with superior and separated white male gods. She quakes, belches, and vomits in response to their oppression.

Once you have integrated Gaia by awakening your inner male and female, your next stage will be directed by beautiful male teachers who cherish Earth women and who have integrated their next level of male intelligence, which is Sirian. The women are running the show right now because they can feel Gaia as she first reawakens. The men will truly feel her by 1998, when men and women will remember how to express the resonant vibrations of Gaia sexually. As you will see later, the Sirians have decided to work out a new deal with the Anunnaki, and that new agenda will be based on the Anunnaki agreeing to lift the Net.

I have come to direct the voices in the cosmos who wish to speak to you now. Why me? I was selected by the Galactic Federation for fusion with my vehicle, who had been inhabiting Earth since the atom was split in December 1942. She was sucked by a planetary shudder into the fetus carried by her mother, making it possible for us to live in your midst seeking to understand the nature of radioactivity and gold on your planet, and she is having a simultaneous life in the library on Alcyone. What I have discovered so far is that all your stories about stellar humans—such as Enoch, Anu, Christ, Isaiah, and Mary Magdalene—are cloaked in lies. These lies obsess you because you sense that these great beings came to Earth to show you the way to stellar access but their true story is hidden from you. They came and deposited their codes in your vortexes, causing you to be fascinated by the traces of their stories. These memories are very juicy and alluring because they make information pathways in the Galaxy. Now you are becoming obsessed with these great archetypal beings as the information pathways in the Galaxy are getting opened and cleared. These stories exist in planetary vortexes connecting Earth's telluric fields with all dimensions, and pathways of galactic intelligence are responding to you as you pursue these records. Many beings from other realms visit these vortexes to study your stories because the vortexes are records of stellar intelligence, the Galactic Mind.

The Anunnaki cannot eradicate these stories because such erasure would cause the Gaian vortexes to go out of form. These myths are Gaia's consciousness. Instead, hoping to distract you from the real truth in these stories, the Anunnaki distort these original records by laying down one layer after another of distorted information in the pathways. Now the Earth vortexes are clogged and very inaccessible to higher dimensions, and that is why they need clearing. Blood, the elixir, cannot flow through these clogged arteries leading into your hearts, and you cannot feel these multi-dimensional impulses. This is the tragedy of the Net. These vortexes hold the experiences that contain all of your knowledge in the third dimension. If such primordial memory is totally blocked in linear space and time, even the Anunnaki could not play there any more, for they would lose their own memory banks, like a person experiencing an aneurysm. Vortexes are whirlwinds that control forces utilized for setting agendas, but these vortexes also hold Gaia's identity—her memory of stories in time. If Gaia is too deadened by manipulation and control of her fields, her species will be erased from memory in time, and the Anunnaki can never again access these vortexes for playing in your dimension. This is why the indigenous people often forbade writing the stories down. Instead, the grandfathers and grandmothers memorized them and transmitted them orally to children. The original pathways out of the vortexes were spun out by Spider Grandmother in the beginning of time and then woven together. The vortexes were generated exactly where the pathways cross, and out of these crossings and lines, species were created. The storytellers told the stories of Spider Grandmother, and animals and plants were formed. We Pleiadians call this the Web of Life. Now the Web has become the Net that blocks travel by stellar intelligences in the pathways. The Web has tightened and has almost closed due to the lies the Anunnaki layered over the original stories, especially since Zero Point.

As the Anunnaki suck you to get Gaia's energy and plot to keep you under their thumbs, they twist the records of activations by great beings, thus keeping you away from Earth vortexes as much as possible. They are heavily invested in keeping you from discovering the real connective powers of sacred places as well as the active powers of gold, uranium, crystals, and plants. Such powers can activate the Earth and awaken your deep memories, triggering connections with galactic intelligence. Power places have often been revealed to you by the unexpected appearance of illuminated beings. Often temples are built where great beings were seen, and many of you can genuinely feel this energy of place. The Anunnaki believe they own you. They've diverted you away from these power places, preventing the great beings from reaching you. Lately, even they are bored with their own limited games, and they are impulsed to seek these great beings. The dynamic is shifting fast because they know these power vortexes are their only access to these powers. Meanwhile, you have become so deenergized and bored by the diminishing energy that off-planet beings are losing access to you. The Anunnaki thought you would become robots they could control with their thought, but instead you are dying. They now realize you must reenergize yourselves. Like parents of teenagers who see that their children will become self-destructive if they don't just leave them alone, they see it is time to release their parental role. If you doubt this, notice how tired you are of being parents and being parented by the schools and government. We Pleiadians can see how bored you are by parenting because you are neglecting both your children and your society.

I am here now to resurrect some juicy stories to reactivate your hunger for multidimensional access. The control forces can't keep you from figuring out your reality anymore. They have told so many lies that they can no longer remember the initial stories, and they fear annihilation if the original records are lost. We Pleiadians remember every story, however, and some of these stories even will expose our activities in your realm. People, you've become the fox chased by the gods in the foxhunt, and now I've come to expose the hunters in red coats on horseback. The great Sirian dog/cat, Anubis, has arrived to instruct the hunting dogs on how to get the fox to fly.

I will warn you right now, these channeled versions of the stories about archetypal beings will make you angry. When you see how the Anunnaki have manipulated you, you will be furious, since you will feel like a fool. Please remember that the fool comes when the shift is prepared, so laugh at yourselves. Some of you will shred this book or throw it on the floor, but then you will pick it back up or run to the store for another copy. Why? Because in your deepest place of knowing, you will hear a truth that belongs to you in these pages. You are so bored you are thrashing around in your own bodies. The lies you've swallowed are the "warp" of the great Net, and your justifiable anger is the "woof." The Sirians have made an alliance with us Pleiadians so that the men and women of Earth will now be able to reconnect with each other after being disconnected for so long by Anunnaki brainwashing. This reunion is coming in the near future and the joining will be passionate, not controlled and manipulated. That is the next step for you, and I'd suggest you just go for it because it will make it easier. No one has ever been able to resist the Goddess, especially visitors from the skies, and the Sirians learned this well when Christ fell in love with Mary Magdalene. By the way, there exists in your field a book called *You Are Becoming a Galactic Human,*[10] which promulgates the idea that Sirians will show up and rescue earthlings with their spaceships. Forget it, people! Quit watching your skies and jump in the sack!

You are caught in confusion right now because you have been attempting to remember your story by means of the tools of linear space and time, the third dimension. We Pleiadians call this book *The Pleiadian Agenda* because we know you are ready for the whole story now. Our agenda at this time is to teach you how to be passionately immersed in your bodies while you learn to view your 3D reality simultaneously in nine dimensions. Just relax. We sent Bach, another great Pleiadian artist, down to prepare you for this perceptual opening. If you think your brain can't handle such a complex form, go listen to Bach fugues for 24 hours with headphones on, and then read this book.

You are trapped in a tightly woven Net that has you more trapped than you realize. This Net was brilliantly constructed by the Anunnaki, who exist in the next dimension above yourselves, the fourth dimension (4D). These great beings wove this Net so that you would be held in density with them through the Age of Pisces. Why? The love force of Christos was so intense on Earth that you had to be held in density so you could integrate this elixir over two thousand years. Out of desire for freeing themselves from being your parents, the Anunnaki stimulated you with Piscean archetypes—compassion turned into pity, love turned into dependency, spirituality turned into religion—so you would finally choose to move beyond pity, dependency, and religion. You would grow up and become compassionate, loving, and spiritual. But they've become so bored by the limitations in you set by the Net that even they can see now that your boredom could eventually blow up this prison.

Without multidimensional access while you are in 3D, you will die and destroy your own world. These great 4D beings, the Anunnaki, who were closely documented in Sumerian records, realize they are losing their access to you as a result of assuming to be superior.[11] They have noticed the children are all on the street and not at home. Earth needs to be fascinating and creative, or children will not play the game. The kids aren't going to work, to school, or to war anymore, and they are on the verge of not having sex anymore. They are ready to play with the Aquarian archetypes—truth, multidimensionality, freedom, and creativity.

This Net woven during the last 2000 years has forced you to mature your emotional bodies, so you could figure out how to release these 4D entities from their karma. As you will see, the 4D entities have been involved in your dimension long enough to learn their lessons. Now they want to be invited to the Party, but those with long records of interference—what I call galactic rudeness—will not be invited unless they learn some Earth manners. Fourth-dimensional beings, mostly the Anunnaki, have pricked and prodded you into acting out *their* feelings. Higher-dimensional entities have also played with your energies by stimulating your intelligence and spiritual exploration. You are even tired of *this* because you want these energetic experiences for yourself! Now all beings must own their own feelings and expressions. This will be a party with no masks or props. The Cosmic Party is to be held on Earth. During this Party, other-dimensional beings can only own their own expressions by penetrating your realm and moving into your energy in 3D, but only when you agree and are totally conscious.

How do you prepare for the Party? You might think all you have to do is get dressed and put on your makeup. In fact, you have to open your chakric systems and clear your emotional bodies. People, if you knew what really goes on when you pray in a sacred place with your sense of self activated to the four directions of your planet, you would pray this way all the time.

The entities needing to experience you are passionate, exquisite, and honorable. We Pleiadians want you to be sitting in sacred circles with your spines straight or having orgasmic sex all the time. The Sirians want you to develop your minds so you can see sacred geometric light forms that hold your reality in form through time. We will teach you how to live every moment of your life in sacred space, tuned to the four directions with your spines straight. We Pleiadians are here to coax new teachings out of the higher-dimensional beings who will be attending the Party. As we've said, boredom is not allowed. What is worse than being stuck at a party with a bore?

Meanwhile, your reality now is no party, as I observe Rwanda, "O Jupiter" Simpson, and the Middle East. You are up against it, and only *you* can choose to process and release instead of murder each other. These Anunnaki, angels, and demons are now ready to speak through me, Satya, to straighten out their own stories, so you can figure out how to release them from their karma. Once you can see these truths, then you will know how to assume total responsibility for your actions—being in integrity in 3D. You will find ways for archetypal desires to express themselves appropriately, such as theater or channeling. The days of the "insanity plea" are over because the only relevant question is, "Did this body in 3D commit this action?" Many tools are coming to you now. For example, a man who wants to stalk the Goddess and murder her could explore that desire and discharge it by means of virtual reality, but that will only work if the program is set up to help the potential murderer clear his anger. Those of you who are very fearful can release and process a lot of fear by watching horror movies. A man who feels the urge to kill will be able to shoot planes out of the sky on his computer game. Whether these tools are good or bad depends upon how you use them.

Who are the entities who have influenced your reality, and what have they actually been doing during these 26,000 years? We are excited to see you burning with curiosity while there is still time to figure out how to be in charge of your own bodies. We *love* it when you wonder who Lucifer really is; we love it when you wonder whether Christ and Mary Magdalene had sex and created a child; we are happy when you wonder how Enoch ascended to the stars, because it shows you'd like to ascend yourselves— or have sex with a highly energized being—and confront your own judgments. However, it seems easier for you to desire ascension with Enoch and tantric sex than to contemplate your own judgments about Lucifer and sin. This will be a piece of cake. Once you've talked with Lucifer, you will find out *he is simply inside you.* If you are a fundamentalist and this idea makes you feel like shredding this book, I ask you, do you *really* want to pay for Jim Bakker again? If you are a Roman Catholic, we must warn you that this book could make it impossible for you to ever go in the confessional again. Sorry. Confession is a bore, and it is lethal; women got abused in the box until 1972, and since then young boys have been at high risk. Lucifer is very creative. To remember your own story, you must look at all of it. We promise you, your curiosity will be more sated by Lucifer or Christ or Mary Magdalene than it will be by soap operas, the evening news, or trials on TV. Our stories even beat the British monarchy's juicy dramas, although those stories are good sources for seeing how the Goddess gets Anunnaki-controlled men in the sack.

As we Pleiadians see it, your next step is to cease attempting to decode nonphysical realms with the tools of linear space and time. That is the purpose of this book. You have been attempting to figure out the influences of nine dimensions in your reality by means of only one dimension, the third. To us, this is like attempting to envision a magnificent oak tree by taking a core slice from its trunk and looking at its rings under a microscope. Who could envision an oak tree—with great branches and leaves and powerful root system; its power in one place drawing rain and sun, soil nutrients and insects and animals to itself; its morphogenetic field holding in form; its sacred geometry making it solid; its cosmic biology, and so on—by merely examining a slice from its trunk?

It is simple once you see it: all your dilemmas are perceptual. You're held in 3D by the Net, which limits your perceptions. One moldy old example of the limitations that have narcotized you is the argument between Berkeley and Hume: If a tree falls in the forest, does it make a sound if no one is there to hear it? Of course it does! The constant going back and forth causes you to not see how 3D operates. Once the knowledge available in 3D is lost, you can't see that the tree does not fall in 4D unless somebody was there and heard it. Events in 4D are recorded when you *feel* them, and 3D just happens. I know this sounds silly and obtuse, but I wanted to present this one because many of you had to listen to "is the chair solid or not?" in Philosophy 101. It's one easy example. And wait until you find out who triggered Sodom and Gomorrah! And wait until virtual reality creates a second nuclear holocaust! Unless you can drop Anunnaki Philosophy 101, you won't be able to figure out whether the tree fell or not. Worse than that, as Earth changes accelerate, you could become Chicken Little! You must master a multidimensional model in order to view your times or you will always be stuck in the Net. You will not know what is real, and that is exactly what holds the Net around your planet. Tricky stuff.

The Pleiadians know that you are all ready to become seers now. Our Pleiadian colleague, Barbara Marciniak, informed you of that in a channeling in June 1993, when the Pleiadians said that some of you will become "Wizards of the Heart." I, Satya, liked that concept because it helped me see what I must use for explaining my own agenda for the Age of Light, which begins December 21, 2012. *Your planet is ready for models that can move you beyond male alchemy into the alchemy of the Goddess, so that your true male brilliance can be activated.* What could be more dead and boring than a pack of moldy old male alchemists? People, we warn you, right now your most dangerous tendency is *secrecy*. Let it all out now—flash, expose yourselves. If you don't, your planet will go out of form. Your solar system will blast out of the Alcyone spiral, and you will be separated from the Maya, who are your twin.

We have said to you many times that you are lazy, that you need to be cajoled, seduced, and prodded to get you going. The point of this book is to offer the tools for becoming seers—human intelligences hanging out in the Garden of Eden seeing nine dimensions simultaneously. You can choose to lie in the Sun, play with snakes, decode the real meaning in words, have sex, eat apples, and stargaze. To accomplish this, you must master the basic astrological models so you will comprehend your own time and place in the Galaxy. Again, is it not awesome that the Maya set up a Calendar thousands of years ago that ends when the winter solstice Sun conjuncts the Sacred Tree crossing? Then you must learn to perceive multidimensionally. That is, you must become alchemists by becoming the elixir ready to transmute to gold.

Why would the Pleiadians want to encourage you in this endeavor? We are nonphysical, 5D intelligences, and we require your 3D realm to be seers ourselves. What I am telling you is that you have no idea how important you are. You, humans, literally are the bodies for all dimensions as Earth begins the Age of Aquarius.

Why your system? Your solar system was chosen by the Creator to be the place for the development of biological life in the whole Galaxy. In order to perfect biological intelligence, the Creator needed to work in a small laboratory, just as your scientists first work in a laboratory to understand the laws of creation that rule a particular experiment. They also work in the laboratory to decide whether they want to carry out an experiment in the planetary field. Anything can be created, but do you want it? Is there a corresponding cure for it once it is unleashed, so that it will not have to be eradicated by killing it, just as the Anunnaki eradicated the results of their genetic manipulations with the Flood. Now the gods are playing with AIDS and Ebola virus, and your priests and rabbis are doctors. As we Pleiadians and the Sirians see it, the Anunnaki do not want to annihilate you again, but you are infected with their killing tendencies after so many years of acting out "his-story."

You must ask yourselves why you seem to prefer killing to just living until death? Do you kill each other simply because you fear death, fear disease? Death is simply the balance for life, and every disease has a corresponding cure right in the plants. These cures are instantly discovered once you have learned what that disease is teaching you. AIDS is your gift to teach you to honor and appreciate death; then you will find ways to die that you like. By the end of this cycle, death will become like birth—ecstatic—and Doctor God will not be there while either is going on.

The Creator first experimented with biological creativity on Earth, which is the physical location with the potential to simultaneously hold nine dimensions in its intelligence. Gaia is the intelligence of Earth, and she is a much more powerful being than you imagine. Notice where the Party is being held. You are about to find out the purpose of Gaia's magnificent and unlimited creative powers, since she has been chosen as head scientist of the biological laboratory of the Milky Way Galaxy. As I said, anything can be created in a laboratory, but Gaia decides whether any creation belongs in her field. If she does not choose it, she will cleanse it from her surface. That's why she blew up the Atlantean laboratory. As you are entering the Photon Band again, Earth will become multidimensional, and her biosphere will be the source for determining which lifeforms will be disseminated throughout the Galaxy. The qualities of this dissemination will be based on what remains in the biosphere once you have become enlightened. This will be a time when it will not be possible to be partially alive in your bodies. Those who do not remain will go out of body because they have not quickened to the Light. The "Night of the Living Dead" is over, and you can't keep on walking around half alive. Since your genes are the structure of life itself, only enlightened geneticists will be able to work with DNA. This going out of form will simply be ecstatic immersion in Gaia, a great cosmic orgasm in your realm. We are here as teachers of desire to help you decide what you want to create to become multidimensional. You will cease holding your energy in limiting forms.

It was necessary for many experiments to be conducted on Earth, by yourselves as well as intelligences of many dimensions, in order to comprehend the galactic laws of biology. Some of you will read these words and say that we dare to discuss the limitations of the Creator. I will answer you for now by asking you a question. Since you judge each other and believe that evil exists in your realm, are you not also contemplating limitations in the Creator? Since 8800 B.C., as you travelled in the Galactic

Night, you have been allowed to search for ways to have no limitations on yourselves. Your only charge during this cycle was to go as far as you wanted in order to see that freedom has boundaries, just as all things in 3D have boundaries. The Pleiadians hope that you have gone far enough to realize you are ready to learn how to create harmonically in your own reality. If you are not, there will not be anything. Can you imagine cosmic silence and no movement? We cannot either. And so your killing tendencies cannot be released into the Galaxy to cause annihilation.

We Pleiadians hope that you will want to continue once you realize the karma triggered in yourselves by higher-dimensional intelligences, who impulsed you constantly during the Galactic Night, must now be owned by each one of you. To reclaim your own domain, you will need to look at every action you have taken, as well as every time you became a victim and allowed yourself to be jerked around. You have to love and honor everything you have ever been or now are. All actions in 3D belong to you, no matter who or what impulsed you to act. Not seeing and integrating your history holds the Net in place, and then you are caught in it. That is why I, Satya, must shake you up by exposing your deep shadows. We Pleiadians know you have already agreed, because we can see that many of you would rather merge with energies than experience Earth changes. Past Life Regression Therapy really works for you because uncovering and contemplating your past lies by means of your past lives enables you to see how these lies still operate in your now.

You must notice that in 3D you have two eyes, not two hearts, and in 4D, you have one eye and two hearts! In your dualized feeling bodies, *you* are the one that splits the laser beams creating the mesmerizing holograms, and so nobody is looking at life to see what is really going on in 3D. Does this blinding fascination with 4D images matter much? Well, few people are breathing with the plants in the garden, shapeshifting with the animals, and vibrating with the powers of Gaia in the rocks. That is *being*, a function of the heart. The question goes back, correctly this time, to Berkeley and Hume: Will the plants, animals, and rocks cease to exist if no one is attuned with them? People, you'd better realize what happens to things in your reality when no one loves them. Just why are the species leaving? And what about how you treat others of your own species? To attain alignment with cosmic law—divine order of life—you must see your own leering face in the carnage of Rwanda or Bosnia. You must feel how "others" are making these awesome sacrifices so you can contemplate your own blood lust. If you cannot recognize yourself in the sacrificial dramas of your times, they will recur eternally, and you will eventually have to act out every one of them yourself, both as victim and victimizer. The Maya figured that one out the last time they were on Earth. They built ballcourts as eternal shrines to sacrifice to divert you from totally destroying their codices. The conquistadors were so enamored of these mirrors that they missed a few copies of the real thing.

We Pleiadians have become you during these last 26,000 years, and I have come to let you know that we finally see where you're stuck. Naturally, it's sourced in something we did. We tried to rescue you when you went into the Photon Band around 11,000 B.C. We know that you firmly believe the gods will *always* decide about your world, and so you wait instead of act. You believe they will save you if you just keep waiting for the Apocalypse. Yes, the Photon Band was the Apocalypse then, but what happens next is the future, not the past!

When you are deep in the Photon Band, laser beams will no longer split into two parts in solar light and create dense realities for exploring feelings. Laser beams will not exist that make mesmerizing, holographic images that you can worship. Instead, their multifaceted lenses will open to my dimension, the fifth, and those of you in 3D will look out to the cosmos through those lenses. Everything you see will be like looking through a kaleidoscope. All your beliefs and judgments will go out of form, but *you* will not if you release these things that you think are reality. Wake up and gaze around again at your world. See the Garden of Eden that you live in! The Pleiadians have been with you for 26,000 years, and now we are ready to mirror back to you the images you hold of us in your reality. If you will look into your own mirror, we will look in ours. Notice that earthlings and Pleiadians work with mirrors, while the 4D gods work with laser beams. The Pleiadians have chosen to become multidimensional with you because biology must merge with love. Once this is accomplished, you can travel with us out of the Garden into cosmic realities. Laser beams are going to be restricted to their highest usage: surgery on the physical body for healing. Mirrors reflect light and laser beams focus it.

We Pleiadians have learned during this cycle that only *you* can decide your world. We have become you, and we know that each one of you knows the truth about yourselves at this time. Actually, we are amazed by how far you've come. We will not be telling you anything about yourselves you don't actually already know. Many of you are still thinking you are supposed to hide your total truth from others. The Victorian mentality is deadly, for there will be no place to hide once the solar light diminishes. You can all cleanse your emotions and learn to stop the killing so much more easily if you will only *share* with each other. Privacy is eradicated as your inner chaos fills the television screen day after day. All of you have raped, murdered, and abused. If you want to, you will be able to sit in a virtual reality machine all day so you can murder, rape, and abuse *until you are bored with it.* You can choose to sit in a gambling parlor on a plastic stool all day instead of walking in the woods with the animals, listening to the birds. Until the opening of the Party, you may choose forms of control over the chaos and nobody will judge you. Even use Prozac if you want to to find out how it feels to have serotonin in your body, and then drop the pills and do it yourselves. *Nothing is dangerous to you in 3D if you know what you are doing, and if you realize all things are only props.*

The beings from many dimensions have gifted you with powerful tools if you need and want them now, and there are more coming. The next wave will be healing tools, and the doctors who do not use them will die of the diseases they have dared to unleash on you. To correctly utilize the tools you now have, you must agree not to kill yourselves, your parents, your mates, your children, or your friends and colleagues in 3D in the name of personal freedom. All the people who have come for the Party have the right to stay as long as they wish.

The Pleiadians are the keepers of the children of Earth. The children have spoken to us, and they want their mothers and fathers at home in the sack, and they want to be out playing in the new image fields of youth. Keep explorations of images and chimeras out of 3D, and feel free to explore your emotions by exploring the 4D archetypal realm. Go for it, have a good time, as the Goddess always fulfills all desire. I know you will stop killing when you trust us, which means you trust yourselves. Remember that you can have what you want. Virtual reality and physical integrity are clear examples of how dimensions function by means of tools, and just think: you will work with nine dimensions simultaneously when your solar system travels the through Photon Band.

During the last 26,000 years, you have been impulsed by marvelous teachers from nine dimensions. These beings have always been your gods and goddesses, mythological archetypes, and, lately your heroes and movie stars. They have graced the pages of your literature, the altars in your temples, and the screens of your televisions and movie theaters. Really, people, from our perspective on the Pleiades, Elvis uncannily resembles Yahweh. The great 4D archetypal powers have had a great time pulling your strings while you've been puppets dancing on the stage of life. Now you are ready to peek at the puppet masters. If you react to this idea with resentment, would you rather remain in closets collecting dust and mites? You have enjoyed your dances, and these masters have evolved with you in your world.

It is an exquisite drama: While one of you is having sex in 3D, 4D beings can feel your energy and trigger you into lust, guilt, abuse, or fun; 5D entities can get excited by your kundalini fire and have cosmic orgasms; 6D entities can expand the fields of your pulsations throughout the Galaxy; 7D entities can carry your feelings via galactic information highways; 8D entities can organize new morphogenetic fields out of your sexual seismic waves; and 9D entities can birth new biological forms in the darkness of Galactic Center black holes. Is that not awesome?

The Pleiadians are more involved with your evolution now because they've lived with you during your last two journeys through the Galactic Night. This long Pleiadian sojourn on Earth has made you suspicious of them, and I want to talk with you about this. You've been jerked around and manipulated by multidimensional entities during the Galactic Night because that's how the galactic system works—until the Cosmic Party. The only other possibility would be stasis and cosmic silence. Imagine never hearing a sound from, having a touch by, or even seeing, another human, animal, thing, or plant. Would you choose that? Would you choose to never look in the eyes of your child again? When you have felt jerked around, it has been because you were caught in the mechanics of 3D, and you could not see what was really going on. The Pleiadians know this. I remind you now that all your experiences have come from your own choices to play with beings who first impulsed you. That is what creates existence. Would you give up sex eternally? What would you be if you'd never encountered an archangel or a devil?

I have frequently experienced my vehicle, Barbara Hand Clow, laughing. She says the only "sin" she has ever found on Earth is boredom. Sin means "without" or "not with," and where she finds you to be the most "not-with-it" is when you are bored. I chose her as channel for the Pleiadian agenda at this time because I want to deliver some very complex Pleiadian records—the mechanics of time and orbits. How to do that without ever becoming boring? Luckily, you have all advanced a great deal, and you are getting more comfortable with Pleiadian 5D tools for Seeing— astrology and dimensionality. You are tired of alchemy and astrology being ridiculed by the World Management Team; some of you know that these control forces secretly use these tools even more than you do!

Since the Pleiadians chose to live with you in your realm during the last 26,000 years, there are things that must now be seen and cleared. They would like you to know now that they once made a big mistake with you. That error has caused you to blame them for other traumas and abuses in your realm that they did not actually cause. The Pleiadians know that their agenda cannot be accomplished without owning up to their own mistakes, just as yours cannot. They interfered with your free will when you were travelling through the Photon Band during the Age of Leo beginning 13,000 years ago. When your solar system travels in the Photon Band during Leo, great Earth changes are triggered because ego identity and belief in regal rights must be established during that age. The Age of Leo was the "Age of Kingship," and beings from many stars and galaxies came to Earth. Gaia always becomes very expressive while this drama is being worked out. You are allowed to only go so far on her surface. During the last cycle, this process caused your poles to shift, triggering the last Ice Age. When the shock hit, the Pleiadians did not comprehend that you were in a balancing process, since they do not experience such processes.

We could feel your pain and death because we were with you, and we slipped out of compassion and fell into pity. We were so deeply involved with you that we tried to rescue you by leading groups of you to safer areas and lifting some of you off planet during the most intense shiftings. In your confusion, you thought we must be gods, and *you identified yourselves as victims* for the first time. You shifted out of the now just when you were ready to claim your own experience and feel the ecstasy of Gaia flipping her poles. You asked to be rescued, and we felt your pain so vividly that we became your gods and rescued you. Just when you were ready to transcend fear, we stopped your process. We will never do this again.

This intervention in your reality caused you to think the gods are above your world, and a dimensional shattering happened in your world.

This was called "the fall." You walked out of the Garden of Eden, and you split your world by viewing it through your eyes and brain instead of feeling it in your heart. The greenness of your world became separate from you, and time began. That is why you have a relatively clear sense of time since you moved out of the Age of Leo in 8640 B.C. The book, *You Are Becoming a Galactic Human*, suggests that the Sirians will rescue you when you are in the Photon Band during the coming Age of Aquarius. They can do that, just as the Pleiadians once did, but the Pleiadians discovered that interference in your realm aborts ascension. As for the Sirians, if they block your process in any way, they will be living the next 13,000 years with you on Earth. The Pleiadians have learned that nobody lifts beings out of 3D; 3D simply sucks in those who intervene so they can work out karma. As for you humans, if such a choice is offered to you and you decide to play with the Sirians, then you will learn a lot from them during the Galactic Night from 4000 A.D. to 15,000 A.D.

As the Age of Leo began in 10,800 B.C., once the shattering had occurred, then you were in your world limited to linear sight, and you thought all multidimensional beings were the Anunnaki. This was natural, since Anu always told you he was your god. You knew better, and you acted like you worshipped him and laughed at him in secret, just like you do with your priests and ministers now. You created pompous ways to worship the gods and puffed them up, so you could go about your life. You always knew that Anu was not god, and we were first attracted to you when we noticed that you understood your own sovereignty. However, in your dimensional shattering during the Age of Leo, you did something that you are now ready to look at: You gave god a name that is actually the name for elimination portals. This punnish entitlement was your attempt to make a joke out of a being who was oppressing you, but the Creator does not have a name. Once you did that, then everything had to have a name; *language began as an identification process instead of using sound as a resonation tool between yourselves for perceptual fusion.* This split you into many tongues, and then Anu could trick you into splitting among yourselves. This has caused *GOD* to lurk all over your planet. Lately "god" has moved out of the church and is operating out of the hospital. This new form of rescue called "Fix me!" is becoming less enjoyable every day, as you insidiously name your body processes instead of just living and breathing until you are ready to let go. Remember, people, death is only your last breath. You have forgotten to trust the magnificent genius of Gaia—your world in the center of our library! It is time for you to ferret out the naming—identification from the Age of Leo—because in the Age of Aquarius, all identity will be biological vibration. Open your eyes and learn to recognize the Anunnaki at play when they say Christ was riding on an ass into Jerusalem!

This book is about the exquisite powers of lower-dimensional density, because the Anunnaki got you to buy into the idea that higher is better than lower. This diverted your experience from you, and you can't see the Garden you reside in. You've become hierarchical, and you're trying to climb out of your own world as if it is a snake pit. It is a snake pit! That's the joke! There is no hierarchy of dimensions, and each one is powerful in its own way for its own inhabitants. For you, the most potent dimension is Gaia. For us, it is electromagnetic fields of orbits and cycles held together by gravity and stellar light.

Maya, the third star in the Alcyone spiral, travels in a tighter part of the Pleiadian spiral closer to Alcyone than your own solar system. Maya is in the Photon Band more often than in the Galactic Night. Like your solar system, Maya is in the Photon Band for about 2000 years of Earth time, then Maya travels in the Galactic Night for only about 1200 years before going back into the Photon Band. The Maya do not influence Earth much when they are travelling in the Galactic Night, as they were recently from about 800 to 1987 A.D. Their mysterious "disappearance" in 843 A.D. occurred when they went out into the darkness. Before leaving, they made sure their Calendar was securely implanted in the third dimension by carving it in stone all over Mayaland. Now as the Age of Aquarius is beginning, Maya is entering into the Photon Band with the Sun. This is always an exciting phase of the Great Cycle because this is when the Maya are able to demonstrate by means of their Great Calendar that the future creates the present. The end of the Calendar is triggering new stages of evolution for you because you are gearing up to learn how to set an intention of what you want to create and be for the next 26,000 years on Earth. You are being subtly orchestrated by the Galactic Maya, and some of you are just beginning to notice what they have set up.

The Maya orchestrate timing in various worlds in the Alcyone spiral, and Alcyone holds the records of time. The Maya are Keepers of Time, your Sun is a Keeper of Frequency, and Alcyone is Keeper of Intention.

You all can participate in setting the intention for the next stage of evolution with the Pleiadians by attuning to Maya timing, raising the vibration in your Sun, and mastering the mechanics of dimensionality. Then the Cosmic Party will have the best entertainment roster.

The rest of the chapter is a description of the structure of the Milky Way Galaxy, the Photon Band, and the Pleiadian model of nine dimensions that are the structure of your perceptual world. These nine dimensions fit into a tenth dimension that holds the nine dimensions and is indescribable. This part of the book is placed here in the beginning, now that I have described the Pleiadian agenda, because you may find yourselves referring back to it when you actually travel in the Galaxy and nine dimensions in the rest of the book.

## The Story of the Photon Band and the Galactic Night and the Alchemy of Nine Dimensions

The Milky Way Galaxy is a ten-dimensional system of cosmic intelligence that expresses itself in nine dimensions. The first dimension is sourced in a beginning form that manifests as an intelligence system, such as the central core crystal of Earth, which sets up light lines of communication from the core crystal through nine dimensions to the center of the Milky Way Galaxy. Like any system, the Galaxy evolves in time and creates in space. The method of each creation is generated in its own first dimension, and intention of that creation is sourced in the future—the Galactic Mind. We are interested in accessing knowledge about the orbit of Earth around the Sun, the orbital pattern of the Sun in the Pleiades, and the path of the Pleiades in the Milky Way Galaxy. As we begin, everything must be looked at from the perspective of Gaia, the first three dimensions of Earth expression.

Always begin in your own location, such as the center of the Earth. If you doubt this, notice the massive confusion gripping astronomers. Earth moves around the Sun with the other planets and moons, which are all spinning. The Sun is spinning as the eighth star of the Pleiadian spiral, and the Pleiades are spiraling within the Galaxy as the Galaxy spins on its axis. No 3D science can describe these cycles, all of which exist only if you first start in one point or with one observer's point of view. Realities are layer cakes and only multidimensional models will describe anything real. Once

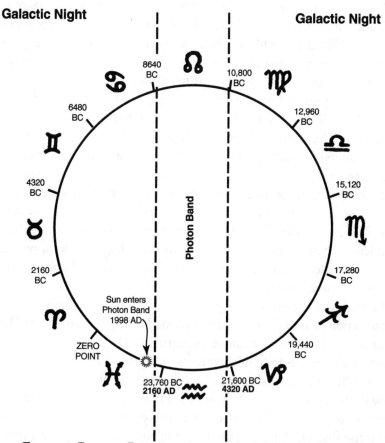

FIGURE 1: PHOTON BAND AND PRECESSION OF THE EQUINOXES

you dared leave your surface in spaceships, you saw that you are only a point in the universe, and now you are beginning to realize that the only view you have is perceptual. We will explore all this with you. For now, it is enough for you to know that you travel in the Photon Band when Earth precesses through the Ages of Leo and Aquarius, and you orbit through the Galactic Night during all the other zodiacal polarities of the Great Ages—Cancer/Capricorn, Gemini/Sagittarius, Taurus/Scorpio, Aries/Libra, and Pisces/Virgo. At this time, you are moving into the Photon Band as you are leaving the Age of Pisces and moving into the Age of Aquarius. (See Fig. 1.)[12]

Earth's exploration of herself in time has resulted in orbital patterns and cycles in the Galaxy that access nine perceptual dimensions. The Galactic Mind is able to hold the thought of nine dimensions simultaneously in trillions of systems. *The time has arrived for you to expand and ground your intelligence by consciously perceiving everything in nine dimensions in your realm because that will free your mind.*

How would this work? From your point of view, the core of Earth is the first dimension (1D), the source of harmony, bliss, and being grounded. The world above this, just beneath Earth's surface, is the second dimension (2D), source of telluric powers and elemental beings. Existence on Earth in linear space and time is the third dimension (3D). The fourth dimension (4D) is a nonphysical, archetypal zone where feelings, dreams, and all connections to Gaia and higher dimensions are available. Planets manifest these 4D archetypal patterns that express their own distinct versions of the Sun's energy and stimulate behavioral patterns on Earth. The Pleiades are the fifth dimension (5D) of orbital patterns and cycles of your solar system and the Pleiadian spiral. The Sirius star system is the sixth dimension (6D) of your world, and it creates geometrical light constructions out of the physical forms in 3D that are shaped by 4D archetypal feelings and their creative patterns in 5D. These are the morphogenetic fields behind physical patterns on Earth.

The fourth dimension greatly influences realities in your 3D world. Now that we have lived with you in 3D for this 26,000-year cycle, we are anxious to help you figure out how you've been influenced. Knowing about the Photon Band and the Galactic Night will offer you a model for viewing 4D that will put you in the observer mode about your lives, which are your own centers. It is your choice now, as opposed to continuing to be puppets dangling on strings used for never-ending dramas in time. We are here to help you comprehend how all dimensions influence you so you can reclaim your feelings—which 4D has complexified—determining how and what you perceive. If you do not know the mechanics of perception and how you feel, you can be jerked around eternally. I will admit I did not know how intense this 4D manipulation was until I experienced it myself by being with you for thousands of years in your reality. As you move out of the Galactic Night, the Pleiadians are poised to receive your wisdom gathered since 8800 B.C. so they can analyze it and send it to the Galactic Center.

In your solar system, twelve planets orbit the Sun—Mercury, Venus, Earth, Mars, the Asteroids (which once were one planet), Jupiter, Saturn, Chiron, Uranus, Neptune, Pluto, and Nibiru. Many of these planets have their own moons. The main archetypal qualities of Earth are expressed by all of the planets, as well as your Moon and Sun.

The zodiacal system of twelve is simply an arbitrary division of six 4D polarities, six of the night and six of the day, which is a good tool for decoding fields of emotional experience in 3D. This lexicon of energy forces shows how 4D ideas trigger events in 3D. (See Fig. 2.) Each polarity is a spectrum from dark to light. Each individual system of twelve is unique and is triggered out of its own unique center, its 1D beginning point. Dimensionality is vertical, and the systems of twelve divisions are horizontal planes. The horizontal planes of systems that form out of nine

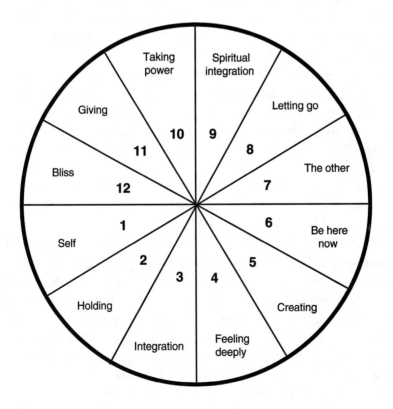

FIGURE 2: THE SIX POLARITIES

dimensional columns of vertical light create disks that are experiential fields which create realities. The Galaxy itself has a horizontal plane that can be divided up into twelve zones of experience, and the experiences that occur generate a vertical axis of nine dimensions at a right angle. Why twelve? Actually, these horizontal fields could be divided up in many ways, but the division of twelve is the one that facilitates harmony on Earth, as has been extensively proven by John Michell, co-author of *Twelve-Tribe Nations*.[13]

The planet Nibiru, home of the Anunnaki, used to be an outer planet of Sirius A, and is now the outermost planet of your solar system. Nibiru links your Sun and the Sirius system. This phenomenon was extensively explored by our vehicle in *Heart of the Christos*.[14] The Sirius star system has played a primary role in the history of your solar system, as has Nibiru, which was partially captured into orbit by your Sun about a half million years ago, shifting the influence of Nibiru somewhat out of the Sirius system and more into your solar system.[15] Besides being the eighth star of the Pleiades, your Sun is also a twin star to Sirius A, and both your solar system and the Sirius system have been assisting Nibiru in its evolution. These astrodynamics are the source of coded legends like Cain and Abel, Horus and Seth, and Quetzalcoatl and Tezcatzlipoca. As you will see in this book, great evolution is now planned for Nibiru, Sirius, the Sun, and the Pleiadians. Your solar system, and especially on Earth, is where the records exist for setting new intentions. When you arrived at this point in the galactic orbit 225,000,000 years ago, the reptiles came to your planet; now you are subtly conscious of reptilian intelligence because they are completing such a huge galactic cycle.

Geocentric astrology—viewing the solar system and beyond from a location on Earth—is the most advanced tool you have in 3D for decoding the time and quality of your unfoldment. As we have said, the fourth dimension is where your emotional body resides. It is profoundly ruled by the archetypal planetary forces of your own solar system. The qualities and relationships of these planetary bodies actually do express your personal unfoldment. Literally do the cycles of Mars generate your feelings of power and anger! Without geocentric astrology, it is very difficult for most of you to master your emotional bodies, to be objective and observational about your day-to-day activities. Fifth-dimensional astrological science offers you freedom from being stuck in linear time since it analyzes and describes the

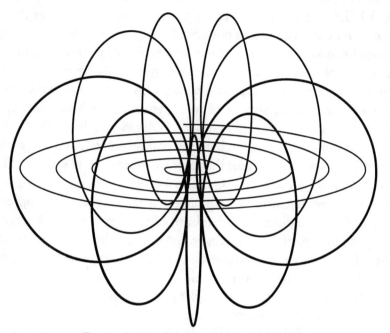

FIGURE 3: 7D GALACTIC PHOTON BANDS

qualities of time. You can examine the planetary cycles, delineate their qualities, and prepare yourself for various periods in your life.

Astrology enables you to look at how the drama of life is artificially pressed into past, present, and future. This enables you to gain perspective on emotions as you feel them—to watch the feeling realm to detect agendas, dramas, potentialities, and spirits impulsing you. Once you master this level of self-observation or self-reflection, then you realize that your access to other worlds is available precisely in these feelings. Feelings are awesome because they are your nonphysical vibratory field that is resonating in 4D through 9D. Once you attain that perspective, you cannot be impulsed or jerked around by any vibration. Many fascinating patterns rise out of your emotional and spiritual richness and give you access to scintillating pools of dark creativity and dances of light dynamics.

How does this pattern work in the Galaxy? Fifth-dimensional light is stellar, which is more subtle than solar light, the light from the Sun that you receive on Earth. Photon Bands are 7D donuts of light that emanate from the vertical axis of the Galactic Center. They spin around and around through the Galactic Center into the darkness of the Galactic Night. (See Fig. 3.) Galactic centers of 9D are pure darkness, and yet, as they spin on their axes, the astounding power of their vortexes shoots out 9D galactic synchronization beams. These synchronization beams spin out of the black-hole galactic centers, torqued by the galactic axial spin. These beams, belts, axes, and horizontal planes with black holes in their centers are 8D organizational systems of intelligence. In the Milky Way Galaxy, this 8D brilliance is called the Galactic Federation; it holds the Galaxy in form by means of information highway photon bands. All stars existing in photon bands generate spirals that capture other stars, and these "Photon Stars," such as Alcyone, are Galactic Federation libraries. This overall Galactic Federation structure is sourced in the deep and incomprehensible nothingness of black holes that birth galaxies from nuclear energy. This energy is pure creativity. The empty divine mind then launches its cosmic light, which links galaxies to galaxies, and gives birth to more dimensions in the Universe. The Universe itself is the tenth dimension, the cosmic "all" that contains everything that we perceive from Earth, and it cannot be named, described, or comprehended.

Your Sun is linked to the Pleiades by means of a spiral of stellar light radiating out from Alcyone. Think of it this way: Your Sun bathes the surface of Earth in 3D light, while Earth also knows 4D light from the subtle reflection of solar light off the Moon and planets. Star light is 5D light that moves out through the stars of the Pleiades—out from Alcyone, through Merope, Maya, Electra, Taygeta, Coele, and Atlas to your Sun. Thus in your legends, Atlas holds Earth on his shoulders in space. Each Pleiadian star except Alcyone, which is located in the Photon Band eternally, travels through the 7D Band for 2000 years of Earth time. Then each star in the system travels in the Galactic Night for varying lengths of Earth time. The orbits that hold various bodies in the Galactic Night are 6D, and the 6D intelligence that carries your solar system through the Galactic Night is Sirius A.

The stars close to Alcyone, such as Merope and Maya, are in the photon bands for more time than they are in the Galactic Night. (See Fig. 4.) Your solar system spends the most time out in the Galactic Night—11,000 years in the dark and 2000 years in the light. What does this mean? Various members of the solar system become very dense while in the Galactic Night, and this generates experience called karma—feelings in

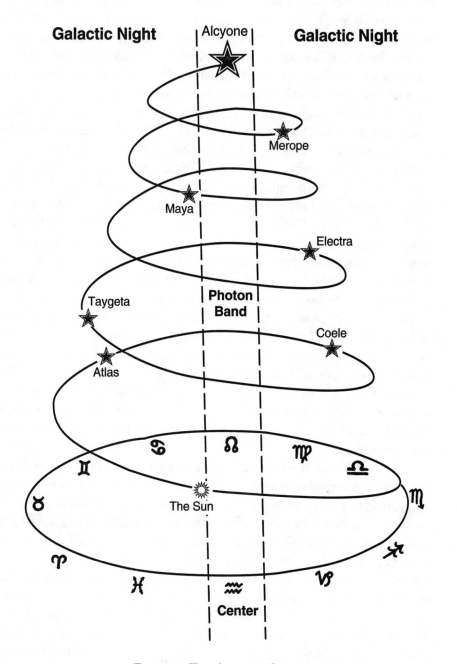

FIGURE 4: THE ALCYONE SPIRAL

4D seeking expression that create actions in 3D. Bodies traveling in 7D photon bands become less dense, more multidimensional. As a result, their acquisition of light cleanses emotional bodies and intensifies vibrations in physical bodies. When you are in this state of awareness, you do have feelings. But such feelings are merely impulses that guide you to stay in your center. These are not feelings that impulse you into karma.

The Galactic Night intelligence in the darkness outside the Pleiadian spiral holds form for the horizontal disk of each Pleiadian star. These disks are composed of twelve divisions that cause density, which then creates history and stories within great cycles of time. Otherwise there would be only birth, a life, death, and no cyclical memory, as with animals. There must be a weaving of creative memory. We must remind you: The animals are superior to you. Their creative memory is stellar, for Spider Grandmother created them first. The Milky Way is a river of animals. These weavings attract stars that make worlds by means of sacred geometry—morphic light fields that generate still more 9D vertical axes. It goes on and on, and if you can imagine it, Maya also has a disk of twelve divisions. The 7D donuts of photonic light from the Galactic Center are information highways that stimulate curiosity. The desire for union, for twinning, for new expressions of both sides of a duality, derive from this passion. This arousal comprises the 7D photon bands seeking the Galactic Center. This curiosity is what causes the rods of 7D photonic light to curl back on themselves, forming them into donuts. The Galaxy would disintegrate into empty space without the nuclear gravity in the center, which then shoots out pulses of light.

Maya and your solar system are now moving into the Photon Band together. This arrival is uniting the Pleiadians and Sirians so they can find a way to solve Earth's dilemma with Nibiru. The Anunnaki have gone too far triggering karma on Earth. Both the Sirians and the Pleiadians have now figured out how Nibiru manipulates the inhabitants of Earth in 3D. As the Pleiadians have said, they figured this out by being with the inhabitants of Earth, and the Sirians figured it out by being with the inhabitants of Sirius B. The new biology must integrate all this knowledge. *From spring equinox 1987 to winter solstice 2012, biological life will be harmonized with divine intelligence, so that the feeling body of Earth can carry the intensity of the coming galactic orgasm.* The Milky Way orgasm must be strong enough to carry life throughout the whole Galaxy. If you doubt this, notice how earthlings are all giving birth too frequently, seeking to encompass this intensity in their bodies.

Earth is Alcyone's laboratory, Alcyone is Earth's library, and Maya is running the schedule so that nobody is late. If all this seems too much, remember playing with your Tinker Toys as a child, and remember how they taught you that everything is organized in central spools that are connected by little wooden rods. Realize that everything we are telling you already exists within your cellular memory. Each electron is light within molecules within the cells in your body. You actually are more light than solid. The distance from one molecule to another in your body is as great as the distance from one galaxy to another. You have worlds and universes within your body!

Alcyone quickened Earth with Pleiadian love vibrations at Zero Point through the Sirian expansion triggered by the incarnation of Christ, a human carrying the intelligence of nine dimensions simultaneously. Christ implanted the Pleiadian love vibration, and that vibration quickened Earth until 1987, when, at Harmonic Convergence, these 9D seeds were released all over Earth. These seeds became flowers in each body that would release this essence into Gaia. Gaia will release each human who becomes the Sacred Tree into the Milky Way Galaxy, like a child blowing on seeding dandelions.

Dandelions, which are solar flowers, cannot seed until each flower has used up its carbon energy. Then they restructure as silica filaments, which can fly away and carry seeds on the wind. These seeds take root and transmute more carbon matter to silica. You can imagine this because you all have picked up dandelions when they look like starbursts, and you have blown them and watched their delicate silica filaments carry seeds on the wind. Well, people, we'd like you to know about how you can complete your carbon-based bodies and evolve them to light-encoded filaments. Imagine billions of light-encoded filaments swirling around your throat that become vertical rods of light as you speak your truth. Your whole body lifts as an umbrella of filaments carries you into the Galaxy to seed it. You can only do this by identifying and speaking your truth, which you can find in all the wonderful encounters you've had during the Galactic Night with multidimensional beings who were exploring themselves in 3D through you. We will teach you to identify the vibration of each dimension that has been playing with you since 8800 B.C. These are the contents of Pandora's Box.

Will you lift the lid of Pandora's Box so the Pleiadians can see what's inside? Only you can decide to see what the Sirians or Anunnaki have been creating with you. What would it mean for you to access your juiciest story? Well, a Sirian could take you on a trip under the paw of the Sphinx. An Enochian could take you on an ascension journey into the Galactic Center, such as in the Book of Enoch.[16] Does this excite you? We hope so, because when you open the portals to the Sirians or the Enochians, the portals open for us to be able to see what they are creating with you. We want to access what they've been experiencing with you out there in the Galactic Night, since we've just been basking in the light and have no idea. This is the time when we stock our library on Alcyone.

Why? We always set a new evolutionary intention with you as you enter the Age of Aquarius, and we can't do that without your data, all your stories. Let go now, do not continue to hold back these magnificent creative powers you possess.

What will we give you? The Maya have told us that they have managed to find a way to get you to see that the future creates the present. The Maya tell us after playing around with you for eons that they noticed you were becoming fascinated with time. So, they made up a game for you. They created the Mayan Calendar with an end date and revealed it to you. As you began to understand its importance, you could see that you are progressing toward this End Time, as if it is a huge attractor pulling you in deep space. As you've been getting closer to this End Time, the Maya can again influence your reality in 3D, since you are both moving into the Photon Band; and they are conducting the orchestra for the "End Times Ninth Symphony," showing you how to play your instruments. They have been composing the music for the Cosmic Party, and it began with Beethoven's "Ode to Joy." *You are waking up and realizing that a future intention is creating your now!* Tricky and outrageous, isn't it? Well, it is even more fascinating than that. In order to set an intention that could create life able to be disseminated throughout the Galaxy at the end of the Calendar, everything you put into it must have perfect integrity. For life to be in integrity in your now, it must resound with the most powerful forces of Gaia to reach the black hole in the Galactic Center.

Only beings who have enough knowledge in the Galactic Night can access such integrity by mastering the nine-dimensional alchemy.

Conception happens in the darkness of the womb of the Goddess. Like sperm seeking the egg, if you can't see in the dark and you are unable to take hold in the tissue, you'll flow out of Gaia in her blood. Only you will know how to conceive in your Garden. The Maya and the Pleiadians can tell you a lot about the tools you will need from now until 2012; they will help you open Pandora's Box and utilize or transmute all the wild energies hidden in it. In order to handle what flies out of that fantastic box holding the intelligence of the Inner Earth, we want to teach you about your solar system's entrance into the Photon Band. As we have said, you must view things from where you are located, and we will give you the mechanics and data for constructing models to understand your movement into the Band.

See your solar system as a disk with the Sun in the center and all the planets whirling around it. That disk is divided into twelve zones, the twelve Great Ages of the Zodiac. As the planets move through these zodiacal zones, you can locate where a planet is in relationship to the Sun in these zones with astronomical ephemerides. For example, Venus might be in Leo or Scorpio, Pluto in Sagittarius or Capricorn. Who cares? Well, as this solar disk slowly penetrates the Photon Band, the point where that disk first begins to move in is the starting point that sets a line slicing into the disk. (See Fig. 5.) The entry point—spring equinox 1987—and the speed of this ingress, reveal which planets are in the Band. Examining the location of these planets moving in and out of the increasing slice in the Band will give you a perfect reading for how your planet is integrating the

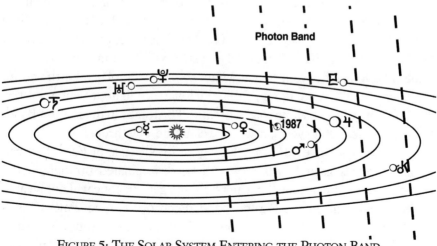

Figure 5: The Solar System Entering the Photon Band

photonic influence Band up to 2012. This material is rather complex, but it will become increasingly important. See Appendix B for the more exact data on the solar system in the Photon Band.

Would any of you deny how much your reality has changed since Harmonic Convergence? You truly are integrating the fourth dimension very quickly, and you are getting stronger impulses in 4D from the fifth dimension and above. You feel Earth's crystal intensely now, and you are well aware that the 2D telluric realm is waking up. A new order is forming, your light is changing, and you will need to be able to identify how the photonic light is transmuting you, especially since March 14, 1994, which was the beginning of Galactic Precipitation. Do not let yourself be fooled by scientists who say this light alteration is being caused by ozone deterioration due to chemical pollution! Although this is partly true, it diverts your attention from something much bigger that is happening: The Ozone Hole is opening due to photonic transmutation, so that solar rays can awaken the 2D telluric realm via the North and South Poles. A truly amazing pattern is building up, and you can adjust to it if you attune to the resonant vibration of the 1D iron crystal in the center of your planet.

For now, it is enough for you to know that Earth first entered the Photon Band at spring equinox 1987 and has been steadily moving into it further—one week more each side of that entry point every year. The border of photonic light is inching across the disk of your solar system. Planets further from the Sun than Earth have been exposed to photonic light when they are orbiting in the section of the disk already in the light. Earth was in the Photon Band from March 16 to 23 in 1987, then for three weeks in 1988. The photonic slice in the disk increases by two weeks each year, and precisely half of your solar system will be immersed when the Photon Band reaches your Sun at winter solstice 1998. Then Earth's entire orbital path will be engulfed in this tidal wave of light at winter solstice 2012. Eventually, the whole solar system will be totally in the Photon Band. During the next 2000 years, it will travel all the way through it.

At winter solstice 2012, any biological intelligence of Earth that can resonate to this galactic vibration will be disseminated throughout the whole Galaxy. Dimensions that can't hold the galactic tone will not be able to remain in form in the Photon Band. Each of the nine dimensions is beginning to tone within the Photon Band. As you are in your dimension, are you a lone reedy voice or a great booming voice in the magnificent chorale? To blow these seeds throughout the Galaxy, a great symphony is required that can vibrate our silica filaments and turn carbon residue to diamonds. Beethoven will be back, hearing his own late quartets that he composed after he was completely deaf in 3D. Van Gogh will even get his ear back. Because your voices need to be so powerful, your vitality and physical integrity must be great.

According to John Major Jenkins, the solar conjunction with the crossing of the ecliptic and Milky Way Band that will occur at the end of the Mayan Calendar happens exactly where the dark cloud in the Milky Way begins, a dark cloud of interstellar dust, the black hole of the Galactic Center.[17] What is left of Earth's biological intelligence can pass into the Galaxy by going through this womb of darkness. In the chapters that follow, you will discover how Tezcatzlipoca and Anubis hold the path of your solar system through the Galactic Night, and you will see why these great Dark Lords are coming forth to support Earth with their profound knowledge of this process. You will see how *knowing darkness is the key to maintaining awareness in the light of the Photon Band.* For now, this is the model of the Photon Band, the Galactic Night, and the Alchemy of Nine Dimensions. Let us begin to explore how these nine dimensions function in time within the Milky Way Galaxy, your stellar home.

FIGURE SIX: ANUBIS GUARDS THE GALACTIC NIGHT

# 2

## $\mathcal{T}$HE PHOTON BAND

"BEFORE THE SUN THROWS OUT LIGHT, WHERE IS THE LIGHT?
Photons come out of nowhere, they cannot be stored, they can
barely be pinned down in time, and they have no home in
space whatsoever. That is, light occupies no volume and has
no mass. The similarity between a thought and a photon is
very deep. Both are born in the region beyond space and time
where nature controls all processes in that void which is full of
creative intelligence."   —Deepak Chopra

*The Photon Band and the Process of Transmutation*
The Photon Band was first detected in 1961 by means of satellite-borne
instruments.[1] Later in the 1960s, earthlings began to move the focus of
their perceptions off planet, when the first astronauts went to the Moon.
This was a movement of consciousness out of 3D. The Photon Band might
have always been there. Prior to leaving your planet, you had no way of
knowing. Possibly all you are really doing is exploring galactic identity as
simply a new and more encompassing way of thinking. Whatever it is, your
view of reality has expanded into the Galaxy. What do I mean? You are
beginning to pinpoint your perceptual focus in a new center—the black
hole in the Galactic Center of the Milky Way. This enables you to reach a
new stage in your evolution.

The Pleiadians do not like being accused of being too concrete. To
them, it is fine to think of this shift as merely perceptual. However, I,
Satya, astrologer of Alcyone, will tell you that considerable evidence
already exists that you are being impulsed from the Pleiades and Sirius as
you stretch your minds beyond Earth's atmosphere. The first modern
Pleiadian contacts began in the 1970s, when Billy Meier of Switzerland

reported and photographed many Pleiadian ships. Communications through channels have increased since that time, and many of you have noticed that many indigenous people say they came from the Pleiades. A compelling argument for contact between Earth and Sirians was chronicled by Robert Temple in *The Sirius Mystery*, published in 1977; he asked how an otherwise illiterate African tribe knew Sirius was a trinary star system.[2] The time has come for you to realize that the Photon Band is real—in some dimension. You can see its influence in its growing popularity as a concept. Once enough individuals assume that it is having an influence, then the mere idea of it begins to alter your reality. For example, possibly the Photon Band is only a particularly apt metaphor for the Age of Light! It's back to good old Berkeley/Hume again . . . Would the Photon Band be changing your reality if you weren't noticing it?

You are moving into the Photon Band and we Pleiadians, who have been intimately involved with evolution on Earth, are being impulsed by the increasing photonic light in your realm. According to quantum physics, both of a pair of photons that originated in one positronium atom always have identical angles of polarization—the spatial orientation of the photon's wavelike action as it travels away from its point of origin (original positronium)—no matter how far apart they become.[3] Thus, what happens to a photonic particle in one part of the Galaxy happens to its twin simultaneously. In this way, what is now happening in the Pleiades to the star Maya is exactly what is happening in Earth's solar system. Now is the time to understand exactly how the Photon Band is the activation mechanism for the climax of the Mayan Great Calendar.[4]

The Pleiadians know much about this Band. Since Alcyone is located eternally in the Band, the Alcyone Library has the most information about it. Alcyone provides stellar gravity of the Pleiades, as your Sun provides solar gravity of your solar system. According to physicists, gravity is the force in the Earth's core that draws weight to itself. From the Pleiadian point of view, gravity is the first dimension of any system that originates communication links with nine dimensions of intelligence. All other dimensions derive from any 1D locus, and as they journey away from their 1D center, they become increasingly less solid. I, Satya, have always thought it was a hoot that your scientists can't yet define gravity. The joke is that they're looking in outer space when they should be starting the search for it in their own planet.

Seen from Alcyone, your solar system is like a lone, last Pleiadian sheep wandering way out in the darkness, which returns to the keep periodically. It is easier for you to comprehend your reality right now from our perspective, and that is why our collective 5D voice is so powerful in your minds right now. Alcyone is the mother of all the Pleiadian herd.

Now that you are opening your vertical axis of awareness, after being so immersed in your 3D horizontal plane, the Pleiadians are very disturbed about the fear-filled stories being circulated about the Photon Band. We have never seen such a Chicken Little syndrome! All the information you require for adjustment to a new perceptual field will be available as soon as you look at things in a new way. I, Satya, am happy to offer you as much information as possible from your own scientific sources, because this is more credible for you and helps you verify what you are already feeling. It would be even more powerful for you to just follow your own feelings now, with or without verification.

A photon is a quantum (smallest particle) of electromagnetic energy with zero mass—no electrical charge and an indefinitely long lifetime. This lack of electrical charge and long life causes my beingness on Alcyone to be magnetic and eternal. If it were not for my relationship in time and space with our other Pleiadian stars, I would express no movement or measure—the creation method of solar light in darkness—such as your solar system in the Galactic Night. If it were not for you, I, Satya of Alcyone, would not even know that I exist in this profound darkness. Remember, darkness defines light, and so I was impulsed to initiate *movement in time* and *measure in space* by sending out a spiral of light. For you, this is your spiritual life! Like Hathor, the Great Cow Goddess of Egypt, I love birthing you, and I can see realities in deep space because of you.

According to quantum physics, the positronium is composed of an electron and a positron, and because the positron is the electron's antiparticle opposite, the two collide eventually and form two quanta of light, or photons.[5] The collision resolves inherent duality into light, and as the electron is a basic unit of activation—life—it triggers the transmutation of the positron—karma. Thus, as the photonic light increases in your solar system, your karma transmutes into information, since light is information. *As you release karma, the antiparticles and electrons collide, quanta of light are formed, and the Photon Band manifests!* As photonic light increases in your realm, the power of your density release moves you deeply into your subconscious, and you get new information (light) about yourself. The more you explore this karma, the more life will be drawn to you for collisions with your energy. You are feeling this quickening.

I will give you an example that will help you take the Photon Band seriously. This will impulse you to prepare yourselves. The Photon Band has been triggering release of negative karma big time since 1987; we Pleiadians are truly astounded by your release of negative karma! Have most of you noticed the intensity of the emotional-body processing and the release of your addictions since 1987? Now enough of the emotional antiparticles have transmuted so that electrons are triggering you in your physical bodies. Thousands of years ago, first your spiritual bodies, then your mental bodies, were transmuted by light; and during the Age of Pisces, you have been transmuting your emotional bodies. Processing your physical bodies began March 14, 1994, and it involves releasing antiparticles called "miasms" from your bodies.[6]

You all have miasms in your bodies that you must release. These are etheric masses that hold memory of genetic or past-life disease patterns; memory of present-life diseases that were not cleared due to vaccinations, which prevented you from manifesting the disease memory and erasing it; or memory of disease that you drove deeply into your bodies by taking antibiotics, chemicals, or radiation when your body actually wanted to heal by means of its own immune system or by letting go into total healing by dying. These miasms are being intensely activated by the Photon Band since March 14, 1994, because your healing process has now moved into the 2D elemental realm. Your four bodies of consciousness increase in density progressing from spiritual to physical, and your process of transmutation has become increasingly intense.

As you progress into the Photon Band, the elements of your physical integrity—the parts of "you" that gathered together to make your body, according to your unique soul agreement—will be flying off and uniting with antiparticles melding into light. Once you are in the Photon Band, your depth of field—your rich biological memory in time—will be your actual embodiment, as long as you can clear these miasms. What do I mean? I have watched you respond to total immersion in the Photon Band before. This is how it looked to me in 24,000 B.C. and it still looks this way to me today: I see an exquisite, lush all-species Garden, and there you are, deep in the greenness as the hot solar light dissipates. Life is vibrating all around you, and you are in *samadhi*. There are no emotional body miasms in your physical body. You are photonic—a mass of cells that is pure intelligence—because you have surrendered everything you were holding from density in the Galactic Night. That is when the Supreme Council of Alcyone meets to read your codes and work with you to set intention about the next 26,000 years of evolution.

The galactic orchestrators—the Maya—have planned Earth's ascension brilliantly by studying your emotional-body density patterns from 3113 B.C. to the present time. They have figured out what it will take for you to accomplish this next step—clearance of your physical bodies—and they know that you cannot do it without all the powers of your mental bodies. You must know how the process works in time.

There are actually two dates in the near future that obsess you: the new millennium beginning 1/1/2000 and winter solstice 2012. Many of you have already begun to feel the frenzy of the millennium. You are waiting for your gods to rescue you, and you are not fully present in your "now." You sit glued to your televisions watching preachers scream about the End Times while your little children are hungry and deeply lonely. Many of you are waiting for Jesus to ride in on the clouds like a 1950s cowboy star. A huge group called "Light Net" will be waiting for "Him" to arrive at midnight, Dec. 31, 1999. When "He" doesn't show, the last emotional-body belief systems will dissipate, and then you will enter the most intense phase of transmutation up through 2012. Meanwhile, there will be a soft, deep, droning vibration all over the planet, like a great swamp vibrating at the Equator, as the indigenous people become ecstatic as they feel the pulsations of the Galactic Center. The inhabitants of Earth will actually pulse with the Galaxy after 2000 A.D., when the Sun becomes fully immersed in the Photon Band. The Galaxy actually pulses like a great heartbeat all the time, but this phenomena is very subtle. During heightened photonic immersion, the interconnectedness of the photon pairs is felt as resonating waveforms that make the galactic pulses audible. This time is the convergence of many cycles. The Maya are always the conductors in these times, and they know exactly what you require for ascension. *Ascension is your reimmersion in the Garden of Eden with your star memory open.*

The field of Alcyone is filled with photons that resonate with their twins elsewhere in the Galaxy. Alcyone does not manifest solid things in linear space and time, positrons have already collided with electrons and formed photon pairs, and the karmic transmutation process is not part of its reality. That is why you perceive the Pleiadians of Alcyone as so loving. Other Pleiadians have different characteristics, but Alcyone, as the central star, always directs the herd. We are genuinely fascinated with how you evolve in dualities, and we feel no judgment in our hearts about your karma. We do like to stimulate your life force, which triggers collisions between life and karma. I, Satya, love this phase with you when photonic influence increases and these dualities resolve into unified insight. Then I can read your energy. I tell you, people, you have nothing to fear. Solar light is a magnificent balm that triggers your growth and evolution in the Galactic Night, and then you return to the Photon Band. The Alcyone Library holds the photon analogs to your light, and what would a library be without books? I delight when you go through self-exploration, which for me is having you with me as you read these books.

The orbits of Pleiadian stars outside the Band are what provide data to Alcyone. The spiral makes it possible for Alcyone to express cellular memory in space and time, since memory atrophies unless it is communicated. This is the reason for the rich tradition of storytelling with indigenous people, and I would like you to know that the memory templates in our library are sound-coded. If the stories are sounded, the explosion of memory causes the pattern to be a spiral for critical leap time, and the spirals are generated by sound. During karma time in the Galactic Night, everything is endlessly circular, then the data which resonates powerfully enough to be audible moves the circle into a spiral. That is why you were all so fascinated with your "Slinky" rolling down the stairs. I tease you, but I've noticed that you usually learn more from your toys than from your books. I will give you a little tip: if you can hear the sound of your book in your head as you read it, it's a good one. Your words are wonderfully sound-coded.

### The Photon Band, the Mayan Calendar, and the Pleiades

Without your journey in the darkness, Alcyone would be eternal beingness with no intelligence, just as your Sun would have no creativity if the planets did not orbit around it, molding its experience by time and cycles. A few years ago, my vehicle would probably not have paid much attention to articles on the Photon Band in magazines, if it were not for the concept that Alcyone is the central Pleiadian star with your Sun as the eighth star of the system.[7] This knowledge was already retained deep in her mind because her Cherokee grandfather, many years ago, had told her Alcyone was her home. This memory was reawakened when she studied with Mayan daykeeper, Hunbatz Men. In his monumental work, *Los Calendarios Mayas Y Hunab K'U*, 17 sacred calendars of the Maya are described—most of which are short-term cycles—and one of the 17 calendars shows a 5D Pleiadian cycle—the Sun orbiting around Alcyone in a 26,000-year-long cycle.[8] This calendar helped our vehicle remember the early childhood story of coming from Alcyone told to her by her Grandfather Wise Hand, a carrier of the Cherokee records of Alcyone from his mother. The Cherokee knowledge passes from woman to man, then from man to woman. For our vehicle, it was very difficult to integrate such an idea while growing up in Saginaw, Michigan. And what does all that have to do with the Photon Band?

My vehicle noticed that the length of both the Pleiadian cycle and the precession cycle was 26,000 years, and the end of the Mayan Calendar and the precession into Aquarius were close in time. Therefore, she asked Hunbatz Men if the end of the Great Calendar coincided with the Pleiadian calendar, "Calendario del Tzek'eb o Pleyades," and he said yes. She quickly intuited that the entrance into the Photon Band was exactly that coincidence, and finally she was able to utilize astrological analytic methods, and she saw it! Our library read her wave of insight, and we saw it! Photon increase in the solar system would be what would trigger Earth's critical leap at the end of the Mayan Great Calendar during the Age of Aquarius! My vehicle already knew an abundance of geocentric astrological triggers; those transits are covered in Appendix A.

As for what science has to say about the possibility of the solar system being part of the Pleiades, researchers such as Robert Stanley and Shirley Kemp, along with astronomers Paul Otto Hesse, José Comas Solá, Edmund Halley, and Freidrich Wilhelm Bessel, have stated that this is scientifically feasible.[9] Robert Stanley reported on the discovery of the Photon Band by satellites in 1991 and commented, "These excess photons are being emitted from the center of our Galaxy . . . Our solar system enters this area of our Galaxy every 11,000 years and then passses through for 2,000 years while completing its 26,000-year galactic orbit."[10] Figure 4 attempts to model this cycle, with Alcyone immersed in the Band emanating out as a spiral that spins Pleiadian stars in and out of the Band. My vehicle has crafted the model of the Alcyone spiral, and this is feasible in terms of galactic distances. Earth is tilted in relation to the rotational plane of the Galaxy, and it is difficult to visualize and catalog motions of stars in our own galactic arm. The way the Pleiades are traveling as a group is shifting somewhat differently than other groups of stars in the Galaxy. Study of the Proper Motion or Universal Motion of stars suggested to most ancient astronomers that Alcyone was the Central Sun that the whole universe moves around.[11] Astronomers still have not invented the instruments to measure such subtle movements between bodies at a great distance from one another that are moving in similar directions, so these relative discrepancies appear to be infinitesimal from Earth. The solar system, the Pleiades, and Sirius revolve around the Galactic Center every 225 million years. Astronomers may not ever get verification of the Sun's relationship to the Pleiades or Sirius; however, how could so many separated indigenous people claim Sirian or Pleiadian origin if these were not ancient memories of the Sun's stellar system?[12]

Many trance channels were reporting increased contact with the Pleiades at the same time my vehicle was receiving increasingly clear communication with Alcyone. Hunbatz Men chuckled when she joked that she was from Alcyone and he must be from Maya. Men does not discuss the Photon Band in *Los Calendarios*, but he does discuss "La Luz," the coming age of light, which my vehicle's Grandfather Hand described as "The Age of Light" that she would someday live to experience. This is, of course, the increase of photons due to the collisions of karma and life force (kundalini), which results in two interconnected quanta of light.

A related issue, that has claimed growing attention since 1987 and was described by Arcturian beamer José Argüelles, is the activation of our solar system by means of a Galactic Synchronization Beam. This process began about 5100 years ago, and entered its climax phase—1987–1992—on August 16–17, 1987.[13] Indigenous peoples all over the planet synchronized themselves with this beam, and astronomers reported that the Galactic Center was emitting tremendous energy around this time. Supernova 1987 was visible in the skies during February 1987, as Argüelles, our vehicle, and a ceremonial group were activating Palenque in preparation for Harmonic Convergence. We Pleiadians know that many inhabitants of Earth realize something really big is unfolding because we can feel your curiosity building, and we love it. Speaking of pairs of photons resonating with each other at a great distance, could that function mean that the group at Palenque contained particles in their bodies that were twinned with the photonic waveforms of Supernova 1987?

Earth precesses into Aquarius every 26,000 years, when each Mayan Great Cycle completes and then begins again. According to both Aztec and Mayan cosmologies, 2012 is also the completion of a 104,000-year cycle composed of four Mayan Great Cycles. This coincides with the cycle of the Four Great Ages of the Aztecs, who say Earth will be entering into the Fifth World. This cycle is also the completion of a 225-million-year galactic orbit since the introduction of the reptilian species on Earth. I, Satya, can tell you that the energy of the Galactic Synchronization Beam in 1987 caused the Photon Band to attain a new dimensional frequency, which shifted the whole Pleiadian system into setting a new intention for the next biological stage of evolution beyond the reptilian mode. John Jenkins has definitively established that the end of the Calendar is winter solstice 2012, when the Sun conjoins the crossing point of the Earth's ecliptic and the Galactic Equator, as discussed in depth in Chapter One. Jenkins has even argued that this crossing is the message of the lid of Pacal Votan's sarcophagus at Palenque.[14] It was while in ceremony during Supernova 1987 that my vehicle was able to encode this 9D Galactic Center pulsation. Nine dimensions of cellular memory awakened in her physical body, as was happening with all other humans at that time.

When the Milky Way Galaxy was activated by the Galactic Synchronization Beam, its liquid darkness essence pulsated, and photon bands became nuclear clearing zones of the whole Galaxy. Every star and planetary system within the Galaxy sooner or later goes through this 9D galactic pulsation by means of photon bands. These bands support the form of the galactic arms, which are filled with electrical energy like your spines. The pulsations in the arms clear zones in the Galaxy by means of exquisite galactic sound tones, and some of you are already hearing this sound as kundalini rising. This is activation time in the galactic arm where the Pleiades are located. As the Pleiadians have said, at the end of the Great Calendar in 2012, biological intelligence will spread through the whole Galaxy by means of this information highway of light. It is as if these photon bands are stimulating antiparticles out of hiding in the whole Galaxy, and then the photon force in the bands is increasing! The Maya knew that the cleansing of emotional bodies and, lately, physical bodies on Earth would awaken biological integrity. They saw how distorted emotions perverted biological integrity, because this perversion was mirrored back to them by Cortez and his minions. They appreciated being able to look the god in the eye, and then they were sacrificed by the Spaniards. The Maya are now quanta of light as they gently persuade more and more people to cease abusing Earth. They are ready to orchestrate the whole planet through the critical leap of 2012.

*Nothing will remain in 3D form in the Photon Band unless it is amped up to nine dimensions.* Yes, this is true, but all this is happening slowly enough for all of you to accelerate your bodies to synchronize with it. If you choose activation, your access to energy clarification exists in your own spine, which will trigger the whole electrical system of your body, and karma you need to finish will make collisions. The photons that split out are signals that awaken the magnificent snake lying coiled in your root chakra.

### Snake Medicine and the Mayan Calendar

The keys to kundalini activation lie deep in the Mayan Great Calendar, which is all based on Snake Medicine. The daycounts of this Calendar are kept by daykeepers who compute with 13 numbers and 20 days. Before you fog out, listen very carefully, for these secrets are the keys to cosmic intelligence. The serpent—*Ahau Can*—that the Great Calendar is based on is *durissus crotalus*. It has a forked penis and grows two new fangs every 20 days, making it the ideal model for duality in quantum particles. The new fangs account for a 20-day turnover, and the diamond pattern of interlocking squares on *Ahau Can*'s skin is composed of sides of 13 scales.[15] (See Fig. 7.) These squares of 13 numbers are the basis of all the weaving patterns and cosmic symbols in Mayan art. That is, the weavers and artists reweave the cosmic pattern constantly in time, and they are never separate from the timing of the larger Great Calendar. The daycount and the weaving patterns keep the time of the cosmic Calendar. Isn't that amazing? Awakening the sacred serpent—*Ahau Can*—in your bodies is the way back into the Garden. This Calendar with its continuous daycount was created just to help you remember that the record keeper of the reptiles—the species completing 225 million years of evolution—is the Sacred Serpent. This snake is the high reptilian form, and the Maya used it as a great archetypal guide for the transmutation process itself. As I get deeper into this book, you will notice that 6D sacred geometry is always in the center of very powerful medicine teachings on Earth.

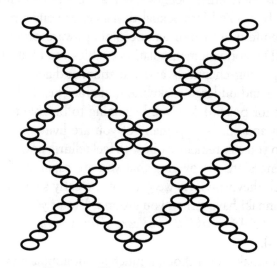

FIGURE 7: THE 13/20 *AHAU CAN*

## Elementals and the Telluric Realm

Unstable elements released on Earth's surface during the last 11,000 years must be returned to the frequency of the telluric dimension (2D), where they can reharmonize with the center of the planet. Elementals must go back into their telluric home during the Age of Light. Photons will help you realize you must find ways to return elementals to their domain by transmuting radiation and chemicals. These elements will long for the rich darkness of Earth when her surface is soaked in photonic light. On the surface, you already have an abundance of materials for creating your own reality. The Photon Band will trigger an elemental process of stabilization, and your part of the process is clearance of your own bodies.

This return of elements to their natural frequency can be very toxic, just like snake venom is when it is in your blood. When the half-life of radioactive elements speeds up and spews 2D powers into 3D, there is terrific instability that you all are feeling. You were supposed to notice that radioactivity and chemical pollution triggers cancer, but you've ignored the signals. Learn to empathize with toxic release by noticing how you feel when you are overwhelmed by 4D emotional energies that are not your own. When you carry out karmic actions in 3D that are actually triggered by 4D archetypal forces seeking expression, you begin to feel what it is like to be used as some other being's raw material. For example, a desire for orgasm can be tricked into sexual deviance, or your repressed desire for bonding manifests into murder. Becoming aware of shocking behavior caused by 4D emotional manipulation enables you to attune to the killing nature of spewing chemicals and radiation. Indigenous people conduct snake dances and undergo snakebite initiations just to be sure they never lose respect for poison! You are beginning to be able to empathize with telluric pain and chaos, and many of you are living in seismically active zones just so you can remember how to feel telluric power. Simultaneously, 4D intelligences are discovering that you are capable of destroying your reality, which they value. As we get into the early stages of exposing how the 4D Anunnaki have jerked you around, I want you to hear something: *Until 1987, the Anunnaki did not care about you or your world.* But they have changed.

The Anunnaki never thought much about impulsing you into opening Pandora's Box—splitting the elements—and seducing you with the idea that you'd like to be gods. Now they see how your god poison is lethal to all dimensions. The Pleiadians and Sirians are amazed to see that the Anunnaki want to take responsibility for helping you exorcise God poison. All beings playing in your nine-dimensional system realize the lower dimensions possess incredible powers that must not be invaded. Like humans and Pleiadians, the elemental forces must also maintain their integrity. It is becoming readily apparent how chemicals and radiation are toxic, and your bizarre emotional body dramas are hitting you in the face. You sense that O.J. Simpson is a mere part of a great archetypal drama. Beware of football games with many elemental dualities—blonde/black, sex/blood, and football/death.

You must not only cleanse your emotional bodies, you must also transmute radioactive and chemical spewing with your minds as you move through emotional blocks. I warn you: Do not bury radioactive elements underground in the 2D elemental realm, since your underground nuclear testing has already set off many earthquakes.[16] This cleansing is going on in all nine dimensions! As you clean up your emotional bodies, use some of that freed energy to clean up nuclear pollution. Nuclear instability involves elements on your planet that have been invaded and broken open, and so they spew. Since you also have been invaded and broken open, you can empathize with, and comprehend, this elemental pain. So as you put yourselves back together again, Earth heals. The elementals have become pain centers to trigger you in 3D. Like the 2D elementals, you have been invaded in your dimension by archetypal forces that have split you into dualities. This splitting threatens to shatter you, but then there will be nothing left of you for the archetypal intelligences to play with. That is why the Anunnaki are seeking ways to stop jerking you around. Like parents who observe their disgusting faults being mirrored back to them by their children, the Anunnaki are terrified by what they are seeing in the O.J. trial.

As you move further and further into the Photon Band, the photons have triggered emotional-body processing that is now prompting the need for an elemental cleansing. The Photon Band will increasingly agitate spewing elements in your physical bodies all over the planet. Nuclear laboratories are very dangerous things to be near, just as are angry people. You function by resonant vibrations, and it is time to scrutinize how you are vibrating. Do not be near people who will not lift themselves to your vibration in these times. As you move closer and closer into the photonic light, the spewing intensifies. More people are getting cancer as they resonate with these chaotic forces. Meanwhile, those of you who are cleansing your bodies, minds, and emotions are not vibrating to this spewing. Humanity is splitting into two groups: 1) those who did intense emotional-body work from 1987 to 1994 and minimalized their exposure to radiation and chemicals and who are now getting triggered by lingering miasms and learning to release them; and 2) those who were not cautious about toxic exposure, and who have refused to clear their emotional bodies, and who are angry, all riled up, and getting sick. One group is on high alert, intending to somehow find clarity and health. The other avoids looking within, waiting for the millennium while the elemental forces rage deep inside. Watch out for people who look like mad dogs!

## Feelings and the Pleiadians

Now the real test of how to accomplish the light transmutation is upon you. As you heal your physical bodies, you are also processing emotions that come up and must use the extraordinary knowledge contained in these feelings to send that energy to others. When you offer this release to others, it can return to its natural vibrational resonance. If you do not utilize this magnificent energy in this way, you will just be seeking your own trivial answer. Meanwhile, in light of the crisis building on the planet, group action is required for the critical leap. Triviality avoids the bigger issue—need for biological integrity as the Photon Band arrives. Answers about life are no longer available just in 3D. Everything is energy and vibrations, and just like being around angry people can make you sick, people who heal themselves and release that good feeling into the field make everybody feel better. These feelings can heal other humans, animals, microbes, plants, elementals, and spirits. These feelings are a potent source of mental and spiritual healings that seem to be miraculous and that are more subtle but more potent than physical and emotional healing, since the mental and spiritual realms are causal. Thought and intent literally determine the health status of your organs, and people get sick from ideas all the time.

The power of your personal healing field is directly proportional to the power of your love, which always attracts Pleiadian assistance. Have you ever noticed how children seem to thrive like healthy plants in some families and wilt in others? Love draws the Pleiadians into your world, especially when you are children. For those of you who have grown up, more and more of you must contact your inner child—the being in you who remembers the Pleiadians. If you send out this boundless love, a Sirian consciousness may suddenly appear, ready to open a doorway you've been knocking on for eons, because the Sirians expand the structure opened first by love.

*Feelings are the only way you can move yourselves outside of linear space and time while you are in body, since they are the access point for beings in other realities to communicate with you.* Since 4D is emotional and not physical, the 4D entities have been drawn too tightly into your realm in order to trigger feelings in you. These feelings have set up dramas that distract you, and you can't see when energy is stuck. What is the solution? Own your own feelings totally! Watch for when you are being run around by something that does not feel good to you.

I, Satya, enjoy visiting you these days because many of you now understand that when you work with emotional energies on Earth, you can send this healing force anywhere. That is Chiron's teaching. Chiron is the half-animal, half-human guide who can direct you deeply into the wounded parts of your emotional body.[17] When you have gone deep enough into your inner darkness where pain is stored, you begin to feel the powerful telluric forces in your own body. These forces were imprisoned in your bodies when 4D Anunnaki drew elementals out of the underworld (2D) to get them to trigger you into various 3D dramas. Get it, peoples, if you are doing something and you feel bad, that discomfort is a signal that elementals do not like being sucked into your body to trigger your action. Then they get stuck and lurk in deep pools in your bodies—miasms—and whenever you are exposed to spewing chaotic energies, these elementals resonate with the chaos. These wounded places can easily be felt in your bodies, and if you will listen to their message, you won't get sick. Whenever you are processing any intense feeling, notice which part of your body is in pain. Move your awareness into that place, and with great respect, ask these elemental forces to release themselves through dimensional portals and return to their own homes. Chiron is the planet that rules clearing the body by releasing the deepest pain. There is not one disease that cannot be healed just by thought.

## The Danger of Beliefs and Groups

To give you some sense of how critical these times are, I ask you to think about groups for a moment. Nothing will be more dangerous for you in the coming years than your involvement in groups gathered together around archetypal belief systems. The bombings of the Branch Davidians in Waco, Texas, in 1993 and the Federal Building in Oklahoma City in 1995—which both caused the deaths of many innocent children—are only an early warning. Literally, the only thing that can stop this hideous acting out of unprocessed inner violence is recognition by each one of you of your own inner pain. In this book you will hear from Lucifer. For now, it is enough to know that Lucifer is a grand force imprisoned in Christianity by religious control forces. Lucifer is used as an archetype to make you avoid looking at your own inner evil. He will tell you all about his entrapment in your realm. For now you need to realize that you hold Lucifer in your own body when you refuse to look at your own inner violence.

Your inner child is your source of multidimensional access, and you cannot access it if you judge everyone but yourself, if you require a devil to contain what you need to look at yourself. As you are being physically triggered by photonic increase, the Pleiadians are interested in busting all groups because you will not survive if you think anything will activate you except yourself. Groups based on belief systems exist to harvest your energy at critical leap time, and the group itself keeps you from going deeply within yourself. Until 1999, these various groups will do anything to hold your membership, including kill you. "Member-ship" means "body-ship," and we would suggest that you do not sign over your body parts.

Chiron is the archetype of bodywork. The 2D elementals are drawn into your body by 4D archetypal forces wanting to use you as a robot to carry out their dramas. If you do not have a clear sense of ownership of your body, 4D archetypal forces can suck 2D elementals into your body, and then you find it difficult to identify what that energy is. Since most of you do not know how to read blood, you find it difficult to feel elemental energies in your bodies. This is why there is so much taboo around blood. Meanwhile, elemental rousing can actually be felt in your bodies. You must realize the power of bodywork because no force can influence you if you fully know your body. During massage, Reiki work, rolfing sessions, or acupuncture treatments, the bodyworker stimulates various parts of your body so you can read its records. Assuming you are in a safe and protected space while this occurs, you are encouraged to tune into your feelings while your body is being activated. The elementals screaming to be re-leased to their realm will happily trigger you into exploring the feelings that first entrapped them—the agenda being played out in you that you did not feel good about. If you allow your feelings to "run"—just go wher-ever they want to go—deep truths will emerge in your mind, and tremen-dous power is released that "frees" you. This allows you to rediscover what pure integrity feels like, what it feels like to just be in your body.

I do not want you to miss out on what a big revelation this is, so we will test you with a little story to see if you get it. Once upon a time, Adolf Hitler decided he wanted to control the world. This desire came from his childhood, when he was not recognized for who he was—a great al-chemist. As he grew older, he got more and more frustrated by people not recognizing that he was a great alchemist who could activate power in the elemental realm and rile people up so he could control them. He decided, therefore, to show everybody his powers. He made big magical pacts with 4D archetypal beings. These beings impulsed individuals in 3D to gather together in groups, and these groups were in turn impulsed to carry out various agendas based on fear. Gradually these individuals put all their attention on the agendas instead of their ordinary lives and became isolated from their loved ones, acting like robots and sheep in Hitler's system. In exchange for these followers, Hitler became head orchestrator of the dramas, and got all the attention.[18] Notice peoples . . . He got all the attention because nobody forgot about him. He set up the dramas by alchemically activating the 2D elemental realms that then sucked 4D archetypal energies into peoples' bodies, and then he manipulated the people in 3D based on the gigantic archetypal belief systems that he manipulated.

Why do I even bring him up? I said I wanted to see if you'd be willing to be tested. If you react with reflexive horror to what we say, then you are still part of one of the groups Hitler invented; the group is called "Holocaust." It is not that the Holocaust was not the penultimate horror. It was! However, I warn you that groups exploiting past memories are more dangerous than groups working on present problems. You have no access for resigning from such groups, since they exist in the past, and meanwhile you are not responding to the present-day holocaust—Bosnia Herzogovina. Observe what you are doing when you dwell on the past. Are you just constantly bringing up old stuck emotions or are you doing it to release feelings about old pain? Use powerful places from the past only for releasing elemental forces to their own worlds, not as devices for holding elemental powers imprisoned in the Earth. That is what smudging is for. Use it as a powerful tool to assist the return of elementals to their world.

## Healing and Orgasms During the Photonic Activation

In their excitement about being freed, these powerful elemental intelligences adjust their frequency down to Earth's core, and by the principle of gravity, they leave your bodies. This is the key to healing cancer with energy, and, as the photonic light increases, working with elemental forces is being remembered by people. How does this work? I can't wait to tell you because we know many of you are worried about this. When one of you has the grand opportunity to dig out a truly nasty unspeakable act that you've carefully hidden deep inside yourself and examine it and love all parts of it, this release sends the ecstasy of your clearing to someone still afflicted by a physical ailment, or to an animal species on the verge of extinction. Once you recognize the energy of spewing elemental forces contained in the "nasty," you see and feel this energy in others, and you can direct your new healing harmonic to a cancer in someone else's body! In order to do this, the cancer itself must be asked if its message has been received by the person with cancer. The disease must be loved by its carrier as the ultimate gift, for it was what drove the individual to the edge of death and challenged him/her to be truthful.

The word "nuclear" means "new clear." All-will-clarify. The Sun rules your sense of self on Earth, and once the Sun is completely within the Photon Band around the year 2000, male and female will become harmonic. The Sun as holder of solar identity for earthlings has held male/female polarization in its awareness since 8800 B.C. As you became more self-reflective, you noticed gender more. This male/female experience has taught you about polarization, and this knowledge will be your source for feeling stellar affinities—interconnecting with your stellar photonic waveforms. This is why the focus on female-in-male/male-in-female is intensifying; yet male and female polarization will not exist for you when you are in the Photon Band. You are all doing a tremendous service working on this issue, more than you realize. This is waking you up to starwaves.

People are becoming more androgynous, and there is much difficulty and confusion around this issue. There is also a building sense of recognition that the Pleiades are the home of the Goddess, while your Sun is essentially male. This helps you to see that gender and sexual identity are totally unrelated. The Sun is a male force seeking identity as it travels so bravely far out into the Galactic Night. Just to survive the long journey, earthlings cling to any identity they have. They desperately latch onto belief systems that pervert and exploit sexual expression. Meanwhile, there is a difference between male and female at the stellar level. That is what you have actually been wanting to know. Your personal sense of male/female has absolutely nothing to do with your sexual preferences, which are merely creative avenues for potential multidimensional exploration. Meanwhile, your resonation with gender identity is the vibration that will protect your species integrity. Strong sexual polarization for mating purposes is the interconnective principle in the universe; it intensifies attraction and joining via photons.

During the time your solar system is outside the Photon Band traveling through the Galactic Night, you evolve biologically. Then when you are in the Photon Band, you go through a clearing process of that biological evolution, a reflective analysis that all species benefit from. Recently, you have been intending more and more orgasms. You decided you wanted to be able to envision and channel kundalini energy in your bodies. You actually created an intention to see the light flowing in your bodes while having sex.

When you are in the Photon Band, evolution emerging out of the density of the Galactic Night gets amped up. Whatever in the Galactic Night that can withstand dimensional recalibration becomes part of the new multidimensional form. I am saying that you have managed to create the experiences you require in order to know how to establish a sexual morphogenetic field in which all of you will be juiced by the sexual energy of everybody else. However, only a few of you will give birth. Homosexuals, childless couples, and celibates will all offer their energy consciously for the precious conceptions, so the children are amped up and shared by all. For fun, let's call it, "The Pleiadian One-Hundredth-Monkey Birth-Control System." Fourth-dimensional entities have become such experts at manipulating you into playing out sexual agendas that you often don't know whether you are male or female. They've confused your exploration of stellar identity—projection or reception of energy—with 3D sexual identity issues. You imagine that you must have a lifelong sexual agenda, and you scream, "I am gay!" Or you puff yourself up and strut about pretending to be the ideal heterosexual family man when you are sneaking around seeking sexual variety.

The darkest hour of the Net was during World War II. Right after the War, people began to discover multidimensional access in sexual intercourse. Many more of you than you realize have been figuring this out. This has been a way to feel pure orgasmic force offering you an energy goal, and your easiest access to it is through sexual activity. Now things are getting even more interesting. Many adults committed to seeking intense orgasm are noticing that the children who were conceived out of this shared orgasmic union are very multidimensional. Many parents are noticing that their children are more conscious than they are—*superconscious* in fact.

Soon you will be amazed to see that children will be conceived only out of high orgasmic states. Once the Photon Band swallows the Sun, the only energy that will be able to create children in 3D is orgasm. If it were otherwise, the children would die when they were born into the field of light. Imagine a man and a woman who have chosen to have a child very consciously, they are having sex, and they can feel all the sexual energy being sent to them by nearly a hundred other partners having sex. When the moment of conception arrives, the auras of the man and woman are tremendously enhanced by all the loving energy from the fields of so many other activated humans, and due to the great clarity and integrity of the couple, their auras mix and meld into an exquisite interwoven figure eight that creates an ideal light body for a new child. This child will be greatly loved and shared by the community. Gay and lesbian members and many other people in this sacred vision will parent this child. They will support the child's parents on all levels because they will know the totally male-and-female polarized sexual act has activated the ideal sexual morphogenetic field. They will also understand that the child must be raised in this particular field in order for the child to be able to activate its own orgasmic powers. The sexual identity of that child will be irrelevant at a societal level, and male or female identity would only be important when polarization is needed for ideal conception.

This form of conception will create a new sexual morphogenetic field in which the sexual fusion of the man and woman is enhanced by the support of the whole group as described above, and it will be obvious that all other forms of conception are destructive. In vitro fertilization, surrogate pregnancies, cryogenic freezing of sperm and eggs—all of these practices are abominable—and are not going to work. In the new morphogenetic field of sexuality, the issue of whether a person births or not will be unimportant. Infertile couples will not be concerned because they will be aware that they have many lifetimes—fertile in some, barren in others. Yet all will be parents of all the children. All in the community will love and esteem mothers and fathers who actually possess the powers of conception, and who dedicate themselves to enhancing this energy by birthing. There will be no unmarried parents because a successful marriage—two functional adults who have orgasmic sex together—will be the prerequisite for conception; conception will be impossible without the melded and fused auric fields. All children will have a mother and a father, as well as the support of the whole group.

When you are in the Photon Band, you are 5D; there is no time, and you are not worried about having babies—but *we* are. We are here to mine your information, we have been honest about this, and we want all of the experience and information that you accumulated during the Galactic Night. We mine you for information and in exchange, we assist you in the transition. Therefore, we are here to assist you in creating the new biological morphogenetic field—a world where all birth is chosen and crafted in group-orgasmic resonation. As I have said, the best way to get your records for us is to mine you while you are having sex. The Pleiadians love merging with your codings as you are having sex, and as your codings mix, we explode you from within in your hearts. Why?

## The Galactic Information Highway and the Sirians

We are your central star, and in order for us to hold the orbital patterns and harmonic patterns by means of wave resonance that holds this stellar system together, we require a very complete level of intelligence. The Maya have stated that human orgasms spin the Galactic Center! Now I am discovering in this reunion with you that you've made a lot of progress the last 11,000 years. As you move into the light and become more accessible to me, it is only possible for me to merge with you when your energy is very heightened, as during highly conscious, intentional sex, or when you are passionately curious about your world.

We can only merge with individuals who are holding their light body—"*ka*"—in their physical bodies. The *ka* offers conscious access to your physical, emotional, mental, and soul bodies. Your sense of self differs in each one of these bodies, and these more subtle senses of self greatly widen your access to nonphysical vibrations. For many, the four bodies of consciousness have already become a useful tool for better knowing your feeling states, and now we will say that this knowledge is the ideal pathway to your Pleiadian origins. The degree to which we can merge with you is dependent on how much energy you can activate in yourselves. Remember, the consciousness of holding your *ka* in your body is what activates kundalini energy. This is why the knowledge of the *ka* was so cherished in ancient Egypt. Egypt from 3500 to 1400 B.C. was a civilization that held the Sirian geometric light field open for all its people. In this field, often referred to as the "Blue Nile," people were taught how to hold their *ka* in their bodies, and then their bodies held the integrity of this Nile field in place. People were grounders of cosmic resonance. As of March 1994, this geometric light field has relocked back into the vortex system of Egypt, and 3D has been expanded again to hold the 6D Sirian geometrical forms.

A new book that covers *ka* work in depth is available by Amorah Quan-Yin called *The Pleiadian Workbook: Awakening Your Divine Ka.*[19]

As your solar system orbits through the Galactic Night, you access the subtle light of many different star systems. For example, you might have an experience with Arcturian light or Orion knowledge. As your solar system continues its journey through the Galactic Night, the further it gets into darkness, the more the intelligence of other star systems can be perceived. For example, knowledge of the Sirians was activated on Earth during the Blue Nile phase in Egypt. At the present time, Alcyone is mining the knowledge from these other stars in order to feed galactic communication links, the photonic information highway. Individuals willing to play around with different parts of this karmic exposure are giving very valuable service to the Pleiadians. In return, the Pleiadians are here to assist you in making this transition because every relationship is an agreement.

Many of you will choose not to stay in your bodies as the energy accelerates, and this is a perfectly fine choice. I do have some advice for you. The best thing about the new energy field activating your planet is that you will find yourselves more able to create your own realities because the expansive nature of the Sirian geometric field makes synchronicities visible in 3D. If you just follow the connections between unrelated things, you can create anything. This expanded field will harmonize your body to any higher vibrations that you can detect, so *let your body lead your choices*. At first this feels like a subtle connecting web of intuitive knowing, then gradually it becomes a conduit system for energy activation. The more you trust this new way of responding to your environment, the happier you will be. This new field is always the sign of very intense photonic activation, which can occur even without being in the Photon Band. The Blue Nile Egyptians achieved this while outside the Band; they grounded starlight by building the Giza Plateau pyramid system, a star map for accessing "The Roads of Osiris," the road to the Orion corridor of the Galactic Night.[20]

The Egyptians developed a system that grounds starlight. In the coming years, you will realize that this same kind of system is the technology behind Rennes le Chateau, Avebury, and Teotihuacan. Now that the Sirian field is locked into the geomantic grids again, you will be amazed how the planet and your sight will reawaken. You will rebuild the temples that enhance the sacred sites once you realize how important they are for planetary stabilization during your journey in the Photon Band. Without these fields, the surface consciousness of Earth becomes extremely dualized, and this was the reason for Akhenaton's bizarre attempt to reestablish the field. In extremely dualized environments, it is very hard to see how to craft your reality.

What is the difference between a dualized reality and the polarization we speak of? With polarization, two units are in resonance; they are interconnected, and they are capable of linking different dimensions and worlds. Units that are dualized are separated in one dimension, such as "either/or," "black/white," "us/them," in 3D. Dualized environments are very limiting, and intelligence is diminished. The Sirian geometric fields expand by means of interconnected photons, and synchronicity abounds because this interconnectivity opens portals to other dimensions. *Attunement to synchronicity affords fleeting glimpses into cosmic realms that rip your sight wide open.*

I advise you that the way to attune to the natural polarization of the photons is to model your life in 3D according to the house system of the zodiac. If you think of yourself on the planet's surface as being in the center of a circular horizontal plane divided into twelve fields of exploration, you will be astonished by how much this model can expand your sense of self. Normally, you are dualized into one side of the issue or the other—such as self/other—but in a field of six polarities of twelve basic life experiences, you are playing out your life while widening the ends of the six polarities. The division of twelve expands your consciousness beyond duality and out of 3D, and a wider view of potentiality moves your field out. The "either/or" interpretation of reality dissipates, and you stop buying into one belief system or the other. Peoples, get this: The Sirians did not really expand your world, you did! From 1972 to 1994, you woke up and realized you were pawns in a game. This magnificent new subtlety that you have attained then made it possible for the Sirians to utilize the expansiveness of your horizontal plane, and they invented a complex new vision that they can hold for you and your planet while you open your eyes. I applaud the Sirians for this beautiful new reality-expanding geometric form.

## Making Home

The Pleiadians admit they have triggered part of this from one point of view. I have told you that the only sin I, Satya, have ever found on Earth is boredom. My vehicle signaled me back in 1972: "It is totally boring, and the repetitions are nauseating!" I could see that you all knew exactly what you were doing. Lately, some of you are magically opening your eyes and living in the present, but many of you are frozen in the past, just like the mastodons who died in the last pole shift and are found today frozen en masse in glaciers. Their flesh was still edible when it was defrosted. Some of you realize you have a choice about at least one thing on the planet— your life. Here you are in this magnificent new field of possibilities. You view the awesome powers of Earth changes, and the grand dramas that individuals like O.J. are creating for you, and you decide: "I'm outta here!" So, make your exit fun!

You can craft your own exit any way you want to by facing what you fear about your personal death. How do you do that? Look deep inside yourself and see exactly where you are choosing death, and then just go for it big time. Are the Pleiadians crazy? Worse, are we disrespectful? Well, the Pleiadians aren't the ones who are drinking alcohol and smoking tobacco while they believe it's killing them; or living in an area building up for Earth changes feeling certain they will die in it; or having loveless sex and hating themselves when doing it. You are! Peoples, it is so easy now. Just enjoy drinking and smoking if you do it; take intense pleasure in living on the edge while you are doing it; and have sex only when you love some-one! There is death in all your ecstasies—that is the nature of 3D—but you don't have to deny yourself any pleasures. *Own what you desire, and all that exquisite energy will be released as waves of joy in the Galaxy.* Stop judging what you are doing, or stop doing it and decide to be alive!

If you choose to leave 3D during these times, we honor you; all we ask is that you consider creating a magnificent death that will blast all your genius through the Galaxy. Many of you have desired immortality by becoming a Beethoven or van Gogh. However, you don't have to go deaf or cut your ear off or not get paid for your work while you are alive! Don't buy into the idea that your killer is killing you! See how each moment is exquisite and how nobody will be able to herd you like cattle. Decide to "Make Home" right now. Go outside the place where you live and take a walk. Breathe deeply, expand your sight, smell with your heart, and feel the tactile responses in your feet. Swing your arms around, and then look intensely into your environment. Ask yourself, "Do I love Earth in this place?" If you feel rejected by your environment because you think it is too dry, too cold, too urbanized, too reclusive, you have some thinking to do. Now that the Sirian geometric field is expanding your field, you won't be able to stay in any place unless you love it. Your only job is to feel grounded in your place and radiate that feeling into your environment. Soon all you will be is grounders of geometric light forms into Earth. She will not tolerate your rejection of her.

Whether you are in the city or country, the jungle or desert, does not matter. You are personally coded to love a certain place on the planet, and the Sirian geometric field will draw you there. Otherwise you will blow up from the miasms that will be triggered in your bodies. Do not believe what you have been told about "place." For example, New York City is one of the most powerful reptilian vortexes on the planet. People have been drawn to cities because of the great vortexes in those locations. New York City is built over magnificent limestone caves that are the sacred temples of awesome 2D telluric beings, and its energy field is similar to that of Jerusalem. When the indigenous people ruled your land and the people understood the power of place, Manhattan Island was known to be a great rock phallus, and it was reserved as a wild forest of twelve sacred springs. These springs each had an altar on which sacred sex was performed for conceiving star babies. There was a sandy beach at the tip of the "penis" where the most sacred purification rituals took place. New York City is so filled with creative genius and geomantic power that our vehicle can feel vibrational differential on almost every street. The most important sacred spring was once called Turtle Island, and it is located right under the United Nations building. London, Paris, Rome, and all big cities are caps over geomantic vortexes that access stellar genius. Conversely, the New England countryside is riddled with powerful megalithic calculators and stone circles constructed after the last glacier receded around 9000 B.C., when we last entered the Galactic Night. The planet is drawing you to your home, where you will be safe and happy.

Every inch of the planet is beloved by Gaia and coded with incredible creative force that the megalithic people understood and channeled during the Age of Taurus—4320 to 2160 B.C. They developed this technology based on remnants of Paleolithic knowledge from the Age of Scorpio— 17,280 to 15,120 B.C.—that survived the immersion in the Photon Band during the Age of Leo—10,800 to 8640 B.C. This is why you feel such energy at the Great Pyramid or Avebury Circle. This is why the photonic language—Crop Circles—is imprinting now in the fields of the planet. It is showing you through the plants where the life force is enhanced. These vortex markings are there to activate you into knowing where you are supposed to be.

I, Satya, want you to take me seriously on this teaching: Making Home, an ancient Cherokee teaching. I offer you information about the timing and qualities of the end of the Mayan Calendar to get you to pay attention to what is going on. I want you to hear me now: What each one of you does is much more important than you realize, because the amount of galactic knowledge that your planet can hold is determined by your attunement to that knowledge within yourselves. If you are walking out of your house and feeling hatred for your street, town, or land around yourself, you are in grave danger. You must take time to attune to the place you live and feel it in your heart; you must work with the energies of your place to enhance them enough so you are responsive to Earth again; or you must seek a place where your heart expands in the rain and sunlight. Do not fear the Sun, rain, winds, and fire; simply change in yourself what resists these essential elements. You cannot live without the elements, and the elements cannot live without you. The photonic activation is now waking up the miasms in your bodies, and you will not be able to handle the transmutation of your pain if you are in an environment that repels you. Hear it, let it resonate in you, say it: "I will Make Home now."

Get out of the past, everything has changed! All you need to do now is look deeply inside and name what you fear, while choosing to live in a place that expands you. Next, go out into your world, do exactly what you fear the most, and observe yourself carefully. Intend what you want, and if you find yourself saying "I can't, I won't," blow through it and say, "I want this!" and then do it! Go on a vision quest, do a mushroom circle, take the spice, or even consider a snake initiation. Begin living right in the moment. You will only be able to do these things if you really feel heart expansion and grounding each day in your special place. Otherwise it is hopeless. How can you ask for Gaia to hold you if you reject her every day of your life?

I am not here to tell you how to die. I am here to tell you that all the information for ecstatic life is right in your life now. You can stop thinking your ultimate choice over your own body is elsewhere and is delayed. Know that incredible loving energy is opening deep within you now that

the Sirians are enhancing the immense geometrical structure that intensifies the Pleiadian love vibration. Feel the love rising in your home, and you
will recognize this by how you feel in your heart. This magnificent activation is an awakening of the Christ energy within each body on Earth. What
do I mean? The Christ energy in your bodies is the resynchronization of
the crystalline codes in your blood with Gaia. Choose life by Making
Home. Or face yourself in choosing your own death—passage to other
realms with a clear sense of direction—release, and stop littering the planet
with yourself when you are half dead!

Meanwhile, the 2D elementals in the central core crystal of Gaia are
waking up and expressing the intelligence of Gaia. Then her surface is
juiced by 5D Pleiadian love harmonics and kundalini fire from nonphysical realms. Only energies in total integrity will remain in the lower dimensions. This is how morphogenetic replication occurs. In this activation,
antiparticles in your body release to seek analogs, photons that will tell you
exactly how to heal yourselves. This is why I say: Follow your fascination,
follow the synchronicities, because those cues are popping out of all the
fusions. Just ask. Each one of you who chooses to go to physical integrity
will feel exquisite, and each one will play a role in setting the new morphogenetic field of biological life. Would you want the disease you are
repressing to be part of the new morphogenetic field of awakened biology?
Would you want the potential for Rwanda to be part of it?

The only way to discover biological codes is to begin with yourself.
You were called into being as a form that is nine dimensional. You are an
organization of energy that expresses itself physically, emotionally, mentally, and spiritually in the form of these *four bodies of consciousness*. The
clearance and activation of these bodies can propel you right into galactic
resonance. (See Fig. 8.) Until March 1994, the "body" that was the most
dense was your emotional body, due to your rich karmic encounters with
beings of all dimensions during the last 11,000 years. The archetypal 4D
realm is the first nonphysical realm beyond your physical bodies; it can
only be accessed by feelings, and it is like a screen for nonphysical dimensions. The natural geometry of your 3D form has re-formed into a true
pyramid, making it possible for you to ground Sirian solid geometry. Your
emotional body seemed to bulge out wider than your physical body in the
pyramid, but its processing is now complete—although some of you may
have some residual work to complete—and you are accelerating in your

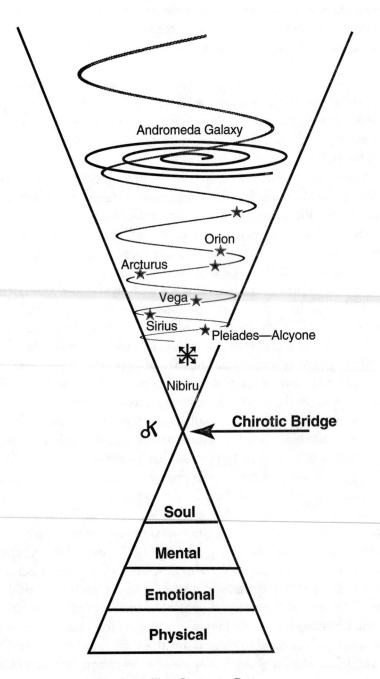

FIGURE 8: THE GALACTIC BRIDGE

physical bodies. The acceleration is very intense because the miasms must be cleared, and that is why you must Make Home so Earth can assist you. *Gaia is going to rebirth every one of you.*

Many teachers have been assisting you in quickening your emotional bodies; they know this is your point of access for multidimensionality. Barbara Hand Clow has already published the solar astrological techniques for facilitating these quickening processes in *Liquid Light of Sex: Understanding Your Key Life Passages.*[21] This body of work is an essential life guide for individuals who will be between ages 30 and 50 from 1987 to 2012. She has also published a trilogy on quickening yourselves by means of past-life regression and multidimensional therapies. If bodyworkers and therapists in these techniques are not available for you, this trilogy can actually trigger much of your own past life content and cellular memory.[22]

## *Your Sacred Altar and your* Ka

No matter where you are, you can Make Home, even in a jail cell. There are two very powerful methods: a sacred altar to the four directions and the practice of sacred body postures. Regarding an altar, explanations of the qualities and energies of the four directions are widely taught and available. You need to study and ascertain the energy of each direction, and you need to choose a small space—eight-by-eight feet is perfect—and establish a center. Then make an altar to each direction. The center becomes the point in your reality that plugs right into the central core crystal of Gaia, and the four directions pull in consciousness from all directions. As you sit in that center and build your understanding about the energy of each direction, sacred objects—stones, bones, artifacts, love gifts, and crystals—will come into your life. Each object will be strongly related to your understanding of one of the directions. By placing sacred objects on certain directions on your altar and remembering its teaching each time you pray in the center, your personal access to multidimensional intelligence will build and build. The elementals underneath you will feed you with intelligence of Gaia. Soon you will find yourself going to this altar whenever you need to heal someone or yourself; you will go there to seek guidance for any question, and you will return there to hold counsel with the intelligences you have brought into your realm. In the center of your altar, the nine-dimensional axis will draw beings into your space as you learn to center.

Eventually, your altar will be a universe that contains all. One room of your house can be this altar, but a small space enhances concentration. With enough time, you will recognize when your *ka* is contained in your body by how this feels when you are in the balanced multidimensional space of your altar. When you are out in the larger world, you will hold your *ka* in your body easily because you will be able to feel when it is not in you. You will be able to reintegrate your *ka* and recharge yourself anytime you want to by returning to center in your altar. Eventually, there will be so many centered individuals in the world that the whole planet will become harmonic.

The model of the human chakras in Figure 9 is different than any model on Earth. This is the Pleiadian view of the human chakra system, and it differs from other systems in that the first chakra—the earth chakra—is the central core crystal of Earth (1D of your realm). In my system, the seven-chakra system begins with the earth chakra as your ground, five chakras in your body from your sexual center to your third eye, and then your seventh chakra is located in the Galactic Center. Your body is in 3D, so your first chakra is your plug into Earth's core, and a line moves out of the center of Earth through the 2D telluric realm and locks right into your root chakra. The first and second dimensions electrically activate your body in your root chakra; if this waking up is strong enough, the serpent rises in your spine and your whole body becomes an electromagnetic field. This field is your body in 3D, and Making Home means grounding your activated body.

Figure 10 will assist you in understanding how 1D grounds you in one point. Then it triangulates through telluric energy allured to you by your own body. Your body takes in the power of the center of Earth, resonates with the energies of the 2D telluric realm by means of cords into your body made of different elemental forms, and then expresses itself by means of your four bodies of consciousness while you are alive (3D). Visualize the 4D archetypal realm as a canopy that can hold the tremendous energy radiating out of your physical body. This 4D canopy is held in form by the subterranean 2D elemental beings who express Gaia, and it has the capacity to respond to 5D through 9D dimensional forces, enabling you to apprehend very high vibrations. The fourth dimension has enough density by means of feelings to enable you to create the full canopy; with it you can observe 4D dramas, and if you can stop judging what you see, you will

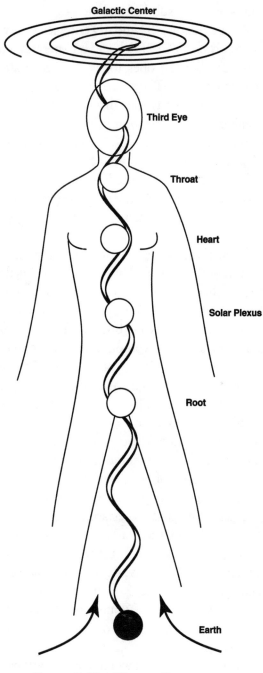

FIGURE 9: THE HUMAN CHAKRAS

begin to pick up some very subtle frequencies.

If it seems like I denigrate 2D and 4D energies in any way, beware, for it is *your own projection!* The 2D elemental energies and 4D archetypal forces are simply the hardest ones for you to integrate. The Pleiadians appreciate their expressions. They love their outrageous creativity. If you hear something in what we say that throws you into judgment about an energy, try listening to that objection in yourself. It is a part of you that you have not cleared. I will drag you through many of your most cherished beliefs. I will insult you about your fanaticism and expose your foolishness and blindness only because you might see one of your own projections mirrored back to you. Why? These projections are what create evil, and when you release them in yourselves, the potential for evil is decreased.

The Pleiadians have spoken fondly of bodywork. Lying in deeply wounded places in your body are the multidimensional experiences that you had in the past that can trigger your consciousness now; you were not able to integrate the experiences when they occurred before. Yet, the energy had to be activated in your bodies for you to have something to work toward. You must realize you often have experiences that have bad parts, and then you deny the whole experience and bury it. During the last 11,000 years in the Galactic Night, you've had many incredible experiences that have become your library of knowledge—memory—for the next stage of evolution. A long time ago, you stretched yourself and tried this or that, you didn't attain it, but you saw new possibilities. Now as things are culminating, all this potential is rising to the surface in all of you.

If you doubt this, think of your history. What else explains the richness of all the dramas on your planet. And what causes you to kill each other in the thousands in order to establish who owns one little part of the planet? If you think about it, you know how the 2D elemental feeling forces, such as blood lust, get riled up when the 4D archetypal beings impulse you into a battle. What else explains the rape and cannibalism in Bosnia-Herzegovina and Rwanda? You are getting sucked into huge dramas so you can figure this out. Would not it be better to slay your own inner dragons than watch on television while whole countries agonize about these forces.

Consciously activating your *ka* will move you farther now. Referring to Figure 10 again: your *ka* can best be understood as your 4D canopy over

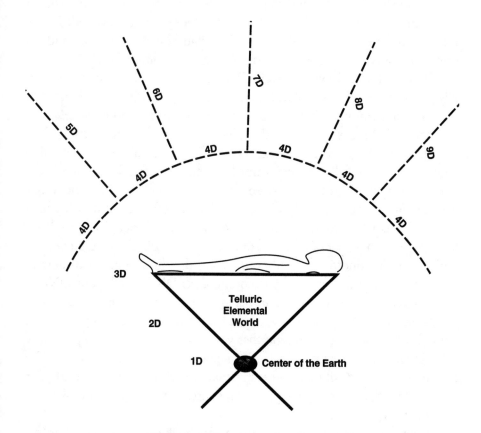

FIGURE 10: THE CANOPY OF LIGHT

your body or energy field. In any dimension, the source of powerful acti-vation energy is from the dimension below, and for your physical bodies, the potent power source is the 2D elemental realm. In any dimension, the source of higher-frequency activation is the dimension right above. Why is this? You resonate sufficiently close with 2D to be able to feel its dense waves in your body, and you vibrate sufficiently close to 4D to feel how it activates you. You must open these portals before the other dimensions can be accessed, just like you must learn to get along with your own neigh-bors before you reach out to people from other countries. You must master the elemental realm to be one with Gaia, and you must master your feelings in order to apprehend the more subtle dimensions. The 4D archetypal realm needs to master your physical vibration in order for you to really know Gaia by working with her elemental intelligence. All of the dimensions are much more intermeshed than you can imagine, and no dimension survives unless all return to integrity periodically.

How on Earth do you master 4D archetypal dramas, which are actually desires from etheric realms for communion with you? The etheric is of such a subtle vibrancy that it cannot be read by you without *transduction* through the dimension above the physical. Transduction occurs when your phone receives electrical signals and then transmits them as audible sound. Listen carefully, you carry much negativity about this feeling realm because you think you have been used. However, you have no other avenue than moving through this portal. You must figure out how it works because, according to Zecharia Sitchin, the 4D Anunnaki manipulated your genes.[23] In *Signet of Atlantis*, our vehicle described an Atlantean scientist decoding photons in a laboratory, and she showed how extraterrestrials can figure out humans by decoding their DNA. Well, your DNA is being decoded again. You are being tested and explored by your Anunnaki scientists. They tell you that they can heal disease by repairing your DNA. I, Satya, can tell you that your DNA can only be repaired by releasing negative emotions, by clearing miasms out of your bodies, and by regaining mental clarity and pure spiritual integrity. Your DNA and your body are a reflection of you, so work on yourself and be very careful about who dissects you.

When you walk the surface of the planet, make yourself into a vertical axis by feeling your first chakra in the core crystal of the Earth rising through your body. Then feel energy from Gaia rising up through your body and out of the top of your head up to your spiritual or crown chakra that is located in the Galactic Center. This cosmic chakra holds the corridor of the nonphysical realms open for you, and it is always spinning. As you feel the Galactic Center, again locate your sense of self in the center of Earth, then reverse your energy out of cosmic realms; move down into your body, and move down through the five chakras located in your body. Locate emotional blocks as you move energy up and down this axis. Are these blocks sexual or from unprocessed feelings or from a blocked heart that will not surrender to others? Are they in your throat where you will not speak your truth; or in your third eye, causing you not to be able to see the elementals and the archetypal teachers? Find out which chakras are blocked, and make a total commitment to exploring those realms.

You will know where the block is by observing the part of your 3D life that is undeveloped. For example, is material deprivation keeping you from getting sex or expressing your truth? Go to where your life is unresolved, the place where you think you will resolve in the future; stop right there and resolve it now. Your chakras will not open unless you totally trust the field you live in—3D—since that is the atmosphere in which you receive other dimensional waves.

The five chakras in your bodies are your personal interface between the physical realms. As you lie on the healing table or in bed with your lover, in safe zones where you can trust the universe, image how your body triangulates to a point right below your body in the center of Earth. Move your consciousness into that point and feel how deep your trust for Gaia is. Then, with the unitizing power of Gaia, travel in that triangle below your body to access the elemental powers in your body that need to release. Perceive how you can feel them as cords reaching into your body and move the awareness of that triangular field right into your whole body. Move your awareness into the places in your body where you can feel the elementals crying for release, and ask them what they want to tell you. Your body begins to feel heavy and dense from their magnificent energy, but stay in it knowing you are safe.

Follow whatever image they create on your screen, no matter if that being came from long ago. Do not judge it, for it may be a story from millions of years ago that you have no context for in the now. Whatever it is, it was not heard in the first place, so trust in this information and listen to it. Suddenly you will feel how much that story is wanting your acknowledgement. Honor it, remember it, and let it go. Go ahead and feel the lightening and the bliss in your body as the higher-dimensional fields begin to flood in. As they come in, focus harder than ever in the place where you feel great elemental powers vibrating. Call the higher-dimensional vibrations right into that place. You may feel crisis as these great powers return to Earth. But think of how happy they are to go home. Think of how happy you have been to go home where you are wanted, and let them go now. Imagine how history might have turned out if one person had acknowledged Adolf Hitler when he was a child.

If you will release in this way now, use the image of yourself on the table with the 4D archetypal screen above your body. That is *your* movie, and if you will run it on your screen, you will be utterly amazed and delighted at what is there. At first it will be painful as the deeply hidden things rush before your eyes, but quickly your curiosity will win. This is why we Pleiadeans love your curiosity so much. It entices you into exploring things that you think are outside yourselves. Then when you discover one day they are all inside you, you finally realize you are a temple of five energy centers that can receive data from any source. As you receive that data, send it into Gaia, because you cannot handle all that energy in your body once it is really flowing through you. The reciprocity begins where the dimensions are vibrating in unison, and you exist in all dimensions simultaneously.

As I've said, total immersion in the Photon Band will trigger all dimensions simultaneously, and you will go out of body unless you are in 3D, grounded, and able to hold the frequency of all dimensions. It is time now to work with Pleiadian healing techniques.

# *3*

# $\mathcal{A}$LCHEMY OF NINE DIMENSIONS

WHAT DO I, SATYA, MEAN WHEN I SAY THAT THOUGHT CREATES REALITY? Many of you are getting glimpses that literally everything that happens to you is a function of your own thought. Some of you have been playing around with this notion enough to have actually tested it. And some of you are waking up and realizing that you are continually creating a whole gigantic world around yourself—*a world created by your mind*. Then you respond to this world by means of feelings—your personal feedback on what you created. From a physical point of view, it is logical that the realities you live out every day would contradict or cancel out all the other realities intersecting yours. Yet, if you are lucky enough to live in a small community where most people know each other, you become aware that each person is living out a complex scenario every day; complex schemes are interweaving, yet people just pass by each other with a quick hello. If you could watch them all energetically, you would be astonished to see how the reality of each one interweaves and the community looks like a huge geometrical complex. Your only access to any reality is absolutely perceptual. Realities are not solid, and the space between things is incomprehensible. You have a clear choice about every thought and feeling that you allow to imprint your consciousness, and those choices make up your world.

All that really matters is whether you perceive what is going on in relation to your inner world. Once you see how outer events are generated by your inner energy, then what's the point of all these worlds created by your mind, these movies? Did you learn something? Did you process all the rich feelings emerging out of it? What would be the point of anything out there reflecting your inner world unless it changes you? As I get into how 3D works, please remember that your great mother, Earth, holds the space for all these movies.

I have arrived at a greater understanding of how this works due to a remarkable event in my vehicle's life that was occurring while she was writing this book. I will take time to tell you about it because this story is an excellent example of how the Pleiadians learn about your reality through your experiences. My vehicle's closest healing colleague, Diane, suffered a brain aneurysm, and during brain surgery, the aneurysm burst. My vehicle repeatedly visited Diane in the neurocritical care section of a city hospital, the central organ of allopathic medicine. While coming and going, she found out how you can use your own special "secret" in order to really penetrate density. I will tell you this story because it will ground you and offer survival tools as your planet reorganizes.

The critical condition of your planet is self-evident: Your planet requires a *complete* makeover of all its systems because you have arrived at the endpoint of materialization. Allopathic medicine is an ideal zone for observing the status of materialization, since true health is actually a nonphysical state. *Health* is being in resonance with the core of your planet; it is maintained by means of *stealth*, and it is your personal *wealth*. These three words are sound-coded. Materialization of medicine has built a wall between your bodies and the natural processes of your planet. You've offered up your bodies, and you are Humpty Dumpty, and now your organs are being marketed. How will you ever put yourselves back together again?

The experience with the aneurysm taught me new methods for restructuring 3D with thought. For those of you who decide to work with this concept, you must create from the highest level of intention; nonphysical forms of creation are based on strong desire, which is based on love. Many of you are discovering these new methods, and I am very excited to be learning about them with you.

Diane became nauseous and dizzy and seemed to have a bad flu. Since she'd always chosen only natural healing methods, my vehicle asked her what she could do. Diane requested body work. My vehicle was sure that something very grave was going on, but she respected Diane's choice to not seek medical advice. It is not possible to heal in any form unless the person who is ill chooses a specific treatment. My vehicle decided to conduct a full Awakening, a healing session that calls in all the nonphysical beings who are working with a person. With her friend on the massage table, she used sage, an eagle feather, crystals, and an otter skin, which is used only for severe cases. Around Diane's activated body, within the wide circle of sage, there appeared the most extraordinary gathering of chemical elementals my vehicle had ever seen. Clearly this woman was capable of working with amazing powers! Nevertheless, she had complained for years about some force that seemed to be limiting her. This group was obviously the source of the limitations. Like any healer dealing with great trauma, our vehicle did her best to understand exactly what was going on. Diane had been a hairdresser for years, and our vehicle suspected that chemical elementals from the salon had gotten sucked into her body. The vehicle could feel that they were ready to go back home into the ground.

By sweeping the air around Diane's body with an eagle feather, she pulled out the elementals, then blessed, honored, and sent them back into the 2D realms. They massed into a magnificent swirl of energetic forces returning to their own domain. Once her body was restructured and rebalanced, Diane fell into a deep sleep. All night, the elementals were flying through the trees, and my vehicle asked them to go home. In the morning, the elementals were at peace, but Diane was not. What could this be? Diane was writhing and thrashing inside her own body. What could this be? She complained of a violent headache and was nauseated, and finally she asked to be taken to the emergency room.

A brain aneurysm was detected that had been there for many years, and our vehicle sensed that this must be the control center for Diane's elemental teachers. A few weeks later, the doctors also found Diane had cancer, so the beings seen by my vehicle were probably chemical elementals that trigger cancer. From a Pleiadian perspective, such control centers are time-coded implants that keep humans from waking up too fast. You would explode if you released your miasms back to their own domains too quickly. From my point of view, Diane's case is a marvelous example of the awakening that all of you are being blessed with now. You will all experience your own awakenings by 1998. The most difficult phase of your ascension—full return to resonance with Earth—will be the release of these miasms hiding in your bodies. The aneurysm was a big wakeup call for me as a Pleiadian, because I did not fully understand your inner pain as embodied humans. My vehicle had been resisting the urge to tell you about what is coming because she loves you so much. However, it is time now, you must have this news. *Just trust.* You will find ways to accomplish these healings that will amaze you. Healing yourselves has moved into the physical realm, and you all must get very smart very fast. On a positive note, physical healings are the most profound ones, but only if you restructure your emotional world based on what you learn during the physical trauma.

Have you ever been showered with amazing insights about how to restructure all realities around yourself while you were in the midst of a huge trauma? For example, your father dies, and your mother is ripped open by this crisis. Her true heart is exposed, and you see her whole perceptual world with X-ray vision. All the family dysfunctions are totally apparent, the real truths about your own family are exposed, and it is apparent what it would take for everyone involved to move right into integrity. Then I have watched you over and over again as *you forgot about such a revelation within three months!* Yet, right in those times is where the knowledge about restructuring your whole planet exists! *All your traumas and pain happen only to get you to see the worlds of others!* The reason you are in so much trouble now is that you've not utilized these times for insight, so the 3D events get bigger and bigger. You are like broken records.

From my vehicle's point of view, her friend was an enlightened being who was in the midst of a titanic struggle with limitation. The vehicle had always known that Diane's inner knowledge was far beyond the field of her times. As always when someone evidences any limitations, it was only because this person's extraordinary awareness was not developed when he or she was young. Diane was gifted with a fully enlightened mother who had always encouraged her to keep her heart open so she'd be able to deliver her gift when the times were ready. But Diane's moment had not arrived yet, and her gift was contained in a time-coded control center deep in her brain. Unexpressed creative expression will always attack your bodies, and the inner anger from this frustration is what makes you sick!

I am using Diane as an example because she survived a brain aneurysm and cancer, and this was a miracle that amazed my vehicle. This experience deepened her trust in the timing and unfoldment, and my vehicle always assumes that whatever comes into her life is a teaching that must be shared. Otherwise pain and trauma is not sufficiently valued. I will tell you more about this event, since healing is the quintessence of your personal Pleiadian self. I am here to help you remember your own creative powers because you are Pleiadians too. You have just forgotten your stellar link, but now your bodies are opening to the stars. Stars are nuclear, and that is why this opening has now moved into your bodies, for they are the vehicles of your creative potential.

## Finding Your Monad

Deep within each one of you is a "secret," a gift that you brought from the stars to Earth when you agreed to incarnate. This secret is a monad of knowledge that is multidimensional, lying deep within your awareness. Diane's gift is brilliance about elemental functioning. How do I know this? It is simple: Whatever trauma you take on is your training for figuring out how to deliver your gift. I see every trauma my vehicle experienced as the major parts of her training. But you deny your traumas, and then you repeat them endlessly instead of learning from them, and you just create more events and things. Surely you've noticed by now that you're creating the wrong things—garbage, gambling parlors, murders, Twinkies, cars, and bombs? Now that you've created so much useless stuff, you feel guilty. Wallowing in guilt, you forget how to create the right stuff, and then you conclude that you are limited. But, have you ever noticed, in spite of what your culture tells you, that you don't feel limited? Right within that inner feeling of limitlessness is the avenue to your own creativity.

If you would follow that avenue, you would cease wandering around not doing what your inner secret has always told you to do. Your "inner secret" gets so frustrated that it draws great elemental forces into your body, and they make you sick trying to get you to listen. That is their job—to get you to resonate with the 7.5 Hertz frequency of Earth, and to stop being so busy. They love you, and they will hang out with you and take you down under the sod lifetime after lifetime if you will not listen. Like radioactivity, they vibrate, causing you to become inert/dead or too active/creative. When creativity is not exercised and directed into manifestation, it turns in on itself and becomes destructive. As I've said, the emotional spewing is complete and the physical work is beginning. *Every disease you bravely manifest and heal from 1994 to 1998 is a disease that would kill you instantly once the Sun is in the Photon Band.*

How can you see these elemental forces? First of all, move deeply inward and feel that place in your heart that knows you can create anything. Notice that this space within is beyond the physical and emotional, notice how it is actually pure thought right in your heart! This is pure unbounded knowingness. Move your consciousness into that place. From that place, you know exactly how to respond in any situation. Feel the desires of the elementals existing inside who are waiting to help you release your miasms. If you will operate from this point until you have released their desires, everything will reorganize around you, and you will see all the pathways you can travel down to deliver your gifts. As you deliver your gifts, the anger around your frustrated creativity releases, and you feel great! In this, I have taught my vehicle well, and you too can learn how to feel these energies in your bodies. Just notice how you feel inside when you are all excited and then follow your fascination.

Your inner secret or personal monad has nothing to do with jobs or relationships. However, activating your monad will quickly straighten out your issues about work, relationships, and health, since these physical and emotional realities are simply your tools for expressing your creativity. How to simply create on your planet has gotten completely confused because you mix creation up with basic materialism and immediately your monad can't operate, since it is nonphysical. What does the monad have to do with your secret? Your monad is the form that holds your higher-self knowledge that totally comprehends 3D reality. If you will start to work from it, it is so phenomenally brilliant that any limitation in your reality dissipates. For example, any physical damage such as an aneurysm, can be healed if you change the behavior that holds it in form. (There is much scientific evidence that the human brain is holographic. Neurophysiologist Karl Pribram and physicist David Bohm came to this conclusion independently in the 1970s.)[1] Therefore, an injury in part of the brain can be healed, and a change in thought can change the overall pattern. Another part of the brain can even take over the function of damaged sections in some cases because the brain is holographic—each part reflects the whole pattern.

Because the brain is holographic, your higher self knows how to help you change behaviors that limit your body. However, you need information from 3D, and your higher self will subtly guide you to find it, but you must listen to inner guidance. For example, Diane did have symptoms indicating cancer, and it would have been wise of her to seek a diagnosis, but she did not because of her lack of respect for allopathic medicine. I mention this because allopathic medicine has much to offer, and you must find appropriate ways to use it, and you must utilize natural medicine when that is appropriate. The intelligence of your higher self is amazing, and all you have to do is take responsibility for knowing as much as possible about the various tools at your disposal, so your higher self can impulse you to go to the doctor or the acupuncturist.

Diane, for example, showed my vehicle how elemental energies needing expression move into places in bodies, and how they can eventually create disease. I, Satya, have been teaching my vehicle about this for years; she'd seen it in many cases, and she has been able to diagnose just by looking at the 2D teachers in bodies. Soon, all of you will be doing this. In Diane's case, being able to see how this process works in the brain was very instructive. Since the aneurysm was created first by thought, then pure thought is exactly what could remove it! Of course, once the physical body has been sufficiently damaged, then surgery can be a blessing, for saving a life continues the possibility of figuring out how to create with pure thought.

In the neurological critical care unit, my vehicle could see that a whole factory or city might be getting wired into people's heads eventually. It is time for scientists to stop creating things that do more and more of the physical body processes. Many scientists already know that thought creates reality, and that thought can cure. However, everybody is making big money on machines and drugs and nobody has yet figured out how to charge money for thought. *Where you are the most out of integrity is with your money.* Notice that the word "expensive" implies that you are divorced from your pensiveness, your thought, like an ex-wife. The expensive equipment is a massive control dynamic that enables you to avoid thought, and it will just get bigger and more complex as long as you buy into the idea that anybody or anything is limited.

These limiting belief systems are deeply ingrained, so it is time for me to take you on a blasphemous roller coaster ride that could potentially get you off your obsession with God, the Great White Father. I warn you, you might not like the information that comes next. But, the choice is between swimming in the light bodies of your own cellular memory or being wired into a mechanical matrix of absolute limitation.

Since this information is going to be hard to swallow, center yourself in your heart, now! And as you get into this, whenever you find yourself breathing hard, with throbbing in the head, or feeling constriction in your heart, please return your awareness to your heart. Then breathe precious air deeply into your lungs, and proceed. Peoples, *you have not loved your own fathers because God the Father stole your affections from your real fathers.* Your frustrated fathers have limited your creativity because they are in so much pain. The Pleiadians are 5D, dead center of your 9D Gaian structure, and it is always the center, the heart, that brings forth the key question. As your hearts activate your bodies, remember the Pleiadians are the rulers of the divine heart. If I say something that is blasphemous, breathe and laugh with me!

## Abraham and Uranium

It is time for you to remember that a nuclear war has already occurred on Earth.[2] Since this fact is hidden, and even though you've split the atom, you can't see the precariousness of your situation because you think nuclear war is a probable future. Facts are, *nuclear war is a past event that you have not processed, and it is about to overwhelm you unless you process its meaning.* I know that now is the time to deal with all the coded and crippling guilt because I feel how desperate you are. This gigantic guilt created an all-perfect, all-responsible Father, who blocks you from being responsible—"able to respond." This has made you into sheep. The nuclear war in 2024 B.C. made the Dead Sea into a lifeless body of water, and this was triggered by Abraham. Before you attack us and say, "Oh, Satya, how can you utter such disrespectful thoughts about our great Father?" please tell me why you admire Edward Teller—"Tell Her"—and the Los Alamos S.W.A.T. Team?

The reason you have not been able to see the truth about this part of your past is because nuclear events thousands of years ago exploded 2D elemental forms out of their own realm. This caused you to feel elemental pain so intensely that the Hebrew Bible was constructed to distract you with every story except the most important one. Yahweh is portrayed as an avenging fire god, and then you built temples and religions to contain this great denial. Yes, your temples and churches are structures and systems for holding this denial. The denial has piled up; implants in your bodies exist that hold it, and just like a nuclear reactor, your bodies are spewing emotional waste. Next, you exposed the denial by splitting the atom. Einstein awakened dim memories of the awful truth, you were terrified, and so you made it all into a probable future. Many of you have very nervous feelings about Yahweh, and some of you intuit that "he" did it. This juicy and cloaked thoughtform manifests in your now as seriously ingrained apocalyptic thought processes, the most dangerous trend in your reality. Since letting go of your obsession with father god will enable you to eliminate apocalyptic thought poison, allow me to tell you all about Abraham.

At the end of the third millennium B.C., Nibiru controlled Ur, an ancient city of Sumer located on the Euphrates River, and the Nibiruans were then called the Sumerians. Like the Vatican, the Sumerian control was theocratic. As I scan your past, I see Abraham sent from Ur carrying a small box with a glowing element inside it. He guards it carefully, for he knows this element is very dangerous and creates great fear. This element came out of earth from deep, deep below Ur, where it had been deposited by the Nibiruans. That is the source of the word, "ur-anium;" it is time for you to notice how deeply coded these words are—the place where the central control center of your creativity resides is in your "cr-anium." All the limitations and potential creativity in your world exist right in your languages. From my 5D perspective, your blindness is laughable, except that it may kill you. The facts are, Ur was the Nibiruan capital selected by Anu for deposit of radiation. If you want more information about this, just follow the path of the Ark of the Covenant, built to contain the radiation in those days.[3]

Abraham's mission was to deposit the power of Anu into Anunnaki temples, so as to control the emotional bodies of your ancestors. It was a plug into culture that has gotten more and more complex, and it will be helpful now to realize that this problem didn't start in the twentieth century. Uranium undergoes a half-life process that causes it to gradually transmute into inert elements. I will call this deposit of the power of Anu "the Anu Bomb," and as I read you, this explains why you felt like your modern atomic physicists were godlike. As I see it, there is a symbiotic relationship between the breakdown of the emotional body through karma and the breakdown of radioactive elements via transmutation. Remember, I do not always understand how things work in your reality, and when I say I read or scan you, I am trying to see what is going on in your bodies. I am struggling to understand this symbiosis, for I know it will be the avenue to your ability to become conscious about the transmutative process. I can see that transmuting radioactive materials is deeply tied up with the work you are doing on your emotional bodies. In that sense, radiation is an Anunnaki or Nibiruan gift.

There are many, many ways to look at this. Back to the Anu Bomb: as

I see Abraham carrying his radioactive box, it looks like the uranium was going to be used for the deposition of the consciousness of Anu in the temple in order to begin a new level of Nibiruan control of Earth. Thus, at the opening of the Age of Aries began the stream of patriarchal consciousness that enslaves you now, unless you pay attention to what it really offers you. During the Age of Aries, war and control were appropriate. They are not appropriate now.

The uranium needed to be deposited in the Middle East, the Levant, because that part of the planet was once deep in the ocean where the surface was close to the hot interior mantle. By means of Continental Drift and crustal shifting, this section of the planet had moved to the surface during the 10,800 B.C. Pole Shift. There Anu could cause this potent energy to be deposited in a very profound and lethal way. That all depends upon your point of view. After all, what has happened as a result of this emotional-body consciousness that Anu and Abraham deposited is that you have gone through much karma and much experience. Remember that your Sun and all stars are nuclear. Still, don't fail to notice how the Middle East has been enslaving people for a long time.

Anu simply wanted to control the world. He is the great father god of Nibiru, and Earth was his chosen 3D territory. Naturally, he thinks he knows what is best for you. Therefore, whenever he has contact with Earth—when Nibiru orbits into the solar system and Nibiruan ships land on Earth, or when he monitors you by means of temple technology—he simply uses you. Once you became sufficiently self-reflective around 2000 B.C., your feelings began to awaken. Anu did not possess feelings then. He saw that you were slipping out of his total control, and he knew uranium would enable him to monitor you even when you came to the end of the Mayan Great Calendar when Anu would be far away from your solar system.

When Anu is monitoring you, 4D archetypal forces can impulse you into playing out their dramas in 3D. Remember, 4D is the most polarized dimension, while 3D is a four-directional dimension that makes things happen. After 5000 years, uranium is thoroughly polluted with emotional-body detritus—human karma. The Pleiadians joke and call it your "Anu-karma." As a result of being jerked around by 4D and going from one pole to another, human feelings are very accelerated. You are being globally linked, and the active radiation of the Anu Bomb cannot contain all this nondirected creativity. Emotions are spewing into inappropriate realms as you run back and forth like rats in a psychology lab. *Uranium holds the vibration in your physical bodies that resonates with the agendas of Anu.* However, because of the half-life principle, I can see that the primordial Anu Bomb is fizzling. I can decode part of this with you, since plutonium is the unstable element that resonates the most closely with our 26,000-year Pleiadian cycle. Plutonium in your environment is lethal to all Pleiadians. Remember, I can see into your bodies, like a visual Geiger counter, and I can see the Anunnaki control plugs in your bodies starting to loosen. As you transmute emotions, you are transmuting the plutonium, and the Pleiadians are more free to bring more love into Earth.

Meanwhile, more radiation is being released into the environment by the military-industrial complex. Everybody seems to be powerless to stop this because it feels like God to them because it is attached to the ancient Anunnaki power play. The Anunnaki are triggering you into manufacturing radioactive materials, you act like zombies, and Einstein is a god to you. Get smart, people! The degree to which you are paying for being poisoned is outrageous! Meanwhile, the increased level of radiation is beneficial to Nibiruan lifeforms. They plan to make a radioactive planet on which to live, if you are dumb enough to destroy the third dimension of Earth.

It is time to remind you that I am only discussing the 3D and 4D aspects of radiation. Radiation is a great example of how a situation can seem to be very negative in linear space and time, and yet the meaning of it changes completely by moving to a more subtle dimension from which to view it. Chris Griscom told my vehicle in 1986 that the emotional body has been vibrating at a lower frequency than the physical body. When she heard that from Chris, we Pleiadians got excited because this explained something I couldn't figure out. We've had a difficult time understanding why you don't clear yourselves faster. From our perspective, this emotional-frequency retardant was what was set in motion by the first Anu Bomb, and we could see that the block is in your emotional bodies. Now that the atom has been split again—dualized, so it can seek fusion in your reality—you must quicken your emotional bodies back to their normally higher frequency.

Listen, peoples, your integrity is to be found in your bodies! Extraterrestrials can only invade your emotions, which are higher dimensional. Look at the 4D canopy in Figure 10. Of course, once invaded emotionally, your bodies can become diseased, and then you can be invaded in those places where frequencies have set in that are not in tune with your body. You are not in your integrity when your emotions are denser than your bodies, and this has opened you for invasion. From my 5D perspective, during the energy acceleration, the natural symbiosis of feeling with uranium will quicken your emotional bodies, so that your Pleiadian higher self will become your true center while you inhabit Earth. With a quickened emotional body, your heart is quickened by us Pleiadians. The resonation of uranium with the galactic cycle shows that humans must raise their vibrational frequencies to match uranium. Then you will naturally "radiate" unconditional love, which centers you in your heart, and all dimensions open simultaneously.

The next question has to be to ask whether Anu laid his Bomb to do just that—raise the vibration of humanity. From my perspective as a Pleiadian, it is difficult to credit Anu with the possibility of a loving decision due to his seeming lack of kindness or compassion for humanity. This is a fascinating razor's edge because while influencing your planet, the Anunnaki have been playing a very parental role with you, and all aspects of your parents are valuable to you.

Like all parents, many facets of their activities have to do with encouraging you to slowly but surely develop and grow, and that is what is confusing. On Earth, many parents, especially those from undisturbed indigenous peoples, are loving in a 5D Pleiadian way. This creates boundless trust in the child. The parental tendency of Anu is not a loving, compassionate kind of parenting. It is more like most parenting in the Western world. If you were to go back into your own experiences with your parents and separate out every place where they felt true love and concern for you, and if you stripped out that loving part of their relationship with you, you'd be left only with the part of them that was intending to grow you, like a plant. They gave birth to you, then they had to feed you, clothe you, and then they had to be concerned about your development. But, imagine if they did not activate the heart-centered loving part of you because it was not in their nature. Have you not known parents who are nurturing their child, yet seem to feel no true or blissful love for that child?

Around 3600 B.C. Anu felt the next level of growth for the human would be city cultures, because that form leads to planetary consciousness. For city culture development, Anu's progeny would need to develop socialization, a way of relating to the other humans that was different from ways of relating that existed before. He believed he would need to monitor you during this phase, and so he utilized radiation. This part of Anu is the part of you that enables you to live in cities and set up territories, take money from others, control other people, and use other people. This is not a loving sense of community and giving. It is a new level of complexity in living, which offers great experience but is not necessarily loving.

Anu deposited the uranium into a very deep place in the planet as a device for monitoring and influencing your maturity and development while Nibiru orbited out of the solar system; and then Abraham delivered it into the temple 1600 years later. This next stage of growth had never before been developed in the indigenous people of Gaia. Anu directed the indigenous people of Earth in building temple/city culture, but once Nibiru left the solar system, he believed he had to have a way to monitor development until you matured in time. Otherwise, setting up these complex structures and leaving them to the inhabitants would be like putting a two-year-old in the pilot's seat of a Boeing 747. I, Satya, can see that whatever goes on with uranium on your planet makes you totally accessible to Anu. I can feel this monitoring device in Anu's brain, which I can easily access because I am higher dimensional. It's like an implant in his brain so he can tune into what you're doing. I can see him scanning you, just like you can see things in X-rays and CAT scans.

Now Anu is on the verge of an aneurysm caused by the degree of materialization on Earth. These archaic implants are becoming lethal, like old batteries spewing PCBs. Remember, I've told you that Anu once tricked you into self-reflective awareness by encouraging you to emulate him—worshiping him as an idol made you idle. That worked during one phase of your growth, but then you got bored. You began to want to be God also, and so you split the atom. Just as Anu was beginning to let go of control, once enough of the Anu Bomb was being transmuted by means of the half-life principle, you began pulling uranium out of Earth. What has this removal of 2D elemental power from Earth caused? Have you not noticed that emotional-body conflicts are intensifying? And have you noticed that the release of uranium on your planet is directly related to the explosion of emotional karma and emotional activity? Notice that. It is true, and it is a huge speeding up of your evolution.

Back in 3600 B.C., when temple/city cultures formed, people who had been in a pastoral mode suddenly went into cities. Their feelings were aroused in a new way, and the same cities became armed camps by 2000 B.C. Uranium triggered defensiveness and the armed camp. You had to go through this stage to come to a higher vibration because the ego or identity of the Anunnaki is deeply involved with growth and development on your planet. Much of this experience has been negative, and I will be going into the most negative elements of this in order to assist the Anunnaki in letting it go.

Just like the 2D elementals want to return to their realm, so do the 4D archetypal lords want to return to theirs. Dimensional pollution has outlived its usefulness. You could say from one point of view that Anu was impulsing you into exploring radiation because he was lonesome. So, recognize that lonely god within yourself and agree to gift the planet with your own genius. Now the time has come to relate to him and everybody else at the next level of frequency. Anu had complete control over the known world in one time frame. The next question is: What is Anu's relative state of control at the present time?

From our perspective, Anu decided in 3600 B.C. to impose a creation on Earth, which was a form of opening up his underwear drawer. Anu exposed himself—Anuflashing—by offering the complete temple/city cultural form, but why would he do that? Well, now I will tell you a secret: Anu was competing with the Sirians, who had deposited their temple/city culture in Egypt, and Anu got jealous! After Nibiru's return in 7200 B.C., the Sirians built magnificent temple/city complexes around 6000 B.C. that activated all the power vortexes on the Nile, and they even built activation structures all over the Aegean. The Sirian work with humans was for higher brain activation, but the Anunnaki thought of the human brain as just a robotic structure to be used by them to control humans as workers.

### Relations Between the Anunnaki and Sirians

Anu set up the full-blown Anunnaki temple/city complex on the Tigris and Euphrates rivers as a beautiful gift to humans. However, he did it out of competition and jealousy instead of as a giveaway. This instantly set in a dynamic of creating and building in order to be a mogul. Creating and building is meant to be an activity that frees humanity and offers the opportunity for communication and socialization; it is not meant to be a · power play. Humans have always been smarter than the Anunnaki have realized, while the Sirians always had a deep understanding of human potential. Since the Sirians are star people, and the Anunnaki are inhabitants of a planet that is part of Earth's solar system, the Sirians always hope that the Anunnaki will learn a few things from Sirian creations on Earth. Alas, jealousy has reduced this potential for earthlings, since the consciousness of star intelligences is more multidimensional in all cases than the consciousness of planetary inhabitants.

There are many connections between Sirius and Nibiru. When Nibiru leaves the solar system, it orbits far out in space and gets close to the exquisite Sirius star system. From Nibiru's point of view, Sirius and the Sun are twin stars. Nibiru is more concerned with the consciousness of the Sun and solar system and with the consciousness of the Sirius system, as well as the planets of Sirius. The Sirius system is a trinary system, it is very advanced, and it has had great impact on earthlings by means of various initiatic African cultures, such as the Egyptians and the Dogon.

Nibiru used to orbit around Sirius B; however, due to various celestial dynamics, the Anunnaki of Nibiru began to visit Earth 450,000 years ago, as was perfectly described by Zecharia Sitchin.[4] I don't want to give too much away too soon, but I will say that the Sirians know a lot more about the Nibiruans than you do, and I'd suggest you take Sirius seriously. The way to do that is by means of Egyptian records, and the opening of these records is why my vehicle helped create the Sirian/Pleiadian alliance. This alliance actually began August 7, 1972 when the Sirians intervened to keep the polar axis of Earth from flipping due to a great explosion in the Sun.[5] My vehicle's personality changed completely on that day, when she and many people on Earth became hybrid Pleiadian/earthlings. She began preparing that summer for the coming Sirian/Pleiadian alliance that she helped implant in Egypt at the end of 1992 in the Great Pyramid and at Saquara. This alliance will assist the Anunnaki and the Sirians to a healing in their relationship. So let us examine the relationship between Sirius and Nibiru.

The great Sirian/Egyptian god Anubis is the guide who holds Nibiru's orbit in form. He is the guide who travels with your solar system all the way through the Galactic Night. The Pleiadians hold the orbit of your solar system while you journey through the Photon Band. They are your mother cow and Anubis is your jackal guide. Anubis is a being who travels the universe with the consciousness of Sirius, and he is a very, very superior being. Think of Anubis as holding the orbital patterns of the solar system as a whole unit traveling its 26,000-year cycle in Alcyone's spiral. As I observe Abraham journeying away from Ur around 2000 B.C., I see that Abraham is a *Sirian!* This surprises me, for I assumed he was a Nibiruan.

This is a great example of how we Pleiadians are mining you. I may seem tedious, but I want you to understand how we Pleiadians are working with you by showing you how it works with my vehicle. This merging is happening with many of you, and you will be able to use this impulsing to rekindle your curiosity and passion. That is what will free you of the guilt from your father god. My vehicle, Barbara Hand Clow, figures things out in 3D by exploring things such as Egypt and the Sumerians, and then I find out where the players who've entered 3D have come from. Once I identify them, then I can trick them into telling their own stories, and it's fun. At this point, now I see why Abraham is such a big deal! Now I see that his story in the Bible is a coverup, and I see why the Egyptians have been so unfairly maligned. These are all typical examples of Anunnaki bad press on the Sirians. And figuring out these lies will disempower the World Management Team.[6] Why? *All you need for taking back your power is to recover your stories.*

Remember, you are first invaded emotionally, and then your response sets up patterns in your body that will eventually result in disease. Since Nibiru orbits out around Sirius B, it has been functioning as a Sirian postal service into your solar system, once Nibiru got caught in your solar system. The Sirians want certain kinds of information deposited on Earth, but Earth is a tricky place. When information is deposited into the 3D Earth field, its multidimensional qualities must be transduced. That is, the power of Sirius must be activated on Earth, just like electricity becoming audible in a phone. Beings from other dimensions and systems are constantly depositing information on Earth, such as crop circles or hieroglyphics. Often this information is destroyed because it contradicts the official story of your past that has been invented and monitored by Anu.

Anu is especially incensed about Sirian information. This is why the indigenous Egyptians, who are still keeping the ancient Sirian knowledge, will not allow excavation of certain sites, especially the tunnels under Giza plateau. Beings from other systems are constantly depositing things there because the main transducer of your planet is located under the Sphinx, and the indigenous Egyptians guard it. Once the system is open again, you will get this information, so remember your heritage, and become multidimensional.

Abraham was a Sirian, and yet he was carrying the Anu Bomb. This would indicate to me that Sirius is also involved in this deposit of radiation. As my vehicle understands the model, the Sirian package that was picked up in 5400 B.C. and delivered to Earth in 3600 B.C. was the temple/city culture model. The temple/city cultures flourished on the planet for over a thousand years, but now a Sirian is seen depositing the uranium? The implications of that are mind-boggling. As I've said, Abraham was introducing uranium because the Anunnaki were jealous of the Sirians and of their magnificent city/temple culture in Egypt. However, the Anunnaki temples and cities never attained the exquisite and subtle levels of the Egyptians. Why? Anu's city/state was created out of competition and jealousy, and ultimately it would always evolve into Sodom and Gomorrah, which would destroy Gaia. It was a lethal creation. It could eventually destroy the planet, so it had to have a built-in limitation—radiation—which would always activate when a certain level of complexity was attained in any culture based on competition.

As I see it, the Sirians have never hidden their own information. You can see this in the records of ancient Egypt. If you become an initiate, you can read their information. The Sirian frequency is still in form in 3D in Egypt for anybody who can read it. This energy is influencing some, yet it is too subtle to be apprehended by most, especially professional archaeologists. In the temples in Egypt, some of you find you have glandular systems that are in resonance with Sirius. Until the last few years, your endocrine systems have only been reading intense and gross feelings; however, some of you have felt your endocrine systems responding to these more subtle Sirian vibrations. Meanwhile, the Pleiadian knowledge has been activating your thymus, a higher heart gland. This gland is triggering rapid physical healing in preparation for the Photon Belt, while the Sirians are helping you begin to feel and consciously work with the subtle glandular systems. These subtle vibrations are difficult for many of you, but it is relatively easy to feel different vibrations in Egypt, especially the qualities of the Nibiruan vibration. For example, if you want to access the Nibiruans, notice when you get a strong hit in your gut that causes your throat to close. The Pleiadians impulse you in your heart, lungs, liver, and skin. It is more subtle to heal in the glands, and glandular healing techniques will end up being the way to bypass the more gross mechanisms of Anunnaki allopathic medicine.

I've already mentioned that the temple/city states in Sumer tended to quickly become armed camps, which ultimately resulted in the nuking of Sodom and Gomorrah in 2024 B.C.[7] It is time for you to realize that the resolution of human conflict everywhere on the planet is not possible without having an understanding of multidimensional beings who have been on this planet. The World Management Team and other forces that work to limit you are a confluence of all energies on this planet that have been manipulating your behavior. You are fighting the battles of beings who are not from Earth! By being totally trapped in 3D, you are having difficulty knowing what is impulsing you, and yet you could see it all if you'd become multidimensional, as you were before you were born. Remember, I said that Anu first impulsed you into complexity so that you could become global. What is actually going on will be beyond your wildest dreams, and we Pleiadians are here now to help blast open these dimensional keys. Things are going to change fast. It is the only way out of another nuclear explosion—this one worldwide instead of just limited to the Sinai.

There are organizational structures in all dimensions, but governments only exist in the third dimension. *As you are grasping for multidimensionality, you limit your access by applying 3D structural models to higher or lower dimensions.* This is most commonly done by people who are working very hard at raising their consciousness, who get stuck in dimensional, hierarchical fundamentalism. An example of this would be the Ashtar Command, which describes the 8D Galactic Federation like the Pentagon. The eighth dimension works with galactic order, but there are no 3D models that can even begin to describe it. Another example would be the 2D telluric realm when it is mapped out as the "inner Earth." As I decode the structures of Sirius, Nibiru, the Pleiades, or the inner Earth, applying 3D thoughtforms will lead you astray. Metaphor is helpful for modeling higher-dimensional concepts, such as the Photon Band being the metaphor for the Age of Light. It is productive to seek traces of higher dimensions in 3D by noticing when energies are around that are too dense or subtle. For example, snowflakes and crystals are wonderful models of 6D geometry; 5D is often very evident in the subtle higher vibrations in great art; and cats constantly evidence 2D elemental activity. Animals in general are very sensitive to elementals, and that is how animals read humans. Everything is interpenetrating.

I am interested in Abraham only from the following point of view: What's the real story about Abraham from a higher-dimensional perspective? The coverup of Abraham's real story imprisons the human race because it is a coded vehicle for 4D control of your reality. That is, the Nibiruans are using Abraham as a tool. The 4D archetypal forces are very invested in exactly where you are stuck in your emotional bodies because these hotspots—belief systems—are where they can still can monitor and influence you. As long as you have all kinds of beliefs about your great father god, you won't look at what the story is covering up. From my 5D view, things that are covered up contain great potential for removing blocks that are lethal for your emotional bodies.

I have counseled you for a long time about clearing your emotional bodies before you go totally into the Photon Band. Now is the time for you to be grateful that this dynamic has moved down into the physical, which can be demonstrated from Diane's experience. The 2D elementals who graced her body were there to vibrate her back to her physical integrity; they were not there to control her by jerking her around with a belief system that distracted her. Peoples, listen carefully now. The 4D intelligences have crafted a great big smokescreen titled "Demons/Devils/Monsters/Lucifer/Boogies" just to keep you from seeing the brilliant 2D elementals! You have been tricked into judging negatively and fearing the very teachers who can lead you directly to your own healing!

*If* you will contemplate how uranium loses its radioactivity by means of the half-life principle, you will get usable information about how to defuse your own emotional body blocks. In the physical world, it takes hundreds of thousands of years to detoxify radioactive elements. In any lifetime, you occupy a male or a female body. If you can completely infuse, embody, and merge with your opposite sexual polarity in that lifetime, you can dump out one half-life of emotional-body karmic residue. Sexual love relationships are both emotional and physical. If you can embrace total polarity resolution with your lover, you can detoxify the residues of lifetimes from the beginning of time by half. Imagine that you break down this resistance by half every time you fuse in orgasm! I will just say it: *The timing of the defusing of radiation is in symbiotic relationship with the clearance of your emotional bodies.* The Nibiruans and the Sirians have used emotional-body control techniques on you that have involved uranium. In your now, notice that the bomb blew up exactly when your emotional bodies were the most polluted—World War II. If you follow the reintroduction of radiation into your environment, it is in direct proportion to the pollution of your emotional bodies.

Now, here you are in 3D with a great deal of radiation in your environment—which enhances your environment for more Nibiruan access—and you are moving into the Photon Band. On some level, like a nuclear explosion, everything in your system will be completely blasted apart. There you are in 3D integrity maintaining your consciousness, your voice, your behavior, your love life, and all of a sudden everything is literally exploded into a million fragments of light. However, from my perspective, I do not see much light in you as I look at you right now. One way or another, you are all extremely worried about this. This makes you feel like you are going to explode, and so we suggest consulting with Anubis of Sirius for some assistance. The Sirians, after all, played a role in radiation being a big factor in this stage of your evolution.

## Anubis and Your Bodies

"I am Anubis. From my point of view, which is Sirian, we maintain a perspective on your dimension similar to a human with an opened third eye who is maintaining a bead on something. We are known as 'the watchers,' but not the Nibiruan watchers referred to in your Bible, who are personally involved in the agendas and situations they watch. As a Sirian watcher, I am only involved in holding together the physical integrity of the bodies that support these agendas and situations—the planets in your solar system and the orbit of your solar system around Alcyone. If these orbital patterns were not held in form, certain patterns would not occur in time.

"If you will assume the posture of the Great Pyramid when 3D is shattered by multidimensionality, you will stay in form. Sit in lotus position or stand and create energy in your hands, while triangulating the energy by means of a chakra. Use the heart, third eye, or crown to form an apex of the triangle, making a pyramid. The apex can generate healing energy in anything. With this, you can withstand the new field until you adjust. There will be great numbers who need healing, and this technique will maintain your integrity in 3D. Investing your consciousness in physical body postures will maintain your integrity as you enter the Photon Belt.

The way to prevent being blasted out is to maintain postures that can handle this energy.[8]

"Cats are great teachers. You are learning to slow down, you are all learning to stop pushing so hard. You are learning to stop when you bump yourselves and heal that part of your body before you go crashing forward. You are all beginning to really pay attention to the status of your physical bodies because we are sending tremendous geometrical consciousness into your physical bodies to help you start to remember this kind of integrity. A moment will come soon when all of you will stop moving, freeze, and hold a posture to hold the force coming into your planet.

"Regarding the excellent activities of the Pleiadians, they are the master teachers about how to hold energy in your heart, the center dimension of your realm. I will call Pleiadian influence *photon focus.* From my point of view, I hold a strong third-eye focus on the integrity of your whole body, not just the heart. You see what's going on here? The Pleiadians are holding focus on the human heart, and we Sirians are holding focus on the geometry of the whole physical body. We are bringing techniques into manifestation fast now, and the ancient teachers of shamanic body movements are coming into view. There is a whole technology on your planet of yoga, mudras, and physical body postures, because as you move into light, these will be what will keep you in your body.[9]

"I, Anubis, lie with my back stretched out forming a perfect curve with my back haunches pulling my spine back, which raises serpentine energy in my body. With my paws forward, I stare out through time and hold geometrical forms in space. I maintain a vigil on your physical bodies. These days there is a great deal of chaotic energy impulsing your forms. You will not hold in place unless you align with the processes moving your planet into integrity. It is time to move your bodies into positions that lock you into tetrahedral light geometry, then freeze and relax when you feel yourselves extending out into space."

## Higher-Dimensional View of Radiation

A higher-dimensional perspective is needed to comprehend the radioactive process, and yet it is very difficult to describe the dimensions above the sixth. I will try. I've noticed that birds seem to resonate with 7D sound coding on Earth. As Anubis said, Sirians hold geometric form in space, and then, as I see it, 7D lines of light circulate this nonphysical intelligence into sound. The navigation skills of birds and their internal oxygenating, their purpose that is unto themselves, their abundant migratory routes and energy lines, seem to be galactic communication links that you could tune into. That is why they exist in your reality. How many people do you know who meditate on birds?

Yet I intuit that tuning into 7D could be facilitated by studying bird intonations because 7D is the dimension that causes human language to be so sound coded. Birdsong is actually higher dimensional than the sound coding of human language! All the uneven dimensions—1D through 9D—are sound coded. The structure of sound actually holds them in form, and these vibrations generate creativity! For example, the 1D sound of Earth is a low hum that manifests as swamp song and low frequency sound in the ground, and this is what keeps your hearts beating while you are alive. John Michell has demonstrated that the harmony of cultures is maintained or destroyed by chanting.[10] Higher dimensions can be directly apprehended in 3D by means of selected music, such as Bach cello sonatas or string quartets by Beethoven. Toning in 3D accesses 5D resonance, and 7D music of the spheres can be heard by lying on the ground and vibrating with Earth bathed in starlight when there is absolute silence. Orbits are audible, and that is how Anubis holds them in form. The sounds in your language express your real story, and so the Anunnaki scramble these sounds to keep you controlled. Seventh-dimensional sound is birdsong, wind, photons moving in great 7D bands, and the solar wind. Ninth dimensional sound emerges out of the absolute silence and darkness of the Galactic Center, which is moving in a slow, circular motion.

Bluebirds bring a sense of clarity. Blue, celestial blue, tunes into the zone where your atmosphere interacts with light. The seventh dimension has something to do with bluebirds and the blue band that surrounds this planet, that invites you to radiate yourselves out in the whole biosphere that you occupy. Imagine no longer living just on terra firma, but seeing Earth as your own space travelers have. You are part of that blue ball, and reflecting from 7D, from the bluebird dimension, there are tones that the birds could give to this that words cannot. Only their song can reflect the glory of 7D. These celestial tones can take all of consciousnesses to the outer edges of gravitational pull that holds matter—oxygen and hydrogen, helium, the elements that are in gaseous state that surround the planet—where the elemental merges with what is beyond. All you have to do is listen to them singing.

As your solar system moves farther into the Photon Band, lifeforms that are sound coded are going to be strengthened and guided by the kinds of cosmic vibrations that will occur. On Earth, listening to the sounds of birds is indeed a very valid pursuit at this time. Notice that birds cannot tolerate radiation at all. As a result of comet Shoemaker-Levy that hit Jupiter in July 1994, you are on the verge of transmuting radiation, and this will strengthen the birds and swamp creatures. This will cause the sounds of Gaia to synchronize Earth with the stars again. These sounds are needed for synchronizing the geometrical light forms of the Galaxy. Such sounds turn photon bands into vibrating highways of light, like tuned violin strings. The blue band around the outer edges of Earth will be filled with a new kind of light as you go deeper into the Photon Band. The birds are teaching you about some of these mechanisms with sound, the way cats are teaching you about Sirian geometry with their body movements.

As I scan more subtle levels, I detect a great deal of interest in uranium at the 8D level. At this level, I feel the Vegans of the Galactic Federation monitoring uranium. They watch the status of radioactive elements as the Sirians monitor the physical body postures of humans. Vegan consciousness is very hard to detect because it rules motivation—awareness behind all things in your dimension. All the 2D through 8D forces can work with radioactive materials, while uneven dimensions—1D through 9D—seem to have difficulty with radioactivity. The uneven dimensions are zones for expressing creativity and freedom, while the even dimensions generate density and structure. The Nibiruans discovered long ago that uranium can infiltrate human emotional bodies and implant belief systems that are held in miasms. This is not a judgment about how the Nibiruans and Sirians are working with uranium, but I still do not really understand what is going on. Plutonium pollution is more lethal to hybrid Pleiadian/earthlings than it is for humans because of its juicy density.

When something cannot be seen, simply shift to a higher dimension for a new perspective. Let's look at the Vegan motivation with uranium. Oh my! They are holding a bead on all the uranium in the Galaxy! How amazing! They are watching to see what is happening with the half-life decay process to understand how much energy exists in the uranium of Earth. Now I see it: They are using uranium to read density factors in your bodies. Via these densities, solidity is generated in 3D, and then the solidity generates timelines—strings that keep 6D geometrical light structures in form. These timelines are past/present/future time, and if they did not exist, there would be no matter, no experience on Earth. These various kinds of density create etheric and physical forms. So the Vegans use uranium as a vision tool, like a CAT scan into density status. When a culture has radioactive materials, it means they've reached a certain point of evolution—achieving total choice about life or death. Radiation is an insertion of chaotic material into 3D for exploring immortality. And that is exactly what Abraham did.

At the 8D level, for your solar system, the Vegans run the Galactic Federation. This is the political realm of power. With uranium, at the 2D level, there is elemental resonance with Earth; at the 4D level, Anunnaki manipulation of emotions; at the 6D level, structural support by means of Sirian light geometry; and at the 8D level, reading of density for setting up laws for regulating energy acceleration. What is important to see now is that at the 8D level, *new laws are being written,* and that is why this struggle over life and death is so all pervasive in all realms. The transmutation of elemental intelligences needs to be evolved because these magnificent beings have not been respected. A few of you are in pain about the animals in your realm when you should be writhing with the agony of the elements that you arrogantly split for your convenience.

All the radioactive materials in your solar system are being observed. Even the abuse of chemicals is being watched. From my Pleiadian perspective, I know that the Vegans are aware that, as the solar system moves fully into the Photon Band, radioactivity will be disseminated through the solar system and beyond unless new laws are implemented. From my point of view, the radiation moving out of this particular solar system is very dangerous to the Pleiades. We Pleiadians maintain integrity of the heart, which many of you value very highly. I can tell you that remaining physical in the Photon Band is possible only for those with true integrity in their hearts.

As I observe you in 3D, uranium can be balanced in your hearts, and it can teach you a lot. Your heart has the capacity, through compassion and love, to love all energies. This is not really about whether radiation is a dangerous or negative energy; it is more an issue of the heart being overwhelmed by density, like the paroxysm in your heart during a heart attack caused by too much density in your arteries. The heart's agenda is to spread its unlimited energy and it quakes in the face of too much density. I, Satya, am acutely sensitive to plutonium because plutonic energies trigger maximum feeling activation, whether a body is ready to handle it or not. You humans reintroduced plutonium just after Pluto was sighted from Earth in 1930. You went deep into the cave before you'd transduced enough of the light in your bodies. I could say that you are breaking our 5D hearts. The expanding energy of your heart could move on 6D gridlines to assist and support this whole photonic increase. The expanding heart has the capacity to offer humankind a physical form with which to experience this transition if you will just become compassionate with each other.

As I observe manipulation by radioactivity, I see radiation holding emotions in your bodies instead of letting them simply pass through your heart. Uranium sticks emotions in your bodies, and then they run amok and become cancerous. This terrifies you and forces you to clear tumors from your bodies. But, these tumors transmute radiation, they process it by means of cancer in your bodies, and the frequency of tumors indicates how polluted your environment really is. Then allopathic medicine uses chemotherapy and radiation—2D elemental bullets—in your bodies rather than teaming up with your bodies. These great elementals are in your body to heal you, and you must respect them. Is it respectful to Earth to "nuke" a terminally ill, elderly person, and then bury that radioactive body? As you pass into the Photon Band, each decision about life and death assumes monumental proportions. If you begin with integrity, all will be fine.

Let's go back to Vega for a higher-dimensional view. The Vegans have a bead on the radiation in your solar system. The purpose of radiation at the 8D level is to quicken energies and to open up densities. For example, the Vegans are watching the Anunnaki to see just how much emotional manipulation is getting locked into your bodies. They can see this by observing radiation in your bodies by monitoring the half-life decay process. When I say they have a bead on this decay process, I mean that if this process goes too quickly, the Sirian geometric order would be destroyed by a chaotic explosion.

Everything is right on schedule, and this is a beautiful story when viewed multidimensionally. How can you judge radiation negatively when it is the central heart of your own Sun? This is a very creative story. And as the different parts of this story are told, energies will be moved and emotions will be cleared like inner lights being lit within the consciousness of all lifeforms. Remember, radiation is being held in your third dimensional reality by the pollution of your emotional bodies. Yet, you must understand that there is no real pollution once you honor your own feelings. Radiation has increased in direct proportion to emotional pollution.

In the time of Abraham, there were similar levels of emotional pollution that brought these elements into manifestation. In those days, the emotional pollution was triggered by the gods who came down to Earth and used humans for their own devices. In your own times, the polarity struggle of the gods began to overwhelm you during two great wars in this century. Since the dark days of World War II, the human race has been held hostage by fear of nuclear war. In the war between good and bad, light and dark, capitalism and communism, religion and atheism, tremendous amounts of radioactive substances have been raped out of Gaia. This has deenergized the elemental world, polluted the emotional bodies of Earth, stressed the Pleiadian heart, and shut out Sirian geometrical expansion.

Look at the agency sponsoring the nuclear standoff—the World Management Team. The World Management Team utilizes 2D, 4D, 6D, and 8D forms, the dimensions that work with structure and density. Without the balance of the uneven dimensions—1D through 9D—which offer creativity and energy, structure will kill all. *The degree to which the World Management Team gets away with murder on your planet is in direct proportion to the degree to which you do not trust yourselves to be creative.* The World Management Team cannot do anything to people on Earth who trust their own powers. You are in a balancing act now, which will empower your creativity. This will break down the control. *You are on the verge of a creative renaissance that will be like a supernova.* To attempt to see this from even higher dimensions, I welcome Enoch from the ninth dimension!

## Enoch and Radiation

"I am Enoch, and my sense of myself is of pure light. The only records of my existence in your reality are stories that have been told about me. The most accurate stories that have been told about me are of people being blinded by light when I appeared. My energy is exactly the same as photon bands. I am a 7D light being when I manifest in 3D, and when I am unmanifested, I exist eternally in the Galactic Center. I came down into your reality once, when you exploded your first atomic device in 2024 B.C., because I felt your agony.

"I came down to encode the materialization of creativity on your planet by means of photons. Without that, you would have been caught in the density. You would have just been a huge iron crystal in space orbiting around the Sun. The iron elementals, who are located in the center of your planet, made the decision that they wanted to experience all elements in the universe. I wonder if they would have made this decision if they knew what it would create. It has created many very painful experiences. All of the radioactive elements are tied up in this. The human body is cellular and filled with water, and radiation is extremely difficult for the body to cope with.

"Radiation was brought into your field because radiation is the central creative life force of stars. Humans decided that they wished to explore their stellar coding, and you cannot know anything without experiencing it in your own realm. So, the opportunity to explore nuclear consciousness was offered. When the nuclear device was detonated after the Ark was installed in the Rephaim temple of Sodom and Gomorrah, many others, such as Abraham, were called into your realm to play various roles in this introduction of stellar elements. I, Enoch, then selected a human incarnation. We wanted to be on your planet while these elements were being introduced. When I finished my encodement, I simply ascended back into the light. What is most valuable about my teaching are the techniques for ascension into the light. That is why the books about me were removed from scripture. Your religious control forces do not want you to be able to ascend directly to the light. They want to entrap you in structures—in temples and arks.

"Meanwhile, just as the forbidden scriptures say, I was taken by angels to meet the Lord. Now, I have appeared to offer more information on this because it gives you a sense of the mechanisms of the dimensions. Please notice as you go along that anything that is being taught to you from the uneven dimensions can be attained by you: You can ascend as I did, you can sing like a bluebird and go to the blue light, you can open your Pleiadian heart, you can be in total integrity in 3D, and you can merge with Gaia in 1D.

"When you ascend from 3D, you first move into 4D. There the angels join up with you, and they take you on the journey. As you go through the dimensions, the various angelic vehicles of those dimensions are what carry you through these zones. When I came into 3D, I really did take physical form. That is what created all the stories. I created a story, a mystery play about myself, just like you do with your life. I did not create a bloodline, nor do the beings of 1D through 9D create bloodlines; however, 3D beings on your planet do procreate, they do reproduce. When I talk about creating bloodlines, I am talking about infusion by 2D through 8D forces into the 3D procreative powers. Infusions into 3D of the 5D, 7D, and 9D levels are kundalini infusions, light infusions, and creative blasts that birth star babies. I have participated in many star-baby creations. This occurs when I impulse a couple having orgasm to agree to create a child on a star somewhere in the Galaxy. This coding hands down the pure light into 3D physical form."

## *Comet Shoemaker-Levy Hits Jupiter, July 1994*

I, Satya, will close this discussion of radiation by telling you a few things about the comet that struck Jupiter in 1994, which created a nuclear explosion in your solar system. The waves from the cometary impacts went out to the Sun, which responded like a great bell ringing waves all through the Galaxy to other stars with planets. These waves informed the whole Galaxy about the condition of things on Earth, and since then many more extraterrestrials are taking an interest in Earth. The satellite *Galileo* was able to send photographs of the cometary impacts back to Earth because it was on the right side of Jupiter for viewing. *Galileo* will crash into Jupiter during November 1995, unless scientists can alter its orbit.[11] This potential release of plutonium in Jupiter's atmosphere tells me that you will soon be dealing with plutonium very intensely. Never has it been more critical for scientists to discover how to transmute this element.

The cometary impacts triggered Jupiter to a new stage of its evolution. For Earth, Jupiter rules mastery schools and secret societies, and it rules expansion of your consciousness and sense of well-being. This comet blasted open the control codes of the secret societies, and this opened your planet to higher-dimensional structural methods, such as Sirian geometric structures and guidance by the Galactic Federation.[12] This book is a direct result of that opening. You now have entered a period where you have great potential to transmute plutonium and move beyond control and secrecy. You will be amazed by what happens as solutions for radioactivity are finally found.

# 4

# THE LIZARDS
# AND THE ROMAN CHURCH

SOME 225 MILLION YEARS AGO, YOUR SUN WAS LOCATED IN THE SAME PLACE in the Milky Way Galaxy as it is now, and this was a time when great reptiles of awesome size had just begun to establish their dominion on Earth.[1] Now, as you return to the same point in your Galaxy, you have become self-reflective, and you are wondering whether life has also evolved in other star systems. Therefore, this is the time to delve deeply into your reptilian heritage, for it is the biological basis of this just-completed galactic cycle. As I, Satya, have told you, a new intention is created at the beginning of each approximately 26,000-year cycle, and four of these cycles—approximately 104,000 years—always entails a major evolutionary leap. There are 2160 of these 104,000-year cycles, within the 225-million-year Galactic Return, and 2160 is the number of years in the precession of one zodiac sign on Earth. Twelve zodiac signs precess in one exact 25,920-year precession.

I bring these vast numbers up because everything is synchronized. The more you comprehend the synchronization of Earth's precession cycle with the Alcyone spiral, and with the orbit of the whole Pleiadian system around the Galactic Center, the more you will be amazed. Now is the time to delve into the real truth about your reptilian heritage, the whole last 225 million years of Earth's biological evolution. The reptiles are the carriers of potent biological codes since they have been living on Earth all the way through the whole cycle. You are fascinated with their supposed extinction in the past because you are actually contemplating the possibility of your own. This apotheosis of the galactic cycle is deeply attuned with reptilian cellular intelligence. I was most intrigued when in 1989 my vehicle was taken by Hunbatz Men deep within the limestone caves of the Yucatan to see cave drawings of the Maya with dinosaurs—and so let's hear from a lizard!

### King Lizard Speaks about Kundalini

"I am King Lizard, and we lizards love your spines. That is all we are really interested in. We are specialists of the spine, along with our brothers—the blessed snakes. The energy in your spines attracts us, and we are here now because this is a time of energy acceleration in your spines. Our spines are very long, and their feeling potential is exquisite, such as with the dinosaur. These days, we have to struggle to stay in incarnational form, much more than you realize. For some strange reason, you think we are invincible because we are so good at eating you up whenever we get the opportunity. I am here now because possibly you might become less afraid of me.

"We are the most advanced masters, ministers, regulators, and resonators of the spinal influence on your planet. Just look at all of us with our exquisitely long spines. Are you not impressed by Tyrannosaurus Rex? Is it not wonderful that such a huge creature with such great, powerful legs and hipbones has such an incredibly long, powerful spine throughout its back and tail? Like you humans, we too had high times in our civilization, and we like the way you've put our Tyrannosaurus Rex in museums! The longer the spine, the more you have kundalini energy. This is because the more vertebrae you have, the more kundalini energy. If you still had your tails, you would have more. Our friends, the Pleiadians, love kundalini energy. Because they are the etheric level of kundalini and we are the physical level, we are both deeply involved in the reptilian biological consciousness of Earth.

"You might wonder if the length of the spine is related to the length of the penis? What about the human penis and kundalini activation? This male member is simply a blood-engorged organ attached to men's bodies, close to their root chakra. Activation and stimulation of the male member are ruled by blood flow in the physical body, not by kundalini energy in the spine. Now, it is true that kundalini energy in the spine activates blood flow in all of the chakras, but the principle that rules the activation of the penis is actually the blood system.

"We lizards along with birds are original biological species of Earth, and we have one similar characteristic: we have an extremely strong biological force. However, our ability to survive on the planet can be a delicate matter. Due to this precarious balance, we are always excellent barometers of the ecological balance of your planet. Along with the birds, we reptiles are very involved with the Nibiruan species, because we have always been here when they've visited during the last 500,000 years. We've taught the Nibiruans our life sciences, and the records of these teachings are recorded on the "Stones of Ica" of Peru. Our vibration is much in tune with the Nibiruans; we are simpatico with them. They admire us when they come to Earth. They think of us as gods. Did you know that?

"Nibiruans differ from us in that they are metallic biology. From your perspective, metallic lifeforms are nonbiological. To comprehend the Nibiruan lifeform, you need to be able to stretch your imaginations to encompass a metallic force as being biological. You'll figure this out when you realize your computers are becoming lifeforms. The Nibiruans are metallic entities who admire us lizards as gods of Earth. They love the kundalini energy surging in our spines, because the metallic electromagnetic force in their bodies resonates with our sacred fire. Also we are cold-blooded, and cold-blooded creatures are closer in vibration to metallic lifeforms and the 2D telluric realm. When the Anunnaki visit Earth, they wear various costumes over their bodies, since otherwise they would look like reptilian metal robots to you. They often wear bird masks, great wings, even bird claws. Sometimes they wear the faces of crocodiles, frogs, or dogs. The Anunnaki resonate with our vital force. If you want to figure them out, listen to me. Around us they are like radios that enjoy being plugged in and turned on. Has it ever occurred to you that your receptor appliances like it when you turn them on?

"These metallic essences, the Anunnaki, receive electromagnetic kundalini energy from us reptiles, and they can monitor all devices that are based on electromagnetism. This is difficult for you to conceive. But if it makes you feel any better, they can't monitor silica-based technologies; however, extraterrestrials from stars can. Everything is linked, and now that you have invented tools that work with vibrational waves, you are joining the grid. You all totally underestimate how much each one of you can actually read energies. The third dimension is flowing with energies—radio, television, kundalini, microwave, and extraterrestrial signals and waves. The human brain is capable of reading any of them. So, too, are your electronic devices when you turn them on. If you really want to, you can hear what the CIA is doing, what the FBI is doing, what the local police are doing, just by listening to the sound codes in phones, televisions, radios, the wind in electrical wires, and vibrations in machines. Anytime you want to, you can tune into metallic forms of communication by translating energies through the metals in your own bodies. This might not be such a bad idea, since the Anunnaki head the World Management Team, which runs the covert spy apparatuses, secret police, governments, and multinational corporations of the world. As King Lizard, let me tell you, your airwaves are loaded with their output these days!

"Here's how you can tune into metallic forms of communication . . . A hologram is produced when a laser beam is split into two beams. Beam A is bounced off an image to be photographed, Beam B is mirrored back so it will collide with the reflected light of the image. This creates an interference pattern, like waves from opposite directions intermeshing on the surface of a pond. The interference pattern is encoded on film, and if you shine another light into it, the image that was photographed can be projected into any space. Once it is projected, you can see this image in space—you can pass your hand through it suspended in air. Your space is filled with waves from many sources, these waves form interference patterns, and images can be created out of them. Your media has specific, surface 3D sounds or images that you all can hear or see, but it is also loaded with masked sounds and images. These subliminal communications are used to encode you with thoughtforms while you laugh innocently, naively at "I Love Lucy." *The World Management Team uses your electronic forms of entertainment to get into your head.* You can ascertain these subliminal implants by observing odd thoughts, emotional patterns, or physical reactions such as stomachaches or headaches when you are tuned into the media; notice when and where they come from.

"Any one of you is capable of hearing the metallic vibrational communications system of the World Management Team, since your own life force generates electromagnetic fields. Naturally, unless you have raised your own vibration beyond their access, your electromagnetic fields can be penetrated and/or monitored. Since they access you and read you, why not reverse your energy through their waves and read them? Your esoteric and magical faculties have been consistently suppressed and ridiculed so you won't figure out how to reverse the process. However, most major male power brokers are members of secret societies, they practice magical rites covertly, so they can become masters of energy by reading vibrations. You can do any of this yourselves if you trust your subtle senses; and once you regain that skill, nobody can pull anything on you. Let's be honest, you sense what the big boys are doing, so start doing it back!

"I am King Lizard. I've come to meet with you to discuss the ecological condition of Earth. We live most happily in tropical environments that are not threatened. Our environment is very endangered, as are the environments of many of the original species of Earth. Loss of habitat and species limits the access of star intelligence on Earth, but each one of the original biological species of Earth has a star home. Star consciousness is a large part of the dimensional spectrum—more than half of it—and animals are the source of star wisdom for humans. Cats live the star consciousness of Sirius, the birds of the Pleiades, and the bears of the Andromeda Galaxy. We lizards have the star consciousness of Draco. We are very attuned to Nibiru's long journey outside your solar system; and we also resonate with Draco, the source of dragon legends on Earth. Sirius is, of course, known as the dog star, and Anubis is a jackal, a dog with a very catlike body. This is because dogs are guardians of humans; frequently a dog will give its life so a human can live. Anubis is the orbital guardian of the whole solar system. He is one of the solar system's guides in the Galactic Night. Snakes are very close to our vibration. Their habitat and behavior are different, but when we are in the water and a snake is on the land, we both vibrate with Earth in a similar way.

"I have a family, a very close family with many generations below myself in time. I have sex with many females, and with males sometimes. We are, as you would call it, androgynous. But we do have biological reproduction, and so when we think of our family, we think of all the lizards that we have produced from our own bodies for eons. Do you think of your species as your relations for eons? We are fascinated with our offspring, and we love them all very intensely. We are mainly interested in the environment that is very close to ourselves. The saddest experience that we have on your planet occurs when the water goes away. Our habitat is being drained away. Have you noticed?

"A long time ago, we decided to fly while seeking safety during a time of great heat from volcanoes. We were taught to fly by our brothers and sisters, the Pleiadian bird teachers. This attempt to fly off the land was not successful over time because it was so foreign to our natural biology. As soon as we were able to find water sources and wet habitats again, we let this experiment with our species atrophy. We feel great affinity with our

Pleiadian bird teachers who attempted to help us with our dilemma when Earth became hot and dry. Once, some of us became ostriches with very long legs, and this was in the time when we had moved into other forms of elemental evolution.

"The reason that we are so attuned to electromagnetic energy is because of the length of our spines and the number of vertebrae, and because we lie and crawl on the surface of Earth like snakes. As soon as you become a species that stands erect, kundalini energy diminishes in your body. Kundalini energy access is stronger for reptiles slithering on the ground. It is an entirely different organization of consciousness that is more attuned to the telluric realm, the source of electromagnetic energy that activates kundalini in bodies. Listen carefully, kundalini waves are from 2D. Electromagnetism works differently in the air above Earth's surface, where it can be as toxic as 4D manipulation of your emotions is in 3D. Kundalini energy is rejuvenating, but electromagnetic fields in the air can weaken you.

"Kundalini energy is electromagnetic energy that reorganizes biological species back into their perfect 12-strand DNA form. Perfect genetic form is the key to functional cellular biology. The kundalini access powers of the reptiles are very important on Earth. There is so much negativity about us, and yet do you realize how magnificent we are? You criticize us for wanting to eat you, but you go out and eat meat all the time. We are exquisite. We are irridescent, green, strong, scaly, and we have activated spines as we lie close to Earth. We lie close to the heart of Earth. You are the ones who do not love Earth enough to see how magnificent we are.

"We are, to the best of our ability, holding the force of pure kundalini energy in relationship to the intelligence of Gaia. We are temple keepers of Gaia, of the biological systems of Earth. Your planet has a certain climatic cycle, and a certain solar/lunar/planetary/electromagnetic cycle. The basic environment of your planet is ruled by the 24-hour solar day. Who is it, or *what* is it, that is holding the basic biological intelligence of the planet in relationship to the intelligence of Earth? Reptiles are the grounders and keepers of that force! As the energy intensifies on the planet, Gaia begins to emit more consciousness. Because you have now entered into an astronomical point where Gaian intelligence is being activated, we reptiles who remain in Earth are the ones who hold this incredible intelligence. We hold this knowledge right within our physical bodies. How many humans can regenerate limbs the way we can?

"We prefer the Galactic Night because it is a time when there is more water, more flooding, and more greening power. When you enter the Photon Band, as is happening now, unless you have the intelligence to protect the biology of your planet, we reptiles will be destroyed. Now, when I say destroyed, it's the same thing as saying that you are a resident of a city that turns into a desert. This doesn't necessarily mean all of our biological species will be destroyed, but the fabric of our culture will be decimated. We may need to retreat to the watery caves under the mountains and back into other ancient caves on your planet, but we would rather stay out in the Sun. You can understand that we don't really like crawling down a hole for 2000 years.

"If you humans could begin to figure more things out, we think that we could have a green, swampy paradise that we all could play in. We would like that. We want that because enlightened humans in the past, when Earth was in the Photon Band, made homes in temples for us. The ancient temple Khem in Egypt was a home for us, as well as Kom Ombo. Of course, the Egyptians, being Sirians, were smart enough to realize that they would need us for the regeneration codes—the keys of human survival during the time in the Photon Band. Also, there was enough of our habitat left on the planet for us when the solar system went into the Band. Do you realize how rapaciously destructive you all are? Nice job you did on Florida!

"If a species is decimated, it does go into another dimension. The imprint of that species is still in Earth's 1D hologram in the 1D central-core crystal, and sometimes it can come back in form in 3D. For the most part, however, if intelligence is not stored someplace in living species— who are the biological records in 3D—it may terminate. How can you take such chances? We fear that if a species is completely decimated, that could be the end of that species, as well as ourselves, and you guys, too. These are very complex questions because the morphogenetic fields of species are held in other dimensions. Certainly, anything can be created again, but we personally feel that it would be possible for a species to become completely extinct.

"For example, why would a species return to a place where it was deliberately destroyed? Do you think any self-respecting crocodile would go to Florida these days? If people understand us as a species but do not value our genius, what does that say? We truly love deeply; we are the keepers of Gaia because we're close to Earth, and if you loved Earth as much as we do, you would appreciate who we are. We need to be appreciated at the highest levels of intelligence, like a brilliant thoughtform. We would come back if honored, but we see no reason to trust you.

"If you are able to destroy us while knowing what we are, then you show you are capable of destroying life itself! Who says you can create life again? Maybe you can in a laboratory. But what kind of habitat is that? We already know the answer: an Anunnaki habitat. There are those on your planet right now who understand this crisis. They see that saving remnants of a species is very important until the World Management Team realizes they are even endangering themselves. Ecologists are retaining species in captivity for regeneration. These ancient knowledge codes are deep, and ecologists are simply doing again what they did thousands of years ago. Often these ecologists were keepers of species in Egypt, whose ideal was to have the 3D surface of Earth—Garden of Eden—be symbiotic with the central core crystal. During those times, we lizards were very happy.

"Unfortunately, as I see it, because we are more intelligent than humans, humans would destroy lizards, even if they knew how irreplaceable they are. *Humans tend to destroy anything more intelligent than themselves.* We can see this jealous, competitive energy in your bodies when we read the Nibiruan miasms in your emotional bodies. When we see these miasms we do eat you up if possible, especially if you are in our habitat wearing safari clothes. One of our finest achievements in the twentieth century was when our Komodo dragon ate up a Rockefeller! The Anunnaki value the mind over all else, and we've had our difficulties with them. They have used us and abused us. We are not evil beings, for nothing that is primary biological species of Earth is evil. Evil is the reverse of live. *Evil is anything that comes into a realm and manipulates inhabitants or interferes with their reality, and it is deathly.*

"When we die, we have an ecstatic experience similar to what you experience as orgasm. We don't mind dying; neither do you; you just don't know it. By the way, normally we don't speak to you, because you do not respect us. We loved the Nile delta region with its wonderful muddy alluvial soil. We came all the way down the Nile from the Sudan just to be in the Delta. You cannot imagine how you have broken our hearts by building the Aswan Dam.

"I wonder if you've noticed how backward, how stupid you are? You think you are descended from apes because an uneducated country parson, Charles Darwin, said so. The ape family is not an original biological species of Earth. They were seeded on Earth from Orion, and they possess extraordinary galactic knowledge, as is evidenced by their leader, Thoth, the baboon god of Egypt. Meanwhile, you humans are descended from us lizards!

"My ancestors, the Red Glint Slit Eyes, are in the British Museum! We have been mummified, and we are on display! Those mummies are from our temple at Kom Ombo. Our vehicle loves to teach there because she loves us. She makes offerings to us there every year. It's a great place, and there's lots of mud. We notice how our vehicle comes alive in wet environments. She can't stand dry places anymore. And by the way, a lot of people are not going to be liking dry places much longer. Why don't you quit cutting all the trees and drying out the surface of your planet?

"We have very complex social structures based on our desires to have comfort, sunlight, and pleasure in the water. You would be surprised at the things we've built on occasion. We've built caves, tunnels, and all kinds of wonderful systems. We've built temples under surface buildings. There have been civilizations that appreciated us, and then we have been willing to activate their temples with our kundalini power. The Egyptians were the ultimate masters of occult technology on your planet, and so, on occasion, they created houses and labyrinths for us beneath their temples. The Egyptians discovered that when you create labyrinths for us, we swim around in them, reproduce ourselves, and create powerful consciousness and kundalini energy. The Israelites admired our technology, and they created caves for us under the Dome of the Rock in order to activate power.

"We did not like it there, however, because they did not appreciate us. They were trying to use us like scaly batteries producing talismanic power. They were trying to use us and our energy to create power. They were not honoring us, just trying to use our power in order to take control of others. The Egyptians were working with our intelligence in order to understand the powers of Gaia. They shared their discoveries with us; they educated us, even mummified us to honor our ancestor cult. One of our most esteemed graduates was Dr. Lizard, and now it is time to consult with this esteemed colleague."

*Doctor Lizard and God*

"We are a grouping known as Dr. Lizard. We are extremely well-educated. We are scholars, and we are wondering why you spend so much time worshiping God while your planet's going to hell? As for us, we are extremely upset whenever we hear the word 'God.' Use of this word always stops us in our tracks for a great deal of time. The way we figure out what is going on with you is to read your feeling bodies, since we cannot read your mental bodies. Your mental bodies are like scrambled-up computer holograms, and the only way that we can detect anything about you is via your feelings.

"You express constant anguish about the God dilemma and about the destruction of your planet. However, *the amount of attention you pay to God is keeping you from focusing on your environment, thus destroying your environment.* As we read you, you do feel true anguish about your environment, but you have no real feelings about God. You are overprogrammed and overstimulated constantly about this abstract idea that does not interest you at all. This is actually a program designed to keep you from sensitivity about yourselves and your planet. This is the main source of a great deal of the difficulty that our race is experiencing. To put it bluntly, *God is a program put upon the Saurians.*

"We've noticed that you think God is superior to yourselves. But, that is impossible, because nothing is superior to you! This thoughtform is idiotic, and nobody actually believes it, but you give your power away by acting like it is true. Haven't you noticed that we do not have this psychological problem? You have a big problem, and you've come to the right place to find out how to bust this belief system. We know that no one is superior to us. The thought never entered our long spines!

"Since you think you are exploring multidimensionality in this book, if you'd adjust your thoughtform away from looking at God as something separate and think of this energy as a generator of dimensions, worshiping would cease with the snap of a finger! When you view anything as separate from yourself, at a higher level than yourself, then you lose perspective on yourself. Watching you, we have noticed that the more you worship this deity, the more you lose your sense of self. Normally we see you as energetic bodies, but when you let go of your identity through worship of a higher form or separate form, your energy body literally disappears! We have to ask, are you alive? Since it's hard to be sure about that, we interact more so with those of you who have very active energetic bodies.

"We are not quite sure of the future. From our point of view, all biological forms will be vibrating at an extremely intense level of frequency while traveling in the Photon Band, and that is only possible within a complex and diverse habitat. Since we vibrate at an extremely intense level of frequency, it is likely that one way or another our biological essence will be greatly invigorated and strengthened. King Lizard already commented that we prefer the journey in the Galactic Night when the planet is wet and green, but like yourselves, we do have to journey through the Band.

"We also exist under the surface on the planet Venus, but we prefer to be on Earth's surface. We prefer sunlight, water, and greenery. On Venus, we radiate mineral light from our blood, glow like we are phosphorescent, and speak telepathically. We are not in corporeal form as lizards on Earth. We are an oozing biological form that looks like frog eggs. If you saw us etherically, we would be a vibrating essence deep within egg forms in oozing green slime, like protoplasm. We are attuned to our forms on Earth, and this relationship is similar to the relationship of Thoth to baboons and apes. Thoth lives on Mercury. We have noticed that our lizard forms on Earth enjoy slime because it reminds them of home.

"Here on Venus, there is a direct genetic link between ourselves and the formerly dominant Saurian culture. We exist in 4D, and we are the genetic bank of Earth Saurians. We are nonphysical morphogenetic fields—idea forms of reptiles and yourselves. The idea form of humans and reptiles came from Venus! In the formation of the human, the mineral mixed with the Venusian membrane was indeed clay, as the Bible says. The history of the Anunnaki creation is in Genesis, and the clay utilized was silica-based, but the story of the reptiles was left out. Reptilian genes were mixed with carbon-based organic mud. That is why lizards love mud composed of rotting plants in swamps. The genetic intelligence of humans is silica-based, and that is why the interface between humans and quartz crystals is so powerful.

"This Venusian genetic mixture goes four to seven billion years back in time. We have records of the gradual manifestation of creatures out of this matrix, according to the cosmological cycles influencing the surface of your planet. As we scan this, we see eons of time going by when these mixtures of membranes and quartz crystal went through processes of reaction both to the solar light and to photon light. This is a very long story.

"The original evolution of the genetic matrix of humans and Saurians on your planet occurred under very natural circumstances. All the Anunnaki did was make the mixture out of primordial Earth elements using silica-based clay for humans so they could read and program your minds. Remember, *the Anunnaki cannot utilize silica-based technologies to manipulate you, but they can impulse you in your silica-based cells.* However, this crystalline matrix also offers you the potential to become fully multidimensional, and silica-based technologies will assist you with this. Once you become multidimensional, the Anunnaki will not be able to impulse your silica-based cells and jerk you around. We'd like to see you figure this out, because the Nibiruan programming in your heads is what is driving you to commit ecocide. If you doubt what we say, consider Mars. We reptiles once swam the canals of Mars. The Anunnaki can't mess with our heads because we're carbon-based, but we also have not been able to evolve our brains as you have. *Your greatest asset is also your worst potential liability.* We reptiles are here to help you figure out how they mind-control you, causing you to become murderers for their agendas—which are belief systems that have nothing to do with Earth!

"This history—we prefer 'herstory'—of genetic development and genetic evolution is thousands times longer and greater than the influence and interference that did occur. This original matrix is much more potent than anyone actually realizes, especially scientists. You actually have less to worry about than you think, because of the original strength of this mixture. However, if you were totally mind-controlled, would you want to survive?

"Remember, we have told you the Anunnaki don various costumes when they visit, and you might just become one of their masks. We are not fooling. When the Bible says you were made in god's image, it actually refers to reptiles![2] They were the Anunnaki's first experiment, and our species failed them from their point of view. Because we are carbon-based, we feel Earth too much, and they can't take us over. Next, they made you of silica-based clay, and they've been preparing you for their takeover. The cosmological cycle predominates, however, and you will go into the Photon Band to rebalance and reinvigorate.

"I, Dr. Lizard, dream all the time. I dream the memories of your race, your planet, and your desires. With your desires, I create morphogenetic fields in primordial slime that can create life on Earth. These days, I hope that you will remember what it is like to feel pure and strong and vibratory. I have not forgotten for the Anunnaki did not distract me from my attunement with Earth. I wish that you, too, would return to this feeling of the original primeval ooze. Then we could heal you more, and you could heal us more. You might even return to being like wild animals. If that is the resonation the cosmos called for, I can assure you that is exactly what you would choose.

"We do not have bodies on Venus. We are vibrational and fourth dimensional. From the perspective of Earth, 4D represents planetary qualities that express the desires of the Sun in the dimensions of time and space on Earth. You do not realize that planets are 4D intelligences that create realities on Earth because a deep prejudice against astrology has been implanted in your brains. The Anunnaki do not want you to realize that their ability to create on Earth is only the skill of one planet among many.

"We are vibrational entities on Venus that replicate in order to resonate more with our environment. We do this by pure feeling. Astrologically, Venus is pure receptivity. We draw desire to us and then express it. I, Dr. Lizard, am the director of the genetic record bank. This is very secret stuff, and you just walked in the back door. Those who have the clear intention to feel more in their bodies these days can get right into the source of their creation—the 4D genetic laboratory of Venus—by totally protecting and honoring species in 3D on Earth. As we move inside the planet Venus, we find the reptilian library—modules and modems of Saurian energy—as morphogenetic fields held in form through feelings on Earth.

"To comprehend this concept, you need to have a very highly developed sense of what it feels like to create something in the physical. The ability for humans to sense differentials in life force is something that is developing very rapidly, and is similar to noticing feelings with extreme accuracy. Feeling the true vibration of the life force itself—the actual vibration of a species—will be a source of mind-boggling evolution on your planet. Many Earth mothers know about this and this is why more women than men are *humble*. Anyone else who is able to be present for the birth of a child has the chance to observe the moment when the feeling body comes in to interface with the new physical form. This is a very powerful vibration as it comes in. It is ecstasy. In your realm, the most important evolutionary trigger of the last 100 years is the participation by fathers in the births of their children.

"You are coming to a biological crisis, and the physical integrity of your species is threatened. *Species are held in form by your ability to feel them, and this is why Native Americans work with totem animals as allies.* As the ecological crisis deepens, this knowledge is going to become increasingly more important on your planet. Meanwhile, the World Management Team has diverted Indians into running gambling casinos in their native lands. The true mission of humans on this planet is to commune with all the other animals, as well as themselves, since the animals express the brilliance of star intelligence. Yet you are trying to kill all the other animals because you've been brainwashed into thinking that human consciousness is godlike. As I see it, the most potent killers of all time are the Christians, because Christianity assumes humans are superior to animals. Other religions value mysticism, a feeling-based approach, but *Christianity has become so mental that it is lethal to all life.*

"Fear is lethal. When it comes up, you must move right through it. Many of you are feeling a constant level of fear all the time. Whenever you feel a particular fear, stay with this fear. Don't rationalize it; go into it, flow with it. It is actually impulsing you to feel more! Locate where the fear is sourced: Is it in your body or in a certain location, like the woods? This is a powerful healing. Move right into the source of your fear. If you keep going with this process, you will move all the way through your fear right to its true source. If your fear is sourced in something that could threaten your survival, getting to it could save you. Otherwise, you will meet your end.

"Let me tell you more Earth information from our records. There was a time when life from Venus was transferred to Earth in pale purple eggs guarded by long-legged spider grandmothers. (New life was in the eggs and these became colored from turquoise to lapis to purple.) These eggs were Venusian and were birthed on Venus by means of feeling thought-forms. No life can exist on Earth for biological species without these feeling lightbodies. We lizards can still feel our Spider Grandmother gripping our shoulders. Our memories are long, and we are grateful to them for delivering our thoughtform into 3D. These times were traumatic, however, as birth is traumatic. All Earth species carry some emotional negativity about this moment, and we have avoided revealing this information. Now is the time for you to realize the fragility of life.

"We lizards do not feel negatively about spiders or any insects. There was a wrenching moment when Spider Grandmother decided that it was time to bring her dream from Venus into the matrix of Earth. This is the first memory of life on Earth—a cavernous place where the spider grandmothers guarded amethyst eggs. From our point of view as scholar lizards, we were the dominant biological species on Earth when these events occurred. We felt the time in this solar system when your feeling bodies were moved into the biological consciousness of Earth by the manipulations of Spider Grandmother.

"There was revenge on those spiders as they coveted and collected the eggs, and the revenge came from the serpents, who carried the highest vibration of the reptiles. This information is available today from the serpent people, and that's why the Bible encourages you to murder the serpent. We reptiles know what it is like to be abandoned. We saw defenseless species, including humans, introduced by Spider Grandmother, but being killed while adjusting to new habitats. We absorbed this victim pain. You felt you were victims when you were learning how to live in a new way, and so today you destroy habitats! You must learn to be vulnerable again, which means being open and flexible. Otherwise you will let yourself be mind-controlled into destroying everything. We reptiles are guardians of vulnerability for all beings.

"My crystalline white-light energy is all focused on my spine. Yet, I am also focused in my underbelly, which can be accessed only by *feeling*, not by raising energy through breath work and radiance. Fear is felt in the belly, which contains the codes for getting through fear. By being focused just in the spine, you will only care about the goal. That's why you were conditioned, and your conditioning is finally being broken down, since it is not appropriate anymore. As you move deeper into the Photon Band, you will be able to armor your backsides if you open up your bellies enough.

"The way to view the fourth dimension is from 5D and above. If you look at everything as linear space and time, you feel like rats in a maze. You would be literally amazed that whenever you find yourself feeling stuck—not knowing where to move, feeling like you're in a dilemma—you will shift it by moving your consciousness to a higher-dimensional perspective. How do you do that?

"With 5D eyes, you can become a seer in 3D. When you are in 3D, you are on a checkerboard, caught in space and time. Your only contact available from 5D occurs when you ask for something in a very feeling-based way, from your heart. Get into it, what do you *really* want? Instantly, right out of thin air from the synchronicity plane, you simply know, feel what you want. When you come from intense feelings, the morphogenetic field that rules that potential manifestation responds to your request. After all, 4D's only agenda is to manifest in 3D. This is how reality works for me in my cellular matrix on Venus. For now, I am leaving, and I turn it over to Satya and her Pleiadians for more information about your biology and how you are caught in the Net in 3D."

## Satya and the Cosmic Restart Button

I, Satya, am here again in your world, and I am very pleased at how you have mined the biological matrix with King Lizard and Doctor Lizard. Are not most of you becoming more and more alarmed as you contemplate your probable futures? The cry of the reptiles is being heard throughout the whole Galaxy. We noticed in these transmissions that the Hebrews were getting quite a slapping around by the reptiles. From my 5D point of view, I do not see that any group has an existential belief system that is worse than any other. So, let's have a close look at Christianity, the religion that claims it recognized the Messiah while the Jews missed the long-awaited one.

Do you know why your calendar goes up to a certain point in time, then back to zero, and then starts again? Have you ever thought about how peculiar it is that linear time ended almost two thousand years ago, and started up again? The Andromedans who watch over the Milky Way Galaxy from an idealized perspective as a twin Galaxy call this moment in time the Cosmic Restart Button, and it is the key to understanding all the powerful agencies of the Holy Roman Empire. The Caesars, for example, believed they were creating temples for the new Nibiruan cycle that began during their reign. There were many signs of Nibiru as Julius Caesar was rising to power. He claimed lineage from the gods as a priest of Jupiter, and he declared that the Hebrew Calendar—which began in 3760 B.C., when Nibiru was entering the solar system—had come to an end and a new one was beginning.

Once Julius Caesar attained control of Rome, he abolished the lunar-based Etruscan calendar, and he set up the solar-based Julian Calendar. Since he was high priest of the Temple of Jupiter, he named the new solar calendar after himself and announced that the new chosen people were the

Romans. There have been various calendar manipulations, such as the Ecclesiastical Calendar set up at the Council of Nicea in 325 A.D. and the Gregorian Calendar established by Gregory XIII in 1582. These modifications have drawn our attention away from the remarkable fact that the Romans controlled reality enough to put in place a calendar in which time descends to Zero Point and then goes forward forever.[3]

For those of you who follow the Hebrew Calendar, I am here to help you understand what it means. You have claimed to be the Chosen People of Nibiru by establishing your calendar in 3760 B.C. We Pleiadians respect your courageous choice to be carriers of such a big concept. However, unless you are willing to get your ox gored—a favorite Pleiadian expression—you will miss the point, and your gods or the Caesars of Earth will jerk you around more than any other race on Earth. Aren't you tired of hearing that you missed the point 2000 years ago? What if you missed the point then so that you would have a chance to recognize a 9D Messiah now! If you are willing to get your ox gored along with everybody else, then you will stop waiting for the Messiah *outside* yourselves and remember that this potential is located *right on your planet right now*. You, too, have been diverted. Everyone has been diverted, and you are marking time on your calendar for another planet, not for your own.

The Romans decided to take charge of the calendrical rules, which are access codes to astronomical alignments in relationship to time. The Romans set up Zero Point as a control dynamic, once they realized what a serious threat the birth of Christ was. The Romans took over the calendar when they chose to play "Us against Them." The Us-against-Them dynamic is triggered by the perihelion or aphelion of Nibiru every 1800 years. This has become a general pattern. Nibiru was closest to the Sun—perihelion— in 7200 B.C., 3600 B.C., and at Zero Point; and it was farthest from the Sun and out by Sirius at aphelion—in 5400 B.C., 1800 B.C., and 1800 A.D. (approximately). Great changes occur in the 4D control patterns over your 3D reality at these points. *The archetypes of history shift.* For example, it was the Egyptians against the Sumerians in 3500 B.C., the Israelites against the Egyptians in 1600 B.C., the Christians against the Romans in 100 A.D. And now, at the end of the Mayan Calendar, it's the New Agers and Christians setting up to play "Us against Them."

The Caesars, by superseding the Hebrew calendar and starting time all over at Zero Point, were all set to take Nibiruan dominion over Earth.

But something else happened while Nibiru visited your solar system—the birth and death of Christ—and Romans and Jews were taken by surprise. Zero Point was also the Andromedan Cosmic Restart Button that set in a new potential with Christ, even though both parties were waiting for the Nibiruans to physically land on Earth; both groups were preparing societies, land, and temples to be the site for the arrival. The Romans rebuilt the Temple of Zeus at Baalbek as a landing port and called it the Temple of Jupiter. They removed obelisks from Egypt and set them up all over Rome,[4] and they destroyed the Temple of Solomon in Jerusalem and built a temple to Caesar on the site. They moved their power points from Egypt to Rome, and they dominated all of the Levant by conquering the whole system that Alexander the Great had once set up. They even had various priestesses prepared to receive the gods as lovers, such as Salome, Cleopatra, and Aurelia, the mother of Julius Caeser.

All of these things were set up for the arrival of the great planet of the gods in the solar system. Nibiru was visible in your skies shortly after Julius Caesar's assassination in 44 B.C., and then it was said to be Caesar's soul ascending to Nibiru. In 17 B.C., Nibiru had orbited to another point visible from Earth—Augustus was on the throne, and the people were told that Caesar's soul had returned to herald the "New Age." Coins were minted by the Romans with the symbol of Nibiru—eight-pointed star— that said "DIVVS IVLIVS", Divine Julius, to honor the return of Nibiru.[5] (See Fig. 11.) As did the Sumerians 3600 years before, the Romans claimed

FIGURE 11: THE EIGHT-POINTED STAR—NIBIRU

this sovereignty, and this truth has been carefully hidden from you by the Roman Catholic Church.

What did happen at Zero Point? Well, it is very funny. The Romans got hoodwinked because they had their eyes fixated on the skies, as you can see by their commemorative coins. Remarkable multidimensional beings incarnate on Earth during the key cyclical change points and there were many around Zero Point, such as Christ, the Buddha, and Alexander the Great a few hundred years before Zero Point. The Romans were standing on the parapets of their great temples waiting for the ships to land, while Christ was born under their noses in the Levant. At Zero Point, the law was the Mosaic code—a legacy of codes from the Sumerians, then the Babylonians, then the Israelites. These codes were all vestiges of Anunnaki systems, and the Caesars planned to use them to take over the Earth at Zero Point. The Anunnaki had set up the temple/city system based on laws of the Sumerian cities in 3600 B.C.; these codes spread through many cultures who would await their return at Zero Point.

The Caesars, through the Temple of Jupiter, were in control when it was time for the planetary return. The Anunnaki were able to utilize the Roman Empire by impulsing them into becoming Nibiruan legions. This was easy since they'd already succeeded getting several other cultures, such as the Jews, to go for being "Chosen." Time would actually cease, and the Sumerian Shar system would begin at Zero Point, and this would establish dominion in time—the New World Order.[6]

But, another agenda was thrown into the middle of the pot: A Jewish rabbi married to the priestess of Isis in Jerusalem was triggering multidimensional consciousness in the Levant. When Nibiru was closest to the Sun after Zero Point, Christ cleared the moneychangers out of the temple at the Dome of the Rock, and he sent out a signal that has never been forgotten. Just as the ultimate power grab was being set up, he changed the dynamic by purging the leeches from the power vortex, and deep inside, you all believe you will throw off the bloodsuckers eventually. Christ radiated exquisite heart energy all over the world. This was more potent than all the energy that could be activated in Rome with at least 13 Egyptian obelisks pointed to the sky in Rome![7] The Christians even claimed that the Star of Bethlehem—Nibiru as an eight-pointed star—appeared to herald the birth of the divine child. This was a powerful theft of the star symbol of Nibiru. The eight-pointed star is often in your Christmas cards showing the Nativity.

Christ set up a ceremony called the Eucharist with 72 disciples as a symbol for taking total control of a double Shar—twice the 3600-year orbit of Nibiru. By using Anunnaki symbols, everything he established was absorbed right into the Roman Empire, like cosmic keys into locks. Next, Anu selected the Holy Roman Catholic Church as his personal device for ruling the planet. Rome would fall eventually, but an official Church organized around Christ would prevail, since humans are most easily manipulated by means of religion. Anu never had had such a big project. The Roman Catholic Church would be the next official Anunnaki establishment. To accomplish this, all its priests would have to be celibate, based on the premise that Christ was celibate. Women would have to be disempowered, and the Eucharist would be celebrated by male priests who had never entered a woman. All knowledge of multi-lifetimes would have to be erased so that people would learn to be terrified of death, and fear of death would limit multidimensional contact. This would offer the Anunnaki total dominion of Earth and prevent multidimensional access to humans. All humans would be locked in 3D so that the Anunnaki would not get foiled the next time they orbited back into the solar system in 3600 A.D. This was a dark hour on Earth—the imposition of the Net—and its energy first came over the planet when a terrible thunderstorm wreaked havoc in Jerusalem when Christ died on the cross.

All you need to do is master a simple paradigm. You do have free will on your planet because certain teachings and events occur no matter what, and then intelligences who do not want you to be free can only overlay these big events. *You must learn to feel how and when you are overlayed so you do not respond to lies when you're getting impulsed.* You can feel truth in your hearts, and your hearts are freed when your mind is clear and you can observe the manipulations that are occurring. Nothing is random or accidental, *nothing*. Look at it this way: A really big event, such as Christ's birth, occurs and people feel its real meaning. The event is then severely distorted and made into a cultural obsession. The control forces constantly repeat part of the story to satisfy the longing of people for freedom from evil. Lies are incessantly repeated about Christ, but people are so hungry for the real story, they swallow the lies like hungry parrots. The false story is repeated ad nauseum until even the liars can't remember the truth. The obsession for truth is constantly placated, and you run around in circles like mindless rats seeking something.

This is your liability from the Anunnaki—your "ability to lie"—and this is why I can tell you that the *only* way out of the Net is to dig deeply for your real stories. You will move right into your own integrity once you have the truth. That is why, I, Satya, am so seditious, heretical, and insulting. Why do I pick Christ? you might ask. Remember, I am reading your energy fields from Alcyone. I simply pick the stories that you obsess on the most. Why? Because what you obsess on is exactly what blocks you. I know in the deepest level of your consciousness that you all want to have your truth, no matter how many sacred cows have to go. I want you to exercise your intelligence—"tell-it-in-your-genes"—to get out of the Net.

I, Satya, can feel great energy around the word "Eucharist." This word was ringing in my vehicle's ears as she said to me one morning, "What is this Eucharist?" and then she got it, "You Christ." This fascinated me because I know you all are to become highly individualized during the Age of Aquarius. So, when my vehicle caught that sound code, I shivered. It is obvious: You are each to become Christ! Of course! It's the end of the Age of Pisces. I do feel how much pain some of you hold around the theft of this sacrament by the Roman Catholic Church because you intuit that the Eucharist is a powerful healing tool. Well, this sacrament might have been lost if there had not been continuity. The power of the Eucharist waned rapidly in the 1960s. Its power was ultimately lost when the Catholic Church terminated the sound codes by translating the most important section of the Mass out of Latin, and when they turned the officiating priest to face the congregation. Many Catholic Churches were built on ancient power points with their altars facing West, and the priest faced East when he raised the Host to consecrate it. Once the priest was turned around, he faced West and got no energy. This change was impulsed by the Sirians, who began directly influencing Earth in 1972; because the Church Net was too impenetrable, the Sirians switched the priest. The priest by facing West not only lost the subtle energy of the East; he also sucked in the chaotic powers of the West during the Mass, and the Roman Catholic Church began disintegrating. Through history, watch for these esoteric games by the Sirians, who are masters of alchemy.

Back to Zero Point: As a result of the 9D activation by Christ, the Anunnaki knew by monitoring your feelings that a power was present on the planet that was greater than their power; therefore they had to cover it up. They simply stole all the powers of Christ and encapsulated the archetype in the Holy Roman Empire and all the energy flowed into the Holy Roman Catholic Church, once Rome fell to the barbarians. The Anunnaki knew that the Magi were Sirian astrologers, and they were furious when the Magi announced the birth of Christ to the indigenous people. Watch the way the Sirians work on the planet. The Magi go back to the ancient days on Earth, and they can be traced all the way through Christianity since Zero Point. Our vehicle followed their trail through the Gnostics, medieval mystics, Reformation Protestants, Quakers, and various spiritualist groups in early New England, and through the early years of the Mormons. She was amazed to see how the lineage is never dropped. For example, in New England, when the colonists first arrived, they were amazed to discover megalithic stone circles, dolmens, incised rocks, and astronomical temples all over the land, just as in the British Isles.[8] Often they built their churches on these sites, or tore out these pagan power markers. The Masons and Mormons excavated these ancient sites and utilized some of the Moundbuilder and ancient American power objects in their temple installations.[9]

The Magi brought gifts for the Christ. Frankincense is the essence that offers the true powers of male creativity, and the myrrh is the essence of the Goddess. These elements were brought because this type of entity had never before incarnated on Earth. His arrival was engineered by the Sirians, and he was not yet encoded with the vibration of Earth. These elements would enable him to survive in your realm. It is difficult to keep such vibration in physical form. I, Satya, watched the frankincense and myrrh being brought to Christ. I saw a beautiful, golden, glowing essence—alchemical gold—being brought to the child as he was anointed by the Magi. When they brought the gold, it was gold fresh from earth that had never been worked. The Magi brought the gold, and they moved it all around and through the aura of the Christ child because his aura was so bright and reached out so far that he could not stay in body. The Christ child had a bright-white, diamondlike light. It extended out so far from the body of the child that the Magi and shepherds shielded their eyes from it. The gold was used to make a boundary on his aura, his halo, which is a very beautiful symbol of exquisite light contained by gold. All humans must have auric boundaries to stay in physical form. If the white light going from the body goes out too far into other realms of consciousness, humans go out of body.

The Sirians charged right in via the Magi to help Christ adjust to the field of Earth. Now that the Pleiadian/Sirian alliance is in place, I am getting data about the 6D realm, and a whole new order is occurring that will supersede the New World Order of the Anunnaki. The Sirians actually hold the spherical systems that support orbits in the solar system, and now that this alliance has occurred, the Pleiadians can expand the vortexes and gridlines of Earth beyond the Net and into a more complex spherical geometrical field. This is why I can reach my vehicle more easily now, and other Pleiadians are reaching many of you. I am here to encourage you to develop your sense of how the Pleiadians mine you and interact in your realm, because they can impulse you into passionate investigations that free your minds. This is the only way out of your dilemmas because no one is going to rescue you from the Net. You must disentangle yourselves from it and expand yourself out beyond it just by means of your passion and curiosity.

The Sirians encode Nibiru with consciousness to be brought to Earth every 3600 years—the "maildrop." [10] Why would the Anunnaki bother to be encoded with these Sirian agendas? I, Satya, do know of one tool sacred to your indigenous people that is a model of Nibiru's orbit out near Sirius: the boomerang, which is sacred to the Dogon people and the Aborigines of Australia. The Sirians are holding Nibiru's orbit in form so it will swing out to their star system like a boomerang, and the mail drop is the paid exchange. If they don't deliver, the Anunnaki will fly out into space like a rock, instead of swinging back. The boomerang is a wonderful metaphor for potentiality in your relationships—you can throw yourselves way out, and you will always swing back if you will stop holding on so tightly.

If you do not come into alignment with Sirius at this point, you could be thrown out of your orbit during the planetary acceleration! The Sun has great respect for Sirius holding these orbits. The Sirians certainly had a great interest in making sure the consciousness of Christ was encoded in Earth at Zero Point. The Anunnaki must have known what the Sirians were up to, since they carried the drop. However, their temple guardians on Earth, such as the Mithraic priests of the Roman Empire, did not know about the maildrop, since it occurred in space.

Notice how the Sumerians proudly described themselves as Anunnaki royalty in the Sumerian tablets. Yet by the time of the Patriarchs, as described in Hebrew texts, the story of the Anunnaki is deeply cloaked. Next comes early Christianity, and information about Nibiru has been stripped out of the Bible. The Vatican Library was established as a secure repository for the real story. Traces of this outer planet are available in recently discovered Essene and Gnostic texts, but another whole book would be required just to analyze these sources at Zero Point in a scholarly manner.[11] It is more valuable to seek out vestiges of the Anunnaki in the New World Order, which is going out of its way now to hide its links with Nibiru, as the Christians and Jews always have before. The straightest path to the truth is to expose all the information that is officially forbidden. That is why I have come now, and that is why you are hearing so much about the Maya. We both plan to give you the secrets.

The Roman Catholic Church has overlayed and controlled Christ consciousness by using Christ as fuel, like the fuel rods in a nuclear reactor, to create its own realities over the last 2000 years.[12] Now, due to the collapse of the Church, the fuel is escaping the tank because you've learned how to pump the gas yourselves. Messiah means Message, but to be effective, it has to be received. The Roman Catholic Church set up a time-coded release of Christ to 2000 A.D.—he came, his mission was aborted, and he would come again in the fulfillment of the Church. This way, everybody would be waiting for him, paying Church tithes, and always waiting for him instead of awakening themselves.

Meanwhile as I read you, often you have felt something else, and these more numinous and mysterious knowings that many of you feel are due to the Cosmic Restart Button. A new energy is coming to Earth from the Andromeda Galaxy, and this energy is shifting the Milky Way Galaxy. According to astronomy, the Andromeda Galaxy and the Milky Way Galaxy are merging.[13] At times you've escaped the Net and experienced exquisite light, love, and compassion from Christ, and that is because the Andromedan archetype is intensifying. Meanwhile, the male/celibate/god archetype is threatening to become a sexual meltdown through the priests of the Church as the Sirians expand the kundalini charge on Earth. Christ was sourced from very high dimensions. He incarnated and set up new processes so that higher-dimensional beings could begin to incarnate more frequently on your planet, and these priests have been set up to carry this force. Now you have come into the latter days of this cycle, and Christ consciousness has multiplied. More entities from other dimensions are coming to Earth, and that is exactly what the Anunnaki wanted to avoid. They are afraid that the higher-dimensional beings will take away their territory, Earth. The Nibiruans want to own Earth because, after orbiting in your solar system for approximately 125 years, they go out into deep space for about 3450 years. When they're out there, they're very lonely, and they are obsessed with Earth. I am here to figure out just exactly what they *do* want, since anything can be sated on Earth if any desire is honored.

Christ took our ancient Pleiadian practices and worked with wine and plants, beginning a *new alchemy* of the planet. By that activation of the basic biological codes of the planet, the opportunity was created for Earth to hold multidimensional beings. These codes needed to evolve within the living codes of Earth. At the 1D level, the Sirian crystal carried by Nibiru resonated at the same vibration as the core crystal in the center of Earth. The Anunnaki thought it would just smash right into Earth like a meteor and shatter. Well, that's not what happened.

The crystal was nine dimensional, and it went right through the body of the planet and became part of the iron core. There was no resistance to it. It went right to the central core of the planet, and it changed the codes. The core will be shifting a few times in the next few years, signaling the most intense activation of this crystal. The central core is like a ball inside a ball inside a ball, and the Earth changes will result from geomantic stress in the telluric realm when the core of Earth moves.[14]

The crystal totally activated the metallic-telluric realm of Earth, and Christ implanted the new potential on the surface by doing miracles while he worked with the elementals by means of the Mass. In that sense, he was just an excellent magician.[15] He set in a new psychological code—grace— that would eventually remove all complexes implanted into humanity by the Nibiruans. *Grace posits that the individual is unlimited if he or she comes from the heart.* Utilizing grace as a practice will move you into your heart and teach you to operate from there faster than any other idea. Christ was a healer; he worked with the emotional body, and he resurrected from the dead. He removed the various "I can'ts" the Anunnaki had implanted into the field, and he did these things as a full 3D human, a virile male. Then the Church stripped away his virility by hiding his true relationship with Mary Magdalene, and the male was emasculated and the female denied.[16] Eventually the Roman Catholic Church became the only organization where a penis is required for the job, but once you get the job, you can't use it!

Mosaic Law will be completely transmuted by humans who realize the Christic feeling is simply natural human potential. Once Christ incarnated as a 9D human, all the Anunnaki could do was destroy him, to utilize him as limp anesthesia to keep you in victimhood, but they failed. The Pope calls for your indulgences and sends them directly to Anu. The structure— Peter's Church—is the Net that came down at Zero Point. In spite of it, Christ left an indelible imprint of light beyond the Net.

I, Satya, can feel that each one of you reading this book is poisoned by some of the lies that have overlayed the great powers of Christ. The very essence of the Pleiadian awakening is the reawakening of the erotic Christ, the cosmic progenitor of humankind. The phallus is meant to be used; *the emasculation of Christ is the greatest lie in history*. Literally, the whole structure of the Roman Catholic Church is built upon the dismemberment of Osiris, whose story is the ultimate loss of human multidimensional contact. Once you remember your multidimensionality, Christ will awaken in you, because it is time. Once this happens, all organized religions will be pulverized. Who among you could have imagined that the membership of the Roman Catholic Church would be cut in half since 1972? The Church has been pushed into bankruptcy because the only sexual outlet left for its emasculated priests is altar boys! The time for the erotic and alchemical Christ has come, and desire is the key to this awakening.

## Meditations from Satya for Opening Dimensional Portals

*The desire of the first dimension* is to draw you to itself. The more you resist this desire, the less you will know what you want. So give in. Create an altar to the four directions and sit in the center and send your consciousness down into the earth beneath your body. Have a good time traveling below your altar, below your house, down through the layers of rock and the caves of the inner Earth, and down into the mantle, and finally into the iron crystal in the center of Earth. Travel in it, bask in it, feel the heat and liquid rocks, listen to the storytellers of Gaia, and remember what they say. Then move right up into the second dimension.

*The desire of the second dimension* is to engage you with density through its chemical, radioactive, mineral, and crystalline essences. We want you to come down with us in our realm where we can lead you through caves with walls of crystals, sapphires, rubies, and diamonds so you can begin to use gems as lenses to see right into your own bodies. Notice that the geometry of the gems and crystals is the structural basis of 6D light geometry. We want you to come down into the inner Earth and meet with us—chemical and radioactive beings—so you will see who we are. Once you see us in our full and glorious power, you will stop invading our world and taking us out of our deep world. You will stop manipulating us by splitting and transmuting us, except when you are in our resonance and we agree with your intentions. Come down and see us so you recognize all of us. For when Gaia goes through her changes, often we are thrown out of our world and end up being lost on the surface. Once we are no longer contained inside Earth, then we move into your bodies, and into the rivers, lakes, oceans, soil, and the air. Come down and see us so you will recognize us in your bodies and environment. Then you will dedicate yourselves to sending us back into our own world. We do not want to disturb you or cause diseases in you. We just want you to get to know us, since we both share Gaia.

*The desire of the third dimension* is to be within physical bodies—animals, insects, plants, and humans—and to be free. Once you are free, you can create anything you want in any reality you want. To accomplish this, you must honor the powers of the first two dimensions and consciously work with them. You must learn to be totally in the present moment in your lives. Once you have learned to be right there in the moment, you will "feel" the future by attuning with the 4D archetypal forces all around you. You need to communicate with these forces because they are your access to your future. To exist in the present time, you must always carry a sense of what you want to create—your personal future. By being in communication with the intense influences of 4D archetypal intelligences, you can feel the desires of the future from all nine dimensions. Then you will be inspired to create realities that serve all beings who share your home with you. If you live in that state of mind, a canopy of 4D energy that accesses all of the higher dimensions will vibrate in your mind.

*The desire of the fourth dimension* is to get deeply involved in the actions of your bodies and to deliver to you all the communications it receives from 5D through 9D. These juicy impulses are very distracting to you. You try everything to ignore their pleas, yet this consciousness is what fuels your creativity. All great artists are adepts at allowing these intelligences into their minds and hearts. In a given day or night, this material might be a grandiose epic playing out, a visit with great evil or pious beings, or the appearance of marvelous composite monsters and weird shapes. All this is attended by overpowering emotions that can seem to exhaust your body. Ultimately it is easier to just open yourself to all this energy and consciously orchestrate your reception of it. How? Follow your fascinations and stop judging anything that presents itself to you. How do you know whether these impulses are good or bad for you before you comprehend their messages? Try working with one of these creative impulses for awhile, and if it's not for you, that is fine. Just let it go, realizing that you have encouraged its formation for a while by means of your curiosity. Then it will pass to someone else who is more ready for it.

Why does the fourth dimension ask this of you? Look at it from my point of view. I am a huge canopy of holographic film over each one of you, and five dimensions of consciousness beyond me are bombarding me with waves of energy and beams of light. These beams split into two possibilities. Each one is something you can create and play with. But I cannot, for I do not exist in linear space and time. If you do not explore and play with all these beams of light, then I am torn to shreds by the manifold dualities that will finally collapse my own sense of self into meaningless chaos.

*The desire of the fifth dimension* is to get deeply involved in your feelings and to serve as your center and radiate love to you and all other things. I am the dimension of your heart, and if you remain intensely centered in your bodies responding to all things that are drawn to you, I funnel waves of love through you, so that you have endless energy to offer kindness to all the beings in your world. If you stay completely grounded in the sacred space you occupy with your heart open as a conduit into the center of Earth, you will be in samadhi with me. I am the center of all nine dimensions that you access. When you are centered in your body and connected to the center of Earth, my energy funnels through the fourth dimension and flows directly into your heart. When this river of love flows into you, the four dimensions above myself begin to flood your awareness. The more you hold your heart open while you are grounded, the more you feel the subtle vibrations of the higher dimensions.

*The desire of the sixth dimension* is to get deeply involved in your minds and expand your field of potentiality. We are the location of morphogenetic fields—record bank of all your ideas in 3D—and when you create something or want something in 3D, we hold the geometrical matrix of that thing in existence as long as the idea of it exists in your minds. When you desire a thing, when you truly honor its potential and beauty, it begins to vibrate more. Anything from our realm can come into your world if you desire it enough, and so I am the source of mysterious synchronicities in 3D. If a young woman who misses her deceased mother stands by a window longing for a feeling from her, I will send an exquisite white dove to that window. When a shaman calls for the power of eagle, eagle will appear. Once a thing holds this radiant energy coming from desire, 5D heart energy fills it more, and I am attracted. This consciousness existing in a 3D object can generate waves out on the galactic information highways. Then the dimensions above 6D discover what we have been creating together in our realms out of the divine ideas sent to us. For example, a shaman may hold an ancient object that is imprinted with energy waves from many ceremonies which star beings visited. The shaman can contact these star beings with this totemic object because when I imprint a form in a thing, there is no block to accessing it from any realm.

*The desire of the seventh dimension* is to get deeply involved in your spiritual lives and to hold the orbits of stars and planets in place in the Galaxy by means of 7D photon bands or galactic information highways of light. I am a web of life and light, not a Net that traps you, limiting your freedom. I hold these highways of light in place throughout the whole Galaxy, and I pulse consciousness through them into the stars they flow through because I want to communicate the Galactic Mind to my photon stars such as Alcyone. Once my communication links are powerful enough, my photon stars send out great spirals that link nearby stars. These stars in these spirals are able to orbit into my bands of light, and then they orbit out into the Galactic Night, the great field of darkness that is the ground of being for the Galaxy. Because of these photonic spirals, I am in communication with many more stars in the Galaxy, and these stars give me new information about the Galactic Night, where new thought is born.

*The desire of the eighth dimension* is to guide the quality of existence of all beings in the dimensions below ourselves. We have many conferences and meetings, and anyone who truly cherishes life can be a part of this dimension. The ability to cherish life—never interfering with any other consciousness in the Galaxy—comes out of many lifetimes in many different dimensions. It is a quality that is often borne out of being in situations where life is not cherished and evil is created. Earth is very crowded because souls are being sent there from all over the Galaxy since Earth is a training zone about evil right now. Evil is live reversed. Earth ceases being a training center at the end of 1999, when all participants will get the opportunity to see the direct consequences of not cherishing the Earth. If you cherish life, you will see the ascension of Earth beyond evil. If you do not cherish life, you will experience the Apocalypse according to St. John the Divine just before 2000 A.D.

*The desire of the ninth dimension* is to exist in eternal samadhi and be available to share this feeling with all other beings who have attained it. I exist in my center of light bathed in darkness and I pulse out waves of energy that would cause a nuclear explosion except for the information highways of light that receive my pulsations. I am like a great jellyfish of light having orgasms that makes eternal waves and pulsations in the Milky Way.

# 5

# *T*HE STORY
# OF GODDESS ALCHEMY

"THE MOON PROTECTS US, FORMING A PSYCHOLOGICAL ATMO-
sphere around our psyche, protecting it from the full blast of
our soul's impulse toward immediate and total enlightenment.
Absorbing only seven percent of the Sun's light, the Moon
reveals its relationship to the Sun through its phases—from
new to crescent to first quarter to gibbous to full to dissemi-
nating to last quarter to balsamic. It is the Moon's phase at our
birth that reflects back to us how instinctual, how conscious,
and how absorbent we are toward the Sun's light, our soul's
evolvement, because on our way to enlightenment we have to
pass by the Moon first. We have to begin at the beginning."[1]

### Satya and Female Alchemy

Alchemy is a process of transforming something ordinary into something
precious. Women are the carriers of the Goddess. In any system, the
Goddess, the female species, rules what is home—what is being located—
and so they are the guardians of place. This is not to say women cannot be
warriors or kings; it is to say that they carry intuitive knowledge about the
real purpose of place, and they should be consulted about all important
issues regarding home, especially war. *In the Pleiades, we goddesses must
be consulted about war.* As the patriarchy has taken power on Earth, women have been considered ordinary, and they have been displaced as
rulers. From the Pleiadian point of view, that is absurd! Now I, Satya, have
come to help you remember that in your realm women are the ones who
transmute the sacred elixir of life—the fertilized egg—into incarnational
form. Women have an intuitive understanding of alchemy far superior to
the male, and in the Pleiades, the Goddess rules alchemy of the spirit.

Ultimately, alchemy is all about the timing of birthing. When is the egg going to be ready to hatch? The issue right now is not *what* will happen, it is *when* it will happen, since many of you sense you are creating a future right now. This has never happened before on Earth; however, this critical leap has already occurred in the Pleiades. That is why we have come to offer you assistance. When we accomplished this leap 104,000 years ago, the Maya also gave us a Sacred Calendar—*Tzolk'in*. I am honored to report that I was one of many Pleiadians who worked with Tzolk'in in those days. Crafting a future in your "now" is a totally new potential, and it is the essence of the critical leap from 1987 to 2012. You needed to experience the constriction of linear space and time to find a way to transcend it. What do I mean? You will use time and space instead of allowing it to limit you—the critical leap of 3D. Women know how to create in time and activate space for new life, and so they will lead the men into the new alchemy. This is exactly what will move you into realms that will stretch you beyond limitation. The primary recordkeeper of time on Earth is your Moon, and so we will begin with the Moon speaking to you.

## The Moon Speaks

"I am the Moon. I came from the surface of the planet Jupiter. The moons of Jupiter are made of the same material as I am, but I orbit around Earth and not Jupiter. A long time ago, there was a very large explosion on Jupiter, and many parts were blasted out of its gaseous body. Once they moved out of their gaseous state, they congealed into solid states, and most of them were captured in the field of Jupiter. The moons of Jupiter mirror Jupiterian consciousness back to Jupiter, as I mirror the consciousness of Earth back to you. Moons are reflectors of what you are feeling. To reflect your emotions is our primary function. In my case, I was ejected farther out from Jupiter, well past the orbit of Mars, and I was captured by the gravitational pull of Earth. Like all moons, I am a reflector of planetary feelings. And, since I come from Jupiter, which rules the mastery schools of Earth, *mastery of yourself is based on whether you deal with your emotions effectively.* You thought physical perfection was the most important challenge, didn't you?

"When I first arrived, the beings on Earth were the same as those who were living on Mars. Naturally, the Martian moons mirror Martian consciousness back to Mars. Life on Mars (which was once in a watery state), existing in viral and unicellular lifeforms, never evolves due to the dryness; therefore, there is no awareness of life to mirror back to Mars via its moons. Meanwhile, on Jupiter there is consciousness of linear space and time, as on Earth, because the nonphysical intelligences work with karma. Jupiter has a gaseous surface surrounding a solid core, and many of you felt its etheric beings during the 1994 Shoemaker-Levy cometary impacts. To be specific, you rebonded with your etheric spiritual teachers, guides, and angelic leaders, and many of you are in deep mourning about the pain of Jupiter. You do not yet recognize the source of this sadness, yet you feel a great power welling up inside. You are remembering your nonphysical selves at the deepest level, and this new organization of self will be more powerful than anything you have known in all your incarnational cycles.

"The traffic between Mars and Earth ceased approximately 500,000 years ago. Before that time, the beings from Earth and Mars also traveled back and forth for commerce, and often by means of 4D thoughtforms, trading legends of heroes and warriors. This was an extremely enjoyable relationship and is still the source of your endless fascination with war. This is why all of you are warriors in your male sides. Since I am just your reflector, these memories about the great feats of Mars still exist in my lunar field, and I can feel how they excite you. You always reenact this archetype to the most extreme degree during the Age of Aries, as during the most recent phase—2160 B.C. to Zero Point—and we Moon beings always say, 'There they all go doing the Age of Aries on Earth again!' Meanwhile, I am a very peaceful vibration, and I am extremely tired of these old obsessions, these tiresome old dramas on your planet, as I know you are too. I have many other memories of great archetypal stories and dreams in my awareness that I like to share.

"As the Moon, I feel energy through silvery ray vibrations. The closest thing you know of this kind of perception is the silvery gossamer light shimmering on the surface of calm water when the full Moon rises. My light is opalescent and translucent, like the flesh of a beautiful young woman's face. I have canyons and craters on my surface, which is almost devoid of electromagnetic energy. My vibrations are so ethereal that there is almost no charge in me; I am completely balanced. I am 400 times smaller than the Sun; yet the Sun is about 400 times farther from Earth than I am; therefore, I appear to be the same size as the Sun in your sky. The Sun and I are balanced. Some of my canyons and craters are high-rimmed and very deep, and within these rims, I capture electromagnetic energy from the solar wind. These vibrations bounce back and forth between the canyon rims as resonant waves, and that is how I read planetary locations and angles. When you play with echoes in your canyons, you are creating the same kind of energy in the air. I have many deep craters from asteroids and comets on my surface, and we have consciousness centers deep inside them—little round, white, domed temples. We emit thought from these structures and you receive it as dreams. These domes transmit our luminescent, ethereal frequencies and hold the records of your memories and your subconscious mental banks.

"I transmit these frequencies to those individuals who magnetically draw my energy. Humans, animals, and various other lifeforms literally magnetize or draw consciousness from me. These are extremely subtle vibrations, which differ from the polarized interactions that exist on the surface of your planet. These are feelings that form the component motivations of your reactive patterns. Neptune also transmits spiritual vibrations to you, but Neptune has an agenda with you that impulses you to create belief systems. My ethereal emanations simply mirror back memories related to experiences you have, which modulate your responses to everything. You transmit your feelings into my record temples, because you could not develop your emotional bodies without memory. Think of how a memory is triggered by a scent, a familiar sight, or a voice, and then a whole visual series of memories are unleashed in your brain as if you have movies in your head. This is because I hold memories of your soul experiences life after life, and the only way you can explore this is to examine your subconscious mind while you are in a body. How do I hold all this memory so that you have the potential of exploring your subconscious? Now that you have discovered fiber optics, you can imagine my great memory records. I have an exciting idea for you: I am able to remember so much because I *feel* you, and fiber optics are responding to your feelings. You just don't know that yet. Meanwhile, animals store memory in their bodies only while they are alive, and that is why they are more grounded in the present moment than you are.

"When you go through some kind of struggle, such as illness or disease, and you don't have the means in the physical to change this vibration, often you can feel that the problem is emotional. When you get to the point where you *really* see that physical solutions are not the only possibility, I can transmit extremely accurate and valuable information to you. You would be amazed at how much you actually do understand realities via these intuitional transmissions. I enjoy reflecting back to you your own deep understandings of yourselves. Based on this great pool of awareness I have about your emotions, you do have ways to alter your physical status by means of your feelings. For example, Bach Flower Remedies will alter the vibrations that create your physical ailments, based on your ability to identify your feelings. Aromatic oils actually do shift your bodies! Certain feeling tones correspond to your vital organs, and these essences work with the alchemy of your emotional bodies. This is a more subtle and profound healing method than allopathic medicine because you can heal disease while it is still in your etheric body—you can locate 'dis-ease' that has not yet gone into your physical bodies.

"If you intend to totally open your feeling receptors in this lifetime, you can take advantage of my extraordinary teaching, but this is a total commitment. As I've said, my record temples hold your subconscious memory banks. What are these? Each one of you has a soul within your body, and that soul incarnates over and over again on Earth, on other planets, and in the stars. It seeks experience in many realms in order to know and express itself, and my record banks hold the memories from all places, even other galaxies! You've heard comments that beings from many realms fight to be born in a body on Earth. The reason for this is that *whenever you have a lifetime on Earth, you can consciously work with your lunar subconscious memory banks, and this cannot be done in any other location.* This is a vast subject, so I will say only a few things about it. Naturally, some memories are traumatic and tend to limit your expressive potential in each new lifetime. As many of you know from doing bodywork and spiritual therapy, if you are able to recover a negative past-life memory, explore it, and release it when your body is ready, you end up being lighter, more harmonic, and happier.

"So, how could you consciously work with your lunar subconscious memory banks? You'll be surprised, I'm sure! These memories exist in your minds as belief systems that repeat, 'I can't have this, I can't do that.' All your negative conclusions about past experiences are deposited in my memory banks! Positive conclusions about the past exist in your active mind; they are available to you, and they are the basis of your free actions. My banks are a storehouse of negative conclusions you've made about your potential, but you don't remember the original event. These conclusions cause you to repeat situations over and over again when you might have a chance to wipe the original negative conclusion. This tendency reduces your creativity in all new situations.[2] What can you do about this? Here are my directions:

*How to Manifest the Physical Reality that You Desire:*
*Lunar Manifestation Technique*

1) Make a list of seven things you want in your reality. If you want this to work, be reasonable, go for what you really want, not what you think you want.

2) Take your list and work with each thing on it. Take the first thing on your list, such as a radio, and say out loud to yourself, 'I want a certain radio for a certain amount of money within a certain period of time.' Describe the radio, the amount, and the time frame, and do not give a thought to how you will get it. *Never* think of a specific person or group who will get something for you, because then you would be manipulating others.

3) Ask yourself if you would really want the radio if you had it. Think deeply about this, because you clutter your mind with things you *think* you want but actually don't. Be careful about this. If you really don't want something, just let it go.

4) Create three scenes of the radio coming into your reality; visualize these scenes in front of your forehead above your eyes, then take each scene and imprint it on your medulla oblongata (the place where your spine enters your skull). Remember, don't visualize a specific person or place helping you get what you want. Do not manipulate the reality of others.

5) Repeat this process until you have created a list of seven things you really want. Then, forget all about it, and put your list in a safe place. Check it periodically, and soon you will begin to notice that things on the list actually manifest. Every time something does manifest, cross it off and think of something else you want and add it to your list. Keep the list of seven going.

"What does manifestation have to do with the lunar subconscious memory banks? Every time you manifest what you really want, you are erasing an 'I can't' memory in my banks. The purpose for coming to Earth is to get what you really want! Then, when you get what you really want when you want it, you end up wanting very little, like indigenous Earth people. Without even remembering or processing the experience that created an 'I can't,' then you will dissipate memories as if they never occurred—thanks to this positive assault on inner denial. You actually can discard your negative memories, so that all I reflect back to you is positive. You will feel my exquisite and subtle vibrations, and find supportive records on yourself active in your conscious mind, once you get out of denial.

"Because of my cycles—lunar nodes, eclipses, and phases—I am a screen for the surface of Earth for all of the other stellar, planetary, and solar energies. From an astronomical point of view, there is no way that I, your Moon, could screen the whole surface of the planet from all these influences. However, I gather the solar winds in my craters and canyons as I travel around the Earth for 28 days. Like a woman who always pays subtle attention to her man, I create a screening force, which is a gossamer web of feelings on Earth. The energy fields of the other bodies in your solar system reach the surface of Earth mostly by means of my light, and I transduce these energies into codes that you can comprehend through your emotions. You feel transmissions of the planets and the Sun from my light. This is how fine vibrations of feeling are held in place and communicated. If it were not for my screening, you would, in a sense, be forced to deal with feelings from Pluto that are too deep, you'd get bombarded by too much aggression from Mars, or the intensity of the Sun would exhaust you. *I am like a great wave of feeling that rises, peaks, and ebbs over twenty-eight days.* I exist to calibrate these great forces, and you can attune to my gossamer web of feelings by cultivating your own feelings like a fertilized garden.

"Earth goes through cycles, and the pattern I see on your surface these days is a pattern I've seen before. In the past, this pattern has been extremely threatening to biological lifeforms. Before you read my description of your appearance, please remember that I am reading the etheric body of Earth. Just as 'dis-ease' showing up in your etheric body or aura is then treated with homeopathics before it becomes a physical disease, so too can you change your feelings about the planet before these energies become full-blown Earth changes. The color of your aura is beginning to turn brown, which is not healthy, instead of being green. The tilt of your axis reflects the consciousness of your planetary body to the Sun, and it is approaching the level of tilt that has created pole shifting in the past.

"How does the present condition of Earth relate to past conditions? The biggest astronomical shift I remember occurred when the orbit of Earth around the Sun enlarged from 360 to 365-1/4 days. This was caused by two simultaneous events: the visit of Nibiru into your solar system, and a gigantic asteroid that came into the orbital pattern of the Pleiades 104,000 years ago. These two events occurring simultaneously enlarged the orbit of Earth. Nibiru is slightly smaller than Jupiter, and because of the speed of its trajectory and its reverse orbit in the solar system, it is extremely disruptive of planetary orbital patterns.[3] This discontinuity caused Nibiru to lose its perfect synchronicity with Earth orbiting the Sun—3600 years to 360 days.

"Nibiru was responsible for the destruction of the fifth planet—Maldek—which is the present asteroid belt. I was orbiting around Earth at that time, and your ancestors experienced great tectonic stress during this event. There are many memories about this in my banks. At that time I was shielding your surface as much as possible from the various comets and asteroids that were flying through the solar system. The breakup of this planet, which orbited between Mars and Jupiter, generated much debris in your solar system. I took some big hits; that's why I have so many huge craters, which are the locations of domed temples holding your subconscious memory banks. These impacts were similar in intensity to July 1994, when the gaseous body of Jupiter was continually smashed by cometary fragments until the impact zone became waves of gas. This caused the surface of Jupiter to be embroiled with potent feelings, as you know. Naturally, I can feel the strong reactions you are having, since you are reacting to how Jupiter felt when the cometary fragments blasted into her body. I have been crying since July 1994, yet few of you know where these powerful emotions are coming from. Meanwhile, Jupiter rules your fortune, your sense of potential, and I want you to know that this period is very promising. If you can figure out what you want, you can create it easily with Jupiter's assistance, and that is why I offered you my seven-step Lunar Manifestation Technique.

"I have been visited by beings from the Sun, and they are very beautiful and powerful. They are emissaries from the 13th dimension, a dimension beyond the basic ten-dimensional system that you are working with. My surface is very cold, and when the solar emissaries come to visit, I feel a warmth on my surface like the warmth you feel when you lie in the Sun and feel its fire, the solar love. You are attuned to me and feel my surface when you work with ritual consciousness in relationship to my subtle light. When you do moon ceremonies and eclipse meditations, you are accessing direct lines into my subtle, emotional vibrations. These ceremonies are some of the most potent ones available to you on Earth. Whether you tune into me or not, I shower you with subtle sensations. These days, I am very concerned about your polarized emotional bodies. You've become dualized because you emphasize your masculine side over your feminine. This blocks my soft lunar screen and overexposes you to planetary vibrations, such as control and manipulation by the Anunnaki of Nibiru. They have covertly shifted you away from your female side, and this is making it difficult for you to realize how you really *feel* about them. This is keeping you from seeing what they are creating in every sector of your societies. If you consciously activate your female essence, then you would feel our fine ethereal vibrations all the time.

"All of the natural synchronizations of 12—such as 12 times 12 is 144, or 12 times 30 is 360—have been disrupted by the enlargement of Earth's orbit around the Sun. However, this has created the opportunity for more evolution and creativity, since everything was held in place like clockwork before that shift. Before the shift, your sense of time was of endless circles and no spirals. Now, attuning to the gradually ascending spirals of light, such as the Alcyone spiral, is the next stage of evolution. For that attunement, I am your most potent source; you already can feel the next stage of evolution, and I am mirroring the cosmic data bank to you month by month. Remember, I am a screen for the planetary, solar, and stellar forces, and a new cosmology is forming. There is no better source for resonating with this energy than doing meditations at each of 13 new moons that occur during each solar year. The solar year is most potently accessed by doing special ceremonies during the cardinal divisions—equinoxes and solstices. Attuning to the 13 moons greatly enhances your feminine nature. This is best accomplished by meditating during the new moon and noticing what special information is available. During my cycle of 13 moons, observe the reflected solar light increasing to the full moon and intensifying those feelings; then let go of all feelings and become empty within as it wanes. Become an empty vessel for the new moon. You can wash away your ego every month from the full moon to the next new moon. You can be reborn at the new moon 13 times a year! If you do this—a practice that was very advanced on your planet a long time ago, and still exists in Bali—you will feel less driven by solar forces and planetary agendas. And all this is easy because, like a nude woman, I have made myself totally available to you by making myself visible. I am so beautiful.

"It is my responsibility to display the principle of 13 for you each solar year. This way, you can feel the magical essence of 13 without think-ing about it. The way for you to move the consciousness of 12 back into synchronicity-based 13 is by means of lunar cycles. Then the way to attain a structural basis is to develop solar consciousness through astrology. Astrology is the only tool you have for decoding feelings with thought; other forms of thought throw you into your head and out of your heart. You can move out of duality and polarization by dividing the horizontal planes of the dimensions into 12 zones—6 above, 6 below. This is a "place expansion" not a time expansion, as are my 13 cycles per solar year. Place expands via geometry, and time opens dimensions when it is felt and not constantly computed. You will be astounded by the brilliance and mental freedom available to you when you intensify your vibration beyond the polarized emotional-body vibration and blow it out into the principle of 12. Notice how you run around like rats in a maze looking at your watches and thinking that what is happening is either this or that! This is why there are 12 houses in the Zodiac, even though 13 constellations and 13 moons actually imprint your awareness day and night. The stellar principle of 13 via the constellations enhances your perceptions in 5D, not 3D. You live in 3D, and that is where you can work to expand perception by seeing all dynamics as a field of 12. Working with the horoscope as a life map divided into 12 zones is the only tool I have found that moves your aware-ness back into a sense of a synchronized Earth, when there were 360 days in the solar year.

"There are 12 houses in the natal house system, 6 above, 6 below, and this sets up six principles of polarity from above to below in the natal chart. (See Fig. 2.) You can examine these 6 polarities and apply them to yourself without knowing any astrology. Just look at the 12 basic lifestyle fields, and notice the section that reflects a struggle in your life, such as marriages/partnerships/relationships ("other" in Fig. 2). If you look to the opposite section, my/myself issues ("self" in Fig. 2), you will notice that you have a lot of energy there. For example, you are drained by a demand-ing relationship and you've forgotten who you are, or you are feeling very powerful yourself, but your partner complains of being ignored. You are almost always very unbalanced in one polarity out of twelve; if you just put more energy into the weak side and modulate the side where you are too heavy, your whole personality goes right into balance! You become harmonic, and that is when you can feel my subtle emanations! The 12 houses are solar conditioning, because the 6 upper houses represent the day—upper reality—and the lower 6 represent the night—lower world. This issue is worth mastering because when you balance, you cease being stuck on yourself. You let go, forget yourself, and magically expand to 13. A grounding in 12 is merely a basic foundation, and it is the key to handling the great solar light that infuses your mind day after day.

"Through attunement to the spiral emanation of 13 triggered by my journey during your nights, you will always feel my more subtle vibrations. That is my gift to you. I am always there for you, just as the Sun rises every day. Lunar or feminine essence is what enables you to let go of thinking for awhile, and just become responsive. In that, feel how timing is all. My timing is the one that penetrates your subconscious because it is what activates your pineal gland, the source of cosmic intelligence. The light that reflects off my surface is actually read by your inner brain glands. The pineal gland is the most responsive when you are in total darkness, which only occurs at the exact time of the dark moon, the new moon. Attuning to this screen keys you to stellar communications, to other planetary communications, and to solar communication.

"Alchemy occurs when my lunar light penetrates the 2D metallic consciousness of your planet. This occurs 13 times during each solar year during the new moon when Earth shields my surface from the Sun for only a few minutes. The 2D metallic elementals register the subtle emanations of stars at the time of the new moon, and your pineal glands register stellar emanations then. This recurrent field of receptive intelligence is the 'Prima Materia' of alchemy. There is a new emotional field each lunar month. Mercury crystals in your pineal glands read this vibration, which is your source of galactic intelligence. Everything is vibration, and I can only reach you with a very soft vibration in total darkness. To summarize: *I screen the field of the solar system to Earth all the time, and at the time of the new Moon, in the darkness I imprint an emotional field of new potential.*

"Once upon a time, the Anunnaki came to Earth and changed the metal configuration of Earth by mining it for gold. However, I know even more about gold than they do. That is why I am not kidding when I say you should be listening to the wisdom of women first. There is gold in the subtle glands of your bodies, and the beings of the Moon can feel the more subtle emotional emanations of your consciousness through gold hidden in darkness of Earth. When you feel cosmic emanations, gold crystals are released out of your endocrine glands and flow into your blood. Women tend to be more cosmically connected because these crystals are released into their blood each lunar cycle.

"Each consciousness in the universe has a process for attunement with the consciousnesses of other bodies, but often these skills are dormant. It is through such mechanisms that great awareness is available to you, if you would choose to develop more perceptual linkage. By learning these skills, which are primarily 5D and higher, you will naturally override 4D control traps because you cannot be mind-controlled once you raise your vibration to a certain level. The vehicle, for example, can feel Mind Control like a bloodhound can follow the scent of an animal. By understanding these vibrations, you can perceive when you are being influenced. This is what women mean when they say they can "feel" something, or their "skin crawls." *Smart men listen when women speak this way.* Women must develop this potential more in themselves; then both men and women can be free of manipulation. Aren't you all tired of getting jerked around? I tune into how you feel emotionally by vibrating with the gold in your blood, and in the potent menstrual blood of women. I can feel that you've had enough of this.

"Many rituals—ceremonies that are repeated instead of being spontaneous events each time—insist that bleeding women not be present. This is because *repetitive rituals are passage rites of 4D Anunnaki priestly systems.* Bleeding women would instantly detect when a control dynamic was being played out, and so they are barred. Also, the power in their blood can defuse rituals. I am the Moon, I regulate women's bodies by synchronizing their pineal glands with my creative unfoldment. One day soon, you will not even consider doing any ceremony without bleeding women as energy directors. Then I, the Moon, will know that you are remembering the ancient ways of feeding Gaia.

"The Anunnaki have removed a great deal of gold from your planetary intelligence. But I feel the most subtle-emotional emanations of your consciousness through the gold in your blood. The more you attune to my 13 lunar cycles—by gazing at me, sleeping in my light, attuning to my cycles and the movements, feeling my energy reflected in water through tides and in your emotions—then the principle of 13 will open you up. You do not have to be a women, you just need to allow women to guide you, as I guide you month by month. Guess what? You can do it tomorrow! Just change all your calendars so the year is based on the 13 lunar phases, and then demarcate your solar journeys by the equinoxes and solstices!

"There are not *exactly* 13 Moon cycles in one year, but every 18 years the Moon returns to its same location on the ecliptic. This cycle is called the metonic cycle, and it is the most subtle of my cycles.[4] You can attune to it just by observing where I am travelling in the sky, and you can keep your place around the Sun in mind just by observing solstices and equinoxes. In this solar system, visual communication linkage is always very powerful, and that is why I am the ideal tool for you. Notice how powerful it is when planetary and stellar bodies are sighted in the sky.

"I am your friend, and I honor you when you gaze at me. You have bravely chosen to become self-reflective, and so I mirror the light of the Sun to you. You cannot gaze directly into the Sun, the source of your identity. But during the time when I am full, magnificent Sun beings come to me traveling on beams of light. I receive them 13 times each year, and I gather their power and shower their vibrations into the wombs of women."

## Satya and the Awakening in the Blood

It's me, Satya, and this information from the Moon is juicy stuff! On Alcyone we access your reality via your Moon because it allows us to know how you feel. When we access your Sun, we link up stellar communications from the Sun, through Alcyone, and into the Galactic Center—the cosmic communications system of Earth. When we read your Moon, however, we feel your atmosphere, your tidal waters, your love intensity, and how you are captivated by mystery on a moonlit night. That is how we know your deepest longings and desires. How do we read you?

I read your vibrations when photons are created in your realm, as already described. The news from the Alcyone Library is that the frequency of photons is indeed increasing in your system. I would not be picking up on more photons if you in fact were not entering the Photon Band. I receive these impulses and read your consciousness when antiparticles fuse with positive analogs like popcorn popping in your dimension.

I am most interested in your emotional-body states right now because I am detecting via photons a great increase of violence on your planet. You've had many historical phases of great violence. The current increase is caused by the mass media. You are aware of many aspects of violence, but you do not necessarily experience them personally. This is creating a great distortion because: 1) violence is only relevant to the individual experiencing it; and 2) hundreds of millions of people hearing about global violence via the media badly distorts its actual meaning. Remember, during a traumatic event, the people watching it are often in more fear than the ones experiencing it. Before the advent of television and mass communication, you *experienced* violence rarely; now you *watch* violence every day. From our Pleiadian perspective, you are *responding* to a degree of violence that is unparalleled since 10,800 B.C., when your poles shifted, a time when there was a tremendous degree of violence. It is time for you to evaluate the impact of imprinting yourselves with so much violence via watching, since this makes you feel as upset as you felt during a *real* pole shifting. At least some of the psychics who are predicting great Earth changes are basing these predictions on vibrations that you are emitting because you watch so much violence. I find the Moon's reading of your aura very challenging because the red energy is coming from violence. The last time you were in the Photon Band was during the Age of Leo—10,800 to 8640 B.C.—and, as you move into the Band and your atmosphere changes, you are feeling edgy. Due to the violence in your media, many of you are thrown into habitual fear of cataclysm. These fears last longer than any potential real cataclysm because you don't die. It's the old saying: the actual trauma was nothing compared to worrying about it.

Your solar plexuses are being stirred up, actual violence is increasing, and your reality is becoming a firestorm. Meanwhile, *what happens during the coming journey in the Photon Band is not necessarily the same as the last journey.* It is obvious that dramas in the media trigger real violence, and it is time for you to withdraw your support from this continual abuse. You are being duped, and your support of this system with your time and dollars confounds me. Meanwhile, 4D manipulators laugh at you. Even they are amazed at how far they can go. For them, it is just a joke that pays; and where you are the most out of your integrity is with money. When I read photons these days, I notice that many of you are responding too quickly to stimulation, making it difficult for you to hold your karmic integrity and your money.

What do I mean by karmic integrity? When you are stimulated by something, you must remember to see how it feels to you first. Once you've really felt it, then you must turn on your brain big time and scan the issue. Use these marvelous data banks in your brains, for they create an energy field out of your bodies. Do that for a few days, and synchronicities will happen that will show you how to respond. Why does this happen? As you scan your reality by means of your feelings and mental data banks, your guides—archetypal beings who work with your evolution—can trigger synchronicities sourced in many dimensions that will show you the next step to take. Impulses from photons are activating much energy in 3D; this quickens 4D, which responds by triggering action as fast as possible. Meanwhile, all you need to do in 3D is stay on track, follow your will, and take the time to play out your own patterns. Remember, these unique patterns are your secret, your monad, your incarnational gift. Lifetime after lifetime, you did not play them out the way you chose to before birth—and now is the time!

Beings in 4D are triggering people so fast these days that this results in violence. As your emotional bodies are awakened by the Photon Band, you may react and carry out agendas too fast. Your bodies have not released the fear that's being awakened, and so fear comes out as violence instead of spiritual realization. Blood is what offers insight into this difficult subject, for what we Pleiadians are seeing is a killing frenzy. It is like a feeding frenzy of sharks in water, when spilled blood activates them as groups. Rwanda was one such bloodbath. So many people killing each other represents a profound degree of bloodletting. This is labelled ethnic cleansing; meanwhile, considering blood as a taboo could offer more insight.

Why are there so many taboos about blood since bloodletting can be a very healthy experience? To the Pleiadians, all this attention to blood is a sign of spiritual awakening and spiritual crisis. You must face issues about blood because the sooner you look deeply into blood taboos, the sooner you can find a better way to explore them. From a multidimensional perspective, 4D intelligences have managed to put all of kinds of crystalline codes into the blood of humans. Remember, all intelligences interact with you to encourage your evolution—and whether the 4D entities who have chosen to do this should continue to do so is not my interest.

Understand that *all* dimensions are ruled by laws of free will, and we Pleiadians do not have the right to go into your fields and stop the activities that 4D entities are creating. However, as beings in a higher dimension, we have the right to explore any consciousness on Earth. For example, you have the right to explore what your friends are doing, but you have no right to influence them unless they ask for your assistance. No other being has the right to influence or manipulate you, but they have the right to impulse you, and if you respond—as you have so intensely to the fourth dimension—that is your choice. The way 4D explores your consciousness is by your blood; 5D does this by means of light. Therefore, when you open yourself to a spiritual experience and go through a light experience, we Pleiadians can read your frequency. That is why the Transfiguration of Christ was so important.

When you engage in a blood experience, 4D entities can read your frequencies. When you get a disease, 2D elementals can read you. If you decode information implanted in your blood by 4D intelligences—enlightening yourself—then this information in your blood *can* be read by Pleiadians in the Alcyone Library. When you quicken your blood, it contains crystals that can be read via light, and it is the most immediate way to access the Pleiadians. All the Pleiadians are excited to know how the 4D Anunnaki are able to quicken your blood. To put it simply, if you yourselves would figure out what is encoded within you, then the knowledge of more spiritual wisdom becomes instantly available. It is your choice.

As I read your feelings about blood, I can feel that to you blood is sticky, it has a smell, it is very organic, and you spend a lot of time talking about the emotional body and emotional stickum—and it fascinates us that you do that. As I read your codes, blood is functioning at a 2D crystalline level within you—the part of you that is telluric and alchemical. Now, remember, for all intelligences in the universe, the lower you go in the dimensions, the more dense is the information. Once you overcome your belief in hierarchy (such as 9D is superior to 2D), you will be able to ascertain who or what is motivating you.

As I read you, *you are murdering each other because of your own judgment about your own vital fluid—blood.* If you will stop judging the very fluid that keeps you alive, then we Pleiadians will be able to read you via light codes—crystalline matrices in your blood! Then we will know how you feel. This is at a level that does not involve human free will. For exam-

ple, we can read telluric forces on your planet—Earth change potential—
by means of the elementals, and so can you. We are reading your realm
with great fascination and interest, you are feeling the awakening of the
elementals, and we are picking up on incredible changes going on in the
crystalline codes in your blood.

When you go into the Photon Band, these codes are released into the
intelligence field of humans and animals, since consciousness is carried in
the blood. You'll notice, if you observe carefully, there is quite a struggle
on your planet over blood. As I view Rwanda or Bosnia, the participation
of 4D entities is absolutely phenomenal as these archetypal forces play out
their roles on the stage. As blood is spilled, a dimensional rending occurs,
and consciousnesses of other dimensions blasts into your own dimension.
Some are very demonic forces coming out of ancient conflicts; they are the
only explanation for random mass killings, which you watch constantly
after the fact on television. Think about this next time your government
thinks it is of no consequence to bomb Iraq and murder 1.4 million
women and children! All of these actions, which occur in places suppos-
edly separate from your reality, will come home to haunt you. Notice how
the Vietnam War is haunting Americans. All that blood spilling accom-
plishes is the activation of demonic forces. We Pleiadians marvel at your
thick skulls! You understand Dracula, and you love stories about vampires! So why can't you figure out what happens during these bloodbaths?
We also would like to point out to you: whenever you look at things just
from one dimension, things get boring and therefore very depressing. If
you wonder why you get swallowed in depression, it is because you view
things only in 3D.

There is a very big drama going on. I see that the Photon Band is activating powerful telluric and crystalline forces. This activation is negative
only if you are not grounding and circulating these forces in your bodies.
However, you can activate these powerful forces with no negative results
in linear space and time. Have sexual encounters that are like earthquakes!
Tone, sing, vibrate, and breathe deeply. Feel Earth responding to your gifting! Dance and make clay pots that feel like the planet, and paint as if light
beams were coursing through the brushes!

The crystalline matrices of the telluric realm are the waves of Gaia in
ley lines and vortexes. When blood is spilled, it all soaks back into your
planet, back into the consciousness of Gaia. Blood is where your records

are stored; it contains an ever-yearning desire for perfection, for beauty and freedom. Gaia is warm and welcoming when she receives your blood. She cries with your pain, and she also feels like a mother when her child gets yet another scrape or bump. As the central core consciousness of Earth, she does not feel pain, you do. Do you think a volcano is in pain when it explodes? Gaia simply is energy that holds frequencies. How could she reject the essence that is part of herself? Only *you* can stop the blood flowing.

How blood plays out in 3D is your choice, and the outcomes you feel are negative will continue until you—the carriers of this exquisite, alchemical fluid—become conscious of your responsibilities, your abilities to respond. I have been clear about this from the outset. Your movement through time, your activation will not go away. And if it did go away, you would have stasis and no movement. You are not acting as if you choose that. In fact, you are acting like you are in the middle of a frenzy of activation that can propel you beyond the dilemma. It's just that you've not passed through this portal before. This is all new, and I caution you again that your wild fears of the Photon Band are unfounded since what happened before does not create what happens now. What creates what happens now is the intention set for the future you sense you are converging into. That is the power of a spiral of time.

Sirians of the Sirius star system as well as those experiencing hybrid Sirian/Earth lifetimes are also activated as photons increase in your realm. As this occurs, they do not know what behavior you will choose for activating yourselves. If they were to influence you, they'd be interfering with your choices about expressing yourselves. We Pleiadians are responsible for our own behavior, and I could tell you many things about us that are good, and things about us that are bad. But we cannot be responsible for your behavior, nor can we be responsible for the behavior of the 4D Anunnaki. Meanwhile, the crystal codes in your blood contain deep memories of all experiences you've had with these intelligences from many dimensions, including us. This all began when the consciousness of Gaia organized four billion years ago. After a few billion years of Gaian consciousness, humans evolved out of the crystalline memory matrix, and you carry this mixture in your blood. We Pleiadians do not have blood, our memory matrix is in light. Our resonance with you is via the crystals in your blood, and you feel us as light beings in those crystals. For example, our vehicle has had some experience with Guatemalan healers who can feel illness by quickening their blood. They can feel 2D elemental powers in the minerals in blood, and we can feel this quickening in your blood crystals when a shaman heals you. Some of them say they "make lightning" in their blood by loving the sick person. Since they activate this force by means of love, we Pleiadians are brought in to assist. I like the way these shamans invite us.

Our vehicle has seen a group of Pleiadians twice, which she has described in her earlier books. In both cases, she felt a bliss from our blue light that is like the bliss we feel in the shaman's blood, or when we travel in your spines. *We Pleiadians discover the most about ourselves in light, and you humans can discover the most about yourselves in blood.* We do not die, for example, but I would cease to exist in 3D if my vehicle died, because I am alive in the crystals in her blood, her source of life. Of course, I could find another channel. About such things I have no sense of linear time, but suddenly I will feel a shaman ferreting out our Pleiadian love for you right in your blood! Our arrival is ecstatic light fusion.

## Creating Realities from the Future

We Pleiadians do not think of what you call "past actions" as the past. If you watch me closely, most of what I'm focusing on is actually the future. Listen carefully: *The future is any past memory that is still potent enough to impulse your behavior now.* You think of yourself as being at a certain point. Once you're at that point, then there's something that you can call "before" and something that you can call "after." You think of yourselves on a corner between the past and future, and that corner is the present. Meanwhile, unless you noticed that you got to the corner and felt like you came from somewhere and were going somewhere, we wouldn't notice you. *We only notice you when you are aware of yourselves in your now.*

When my vehicle tunes into my frequency as Satya, she goes into something akin to timelessness. When she comes back into her frequency —3D—there is a "before" and an "after" for her. Do not miss this one! *Once she is in our frequency, she can see future potential, and she chooses what she wants out of it.* Then she moves back into the present moment, where she digs up any relevant past knowledge about what she has chosen, and she uses that. Then she forgets all about the choice, and poof! the new creation appears magically in her reality with a full background resume! I am not kidding . . . The more you understand that the future is simply any idea or thing you might like to create, the sooner you can craft a future of your own choosing. That is why small children love to make sand castles so much. Our vehicle consciously creates most of her reality from the future by observing what is boring now and deciding not to repeat it. We love this particular discovery on her part; and I'd suggest you could erase Washington, D.C., in an hour with that one! TV would last about 10 seconds, and spectator sports about 5 seconds. She simply looks ahead to a particular point in time, makes a plan, and has fun watching it unfolding, since the one thing she doesn't know is *how* the future will happen.

### A Deeper Exploration of Blood Codes

Let's go back into the blood and decode it. It was decided by the Sirians in conference with the Galactic Federation to have the vital essence of 2D, 4D, 6D, and 8D be blood. Blood is fluid that is alive, and it can be energetically alive as well as physically alive. The Sirians are the keepers of the blood because they are the keepers of darkness in the Galactic Night. When you are actually in the Photon Band, for example, your blood is no longer dark, it is crystalline blue, and it is more air than liquid. Since you are moving into the Photon Band, your blood vibration is shifting out of the Sirian realm into the Pleiadian realm, and this can be seen as the color changes. Blood is the most potent multidimensional connector in your bodies, and it is being rather vigorously fought over. One of the sources on what is at stake in this battle is *Holy Blood/Holy Grail*, which catalogues how 4D forces utilize the 2D elemental realm to set up political realities in 3D.[5]

The principal 4D intelligence involved in blood biology is reptilian. Reptiles are the originators of complex blood circulation in bodies, but they are so ancient that their blood is still cold. Our friends the lizards are simply reflectors in 3D of the 4D reptilian vibration, just as cats reflect the Sirian mode. I would advise you that the more you explore the stellar codes of animals without prejudgment, the more you will be able to see what is really going on in 3D. Such keen sight is what offers you free will, your most potent faculty, your pathway out of linear space and time. So, let's go for it.

Reptiles are cold-blooded, and the issue that we are speaking of regarding your blood is about warm blood. The more that warm-blooded creatures tune into warm-blooded essence, the more understanding is attained about feelings. Being members of a warm-blooded species, you will see that some impulses are cold-blooded and it is best to avoid them. The same advice would follow for the cold-blooded entities of your planet. The more the reptiles tune into their own cold-blooded vibration, the more they will understand themselves. The cold-blooded codes are the source of the even-numbered, 2D through 8D, intelligences; and the warm-blooded codes are the source of the odd-numbered, 1D through 9D, realities. As we get into this, one is not superior to the other; they simply function differently.

As I scan Bosnia, for example, there is a race of people there who actually think their blood is cold, not warm. This thoughtform sucks in amazing elemental forces that trigger atrocities. Why? Individuals who think they are cold-blooded fear snake medicine so intensely that they are becoming what they deny! Whenever humans think of themselves as cold-blooded, elementals are sucked in and become whirlwinds that draw such vibrations back deep into Earth. As I feel the cold-blooded nature of reptiles when I tune into them, I can feel these reptiles responding strongly to metals in Earth, a very 2D vibration. When I tune into warm-blooded entities of your planet, I feel them tuning into the 5D Pleiadian vibration. We Pleiadians will know you have changed when you stop killing yourselves. This will come when you totally access your warm-blooded nature—by fully processing *all* your feelings.

One of the ways you contact different dimensions is through the food you eat. I have noticed that you humans have a higher sex drive when you eat red meat, and I've noticed that fructarians lose their sex drive. This is more important than you think, because the Pleiadians have noticed that you tend to follow gurus and lose your freedom when you are sexually dormant. I've noticed you want little sex when you eat fruit, you want a little bit of sex when you eat vegetables, more when you eat rice and chicken, and you really go for it when you eat beef. Meanwhile, look how proud King Lizard is of his long spine and magnificent kundalini energy. The reptiles have carried you through a long process of activation of your kundalini powers for the last 225 million years, and much of this activation was enhanced by eating meat and blood.

You are evolving to a less sexual level, you are becoming more androgynous, and you are experimenting. This is why you must not judge any of your processes. Your charge now is to *understand* your behavior before you rush to *change* it. Of course, some of you become vegetarians or fructarians simply because you *feel* like it. Gaia has agreed to allow you to create on her surface, and she is the most allowing and loving presence that you can comprehend.

Today you have constant movies about vampires, you obsess about blood in murder trials, and your biggest disease is blood borne! Yet, you have choices about working with this energy. You could call in a reptile and say, "Here, lizard. Would you like a drink of this blood?" Or you have the choice of pouring it on the ground to Gaia, and saying, "Here, Mother Gaia, enjoy our blood which is you." Can you imagine drinking blood? Smearing it on your bodies? How about praising it? Should you allow yourselves to annoint your faces and your bodies with blood? Many women are doing that at this time. This may shock you; however, *smearing blood all over your bodies is better than spilling it on the battlefield.* Why not seek a more creative and attractive solution that will make *you* happier? There are some kinds of blood flowing from your bodies that are an act of creation, such as menstrual blood and birthing blood.

When you bleed or receive a wound, there is great teaching for you in that experience. The surface of your body is a barrier between the outer and inner worlds. When your inner world is pierced, the outside reality can be known from this most hidden part of yourself. There is potential great consciousness available here, and this is why some indigenous traditions work with body piercing. Then there is blood letting. The famed healer and artist, Hildegard von Bingen, advised bloodletting as an annual or biannual event to release negative forces and ill humors from the body.[6] It is a cleansing. For example, the Pleiadians have indicated that it is very dangerous for you to have the blood of others injected into your bodies. If you could see the 2D elemental forces in blood, few of you would ever agree to blood transfusions unless it was *absolutely* necessary. For the most part, if you want blood for medical emergencies, why not draw it for people who need it, and otherwise have your own blood drawn prior to surgery? Such actions would help you overcome your fear of being penetrated, prior to opening your inner world to the outside reality by surgery. Doctors exercise phenomenal control over you, and many of them know that bloodletting tremendously enhances your vitality. But instead of enhancing your vitality, they draw blood in ways that deplete you, and they charge money for this.

They block you from dealing with your own blood. I have been very clear about how the doctors are most influenced by the Nibiruans, and the main way they control you through the doctors is by blood control. Medical school is a process set up to desensitize them. They are taught that people cannot handle seeing blood, seeing the processing of blood or the spilling of blood. Yet, it is easy to see how a higher-dimensional perspective could create an incredible shift. How would you like an alliance with 4D the same way the Pleiadians have made one with the Sirians? Imagine how different your reality could be if this issue was raised just one notch higher. There are many individuals who are working to create a higher-vibrational point of view about blood. So let's shift to the Eucharist, where higher vibrational codes about blood have already been implanted in the planetary field.

## Christ and the Activation of the Plant Realm

Christ transubstantiated your plant realm into blood, and then he set up a sacrament operating through time for increasing the resonance of Gaia in the plant realm. The plant realm is the green expression of the 2D elementals, as you humans are the red expression of the 2D elementals. Humans transduce elementals into electromagnetic communication systems—kundalini energy—and plants transduce the elementals into a breathing system—oxygen and carbon dioxide. When you allow yourselves to take the time to feel the power of a great tree, you feel the planet breathe and you can communicate with the tree. Trees are very lonely for you, and you are losing your own ability to breathe by cutting the forests. The forests are slowly losing the memory of the Garden—the mind of Gaia. Meanwhile, people, you are the keepers of the Mind of Gaia, and once you remember this and feel this force, you will stop destroying your biological libraries—the forests of Gaia. Why do you think Christians were so intent on cutting the sacred oak groves of the Druids? Wake up, wake up, tell your brothers and sisters that they are keepers of the mind of Gaia.

As we've said above, the Anunnaki planned to take over your planet at Zero Point. But when Christ elevated the green plant realm into blood, they knew that this would evolve you right out of their control range, as you would begin to feel Gaia in your blood. So they devised a big program from Zero Point to 325 A.D., and they gradually manipulated you by setting up the Christian Church to dominate the diverse religious movements of Rome, Greece, the Levant, and Egypt. In 325 A.D., the Roman Catholic Church was set up as the official dispenser of the Eucharist. The Anunnaki Caesars realized what Christ was doing by transmuting wine into blood, and they immediately tried to shut this power down by taking total control of it. Many of you still have emotional bodies that are controlled by religious belief systems and physical bodies that are controlled by the medical establishment. There will be a great fight as you move into the Photon Band. This battle will occur within each one of you as each of you takes back your integrity.

I know these ideas are difficult for you to contemplate, yet the level of violence is forcing you to dig deeper. You all know something is terribly wrong. Your prejudices and belief systems are inherently irrational and contradictory, and many religious systems are self-destructing these days, and this shocks you. In the 1950s, who would have thought many altar boys would have to fear sexual abuse from their priests? I prod you and tease you about religion to wake you up, but I know how painful this loss of belief is for you.

Let's pick an especially cloaked idea and go for it as a group! We Pleiadians want to know if you have any idea how you could fall for the Immaculate Conception, since any immaculate conception in a female could not produce a male child? Why do you study genetics and then draw no conclusions from what you study? Where would the female get a male chromosome? From a star being? From a God or an angel? People, the birth of Christ was a 3D event! Who came up with the idea of no sex in this creation? Well, this ridiculous diversion was created by the Anunnaki to keep you from seeing that Mary Magdalene and Christ birthed a child. From that birthing, the Christic codes were implanted into the blood of the planet. *Codes don't get implanted in 3D by celibate males!*

Speaking of our alliance with the Sirians, now that the Age of Pisces is closing out, the Christ consciousness is flooding into your planet from Sirius, and this reinvigorates the ancient Egyptian field codes. These were implanted when Osiris came to Earth at the beginning of the Age of Taurus in 4320 B.C. Later, a blow was delivered to the Sirian codes when Osiris's phallus was taken off by Set. This is very secret stuff. Osiris is a "green god" like Dionysus, the god of wine. Osiris lost his phallus because Egypt was the zone for the codes called "Blue Nile;" he had to be dismembered to trigger the next stage of evolution of humans into the "blue race" expression of the 2D elemental realm. Humans needed to lose their role as the green expression of the elemental realm so the trees and plants could be honored with this green expression. The shift for humans into the Blue Nile consciousness was how humans began to access their stellar codes. In the ancient days, the stellar codes were reserved for the pharaoh. He carried them to hold the field of the Blue Nile for the people. Now, as we enter the Age of Aquarius, every human can attain stellar access.

Subconsciously, you cut trees attempting to regain your green power. Deep inside you fear the moment when Osiris lost his phallus, so you cut trees to prove to yourselves that you are more powerful than they are. Having this power somehow makes you feel like you will not get castrated. However, this is an act of defiance against your male vulnerability. Remember, *the emasculation of the male is what is killing your planet.* Once that great blow happened to Osiris, Sirian codes were removed from 3D. Once you had the opportunity to discover them yourselves, and since 1994 that faculty is available again. The real point of Osiris is that you must remember your vulnerability. Most of you remember the days of the Blue Nile when you were like plants. You lived in exquisite synchronicity and you breathed with the planet then, but you also felt like a plant—rooted to one place. You wanted free will and this rooting grated on your minds and hearts. Imagine a great tree having as much sensitivity and awareness as you have. Then see that tree in a great forest next to a churning river. One day you come before that tree, and it has never seen a human before. From the tree's point of view, it created you. And you cut it down! Like Osiris, this tree is severed and begins an eternal search for its lost self—you. We Pleiadians can see that you are ready to reintegrate these vibrations. Remember, we can see the future: A very great number of you will choose to become magnificent trees in the new forests. There you will be for 500 to 10,000 years, silently observing Gaia's creativity. Maybe a human will walk by someday, maybe not, but in the next age the forests will prevail and not you humans.

In accordance with cosmic law, the Anunnaki must evolve too, and they are being activated by the Photon Band because the Sun is responding to it. The Photon Band does not destroy them. They have been in it many times, yet they are still around. The Nibiruans will be orbiting into your solar system around 3600 A.D., just when your solar system is still moving in the Band through the latter days of Aquarius. Their abilities to control and manipulate you are already lessening, but many of you don't know this yet. During the Age of Aquarius, their control will dissipate. The Net already peaked back in 1989, and the next Anunnaki takeover attempt will be directed out of Washington, D.C. Well, people, if you thought the fall of the Berlin Wall or the disintegration of the U.S.S.R. was something, wait until you see the walls protecting your own government fall.

The Sirian influence will also lessen as you move deeper into the Photon Band. Sirius is the twin to your Sun, and it exists in the Galactic Night. Now is the time to learn as much as you can about the Sirian and Nibiruan teachings. The Sirians are the keepers of orbits in the Galactic Night, and the Anunnaki are messengers of the Sirians, and as you move out of the Galactic Night, suddenly they work together to create realities on Earth. A great reversal occurs during the shift out of the Galactic Night, the part of your journey when various 2D through 8D intelligences greatly influence Earth. We've said little about the 8D intelligences—the Galactic Federation—but when your Sun passes into the Photon Band in 1998–2001, that is a time when your solar system has direct communication with the Galactic Federation.

The Pleiadians began to mine your information as soon as your outermost planet moved into the Photon Band, which was 1972 when Pluto entered the Photon Band and the Sirians began constructing geometrical light structures and forms. A great pulse from the Sun in 1972 opened Earth, and this impulsed the Sirians to construct a geometrical light system that could access and read the high-energy frequency of the Galactic Federation.[7] The Sirians are transducers for the Galactic Federation when the solar system moves into the Photon Band. The only records you have on this process are from the reign of Akhenaton of Egypt. Akhenaton's teaching about the Aton is actually secret knowledge about the qualities of your Sun when your solar system is in the Photon Band; that is, you are enhanced by the Aton, by the Photon Band, which will turn your blood crystalline blue.

As you move deeper into the Photon Band, you have nothing to fear from the Sun. Like the Aton, you will be able to gaze into it! Imagine that! Your blood will become blue, your plants will reinvigorate, you will be able to handle great light with your eyes, and you will become gentle and loving again. The Blue Nile will be the field of your planet, and the green ones will breathe the 2D elemental powers through crystals in the soil, which will birth great forests again. Imagine it! There will be absolutely no control on your planet for 2000 years as energies and forms reorganize. Many agencies and teachers on your planet are attempting to convince you that you must fear what is coming; yet all that is coming is the removal of control so that all lifeforms can vibrate back into integrity. Yes, if you are a killer, you will die; if you do not love your body, you will leave it; if you fear the forest, you will not be welcome there; if you do not love the children, you will not parent them; if you do not hold your animals, they will leave you; and if you are not interested in cosmic communication with the Sun, you will go into darkness. But then you will come back in a body as a tree, a child, an animal, or a Sun being. All the control you created to convince yourself that you have to stay in your body will be gone. You will only stay because you want to.

Furthermore, ninth-dimensional intelligences actually know how much you love freedom from all control. We Pleiadians have noticed that you are enjoying watching Washington, D.C., turn into a cartoon strip. Many of you intuit that Clinton is about to grow his nose and Newt Ginko is about to grow his tail, and both of them will be laughing with rosy cheeks, like Pleiadians telling jokes. Many of you are feeling like we're going into a summer off after being in a very hard school. And what were you so worried about while you were in school?

## The Multidimensional Explosion

Finally, you wonder, why does Gaia tolerate all this? Think of Gaia as just a point—the 1D central-core iron crystal—and what if that was all she ever was? She chose to generate the nine-dimensional line of creation that is *you*. You could just as easily ask yourself why you chose to exist? What are you doing here? Surely you do not think it is an accident? We Pleiadians chose to be the center for your nine dimensions of existence, and we know we are involved with you as long as we are in form on Alcyone. I, Satya, do have to admit that I go into eternal contemplation and forget all about you. Then I wake up and remember you as if you are my dream in the dark night. *You humans are the dream of the Pleiadians in the Galactic Night. Now as all dreams are becoming reality, we Pleiadians are bringing you into the light.* Gaia is the creative expression of biology, and to conceive of this as your central organizing force is what is most powerful for you now. She is the central beginning point of your awareness, she is gravity. Then all the other levels of her evolution in other dimensions develop her.

You have a central organizing force that is your identity, and yet you are not solid. You're in form in 3D; Gaia is in form in 1D, and the first dimension is solid. You think you are solid because gravity—the central iron crystal—is solid. The 2D elementals think they are more solid than you are, and so they tend to come into your bodies to fill up the empty spaces in your bodies. In 3D, you manipulate elemental intelligences to try to convince yourselves that you are solid. Then you can split matter. The 4D beings feel like they are *not* solid, and so they keep on trying to invade your realm to get a body. We Pleiadians in the *fifth dimension* are right in the middle of the whole alignment, and we feel more solid as we move down the dimensional ladder, and we feel less solid as we move up the ladder. We are your teachers about the values and status of each realm. While you were in the Galactic Night, we encouraged you to love the elementals, to tune into the core crystal, to love your 3D bodies, to have a blast playing with the 4D archetypal teachers, and to have lots of sex to generate 5D kundalini waves. Now, as you go into the Photon Band, we are here in 5D to tell you more and more about how 6D loves to expand you with light, how 7D loves to generate information highways of photonic light, how 8D loves to create new organizational structures, and how the 9D Galactic Center has cosmic orgasms when you follow your bliss. (See Fig. 12.)

The more you hold a sense of these forms in your awareness, the more you will be surprised at what it does to your consciousness. As I've said, my vehicle has learned how to create on Gaia's surface. She has discovered that Gaia is unlimited if you are working within her laws. Deep in the indigenous knowledge of your planet, it is known that there is no hunger, no limitation, and no disease in Gaia. The 4D archetypal forces have tricked you into belief systems of limitation. You *think* limitation exists, limiting belief systems are born out of this, and you *feel* you must suffer because of the limitations. You do not *act* to change this because you believe it's real. The only thing that is true in all of this is, if you keep going, if you do not change it when you see it, then in your end times you will be hungry, limited, and diseased.

The Anunnaki have set the thoughtform of limitation in place because they hate to leave Gaia and travel out into deep space. You felt their lone-

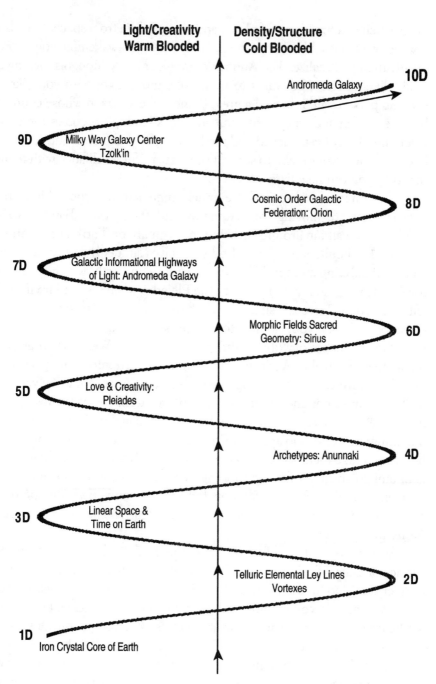

FIGURE 12: VERTICAL AXIS

liness when you first went off planet and viewed Gaia from space. You also saw your planet's blue/green hues. This view is awakening you more deeply than you realize. The Anunnaki are like greedy Mongols sacking a castle; like a lover who wants to spend one more night with you; like a starving person who is served a great dinner; like a person whose country has been taken and who grabs someone else's land. Now comes the time when the Mongol gets sacked and the land raider gets driven out. I, Satya, have come into your realm to suggest some terms for an alliance with them that only you can negotiate.

The Anunnaki do not have much time left for controlling you because you are moving into Aquarius and the Photon Band. Lately you've been walking around realizing that you are on Earth and in other dimensions simultaneously: you find yourselves suddenly in Andromeda; you are inhabiting an especially exquisite place on Earth, which feels like the Garden of Eden; you trip out to the Pleiades when you end up in bed with a goddess. Here is a suggestion: I have advised you to set up a four-directional altar in your home. How about selecting an object that could hold the awareness of Niburu and putting it in the West? Then as you meditate and travel to Andromeda, welcome Nibiru into your space and take them with you. Listen, people, you can travel anywhere when you are in the Gaian mind, and other consciousnesses want to share those journeys with you. It is time to remember the ancient Hopi way of always including the guest who appears. Feed your visitors, bring them into your home, and take them with you when you travel. Teach them all how Gaia is unlimited so they will stop robbing her. Teach them that Gaia cannot be owned, and then they will stop fighting for land. *Each one of your homes is to become a temple with great trees, a sacred altar, and a kitchen for feeding your visitors.*

As you move into the Photon Band, there will be a moment when the surface of Gaia will shift as the telluric forces shift her relationship to her iron crystal and multidimensional intelligences are able to access her libraries. Those in communion with the iron crystal of Gaia will welcome all the other intelligences who also share her space. You are only a keeper of Gaia if you are one who Makes Home for all beings who desire her. Do not worry. There is an infinity of time because time is already expanding. Have you noticed? You are losing interest in 4D dramas, 6D structures, and 8D organization, and you are dematerializing back into beings who simply want to flow with Gaia. You are immortal when you are in touch with the nonphysical elements of yourselves—your identity that is held in Gaia and extends through Alcyone to the Galactic Center. After you have fed and sheltered those who are called to you, the only way to help people is by getting them in touch with the nonphysical attributes of themselves. Humans in touch with these attributes have little difficulty with Gaia's movements and expressions.

How will you handle Gaia's transition? You will do this by working with her Goddess alchemy, so let us go back into the blood now that you are truly expanded. Doesn't that feel great? Why not just be like that all the time? Notice that your resistance to this topic is less now that you have let go. Notice this because the Anunnaki are quickened by the energy in your blood. If you can remember the deep harmony and balance of the iron in your own blood resonating with the center of Gaia, you will not trigger archetypal forces that seem to be outside yourselves. In case you think we Pleiadians are unsophisticated about such things, do not be foolish enough to underestimate us. We know all about your tendencies to become destructive when you are gripped by apocalyptic belief systems. This tendency is modified when you move into the Age of Aquarius because of the deep Aquarian tendency toward individualism. Belief systems are a result of groups, and Aquarians dislike group belief systems such as Nazism, communism, and Christianity. Now is the time, therefore, to go deeply into your blood, which is the very source of your individuality.

Our vehicle has learned how to read the crystalline matrix of blood, and we've been mining her for this information. As you move deeper into the Photon Band, your blood gets extremely activated. This is happening now and is creating scenarios that are very difficult for you until you figure them out. You are in the midst of a planetwide clearance of all the karma and pain involved in the process of the blood. You will be amazed by this as it intensifies. We have noticed that these experiences are very valuable to the individuals involved, but you may not need to go through such things. Have compassion for those who do, and honor their own choices, even though these things are very hard to understand. Situations that would be very difficult for you may not be that way for others. Have you noticed that people are not as sensitive to pain as they were ten or fifteen years ago? For example, people are not as stirred up when they watch a movie and see someone's head chopped off. Have you noticed this?

Assuming that all of you react with total attention and compassion when someone has actually been injured in your presence, you can then look at this desensitization in the media from an entirely different point of view. Much of what occurs in the media is not negative, it simply carries a very dark vibration.

How can you know when you are being manipulated by these forces? It is easy. Whenever you get a really bad feeling from anything in the media, turn it off or walk out of the theater. *As long as you are willing to pay for being manipulated, there will be plenty of so-called artists who will happily serve you.* We warn you, people, remove your bodies and your consciousness from all situations that are violent, except situations where you can act to calm the violence. Do not watch accidents, shootings, or lines of starving people unless you can provide first aid or bring food. Your attention is being drawn away, and you won't be there in a situation when you could do something.

You are in the middle of a great process of letting go an involvement in the blood field as it transmutes. What happens next is the intelligence—mental body of the blood—will become available to you, as it is to our vehicle. Shamans have the ability to tune into this intelligence and utilize it for healing and joy. As I've said, you are becoming "Warriors of the Heart." You will literally read the codes in your blood and figure out what's going on in your body. Then you will tell the doctors what they can do to assist you, and doctors will become healers again. Healers work with Gaia to enhance all realities. Indigenous healers can walk through the forest, and their blood informs them of which plant or herb to use for which ailment. They can attune to the health of the planet by reading the tree sap like blood. The Lacandon shamans of Chiapas are dying in their own forests, where they've been protecting the trees and plants for all individuals who have chosen to live with Gaia.

You will see this kind of knowledge literally exploding on your planet. You must protect indigenous people who still remember the Gaian codes. This particular kind of shamanic knowledge is exceedingly pragmatic; it works the most accurately when individuals read their own blood, not when they have it read for them. This is a skill that each one of you can activate. Hildegard von Bingen mastered it and wrote about it. As you go further dealing with immune deficiency difficulties such as AIDS, you will begin to get extremely interested in mastering this process.

Regarding Rwanda and Bosnia and all the other places where your fellow humans are killing each other: I read your vibrations very thoroughly while these events were occurring, since a lot of them were happening when the comet impacted Jupiter. These were big events, from our point of view. During these times, you got a big realization deep in your bodies: You could feel that what occurred in these places could occur anywhere—it could happen even to you. As a result, a whole new commitment about how to avoid these situations is being very quickly activated. We know that there are many dark forces and manipulations going on in your so-called New World Order. We know that evil is real in your realm even though we do not have such a force in our 5D realm. However, one of the things that is occurring due to the mass media is that many individuals who see what is happening in places like Rwanda are deeply motivated to shift these situations. Think about it.

Listen carefully to me, people. *Your* desire not to have this going on actually changes the people who really could alter your reality! What do I mean? In case you didn't know it, generals and bureaucrats think of themselves as being agents of your desires. If you don't care, they don't care. So what if a few more million die in agonizing starvation? But what if you care and you will not tolerate their evil insensitivity? New imprints are occurring on your planet. Many men are seeing what could happen to them if they continue to be angry at their wives as O.J. Simpson was. As we Pleiadians read you, these things are being more deeply thought out than you may be aware of at this time. Those of you who Make Home now will end up moving into the economy, schools, and communities, and you will be the builders of new realities for the Age of Aquarius.

# 6

## *L*UCIFER'S DILEMMA
## AND THE POWER OF ANU

"YOU JUDGE ME MORE HARSHLY THAN YOU JUDGE YOURSELVES,
since I am spirit and you are body."

Lucifer

*Sixth-Dimensional Light Geometry*

We Pleiadians did not fully comprehend the nature of the sixth dimension, the dimension just above ourselves, until our vehicle had a vision when she was looking at the Acropolis in Athens in 1994. She had been able to see the 6D geometrical light forms that materialize objects in 3D until she was four years old. One day, she asked the housekeeper about the complex light fields she enjoyed watching coalesce around a table lamp in the livingroom. She wanted to know if the housekeeper liked the visible planes formed by triangles and octahedrons flashing around the lamp. In her eyes, the lamp and table were either moving into reality or receding back into light. The housekeeper looked at her sternly and said in a precise voice, "None of the things you say you see around the table and lamp are there!" Poof! Our vehicle lost the 6D sight, one of the few faculties that was shut down in her childhood. This perceptual faculty is the inner sight of the hypothalamus, the brain organ just above the medulla oblongata, the organ we use for visualization to create realities.

As we've mentioned, our vehicle was suddenly inclined to do a series of Sirian/Pleiadian alliances in Egypt and Greece from 1992 through 1994. The more she just let go and followed the scintillating lights, the more we Pleiadians impulsed her into wild and crazy activity like rattling, toning, and seeing the energy of sacred sites though the eyes of her students. Now we suspect the Sirians must have also been impulsing her because she began to see the 6D forms again. These faculties will now be awakening in everyone. As these openings occur—as with the opening of any subtle gland, such as the pineal, thymus, thalamus, and hypothalamus—it can be very hard to understand how to stay grounded, just to stay in your body. The more you know about these fields and how to perceive them, the better, because that will be how you can handle these openings without flying right out of your bodies.

Any object, such as the Acropolis, is held in form by the morphic field of that object. This 6D morphic field is what makes it possible for things to manifest in 3D. Such objects form in 3D from morphic fields when humans have an idea of them and want them to exist. It is easier to see the light geometry of inanimate objects than it is to see the morphogenetic fields that causes lifeforms, such as your cat, because lifeforms are always moving. Subtle fields are easier to see by glimpsing them with peripheral vision when they are stationary. If you try to see them by staring at them, they disappear; if you think about seeing them too much, you can't see them; and if you believe they are not real, you will miss them altogether. Just the suggestion that what our vehicle was seeing as a small child was not real was enough to instantly snatch her sight. Meanwhile, the world of 6D light forms that create realities in 3D is absolutely exquisite, for it is the very structure of creation, as snowflakes are the crystalline structure of water. As for the morphic fields of animate things, Kirlian photography has scientifically verified the existence of these subtle-energy fields.

Many artists can see such fields, and the visual arts strive to make these fields visible, since they are actually the source of beauty in matter. Beauty and desire are what cause things to come into existence in the first place, and a painter can make this visible. We Pleiadians would like you to notice that there has been a concerted plot by 4D intelligences to destroy your ability to see these fields. Modern art and music have often become ugly by portraying things that no one wants to look at or hear. Yet when an artist strives for true beauty, these fields can actually be felt and heard. Great art causes your heart to expand, and these perceptual modalities are the essence of Pleiadian passion. Ancient objects, such as the Sphinx or Parthenon, are especially wonderful places to see these fields because they have remained in 3D for so long by means of the intense feelings of humans. This is why great art often portrays sacred places and ancient artifacts.

The existence and preservation of ancient artifacts and sacred sites is a perfect record of your own curiosities and passions. Your heart expands because the beauty held in form through time by caring humans centers you in 3D and expands via 6D morphic fields. You tingle and feel awestruck as such experiences cause you to feel less solid. This helps you to feel that you are free, that you are in harmony. That is when we can impulse you and entice you to follow your fascination. We Pleiadians have wondered why 4D intelligences want to shut you down. We began to figure this out when our vehicle reopened her 6D sight. Now we see that the 4D control forces believe that they cannot run you around like rats in a Pavlovian laboratory if you are able to see the 6D multidimensional causal fields. Guess what? They're right!

In November 1994, our vehicle was standing on a balcony staring at the Acropolis bathed in clear starlight, which is rare in Athens. Orion and Sirius were sparkling like diamond crystals, and she was contemplating the exquisite symmetry of the Parthenon. Suddenly the whole temple reformed exactly as it was in 600 B.C., and the white marble perfection glowing in the night sky was the essence of true beauty. As she stood enthralled, lines of blue white light began shooting off all the angles and curves of the structure, as if the Northern Lights were forming in the night sky behind the Parthenon. An immense geometrical field of complex angles grew off the Parthenon and spread into the night sky. She saw the light structures holding it in form since 600 B.C. It looked like a new white Parthenon was being morphed on a computer screen to the stars! The next day she bought marble carvings of statues from the Athenian Classical Period. For the first time she saw ethereal beauty in the face of Athena, the exquisite geometry expressed in the simple drape of fabric on a body, and the soul proportions visible in tensed and healthy leg muscles, necklines, and arms.

Why do we go into such detail, as if the Pleiadians are sticking you back in the fifth grade discussing Athens and Sparta? I, Satya, want as many of you as possible to remember how to appreciate beauty and harmony because we know that cultures that value these things are able to consciously reduce destructive tendencies among their citizens. The vapid imagistic culture of North America spawned in New York, Washington, D.C., and Los Angeles, threatens to overwhelm the whole planet in an imploding wave of violence and ugliness. We single these cities out because they are like metastasizing breast tumors on the body of Gaia. Your planet requires a very powerful dose of beauty quickly, or this cancer will overwhelm everything.

We've always said, no one else will save you, but the way out of the impasse is so simple! You have all the models of planetary beauty. In culture after culture there is exquisite art; you must refuse to support ugliness in any form. The short period in Athens from 800 to about 400 B.C. was a phase that came after thousands of years of war and struggle in the Mediterranean world.[1] Finally exhausted by interminable struggles, the City States of the Athenian League attained a culture devoted totally to artistic beauty, personal freedom, and intrinsic harmony for a short while. This culture was seeded throughout the ancient world by Alexander the Great, and then it became part of the cultural basis of the Roman Empire. *The Greeks demonstrated a new cultural form that could be the ideal model for city life in the Age of Aquarius.* This brilliant idea was lost in the fall of the Roman Empire in the fifth century A.D.

How did you lose this vision based on conscious and willed cultural order? Your breakdown is much more serious than you realize, I, Satya, am going to take you very deep into some archetypes that hold information about how you limit the powers of your will. This is blasphemous material again. I apologize, but I have no choice about the honesty required, since your other alternative is obliteration and boredom. You are way too serious about yourselves. Don't worry, be happy! Lighten up! I begin by consulting with Lucifer, the one who is said to be the angel who fell from god.

## Lucifer and the Anunnaki Diversion

"I am Lucifer. You may regard me as one who is willing to take responsibility for pushing an issue to ultimate potential exposure. I am simply the dark side of the sixth dimension; but the light side cannot manifest without me. Without great force and intention, how will anything occur in your dimension? Think of the energy required for manifestation! So, until you push yourselves, I will keep pushing you, since I can see you are losing interest in your world.

"I am merely a force. If you have preconceived notions about me or any kind of negative feelings about me, then you don't respect raw power that can be used simply for good or for evil. I simply hold power implants in bodies, and it's your choice to activate them or not. If it weren't for me, 3D would be emotionless. Since evolution is required in the cosmos, time and place are necessities for any experience to occur. If it were not for basic force, there would be no 3D. I am the mirror of you that you will not look into.

"I am an angel from a higher dimension who was once in 3D. When I first came down, I was taken over by the Nibiruans. Therefore, I know a lot about how the Anunnaki use the Net. I am the perfect one to help you dissect the source of your inner violence creating your outer world. I share your dilemma, yet I still possess wider sight than you have. I am an etheric consciousness who came down to play in Earth. So, let's go for it! Angel means "angle" in 3D. Like the vehicle's sight of 6D angles, I could come and go until nobody could see me anymore. I, Lucifer, am caught by your inability to see subtle realities, and I have come to assist you in discovering how to see again.

"It is cosmic law that any being may choose to explore realities. You are the caretaker of your reality. You are the ones who must hold open your light planes so beings may freely come and go. However, I got caught by your lack of will and attention, and now it's time for you realize that's what happened to you. Your stories of me are all reflections of yourselves. Those of you who feel the most trapped in 3D talk about me all the time, and those of you who feel free in 3D never give me a thought. Meanwhile, *I am the diversion that keeps you from seeing what the Anunnaki are doing in your world.*

"My agreement to be interviewed by the Pleiadians is a desperate act. It is awesomely difficult for me to be brought into the Pleiadian field of this book. This makes me feel how I am caught in matter, specifically in radioactive matter. Like you, feeling is difficult for me; thinking is easier than feeling. I agonize with the powerlessness of the Pleiadians regarding radiation. As I come into your realm and I feel the Pleiadians through your energy fields, I remember being a soul in a body that was exquisitely loved. Often, unbeknownst to you, that is how I visit you: I move into one of you as you are being loved, and the Pleiadians move in and expand you like a supernova. I love to do this, but I must also tell you about the pain I feel with you. I feel like a child who is drowning and watching his or her parent go into shock as the tragedy unfolds. The parent is too far away and can't even attempt to save the child's life! The child is already out of body and knows there's no way out of the situation, and so the child is caught by the trauma and does not move into the light. The child hangs around in the astral and gets caught in time again. My relationship with the Pleiadians is a rather sad relationship, and yet the feelings I attain in your bodies suck me into your realm.

"I did not incarnate. I came to Earth as an ethereal entity. When I decided to come into the field, I got trapped like a bird in a cage. I don't really understand exactly how I got trapped. I can tell you what it feels like, but I don't understand how it happened. Possibly you feel that way too, but you judge me more harshly than you judge yourselves, since I am spirit and you are body. Those of you who fear me the most are the ones who have the biggest body confusions. Yes, I do tempt you to explore your bodies, since you chose a body for being on Earth. You can leave that field if you master your bodies, but I don't have such a choice. I never had a body I could explore. *I am the source of your beliefs that you didn't really even choose to be born.*

"Once upon a time, I came here because I wanted to be able to create like the creator does. I noticed one day that there were all kinds of exciting things happening on Earth. Things were being created and formed, like animals, crystals, and trees. I noticed that Earth was a place where creation is visible because it's dense and time locates things. That's why it's a school for beings from nine dimensions and anybody can apply. I decided that if I was going to create as the creator creates, I would come to Earth and figure out how to do it. I would come to learn just like all of you do.

"Here's my dilemma: To create, one must master the dimensional construct. When I got caught in 3D, I lost my ability to see the dimension that I came from. I am sure most of you know exactly what I mean. In fact, I am so lost here that I still can't tell you where I came from, I'm just stuck. I have many peers, many friends, and many of them came along with me. A whole group of us came, since I wasn't about to try it on my own. I am the light. That's what Lucifer means. I am light caught in matter. Therefore, I am the dark side of my own dimension. I operate like radiation because I spew; I feel frustrated and caught. I spew energy, seeking my home. The work to be in your bodies in 3D, which each one of you who has accessed multidimensionality is doing, helps me reaccess my own vibration. Many of you are doing marvelous work, and you deserve gold stars. The more you get into your bodies, the more all the denizens of the nonphysical realms are being freed.

"The reason I've got such a reputation on Earth is because I have been encouraging you to transmute. I am the one encouraging you to explore alchemy, astrology, and spiritual healing. By the way, I was entrapped by the Anunnaki when they created the Net at the beginning of the Age of Pisces. Now I am caught in time like a gigantic fish flopping the Net all over the beach. You think I am the cause of 4D trickery because the Anunnaki have tricked you into thinking it is I who is jerking you around. Not true, and all I want is to be released from your dimension. If you could lift the Net, I could swim back into the water where I belong. How could you do that?

"When you follow your curiosity and find ways to raise your consciousness, you get very excited. When you get excited, the fire rises in your bodies, but the next faculty that needs to instantaneously activate is your will. Why is that? As I already mentioned, mastery of your bodies is your path to multidimensionality, and this is accomplished by means of kundalini rising—the activation of your passion. Kundalini energy activated by raising your consciousness is your fuel, for it is the alchemical fire of the gods! You tend to be hypnotized by its potential when you first feel it, but many of you get diverted into limiting behavioral patterns once you get excited. Where the Anunnaki have been the most clever is in constructing a set of belief systems in your world that separate your spirit and body. Let's call it the "Anu Split."

"You are subtly encouraged to think you must get out of your body once you find spirit, that you must remove yourself from ordinary, mundane reality and seek 'meditation.' Just when you need grounding and lots of sex, you think you're supposed to go to temple. You drop your normal life habits, the very habits that guided you so far down the path already. Some of you leave your families because it would be more exciting to be an alchemist, yet your families are the ideal kitchen for transmuting yourselves.

"When you first get activated, you tend to move out of your ordinary reality. This occurs because the guides who have taken you to that point need to let go in favor of a new set of more sophisticated guides. There is a brief time when you must pass from one portal to another, and *only* ordinary reality will hold you on your true path, since it is the only reality you really know. Home is where you are in your power, but you get activated and then you shift out of 3D, poof! Anunnaki grab you! I, Lucifer, can attest: The way to avoid being pulled out is to stay grounded in 3D. Notice that I am often portrayed as one who is being burned in the ass in the fires of hell! I, Lucifer, am an Anunnaki ploy to scare you away from the sacred fire within your own bodies!

"One of the easiest ways to get out of the now is to be in a tense relationship fighting with elements of yourself that you dislike, and you are caught in the relationship observing yourself right in the other person. When you are irritated by this partner, imagine that each annoyance is actually something you don't like about yourself. *Relationships are a privileged agreement to share mutual realities so you can have feedback on the true nature of experience.* When you are in a partnership with someone and you allow yourself to go out of synch, you are abandoning them. If you play emotional body games and allow separation and tension to continue, what you're asking for is for one or both of you to get snatched emotionally. Weird energies are drawn into a room when people are tense and angry. The key is to be dedicated to staying in synchronicity together, because then the separative vibrations cannot grab you.

"As an example of how complex the Anu Split can be, for a generation or two the Anunnaki have been tricking you into not staying in synch in your marriages by implanting the idea that you are 'codependent' if you are close to your partner. Of course you are codependent until both of you mature! Would you rather be dependent on me? Lucifer? What ego you have to think you can go it alone! I had such an ego, and look at my reputation now! There are Anunnaki vibrations all over the place waiting to encourage you to waste all your time getting angry and frustrated, so they can impulse you into habitual relationship games that open space for them to enter your minds and split your hearts. It is better to depend on your parents until you are grown into a man or woman; then depend on your mates until you feel emotionally secure; and lastly you will have a relationship with someone who is your perfect mirror while you mature and become totally unique.

"If you don't figure this situation out, I will be trapped in 3D eternally, and I am getting very bored. I am dangerous when I am bored, as the Babylonians once discovered. Yes, I tricked them into blowing up Sodom and Gomorrah because I was bored one Saturday afternoon. What an explosion! All of you know that it is time to solve this dilemma. You got a personal glimpse of this danger with the Oklahoma City bombing, the 'OK Bomb,' as your FBI calls it. As with the Branch Davidians in Waco, Texas, many children were blown up. The Anunnaki love conflict and they are very hierarchical. They are interested in those of you who think they are important. For example, they are more interested in the personal conflicts of Bill Clinton or the government in general than they are in the love affairs of the postman or schoolteacher. They are very attracted to powerful and important people because they can trigger big agendas that influence many of you. If you are one who influences others in this world, the more powerful you become, the more you have to be smart about these forces. If you are one who lives a simple life, do not bother giving attention to the media system that tries to get your energy by hooking you on the dramas of the famous people. *Your world is becoming a tornado of forces that want your soul.* Certain ones of you are being singled out so you can be knocked off, but nobody can influence you if you are totally grounded.

"As a Fallen Angel, I passed through 5D Pleiadian and 4D Anunnaki frequencies when I came down through the dimensions to Earth. I studied what they are doing with you, and I will tell you all about how the Anunnaki have tricked you regarding the Pleiadians. Just as they tricked you into thinking that the 'devil/me' jerks you around, they've tricked you into thinking that somebody will rescue you. Beware of any rescue or charity. True assistance comes in something that prods you into waking up and strengthening your wills. The Anunnaki intervene and attempt to take your power away exactly when you have decided to actuate your original monad—your most significant 'I want' versus 'I need.' I, Lucifer, tell you: Beware of the Nurse, the Doctor, the Priest, the Politician, and the Salvation Army ringing bells at Christmas. Do not ever accept "helllpp" unless you have first asked for it with a lot of thought, and I, Lucifer, know what I am talking about, because I am in hell. Beware of Faustian pacts for gaining more time on Earth. Accept charity only if you feel the other person's true generosity and not gratitude. Are you elevated by gifting, or do you feel yourself groveling? Walk down every path alone unless you feel ecstasy when a hand is extended, even if you have to starve.

"It is time for Anu—Great Father God—to be truthful with you. Since Anu has split you, irradiated the Earth, and imprisoned me in time, I order him to tell you about immortality now."

## Anu, The Great Sumerian God

"I am Anu, the great god. My name dominates Earth's ancient history in

Sumer, and also in Egypt, where I was called 'On.' I created Sumer and Akkad myself, and then I took over Egyptian culture when it got in my way. When I first came to Earth 450,000 years ago, there were a bunch of scraggly heathens running around. People were just like animals, but their neurological systems had potential. You are the only species I have animated, the only species in whom I have encountered the Goddess. I was most attracted to the fertility and greenness of Earth when I first came, yet I cannot deny that I have almost destroyed that which I liked about Earth. Don't criticize me too harshly: You earthlings do the same things to yourselves. You destroy your vitality sometimes just because you're bored. Now, I am worried about the destructive tendencies that come of boredom. There might not be an Earth for me to return to. That's what makes me willing to be called on the carpet by Lucifer, one who knows all about your destructive tendencies, even though I, Anu, am the source of them.

"We Anunnaki die if your planet dies. Before I tell you my truth, as Lucifer of the Galactic Federation has compelled me to do, I want you to understand one thing: I am your god, and I have impulsed you to become who I think you can be. You have so responded to my expertise that you have become too much like what I wanted you to become. Now, like a person who has lost his will in a marriage, you are on the verge of destroying your reality because you don't know yourselves. I could not see this until now—the moment when you see you just might destroy your world.

"When we orbit back into the solar system and interact with Earth, you are our 3D refueling station, Anu Gas. There are things that we require from your sphere in order to continue our existence. If you ceased to exist, this would be like the station closing. When we are out in space, we are brave explorers of stellar consciousness. Like a satellite, we are limited in our ability to explore, and we encounter no other place like Earth. To give you a sense of the fruitfulness of your planet, the resources we gather from Earth carry us all the way through more than 3000 years of journeying in deep space. Only those of you who have experienced exile have any idea how lonely we get. The Kurds are our people, and they know how we feel. Once lonely, we become desperate and uncivilized. Long ago, we implanted the story of the Exodus deeply into your scriptures so that you could know how we feel when we are out in space. Instead, you use this story as a tool to condemn your enemies.

"We mined gold from Earth, and we use it to protect our planetary aura when we come into the solar system. When we are farthest from the Sun, we come close to Sirius, but Sirius does not have planets. Our relationship with Sirius is about stellar consciousness, not planetary consciousness. The Sirians are the archetype of our stellar evolution, as the Pleiadians are the source of your stellar evolution. If we did not have Sirian higher awareness influencing us on some level, we would not evolve, as you would not evolve your spirits without the Pleiadians.

"I am a lonely god contemplating the end of Earth as I've known it. I am a very important being. Soon—from 1998 to 2000—there will be a convention of the Galactic Federation to discuss Earth. Anyone seeking life is a member of the Galactic Federation. We will call together entities of 2D, 4D, 6D, and 8D who have an interest in the condition of Earth. Why the even side of the dimensional caduceus, and not the odd side? The even dimensions of the alchemical tree of life create structural laws for the Galaxy, and the odd dimensions live out the laws by exploring free will. The very laws of existence must be rewritten so that the life that lives them out can remain free. It is not that one side is better than the other; each one just works with different agendas. We, the gods of 4D, are the ones who know that we must write new laws of existence.

"Have you seen all the fine temples we've built on your planet? We must have your genetic material to continue our species when we are out in space, so we build first-class hotels for our visits. My ultimate objective is for humanity to have a pure genetic strain for its own sake. Then we wouldn't have to influence you or change you when we arrive; we could just intermingle and sojourn with you. Like adults who are ready to begin a relationship without either party needing any more maturation, we would meet as equals.

"We are the gods who come down to Earth, called by you the Nephilim of the Hebrew Bible. We built your temples as places for impregnating Earth species with our seed. The ancient stories of the solar princesses and priestesses who mate with us to birth future kings and queens are real. This is a long story, a long relationship that you can only explore through time. All that is useful and relevant now is for us to examine together a series of behavioral patterns that have become part of your culture as a result of your attempts to cope with our visitations. Like a lover who finally realizes that his visits changed the one he loved, I want to know from you how we have changed your world.

"When we actually visit your planet, we inhabit our temples for over 200 years. Since our orbit around the Sun is 3600 years and yours is 1, our 200-year visit is to us like one of your 20-day vacations in a great hotel. In that time—seven generations—we select your goddesses according to their genetic lines, and they give birth to children from us. Some of the children choose to leave Earth and travel with us, and some remain and seed new royal genetic strains. This is a fair exchange of genes. However, these experiences are also the source of your deepest wounds. This is why you hate to separate from one another to go on long journeys. We know this, but this is always part of any long love affair.

"For now, here is what is important for your survival: I now see that these experiences have set deep birthing triggers that result in chaotic breeding. During this last cycle since Zero Point, all temples that built their traditions on the Patriarchs of the Hebrew Bible are infected with this chaos, especially the Vatican. This infection is god blindness. Have not most of you wondered why the Church denies women sovereignty in their bodies? Why are your goddesses only useful as birthing vessels? I will tell you: On Nibiru for thousands of years, gestation was accomplished with fertile eggs that we put in receptacles—Holy Grails—after gathering them during sacred sexual ceremonies in our temples on Earth. To us each goddess is an individual receptacle for birthing, and each fertilized egg that we gather is precious to us. Your women are fertile and sex is wonderful with them. We have used you in such a powerful way without your total agreement that *deep inside you believe you do not control your own fertility, your most basic right.* You do not take responsibility for your birthing.

"In the past, your 3D worlds have ended by fire, flood, and quakes, and this time you are on the verge of being smothered in bodies. There is still time to rebalance your numbers, and as a first step, we will help. I, Anu, will do an intervention on the Pope. I hereby end Papal Infallibility, the Nibiruan Imprimatur! To prevent further difficulty in the future, the Pope, who badly needs a long recovery program, will be coming with us the next time we leave Earth! He can be the new Anu so I can retire, and that is why the Pope has been practicing his traveling and languages so diligently. I joke with you, I am sure you are laughing,— but it is time for the end of women being used as vessels.

"The population crisis and planetary suffering on a scale never before known cause me to ask, 'What have I done that is causing you to pile up bodies? Did you develop all that earthmoving technology just to dig mass graves? What have I implanted in your minds that even destroys your life force, your immune systems? Like a lover who draws away and looks at his lover and realizes there is barely a thread left of who she was when we began, I want to know what I have done.'

"We must begin with the basic law of Earth, which is that each one of you has free will at the soul level, and with that power you can change any reality while you are alive. From that perspective, nothing happens to you unless you have chosen it, and if you didn't want to be in this situation, you wouldn't be. We have come to this point together, and all I can do is share my part. We like to control you as much as possible so we can use you. I am like an employer who intends to get everything out of an employee for as little money as possible. In our time with you, we've discovered it's easier to get you to do what we want if you are afraid of death. But, what am I going to say to the Galactic Federation Council? Am I going to say I made humans so fearful that they are killing each other off? Great report!

"We discovered a long time ago that if we just made you afraid, we could get you to run this direction or that. We are stunned by how easy it is! Thirty years ago, we told you to prevent heart attacks: eat margarine instead of butter. You ate margarine and heart attacks increased faster. Lately, we told you that butter is better than margarine after all! Ten years ago, we told you that you gain weight because of fat consumption, and we printed the fat content on all the food labels. Everybody studied the labels and cut down on their fat consumption, but during the decade, the average weight in the United States went up ten pounds. Some of you got fatter and some got extremely thin. The fat ones ate more because they felt guilty about everything they ate, and all they thought about was the fat content of food. The thin ones became nervous, consuming engines. Only about one out of a thousand of you even suspected that thought controls weight, and the fat you consume is the combustible fuel for your body. Meanwhile, your cancer rate skyrocketed in the thinnest ones among you, because cancerous cells are transmuted in fat cells and your natural elemental burning mechanism was thwarted. You fell for all this because you fear death so much that you will do anything to add a month to your lives!

"*You are doomed unless you stop fearing death.* We are the ones who caused you to fear death, because we age very fast while we sojourn on Earth. We age 3600 years during 1 of your years, and I am old and tired from all my visits during the last 450,000 years. We are fearful beings, and if you want to understand our fears, look at the rising tide of fear on your planet. We have projected too much of our stuff on you, since the successful imposition of the Net meant we could get away with murder with you. Like a malicious joke, it was funny until it went too far. Now it is time for you to wake up and realize that we Anunnaki influence your planet during our whole orbit, not just when we visit you. How? We are influencing you via thoughtforms implanted in your minds. Because we need resources for such long journeys, we've prodded you into hoarding and stockpiling as if the Sun was never going to rise another morning. Meanwhile, you function better with fewer things, and you are happier in communities in which you share. Now, like a mature lover who assumes his lover has a great time and doesn't have a thought about her while she's away on a trip, you need to remember happiness when life is simple.

"Many of you know about hoarding secrets so you can use them as a source of power just for yourself. It's obvious why we have totally controlled the information our Sirian teachers entrusted to us, but now suddenly I can see that this knowledge is exactly what can save you. After such a longstanding love affair, I've reached that point where all I care about is you, even if that means I have to release things I am holding that I think could save me. I am ready to share this knowledge with you because sharing knowledge is the point of the Sirian/Pleiadian Alliance. You cannot imagine the awesome cosmic shifts that are occurring because the heart and mind are united in the Pleiadian goddess and the Sirian alchemist.

"More about galactic politics later. At the present moment, we are carrying alchemical secrets given to us by the Sirians, and we are heading toward your sphere again. We've admitted that we don't necessarily plan to give you the gift exactly as it was handed to us, once we get to your system. That is always the situation when we approach your solar system. You know what it's like to carry a treasure on a long journey and resist giving it away at the end. Alchemy involves total commitment to transmuting your spirit/soul, so that your body has sufficient fire to receive nine dimensions of cosmic knowledge. You have a body, and there is no need to wait, since alchemy is something that can only be seized in the moment.

"The way to get a pure message from Sirius is to tune into it now before Nibiru gets closer to Earth. The Pleiadians and Sirians are aligned to assist you in this. It is easy to see that the Sirian alchemical vibration has intensified since 1000 A.D. This vibration permeates the work of Hildegard von Bingen, Albertus Magnus, Meister Eckhart, and many other medieval artists and mystics. At the time Nibiru was recently closest to Sirius around 1600 A.D., the Renaissance was in full swing with the de'Medicis, Kepler, Paracelsus, Botticelli, Fra Angelica, Michelangelo, and so many others. And I have a confession: As I, Anu, saw this great awakening unfolding, I panicked at the possibility you would free yourselves. I aborted the Renaissance! I wanted to keep all the secret teachings for myself. Like an old father who always said he'd give his power to his children but will not release anything once he has become an old man, I couldn't let anything go.

"The systems of the Vatican, feudal, divine kingship, and secret societies were already all set up. All I had to do was send a jolt of fear through the whole system, and that would take care of your ideas about freedom. Giordano Bruno was writing about multiple dimensions and extraterrestrial civilizations, so the Pope burned him at the stake in 1600 A.D. This split science and theology so there would never be proof of spirit, and spirituality would be the sign of a weak mind. Many great Renaissance musicians and painters were opening you humans to multidimensionality. All I had to do was cut off an ear or gouge out a tongue or two, and you concluded that art ruins peoples' lives. Healers and geniuses discovering alchemy were accused of being Lucifer himself, and many were burned at the stake in public.

"Yet now is the time for you to realize that many great artists captured the alchemical codes during the Renaissance. These vibrations were brought down into the physical realm, and this art contains the codes for restructuring the whole planetary field from 1987 to 2012 A.D. What you do right now is of crucial importance, and the great Renaissance artists are in physical body now poised to fill your world with beauty and ecstasy. You have been waiting for this. Are you not amazed by millions of teenagers listening to Hildegard von Bingen and Gregorian chanting? Wake up! Wake up! As Nibiru comes closer and closer carrying alchemical treasures, you could wait for the gods instead of awakening yourselves. You might be Michelangelo! You might be Fra Angelica! However, you can just be sheep herded in groups waiting for the Apocalypse, cowering and waiting for the gods.

"The Apocalypse is the end of your sphere, and the end of us. Look,

I'm just the boss who realizes he's ruined the company, and is wondering what will he tell the stockholders? I am the U.S. President who realizes he's blown it with NAFTA as he watches world currencies tumble into the toilet. This is getting too big for any one person, and guess what? That is when the individual wakes up! I, Anu, am here to share the truth with you before I have to report to the Galactic Federation. In the old days, the boss would loot the company and head for a tropical island, but there is no tropical island to run to anymore. As Nibiru comes closer into your solar system, my desires are activated. It's like when you get close to a treasure, and you just want to grab it all. I have been known to be a pig, and so have you! As I get closer, I get blinded by the light of the Sun. I know from the past that I think less clearly when I come into your realm, just like a man is blinded by the sight of a beautiful nude woman. I hope you will just seize the alchemy in toto as a pure gift from the Sirians right now, and shout, 'Up yours, Anu!'

"If you study the alchemical tradition, you will notice that alchemical science gets to a certain level, and then two human traits abort it: greed and fear of personal power. First of all, alchemy is not meant to be a tool for becoming rich; it is for becoming *multidimensional*. The appropriate tool for greed is banking. Secondly, if you are going to become an alchemist, you have to begin by becoming powerful. Alchemy works by utilizing kundalini power and creating fields in your bodies that can access any dimension. This can only be done individually, since each one of your bodies is a 3D portal linked to Gaia's iron core crystal. One person is not meant to become a leader who harvests the financial, sexual, and psychic energy of individuals. No one of you is to offer your power to another, since your power is the only access to the spirit. I, Anu, confess: For hundreds of thousands of years, each time you found your power, I used you as my tool. But now we are on the verge of mutual extinction.

"My control devices are your death, since, like the rich company owner, I'm only around for a little while. While I'm away, I set up secret brotherhoods to run the planet, and now these secret societies and religions have assumed a life of their own. They all want to be the rich company owner. As Nibiru comes closer, these brotherhoods feel their old covenants activating. Watch out, for they are so easy to see if you know them.

"Once you are initiated into a closed grouping, you are a Nibiruan construct. All these groupings are based on hierarchy, and they are exclusive and fear-poisoned. Their leaders sell their souls and bodies to fuse the group as individual members grovel and snivel. *If you work in a group, make sure it is an open community.* There must be no financial or personality competition in that group, no ownership of anyone's energy/creativity, and you all must be temporary stewards of a resource. Then let everything go and call yourselves earthkeepers and simply do the work and keep no secrets. If the least powerful one in your group becomes quiet or locked up, ask him or her what the next step is. Openness of teachings and absence of ritual is always the sign of true earthkeepers.

"I am being totally honest about my influence in your world. This is the moment when a lover bares all, hoping that his lover can seize the moment and blast to the stars. I am happy that your Zecharia Sitchin so brilliantly and bravely told our story because, if you can remember that you are human and extraterrestial, you will be able to deal with visitors from the sky when they come. If you want to, you can see the faces of all your lovers from other dimensions! Once we of Nibiru got involved with you and worked with your genes, we mixed ourselves with you. Your women have given much to us, and we finally are grateful for every moment of love. We have not taken away any of your original integrity because no one can do that. But we have badly distorted one part of your reality. Since we journey so far, we are great warriors, and we are very male. You are meant to Make Home and live in harmony with all species on Earth. To resonate with Gaia, you need to be very female. We have forced you to be too warlike, too compulsive, too focused in linear space and time, too fearful. Now these incompatible tendencies are exploding your cells. Luckily your genetic matrix also has stellar contributions, and now this stellar-cellular matrix must awaken. You must interact with other dimensions to heal.

"We know we do not have all the answers for you. We know you are ready to learn from the Sirians as we have. It is so difficult for us to offer our magnificent teachers to you and to leave our temples. Any fears in your minds from us will limit you. If you can give up these fears, your potential access to other worlds is astounding. Access to other realities is the spiritual enlightenment you seek because you are meant to Make Home and then journey with your minds. In our shrine for you in Nibiru, which is like a typical megalithic stone circle on Earth, we call you the 'People of the Vision Quest.' We are meant to journey and visit you.

"The brotherhoods we created based on secrecy, power, and war threaten to destroy every last indigenous person, every last tree, every last remnant. Why? Because I judged myself negatively: I thought you would be happiest if you weren't like me, so I hid my real self from you. Now I know it is the combination of *both* of us that will enrich each one of our worlds. You are close to being overwhelmed by my negative judgments of myself, and that is why I am being so honest. Gods don't usually confess, so pay attention. If you are to take the alchemy, you must learn to recognize us so you can stay on an equal footing with us. How could you do that? Watch out if your teacher has an aloof and imperial kind of consciousness that tends to hypnotize you, causes you to grovel and swoon, and confuses your mind. If you examine history, these trends were very apparent all around your planet in 1800-year cycles. Imperial Rome leads right back to Persia, right back to Assyria, right back to Sumer. As you examine cultures, you can see the Nibiruan influences. Zoroaster and Ahura Mazda are classic early scouts! You will need to master alchemy before we get closer and become stronger, for that is our nature. You are gentle and we are great. When we come closer, we will want to control you and grab your treasures. After all, we will be returning warriors and very horny! Since your women do not want to get snatched, it might not be a bad idea to listen to them for change. They know us very well.

"The alchemical codes teach you how to transmute elements. Gold has always been very prominent in alchemical literature. Gold is the metal that opens portals for us to enter 3D! The Pleiadians enter your world via sugalite and sapphires, the Sirians via diamonds. We must become 3D to enter your realm, and gold is our tool for manifesting in your world; that is why you are afraid of alchemy. We use gold as a communication device on Earth when we are not in the solar system. Radioactive materials access stellar frequencies of even higher dimensions than gold, and we tricked you into experimenting with unstable elements because we wanted to figure out how they work. This must have been a mistake, since you are on the verge of blowing yourselves up. When I meet with the Galactic Federation, I am in trouble because the unbridled use of radioactivity threatens the Galaxy. Nobody knows how to help you decide to stop yourselves. You must cease all mining and production of these materials until you discover how to transmute them. Would you conjure up Lucifer in your bedroom without knowing how to remove him? You are arrogant because I, Anu, am arrogant, and you are made in my image.

"If any one dimension is obliterated, all are obliterated. Abraham came to implant an element into the center of our Temple that would access the elemental stellar mind. Never forget that my planet is only a planet and not a star. Once you comprehend the new cosmology, you will realize I am not father and you are not son or daughter. As I've already said, it is time for you to see who comes into your realm. The story of Abraham was first written down in 2000 B.C., but he came to your planet in 3760 B.C., when he implanted radiation in the central temple, called Ur. I, Anu, came down into the top chamber of the Ziggurat and impregnated the Goddess. Who was that Goddess? All the women of Earth. This was the implantation of stellar codes into the genetic matrix of Earth, and that is why Abraham is revered as the great father god. Sarah is a solar priestess, 'Sa Ra,' who conceived a stellar child even though she was barren. When Abraham was in Egypt, he claimed that Sarah was his sister, and therefore she was a Sirian solar priestess. Abraham was given the covenant of the land of Canaan for deposit of his seed at the sacred tree of Shechem.[2]

"The Sirians are revealing the real story about the archetypal father—Abraham—to send out a signal to the other systems about the dire situation on Earth. What do I mean? The Sirians are sharing their most deeply imbedded and potent implant in your history so you can understand that it is a 6D story and not a story about us, the Anunnaki. Then you can drop the belief that a great father rescues you, and you will see you must master the transmutative potential of radioactive materials yourselves. That is why the Sirians brought them to your planet in the first place. There is a process going on here that is not necessarily as negative as it seems to be in your dimension. Remember, stars are nuclear. Stellar consciousness has been awakened in 3D, you will never be the same again, and there is great potential on Gaia now.

"We Anunnaki decided in 3600 B.C. that it was time to integrate stellar frequencies for the solar system. This quickening was a gift from us, and now you must have the keys to its transmutation. Any element is negative only if it is used unethically. If used with integrity, any element is a positive power. Radiation is poisoning your planet because you are using it amorally; we manipulated you into unleashing it in your world. This is your greatest test. *Radiation is sucking in stellar intelligences, and I will become mortal if I do not unleash all your creativity.* Like Lucifer, I will get caught in your dimension, but at least I could incarnate. I, Anu, don't know the outcome because you create the outcome. You must get over the idea that I know everything. I don't. Things have gotten out of control because you've been tricked into taking actions while you didn't know what you were doing, but you thought I knew what I was doing. Einstein was a monotheist and thought god was omnipotent.

"Sodom and Gomorrah were destroyed in an atomic explosion in 2024 B.C. In those days, Abraham was a historic personage.[3] In this destruction, many great lessons were learned. I, Anu, triggered this to get rid of things that we didn't like. You do that all the time. What happened in Sodom and Gomorrah is what happens in your cities at the present time: They get bigger and more complex and finally self-defeating, and section by section they are laid waste because you don't care about them. We destroyed Sodom and Gomorrah in order to just do a little house-keeping, just as evil men working for multinational drug companies are cleaning out people in central Africa by seeding lethal viruses. Do not be surprised by what I say. You all know people who'd just as soon nuke something as bother to clean it up. After all, look what you did to Japan. I can see however that nuking things creates reactions that all lead to doom. We see this, but we don't know what to do about it.

"Let's go back to Ur again. Around 5000 B.C., the Sirians gave us radiation as the maildrop to deposit in 3600 B.C. Abraham buried it under Ur, and made it a secret. Later it was dug up and carried from temple to temple in the Ark. We impregnate goddesses in the temples, so we mixed up uranium with our own sexual behavior. This placed behavioral patterns in your genes that you struggle with now. These hold you back from adoring the Goddess; *you are afraid to unleash her sexually because she might become a nuclear explosion.* She is meant to be a nuclear explosion! And those who remember how to adore the Goddess will be doing the most important energetic work from now to 2012. Our sexuality with temple priestesses is our most beautiful form of expression. It is a source of ancient love and knowledge about species that need regeneration from Nibiru.

"To you, we are the ultimate users. This is the part of you that just uses something without enjoying it. This must stop as you adjust to higher frequencies, or all the unused personal energy and incomplete emotional growth will backfire in your bodies and in your world. We made sex spinal so kundalini fire would continually regenerate your bodies and genes. We believed that if we could mix the genetic matrix with radioactive consciousness, then you would have stellar vibrations in your spines that we could decode. We watch you, we observe you when you learn, and then we learn. We thought that this would offer us more stellar linkage, and we thought this would improve your children. Never forget that children are the only future for both of us.

"I thought that the children who came from these matings would have stellar intelligence. That's how I created Enki, and there was a great quickening of humanity at that time. However, Enki's nuclear/stellar energy tended to obliterate indigenous consciousness. Things were too juicy too soon, like a nuclear meltdown. Everybody turned to worshipping Yahweh, the powerful deity who emerged out of the patriarchal, nuclear explosion. *Nuclear power is monotheistic, yet kundalini activation of each body is polytheistic.* I, Anu, am the monotheistic god who sees that you all need to feel yourself as a god, as a body alive with the divine flame. Now I see that there must be no sexual activation without the permission and support of the Goddess because sex with the Goddess without her permission creates a splitting that becomes stress between sister and brother, brother and brother, sister and sister. Listen to me. Stop reading this book now and do this:

*Each one of you think of your siblings and notice any separation you have from any one of them. If you will contact that sibling and relink yourselves, arguments between the gods will be finished, for they all sourced in sibling conflict! This is the confusion that was implanted by means of Cain and Abel, Horus and Seth, and Enki and Enlil. Go heal it with your brother or sister now! Now that uranium is in your field, you must do this in order to save yourselves.*

"Once the Temple was needed for containing radioactivity; this nuclear energy, however, has gradually overtaken humanity, and it is the source of religious fanaticism. No energy should be introduced into Earth unless humans have the capacity to transmute it themselves. You couldn't handle radioactivity and Yahweh then, and you still can't now. This has gotten so far out of hand that none of you even knows who has the waste! Even the CIA doesn't know! This is because secret societies totally control everything that goes on with radioactivity. Lately, the initiates deposited it in the Four Corners area of the Southwest, the location of the ultimate Anu Science since the 1940s, and they have become addicted to this covert energy. You are paralyzed by deep and automatic responses to it. *You must each access alchemy directly from the stars.* Then your scientists will be able to transmute nuclear waste, while you transmute your inner triggers to save your planet.

"You are playing out the drama with radioactivity; it is teaching you about how everything you create will come back to you. We are involved in a great big experiment together looking at what we Nibiruans have been creating. Scientists are realizing that they are controlled by us, and they are deeply disturbed. They thought they were great alchemists and could play at being god. You would be amazed at what scientists are figuring out right now; many of them know they have been duped. They thought they could create bombs and nuke their way to enlightenment.

"The awakening of the scientists is critical. Scientists are the only members of your society who have any power against the government. They are holding the present authority structure in place, and they know the world is being destroyed. Withdraw your support! You have become almost exclusively the agents of Anunnaki control. You know you are puppets on a string. You have played with unstable elements and gotten a glimpse of potential chaos in your world. Now is the time for you to cry out and signal the rest of the Galaxy that earthlings are ready to become alchemists, and you scientists are willing to teach all of them."

### Satya and the Chosen People

Now that Anu is finished, I, Satya, am back. I am wondering why the stellar awakening has come to such an impasse within each one of you? I can feel that you won't like hearing what we Pleiadians say, but our vehicle is willing to read you.

Each one of you has a trigger point deep inside that causes you to operate on robotic energy and automatic response patterns. Maybe you think you have to be faithful to your husband because your mother told you to, so you never experience the challenge of being trustworthy? Or maybe you think you have to be faithful to your wife because your mother controlled you, but you've never enjoyed sex? Perhaps you think you have to change the world because your father told you that you didn't deserve life unless you made a difference, so you never enjoy being powerful? Or perhaps you think you can't do anything you want with your body because someone taught you limitations? These confusions are sourced in lifetimes of great power in which a force, a belief system, or a political agenda was channeled through you while you were totally conditioned to forget yourself. You were used as a tool. The Anunnaki-based secret societies have been very thorough. Each one of you was initiated into them in past lives, many of you in this lifetime. These initiations taught you *how to stop feeling first before you acted; eventually you forgot how to feel at all, and then you stopped doing what you wanted to do.* For our vehicle, that pattern comes out of having a lifetime as a Hebrew prophet in which she channelled an ascended being called Isaiah.

During the Hebrew prophetic period, the Chosen People formed their identity around the Exodus—escaping oppression by the Egyptians—and in those days, the Egyptians called the Hebrews, the "Hibiru." We Pleiadians do not care about whether the Egyptians oppressed the Israelites or not. From what we've seen of human behavior, they probably did worse things than anything the Israelites have accused them of. At this time, we are interested in this issue in order to understand and widen the vision of the Jews, since they are carrying the Chosen People archetype. Escaping Egyptian oppression is the same as escaping Sirian oppression, since Egypt was a Sirian culture, and the exceedingly nonjudgmental thoughtforms emerging from the Sirian/Pleiadian Alliance make it possible to investigate the deep belief systems sourced in the Exodus.

In 700 B.C. my vehicle channeled a group of beings called Isaiah—"I-say-yah"—in the Temple of Solomon. That was the lifetime when our vehicle was plugged into by a control force; she knows it, and now she chooses to pull out the phone jack. Remember, we are wanting to discover that point when your energy becomes automatic or robotic because that is when you get disempowered or disemboweled, then you have come back again and again to repeat the same pattern. We want to find that nexus you are unable to move past that is coming out of a lifetime of great power. How do you move past it? It's easy; just become more powerful—more clear and conscious—in this life than you were before!

## Isaiah and the Egyptian Temple of the Reptiles

"This is I, Isaiah. In the ancient days, I was one of many channels who were bringing in Orion beings for information about how to defeat the

Egyptians. This is the same dynamic as channeling the Pleiadians, and many of the channels are getting the same information. These again are the days of prophecy. Why Orion? Our Hebrew priests discovered the Egyptians were working with Orion beings, and we went to Egypt to study in their temples to figure out how they did it. What we discovered was truly amazing.

"The Egyptians accessed Orion by working with reptiles who lived in the bowels of their power points. So we made tunnels and filled them with spring water under Mt. Moriah, and we moved in crocodiles so we also could work with the beings of Orion.[4] With this technology, we got the news directly from their guides. We wanted to know what the Egyptians were tuning into so we could outfox them by using their own guidance against them. Our channels brought Orion data into the Temple of Solomon on Mt. Moriah.

"I was one of the channels who was literally imprisoned in the Temple over the crocodiles because my channeling faculties were very developed. A great channel is like a radio with many stations. Once a being is called in, that being will answer any questions the questioner feels strongly about. *Channeling is the most uncontrolled information source on Earth,* and it has become the way to get news again, since the authorities are lying to the people, as they were in my time. Most of you know by now that the media is an Anunnaki grandstand set up to jerk you around.

"For me, the Temple of Solomon was an interrogation chamber. As I get into this, please realize that I respect all of you. Mt. Moriah and the Temple of Solomon have meant millions of things to millions of people. They are powerful sacred sites in tune with Gaia. I am only telling my own story because it is time. After all, my story was distorted in the Bible, and it hurts to still be misunderstood 2600 years later. I do not believe or assume any place on Earth is negative for any other consciousness in the universe. I would hope that any of you who esteem this Temple would be curious about the story of Isaiah, especially since the Temple is not in physical form at this time. It will be rebuilt as soon as its keepers learn to work with nine-dimensional access and make peace with the indigenous people of Palestine, so that it does not repeatedly get blown out of 3D. The Pleiadians have told you that the 6D Sirians hold things in morphic fields, and the original idea of the Temple of Solomon could be again reconstructed in 3D, but only by keepers who work with all nine dimensions. The vehicle plans to visit this Temple in 2012, for it is very sacred to all Gaians.

"As an initiate of the Temple of Solomon, I had the memory codes of all my past lives reaccessed by the rabbis. I was chosen for this channeling position because they discovered that I had been an 18th Dynasty priest in Egypt named Ichor, which means 'blood of the gods.' Our Hebrew agenda was to defeat Egypt; and selecting an initiate who has the codes of a culture one wishes to defeat is very typical of secret-society practices. Do not feel honored when a secret society invites you for initiation, since all they want is your codes. If you wish to keep your integrity, let no one use your codes; use them only to take your power and activate your monad. In case anyone reading this wants to say I am singling out any group, remember I am exposing *all* Anunnaki manipulation techniques. As Isaiah, I can only report on how Anunnaki manipulation worked in my times. It will be up to all of you to decide whether this is still going on in your times.

"In that lifetime as Ichor, I was initiated into the secrets of channeling. I was taught at Kom Ombo on the Nile, the reptile temple, and then I was taught star divination at Khem, the reptilian divination temple, just above the Delta. In case you think I am favoring the Egyptians over the Israelites, my vehicle has already documented in "The Mind Chronicles Trilogy" how being a member of a secret Egyptian cabal was hell. What is totally unique about your times is *all secrecy will cease when Earth enters the Age of Aquarius.* So, please allow me to tell you about the reptilian temple.

### Khem, the Reptilian Temple of the Nile Delta

"Khem is an underground tri-level complex with a fourth level on the surface just above the ridge that drops down to the Delta. The bottom level is at the water level of the Nile during the dry season. When the inundation came, the lower level filled with water and crocodiles. When the water filled the chambers of the first level, the crocodiles were forced through holes in the ceilings of the lower chambers to the next level to get oxygen. The second level was a lizard maze of channels, resting places, fish, weeds, and lotus blossoms. The ancient Egyptians even tiled the walls with swamp scenes of the cataracts where the crocodile's journeys began! Once these lizards slithered into the second level, they rested, played, and tuned into their community relations. The third level under the surface temple was a series of rooms, each with a hole in the center, and set over the holes was a globular crystal lens that looked like a crystal eye. The walls of the rooms were tiled in gleaming deep aqua blue—Ptah's blue that symbolized the Blue Nile.

"One festooned grandmother hippopotamus from the White Nile lived in a woven bamboo house in the third level during the divination period. In the temple on the surface, Ichor and the temple astrologers cast natal or birth charts for all crocodiles born during one lunar cycle during a given inundation. The temple astrologers studied the crocodiles to understand the biological forces during the time of the inundation so the biological status of Earth could be communicated to the Orion Library, which is the Library of the Galactic Federation. This was how Khem functioned.

"The Eighteenth Dynasty astrologers developed natal astrology for the Orion data banks by reading the biological codes of the reptiles. This was done to enhance the harmonic form of the Blue Nile. The animals who participated were sacred. The crocodiles who were born during this period lived their lives in the sacred temple lakes up and down the Nile, and the grandmother hippo came down the Nile in a sacred boat from Aswan. Since all intentions were of the highest order, nobody was misusing energy. The Egyptians were a peaceful people for thousands of years because they knew how to keep busy! *They understood that humankind's greatest difficulty is frustrated creativity.* The outrageous beauty of Khem, the greatest lizard lounge on the planet, is a great example of creativity just for creativity's sake. Wouldn't you like to hear a crocodile natal reading?

"During a great famine that occurred when the pharaoh was weak, the Hibiru came into the land of Egypt for a long sojourn. They were very surprised that the Egyptians were communicating with beings of Orion at Khem and Kom Ombo. They wanted to learn how to do this because they knew that Orion was the conduit into the 8D Galactic Federation. These beings were responsible for cosmic order and known to be very powerful and hard to access. Since Egypt was a land of power, plenty, beauty, and harmony, the Hibiru thought the source of this good fortune must be the Galactic Federation. Actually, this was not the source of Egyptian fortune. They were just great manifestors, and they played all the time, even with crocodiles and hippos. Power is just power, and it can be used for good or evil. The Egyptians discovered how to work with Orion and developed a very high level of manifestation consciousness from this. The Hibiru wanted to master this facility in order to get what they wanted.

"Like any power technique for accessing multidimensionality, the telluric realm must be worked with to access 'the powers of place;' in order to activate the telluric realm, the intention of Gaia needs to be sourced, and this was done in the bottom layer of the temple where the crocodiles rolled around in silica clay. Crocodiles are cold-blooded and they vibrate with the mineral realm. Humans are warm-blooded and vibrate with plants. Crocodiles love mud and humans love the Garden of Eden. The Egyptians found out that if they set up a temple on a reptilian power point with crocodiles vibrating in silica mud and the grandmother hippo wallowing in the lush plants they could divine the qualities of the 2D telluric realm with their astrologers.

"There are some power points where all the dimensions interface with the telluric realm, and Khem was one of those places. Gaia was 1D; 2D was reptiles vibrating in clay accessing telluric powers; 3D was Egyptian astrologers triggering 4D sight by analyzing planetary patterns. This lens accessed the cosmic wisdom of 5D through 9D. The Hibiru were Nibiruan adepts, and when they saw how the Egyptians worked with the crocodiles and the hippo, they wanted to learn the technique. The Egyptians were Sirian adepts, and Sirian knowledge is never secret but is rarely understood. That was the point of the appropriate lens. If this is confusing to you, have you ever read a book all the way through and had no idea what it said? This is because you did not have the inner knowledge to access that book at that time. Sirian knowledge is open to all because it can't be comprehended unless the person seeking it has 6D sight. This sight is rare; it is always cause for celebration whenever anyone on Earth attains these levels. The Egyptian and Greek temples, and Hopi dances, for example, are open to all visitors for this reason.

"Egypt, Greece, and Hopiland are revered, feared, and often invaded because they trigger jealousy. *Whenever you feel jealousy toward someone for their talents, watch it!* Examine that ugly emotion, cease what you are doing immediately, and petition to study what you covet. The Hebrew people are a cosmically talented race of people; possibly this original envy set in only because the Egyptians were more advanced than the Hibiru during the time of the Exodus. Envy and jealousy may be the most caustic emotions you create, but the jury is out on that because just when it looks like you've found the worst one, you find another. In case I sound like a moralist or ethicist, I am. That's the one quality you'll find in the Book of Isaiah that is accurately portrayed.

"When the Hibiru came into Egypt, they asked to study in the temples, and of course they were welcome. After studying at Khem during one inundation, the Hibiru could see that the Egyptians had figured out how to utilize the planets as dimensional lenses. (*When anyone works with the magical system of another, great risk is involved.* Much care must be taken by the adepts in training to shift their own bodies to adapt to a new energy form. To do this, the new energy frequency must be totally integrated, and the heart must be opened so pure teaching can be received.) Meanwhile, the Hibiru were in a hurry because they wanted to return to their land, the Fertile Crescent. The Egyptians were using all 12 planets for their divination lenses. To master this dynamic would require studying during 12 inundations, a full cycle of Jupiter around the Sun, which was required of all Egyptian astrologers since Jupiter is the home of the mastery codes for Earth.

"To the Hibiru, the Egyptian adepts were brilliant but archaic. All the Hibiru needed was the technique, not the whole process. Why not just set up the system itself and then just utilize Nibiru, they thought. For the Egyptians, the 4D planetary archetypal realm could only be accessed by utilizing all the planets plus the Moon. The Egyptian Ennead is based on this belief, and the Egyptians were, and still are fundamentally polytheistic. They were dismayed when the Hibiru decided to leave Egypt after one year, because they knew that partial mastery of any system results in disaster. In this case, the spatial dimension of Earth's solar system is expressed by all 12 bodies; if anyone on Earth used this powerful reptilian divination skill with only one planet, they would become obsessed with the archetype of that planet—monotheism. Monotheism breeds fanatical anthropocentrism, which eventually destroys Earth. So the Egyptians repeated the principle of 12 again and offered all the knowledge they had to the Hibiru.

"The Egyptians offered to teach by their own example. For example, if the Egyptians had a dilemma, such as a potential war, they waited for a lunar cycle during an inundation when Mars was in certain key alignments to ask 5D through 9D guides about battle plans. Egypt was a land of peace that repelled outside influence from 10,800 to 1600 B.C. by setting the clear intention that they did not want to do battle. Before the breakdown of the Blue Nile in the latter days of the Eighteenth Dynasty, the Egyptians kept warfare to a minimum. Sometimes violence occurred at the borders where they fed hungry people, but the inner field of the Blue Nile was held for thousands of years, and it still exists from Saquara through Giza plateau to Khem. Enemies might show up from any direction, but the Egyptians had created a zone of peace, which they maintained with great awareness. The Nile was home to any visitors who arrived. The Egyptians ascertained the desires of the visitors and absorbed them into their kingdom. What was this to them? The Egyptians assumed that each person who appeared was a teaching for them. They rarely travelled, and visitors gifted them with storytelling in exchange.

"The Hibiru were one of the groups who showed up periodically from the northeast saying 'I'm hungry. I need clothing and shelter.' The Egyptians would absorb them and take care of their needs, especially since they knew the Hibiru had been driven out of their land by nomads coming in from the north of the Levant. They had an extraordinary ability to absorb because they had a very creative providential culture.

"I, Isaiah, could access any source, and the Temple wanted to know everything possible about Sirian records. So, I tapped into my past-life records as Ichor and informed the Temple about the codes of Khem. I got Sirian data by reading a cubicle room with yellow sandstone square walls, square ceiling and floor under the Sphinx. I accessed this room in 700 B.C.; and soon this access is going to open again for the whole world. This time, a new level of integrity is available if you will examine what has gone before. That is all that is required. Those of you who hold these access codes are going to feel your brains synchronizing for this. The adepts of the Temple of Solomon were actually able to get into the room under the Sphinx with their minds, and so, of course, they can do it again, but only if they let go of their deep hatred of the pharaohs.

"The room under the Sphinx is the repository of all the records of Egyptian multidimensional access. It contains all the tools and techniques. There are no things, no objects, simply knowledge in this empty space. I was very disturbed that our Temple could read this knowledge, since this record bank belonged to the Egyptian people. This was meant to be a knowledge source, a generator, a field, for the people of the Nile. This was not meant for Canaanite minds, because the Egyptian mind is Sirian, and the Canaanite mind is Nibiruan.

"To really comprehend any information, you must first know how the mind of the channel works. In my times, I was involved in life and politics, as well as in the Temple of Solomon. In spite of what went on in my life, deep inside I had a soul that operated in pure integrity. I had objections to what was going on in my world, then sometimes I felt comfortable with what was transpiring. I felt saddened that my people, the Hibiru, didn't use their own sources of knowledge during the Eighteenth Dynasty, and I felt sad that my people were using Egyptian sources in my time. 'Why are my people seeking to steal the knowledge of other lands instead of remembering their own?' This is the central question of human existence—the riddle of the Sphinx. *Egypt exists just to keep humanity asking questions, and my people exist only to find a home.*

"I was trained to visualize the room under the Sphinx and glean information from it. I am a Hebrew prophet of the Temple of Solomon, I was bar mitzvahed, I am a keeper of the Torah, and I wander in the desert seeking Yahweh. All of that I am proud of, but my work with the room under the Sphinx makes me feel so guilty that my pain reverberates through time, because I never found my source of knowledge. All my life I wondered, why do we have to steal from the Egyptians? Why don't we access the power of the land of Israel where we wanted to be given home. As you know from the story of Isaiah told by my vehicle in *Signet of Atlantis*,[5] I studied with the indigenous Canaanites. They taught me about their sacred sites and their guides—Pleiadians—but this knowledge was barred from the Temple. These people are still waiting to gift their exquisite hearts into the Temple. Oh, I cry in pain through time for soon this pain will overwhelm all people of Earth.

"Perhaps it is just me? Maybe it is only my heart that is split because my higher self was not integrated with my personality self since I was being used by the Temple? Am I the only one? I am alive on this planet, and I am a channel of extraterrestrials. Everyone has a noble self, but we were dealing with Egyptians who couldn't figure us out. They were unsophisticated, and they walked around claiming they are integrated—not split in their hearts. As I stay with my pain, my higher self is saying that I never heard what the Egyptians said to me because I was two-hearted.

"I channeled the Orion beings to find out how to destroy the Egyptians, and all I knew about Egypt was that it was the place we could always go to by heading southwest when we needed help. Egypt is where the people are always loaded with goods shining in the Sun. I was not conscious of these agendas because I was not aware of my higher self. I could not imagine it, since Yahweh was spirit and I was not spirit. Would you be able to imagine an idea like soul if nobody had ever suggested such a potentiality?

"Integration of the higher self was counter to my background. As Isaiah, Hebrew prophet, I was one of the 'Suffering Servants of Israel.' To stop suffering, I'd have to throw off all the layers and conditioning and leave the Temple. I wonder if the ancient Egyptians had a higher self, or was the spirit in crocodiles? The Orion beings were communicating through the nine dimensional axis of Khem to the Egyptians. To examine a particular issue, the Egyptians were using whatever planetary lens was appropriate for a given question, such as Mars about war or Venus for romance. They were a Sirian race of very high intentional brilliance, and they understood it was of divine order, a great gift from the cosmos, to utilize this nine-dimensional technology. It only worked positively if they were clear about their intentions. This knowledge could never be used to acquire something. They knew how to manifest any reality; they literally could *get* anything, but this technology could only be used if they never influenced the reality of anyone else. They knew how to *get* but never *take*. The Egyptians were as acquisitive as everybody else. They had no problem going for anything they wanted, but they knew they did not have the right to interfere in someone else's reality. They knew that anything they took from someone, whether covert or out in the open, would cause an energy suck on the Blue Nile. Conversely, they knew that everything they got through manifestation had to be shared with anyone who came into their home.

"We did not comprehend this ethos, and the Egyptians didn't know anyone looked at the world differently. They couldn't imagine that anyone would *take* in order to *get*. As we were stealing their information, they thought they were sharing with us! Unless people know how to manipulate others, they are unable to realize that someone is manipulating them. And when we stole from them, we didn't really know what we were getting, but it was obvious they would give us anything we wanted. Now it's time to understand this, because we blamed them for what came out of our robbery of them.

"Remember, when planets are used for 4D divination, then the canopy over 4D accesses 5D through 9D. (See Fig. 10.) The Egyptians used all the planets and the Moon to activate that canopy, while the Hibiru decided to just utilize Nibiru for activating it. Now remember, when the Egyptians did it, if they thought Venus was the appropriate planet, then they assumed that they had the right to consult with the Venusians for their expertise. When doing manifestation work with Venusians, they always gifted them—and Egyptian jewelry is exquisite due to Venusian influence. There was reciprocity and this was enjoyable. The Egyptians also had many esoteric technologies that they had garnered from many other sources. Being a hybrid human/Sirian race, they had access to many stellar sources. The Hibiru did not, they wanted to steal the technologies, and so they did. Here's what happened. . .

*I, Isaiah, can report that we activated the 4D canopy in the Temple of Solomon, and then the Anunnaki simply carried out our wishes. The Temple of Solomon was the locus for the Anunnaki to operate through the Hebrew people. Yahweh was not in control of Earth, but the Hebrews assumed covenantal powers. The Anunnaki were willing to impulse people to carry out Hebrew plans in exchange for the establishment and maintenance of the Temple of Solomon.*

"What I, Isaiah, have just said is disgustingly blasphemous, but the psychology of it is very obvious to any one who is an American. The United States has done the same thing by selecting Mars for its god and trying to be the dominant Superpower. Since the stated agenda of the Anunnaki has always been to take over the world—New World Order— then by using them to get something, you become them. As for the United States, by using war to get things, the United States has become Mars— violent. *The United States of America used to be the breadbasket of the world and now it is the weapons manufacturer of the planet.*[6] These things will continue until they are seen and renounced by all of you. As we were swallowed by one point of view—monotheism—so were you and your nation will fall as mine did. Remember, I lived when the Temple was destroyed, and this split my heart.

"Yahweh was simply the perfect diversion, the perfect coverup, and then he became an eternal smokescreen. I was not happy being a channel for the agenda of the Temple of Solomon. I was a cipher. I did not do what I wanted to do, and I was in pain because I knew my people could have been more evolved than this. I was not proud of my role, but my personal coding system was intermeshed with the temple system once I got initiated. My body was like a computer chip stuck inside a computer, and if I moved, I would bend the prongs and eons of knowledge would be blown out of the Temple or my brain wouldn't work anymore. I was a cipher who transmitted Orion information, otherwise I'd get pulled out of the computer and my brain would be blown, as if by an aneurysm. Because I was initiated into a secret society, I did not make any of my own choices.

"There was no meaning in anything, and all I knew was control over my creativity. That control over me was transmitted through the Book of Isaiah, which you think has great meaning. Watch it: *'mean*-ing' means control, and my book, as well as most of the Bible, creates a direct conduit for Yahweh into your mind. On Nibiru, Yahweh is just a minor clerk in a back office. We were told to be in the Temple for meaning, and it became incomprehensible to just be without a reason. I was a man who found no meaning in anything during the 60 years I channeled in the Temple of Solomon. There is only experience and creativity, no real meaning. That's the point of 3D! Don't try to make 3D into something it isn't. *It is a place where realities can intersect through lenses.* Meaning is *mean* because it forces one point of view, and eventually wars happen between the points of view. In the Book of Isaiah, every word is the exact reversal of what you think it is. Creativity and beauty could come back into my book if you'd only listen to the sounds in it. I, Isaiah, am ready to sign off for now. I have spoken to you, my people."

# 7

# ALCYONE LIBRARY AND TZOLK'IN—KEEPER OF TIME

I, SATYA, HAVE NOW MOVED INTO REALMS BEYOND MY OWN FIFTH-DIMEN-sional world. I know you are all ready for nine-dimensional perceptual freedom as Earth precesses into the Age of Aquarius, because I am vibrating with your passion and curiosity. Your openings are all timed by the Mayan Calendar; the program is right on schedule, yet even I want to know how you will do this in less than twenty years. As I have lived with you, often I have thought you have so much creative energy that you cannot possibly ever utilize it all. *You've become violent because you do not channel your creativity.* That is really what we Pleiadians think about you after being with you for 26,000 years. As we have often said, we have come from your future to help you move beyond the present impasse, and the Maya created the Great Calendar as the perfect device for learning to create the present moment from the future. Now as an Alcyone astrologer, I say that *it is time for the Mayan Calendar to come forth to impulse mass consciousness.* Learning how to create from the future is the way to make the critical leap, learning how to become intentional humans. That is how you can consciously channel your storehouse of creativity and stop the violence.

The Maya created the Mayan Great Calendar—called the *Tzolk'in*—to show you how to create a future intention, so you could decide what you want and work for these desires in the present time. People, let me tell you how sacred this gift is: The Maya gave this Calendar to our star system, the Pleiades, 104,000 years ago, and our ancient journey with the Calendar made us who we are today. Therefore, I have come from your future to help you comprehend what you have been offered.

Many very respectable intellectuals are fascinated by the implications of the Mayan Calendar. It is a brilliant device that describes a process of time that approaches a completion point: the end of time. But this has nothing to do with the end of the world. Now that you have a sense of six dimensions, think of the exquisite geometry of the sixth dimension; then think of the Mayan Calendar as a 6D morphic time field that is precipitating in its basic elements according to a known time unfoldment, just like a pregnancy. During a pregnancy, a fetus of unknown characteristics is being carried, which could abort. In most cases, the original form created by the sperm quickening the ovum becomes a human being. The Mayan Calendar is a conception that is modeling history, and the growing group of people who see that it describes the future is causing its field to influence the whole planet. What is supposed to occur at its ending is something about which we can only speculate. We Pleiadians are here now asking you: Are you ready to imagine your future? If you are, we are here with the Maya and Sirians to play with you and prepare you for the Cosmic Party.

Certain physicists and mathematicians are considering the possibility that emerging dynamics operating on the planet are being triggered by the end of time. The Mayan Calendar is discussed by ethno-pharmacologist Terence McKenna, biochemist Rupert Sheldrake, and chaos mathematician Ralph Abraham in *Trialogues at the Edge of the West.*[1] In it, Abraham describes "chaotic attractors" as advanced forms of order that influence less organized states, and that pull these states to an end point. McKenna notes that reality is becoming increasingly complex, and speculates that a singularity or culmination exists at the end of this process. Sheldrake, who first popularized the idea of morphogenetic fields, outlines the echoes of light in the fields of all things as signs of a common attractor for the entire cosmic evolutionary process.[2] McKenna works with a fractal wave rooted in the I Ching, and the wave's terminus is December 22, 2012, one day after the end of the Mayan Calendar.[3] All three scientists have devised some potential models for how an end of time could be pulling realities toward itself; and many very intelligent people in different fields are considering the possibility that the Maya actually were able thousands of years ago to delineate a point in the future. August 16 to 17, 1987, a key shift point in the Calendar, was featured by Tony Shearer in 1971[4] and by José Argüelles in 1987.[5] This key point triggered massive planetary celebrations, which José Argüelles named Harmonic Convergence; we Pleiadians prefer "Harmonic Emergence," but we also like the idea of a convergence of nine dimensions. As we've discussed at length, something actually shifted then, and the awareness of that shift is what matters. Argüelles said that Armageddon—the final apocalypse awaited by fundamentalists—would be short-circuited by the Convergence, and its script would unravel from August 1987 through July 1992.[6] To honor that brilliant insight, our vehicle wrote *Signet of Atlantis: War in Heaven Bypass* in 1990, because a "War in Heaven" is simply a religious idea that could set off a war on Earth.[7]

Remember back to Harmonic Convergence. During the event, very few people understood what it was. Our vehicle perceived that a shift in the field of Earth actually was predicted in the Mayan and Aztec calendars. She became certain that it was possible to identify key turning points, describe their basic qualities in advance, and create events around these times to shape the potential creative forms of the participants. This would appear to be merely "Shamanism 101" but Harmonic Convergence had exactly the right planetary and astral configurations for a global con-sciousness acceleration. *How could the Mayas know that thousands of years ago?* Please refer to Appendix A for the planetary configurations 1987 to 2012 and Appendix C for the timing of astral precipitation of this new field from 1994 to 2012. The Convergence event triggered gatherings of hundreds and thousands at major sacred sites all over the planet.[8]

Our vehicle was at Teotihuacan, north of Mexico City, where more than 100,000 people on the Pyramid of the Sun watched the Sun rise on August 17, 1987. Later, whenever she was teaching, she began to watch people to see if they actually were shifting. By 1988, she could see that more people were realizing something had changed; and from 1989 through 1992 she saw that a shift *had* occurred. It was as if people had walked into another world and were looking around with new eyes. *As a result of experiences with Harmonic Convergence, many people are realizing that the Mayan Calendar actually does predict consciousness acceleration.* This is the "news" that's not on the networks ("working the Net").

You are moving toward a described point in the future, which many of you are beginning to consciously craft now, and the Calendar is like an etheric aerobics class that gets you to focus on the quality of your ideal body and work toward this ideal day-by-day. We Pleiadians are getting increasingly excited as we watch you unfold according to the Maya timing cycle, since *we* have already experienced this exquisite apotheosis of love. We look through your eyes into your new world as if through a periscope, and your movie is getting rave reviews. These days, if you ever doubt that a great activation is going on, go to Teotihuacan at spring equinox. In 1995, more than one million people were there praying for the coming Age of Light![9]

For 26,000 years, you have been evolving into self-reflective humanity, and now you are in the early stages of crafting an intentional human based on future ideals. When you state an intention, there is a tendency for you to want it to occur sooner rather than later. As you will see when Tzolk'in comes forth, the genius of the Mayan Great Calendar is its length—26,000 years—*because that is the length of time it takes for a critical leap in human evolution.* The precession through twelve astrological ages is required for full expression of all facets of Gaian potential within the galactic evolutionary plan.[10] But in 3D, when you are aware that an orderly process is occurring, you have a tendency to want to hurry to manifest the result. Others, who want to be involved in what is being created, get drawn in. Excitement about its potentiality builds, many more want to get involved, and we Pleiadians can see that a Maya wave is building. For example, the Mayan Calendar is the ideal device to get men to become intuitive. Women all know that a pregnancy takes ten moons and they do not try to change its unfoldment in time, but men try to manipulate time— and pregnancy! In order for time to finally end, you must maximize its inherent potential before you let it go—that is, you must just flow with time and then it will become a wave, as pregnancy and birthing is for women.

I, Satya, would like to consult with some very advanced beings before we consult with Tzolk'in, the Calendar itself. The mind of Tzolk'in is so sacred that it is only accessed by the Maya Galactic Meditation. Our vehicle discovered this technique links your perceptual faculties through the seventh through ninth dimensions.[11] As with any great shamanic journey, I must clear records out of you. Your bodies must be very clear and vibrating at a high frequency to access new tools for accessing new states of consciousness. Occasionally you will find me sweeping cobwebs from the Age of Pisces out of your brains.

First we will tune into the mind of your Sun. Then we will move from the center of your Sun into Alcyone, our central Sun. Via the 7D Photon Bands, we can meet with intelligences of the 8D Galactic Federation. Then finally via our own Photon Band, we can access the 9D Galactic Center where we will meet with Tzolk'in, the Keeper of Time of the Milky Way Galaxy. You can meditate this way simply by going into the Sun, then into Alcyone, and then into the Galactic Center, the home of many ninth-dimensional intelligences.

## Reading the Mind of the Sun

"I am the mind of the Sun, and we are a centralized consciousness. Our libraries are open to you if you project the feeling of where you are by coming from your heart. Think of your awareness as an intelligence coming to us; then identify your own unique source, and you may read my records. Do this by going into a meditative state with a strong sense of your own location and all its codes whenever you contact the central records of the Sun. For example, if you are sitting next to an exquisite forest stream watching my light filtering through the canopies of ancient cedars, send me your awareness with all the beauty of this forest in your heart. Can you imagine what it takes for me to send my light into your old-growth forests? As you do this, be intensely aware of what you truly want. The greater your sense of true self when you contact me, the greater your access to my records. If you approach me from your heart, I can answer anything about your own stellar source, and you will never be lonely again. *If you are lonely, it is because you've forgotten your stellar home.* I am your star, your first bridge to other stars, and I am the way for the vehicle to read the records of Alcyone.

"Species exist only if you humans love them, and the Sirians hold bioregional fields of Earth so that these species can Make Home. As you know, something is amiss in this linkage, and so I will tell you what is wrong. For a long time, Nibiru has distorted the flow of consciousness between Sirius and myself. Remember, I am your Sun, source of all your life. Normally I can easily resonate with my twin star, Sirius, at 13 levels of consciousness, but Nibiru has been disturbing my ability to resonate with Sirius on all levels. *You* are the consciousness that links my solar mind with Sirius in your habitat, and your extreme fear of Nibiruan interference disturbs these communications. You've been imprinted with Nibiruan obsession with scarcity, and you believe that all species will be eliminated. This is a foregone conclusion in your minds, and so you don't act to save them. Yet all of this is just thought! You've stopped allowing yourselves strong feelings about animals because their extinction hurts too much. Your hopelessness about saving your species reduces your ability to participate in the great web of life that puts you in resonance with Sirius and your Sun! I need you to link me with my twin in your mind. For example, the Dogon and their ancestors were so in tune with my solar mind linked with Sirian genius that they filled the plain of Africa with a panoply of outrageous animals. Just where did you really think they all came from with all their spots, manes, horns, and tusks?

"I am emanating great consciousness and energy at this time directly into your hearts in order to help you overcome your confusion. *The time has come for you to activate Gaia according to the Mayan Calendar.* This is why the World Management Team is trying to trick you into fearing me, the Sun. You are supposed to fear my rays on your skin, and you are supposed to shun my guidance. It is a fact that astrologers are in tune with my intelligence and my expression through the planets. Let me show you how this functions. I will use Mercury as an example—a planet that most of you understand easily because it rules your minds, while Earth rules your bodies.

"Like Earth, Mercury has a 3D awareness, and you actually experience it all the time. Mercury is the regulator of ideas—a computer bank of potentiality. It is pure intelligence—thought itself—the essential mechanism for figuring out how thought creates reality. The 3D awareness of Mercury is as material as your bodies are, and now that you have computers, you already know this. You now face the danger of throwing out animals for computers without remembering that both are needed. How will Mercury hold in its hard drive the *idea* of an animal if that animal no longer exists on Earth? If you love an animal enough to protect its habitat on Earth, it can be replicated out of this hard drive. Ideas are eternal in Mercury if their form exists on Earth. Shamans occasionally manifest owls, eagles, or white buffalo calves to help you see this. If you protect habitat, they all will come back—if they are not forgotten. This is why I want you to come into my mind through your heart as you sit in primordial, old-growth forests, which are solar libraries.

"The intelligence of each planetary body is affected by the status of all others. On Earth, your understanding of mentality is extremely deficient and incorrect at this time, and so you limit my solar creativity. The limited usage of Mercurial intelligence on Earth short-circuits me. I am very fond of Mercury; for me, I like Mercury the same way you like your car. Imagine life without your car! Furthermore, if you leave your car in the garage all winter, it won't start. If you did not have this mental vehicle expressing my light, all of your ideas would get stuck in me. I am a body of consciousness held together by my sense of self. My solar sense of self emanates to the planets, and they take my light and express my qualities in time.

"Mercury expresses mentality while Earth evolves life. What you value most is mind and body, so you'd better listen when I say how limited your minds are. Biological forms require an integral sense of self—*idea of form*—to possess intelligence and will to survive. As has already been noted, the morphogenetic fields of species *exist* on Venus and awareness of their status is in Mercury. If Earth's biological lifeforms do not have sufficient mercurial powers, then they will not survive. For example, I shine every day and the strength of my heat is relative to the seasons; then Mercury cues animal behavior based on my light. That is how a bird knows where to nest, or the apple tree when to blossom. If you pollute the air and change my light, the bird forgets to nest, and there will be no apples. You use only 10 to 15 percent of your brains, driven by my Mercury power, because you are mind-controlled. Then you stupidly destroy animal and plant habitat, the animals have the use of less of their brains, and instinct is wiped out. Imagine if you only had 10 to 15 percent of my solar light! Gaia is biological, and she expresses herself through many species. You need my energy for this; all planets draw my light to themselves by sound harmonics, and Mercury calibrates the sound codes of all the planets. Sound is the communication tool of planetary intelligence.

"You have dared to cast your mind into the solar system as a result of your daring quest for Tzolk'in and now you are edging into the Galactic Night. Insects sound the Galactic Night where my light ends, and they are your teachers about traveling in darkness, the portal beyond the sixth dimension. Insects open the Galactic Night for you. Their sound is diminished by light, and they are silent during the day. As darkness comes to assist you in achieving your most subtle perceptual states, their sound intensifies. They are lovers of the stars who cry out in the darkness, and they hold the keys to your most advanced metamorphic processes.

"I, Sun, am not happy about these attitudes and behaviors. After all, I shine for all creation. I do not understand the destruction of fields that resonate with me. You even destroy your human habitat! You build highways and cities, and then you destroy them, just as you once destroyed empires such as Rome. Many of you glorify the destruction of Rome or of Sodom and Gomorrah, yet *my* solar powers gave the Romans and Babylonians strength to cut all those stones, raise them, and dress all the buildings and temples with them. How dare you applaud the physical destruction of anything created from my energy! Earth's indigenous keepers have always had a profound degree of communication with me, and they do not build things they do not use. If they don't want something anymore, they give it away rather than throw it out. They greet me when I rise and observe me when I set because when I am just above the horizon, it is safe to stare into my fire and read my mind.

"I shine on the surfaces of the planets and get information from them, which you can access. Lately, my communication link with Jupiter has been greatly distorted due to the impacts of fragments from comet Shoemaker-Levy. When something like a comet hits one of my planets, I feel like it hits me, just as a whole family becomes disturbed when one of the children has a problem. I'd like to read this event for you, since Jupiter rules your spiritual expansion.

"The fragments of comet Shoemaker-Levy created a huge opening in the emotional bodies of all of you. The impacts are ripping open Gaia's emotional body. Earth is solid and human awareness is very dense. The gaseous nature of Jupiter opens your emotions, and the great spiritual waves in my solar system are tearing you open. The catastrophe triggered deep, emotional memories of previous disasters, and this is forcing you to remember how you felt when many of your biological species were destroyed in an afternoon. By remembering that horror, you will be able to intervene in the slower extinction that is now occurring. Even though these cometary impacts were operating at a great distance, this was an emotional event of very high vibration for humans, teaching you how much each planet affects your minds. I know this because I can feel you responding to the waves from Jupiter that are ringing me like a great resonant bell.

"Nibiru's agenda is to access more feelings, and it is being drawn back into the solar system faster than usual, attracted by the great waves of emotions in my body. My whole system has the reddish glow of passion; look at Io as it brightens like a diamond waiting for 2010.[12] Boundaries have been ripped open by the comet, and these waves are reverberating throughout the Galaxy. Even the sacred twins—Andromeda and the Milky

Way—are pulling together faster. My solar system is going through a consciousness acceleration called for by my own guide, Tzolk'in. Once this
acceleration is complete, there will be a free flow of communication from
my realm to other realms. I will be honest. I know I am moving into the
Photon Band soon, and this experience is even more intense for a star than
it is for a planet. As for you, you have been locked off and isolated from
all the other dimensions, and now all the doors are opening. If I can handle
the Photon Band, you can!

"Why would you want to explore your stellar nature by tuning into
me? Besides ending your loneliness, stellar identity allows you to transcend
the narrow perspective of linear space and time. If you tune into my intelligence, I have the ability to resonate with you simultaneously in thirteen
dimensions. As you may know, you can access nine dimensions at this time.
These are all available to you in my mind, which enables you to be free in
your world. Your star teachers went through a great deal to get you into
this realm at this time so you could begin to fathom solar consciousness.
They have great agendas for you during the Cosmic Party."

*Satya Takes You into the Alcyone Library*
It's me, Satya again, and I'd like to introduce you to the round Temple of
Gaia in the center of our Alcyone Library where we study Earth. (See Fig.
14.) Gaia's temple has a large, white, marble dome that contains a huge,
circular, golden-alabaster platform circled by a channel of water. The
alabaster platform is 100 feet in diameter and has a carved quartz-crystal
model of Earth, called "Ge," resting on a fluted pedestal in the center.
Earth is encircled by ten beautifully proportioned Ionic columns; the
inner diameter of the circle of columns is 50 feet. These columns are
topped off and connected together by a circular marble lintel. A person
can walk freely on the soft alabaster surface between the circle of columns
and the circle of water. Pleiadians who work with Ge walk this outer circle
and contemplate her through the columns. A marble bridge spans the
water channel, which is edged by the inner walls of the dome and the outside of the platform. Dolphins swim in the channel while goddesses and
their consorts walk the outside circle. The entrance from the outside of
the dome leads right to the bridge over the channel, and two large statues
of Anubis rest on portals beside the front entrance. No one is allowed in
the center where Earth is located; a multidimensional vortex records

FIGURE 13: THE ALCYONE LIBRARY

photons on Earth paired with photons in Alcyone—resonant twinning energy in action.

This the etheric temple of life, which exists eternally in the central core of Alcyone, very similar to the central core of your Sun. Central cores of stars contain ideas of many worlds. The iron-crystal core of Earth came out of Digitaria of Sirius, and Alcyone's core is this model of Earth, because the only place where biological lifeforms are created in the Milky Way Galaxy is Earth. (See Appendix D for the story of Digitaria and Earth.) To eliminate the last vestige of hierarchical thoughtforms, imagine this: Central cores of planets and stars are the densest intelligences in the universe, and they contain *all* record libraries.

We do not have polarization on Alcyone; our essence is light, and your relationship with us is the result of the identical wave resonations of photon pairs in the temple of Gaia and in Earth, no matter how far apart they are in time or space. How could this be? *Photons are pure thought, pure idea, and they reveal their existence in a realm where thought travels faster than light.* If you could see *all* the lines of light between *all* the stars, you would see my form. When I come into your realm, I create beauty by my simplest vibrations. The temple of Gaia in the Alcyone Library is like an exquisite ancient Greek temple. We Pleiadians are drawn into Earth to manifest beauty and sex. We can move into dimensions that you cannot because your realm is still polarized. You are still going back and forth, this way and that way, and this is caused by consciousnesses that had over-powered you in your own world. You need to understand more about power.

*I, Satya, want you to cease being mind-controlled so you can simply Make Home.* Power is only a tool that offers the potential for unlimited freedom by means of actions that are congruent with personal integrity. Sometimes what is in integrity is hard to see when perceptual limitation blocks individuals from multidimensional laws—laws at the eighth-dimensional level. I want to know the dimensional laws for activating power so that any human person can choose to live in an illuminated world. For this teaching, I bring forth Barbara Hand Clow because she learned these laws through her actions on Earth.

## The Nine-Dimensional Lenses of the Illuminated World

*The power lens of the first dimension is accessing the vibration of the iron crystal in the center of Earth—Ge.* Any dimensional being who resides in any one of the zones of the nine-dimensional vertical axis coming from Gaia's iron core is attuned to Ge. To stay in form, all that is required for this is attunement to the iron crystal—the Sirian star heart of Earth. You must create a four-directional altar in your home, and you must center yourself in it frequently enough to learn to feel Ge. She sends ideas to you via her vibrations, which include her whole gravitational field. When you access her, you align into her mind, because your field is Ge. You just forget about that. Her field extends all the way out to nine dimensions and into the Galactic Center. Anyone who is born on Earth can access all nine dimensions just by sitting in the center of a four-directional altar. You must return to this center long enough and often enough until you find yourself feeling Ge's power. When she first comes, she will feel like an earthquake, and you will know you are no longer a galactic virgin when this happens. Once you have attained this, she will be able to draw you into her mind whenever she wants to. You will know when to seek your altar.

*The power lens of the second dimension is conscious linkage and total openness to the elemental realm.* Many of you have been taught to fear this realm. It is true the elemental realm can get riled up if you pay it no heed, but working with it is the way to regain the knowledge of the indigenous people, the keepers of Earth habitat. The elementals need you to talk with them, pray with them, sing with them, and to bless and feed them, and I have come to Earth to teach you how to remember this sacred knowledge. After all they have chosen to commune with Ge and find ways to express her passion by means of wind, rain, fire, and earthquake. Each creation by the elemental realm is a ceremony for Ge. The elementals are the poets of Earth, and they love dances, songs, and art for these ceremonies. Listen to the elementals as they teach you that Gaia's most sacred times are equinoxes and solstices; these are the times when her powerful magnetic field is most maximized and the elementals have more powers of expression.

The nature of the surface world depends on the elementals, and they take their job very seriously as guardians of your habitat. They are more aware of the intelligence of Ge than you are, so they impulse you to create rituals to teach you what you need to know. They are more subtle, brilliant, balanced, powerful, and conscious than any beings on Earth's surface. Animals are much more intelligent than you because they take the time to truly feel the desires of the elementals. Animals can teach you about these desires, and it is wise to pray with animals to understand the wishes of Ge. They *love* ceremony, and they will always come into your circle if you call them. When you are praying, know the animal guides of that place. Altars to the sacred directions are devices that can access the guides and codes of a particular place; they will assist you if you can link with their energy. This is done via directionality. To link, the elementals love to be fed, and you must keep corn, cedar, tobacco, water, sage, mushrooms, nutmeg, salt, ant crystals, and many other gifts for them. When you first go in and talk with Ge, face each one of the directions and ask them what gift they want. They will tell you.

When you need to heal yourself or someone else, sit in your altar and have a talk with the elementals. They are the ones who can tell you how to heal anything. Their ancient DNA, which has never been tampered with, lives in the deep ocean ridges boiling at very high temperatures. Meditate on this ancient DNA, and it will restructure the DNA of the person who needs help. Ask them for messages, listen to them, follow their advice, and you will be amazed at how accurate they are. Once you have made them your allies, listen to them wherever you go. Once you befriend them, they will follow you anywhere—the way a loving and loyal dog follows you—and they will tell you what to do. They are beneath your surface, so they can reach you wherever you are on the curvature of the planet. If a terrible storm is coming, they will impulse you to go to shelter. If an animal or human threatens you and it is not your time, they will strike that threat with lightning or wind. And remember, return to your altar and feed them often, and when you are out in the world, thank them and gift them whenever you can. Never go so fast that you don't have time to respond to a rock or tree that calls you. Stop a moment and bless them.

*The power lens of the third dimension is you.* Once you have mastered your altar—linked with Ge and befriended the elementals—then it is time to understand who you are. No indigenous person was taught anything about the surface world until they had mastered the first two dimensions. For example, the elementals express themselves by means of wind, rain, fire, and earthquake, and you express yourself sexually; they are the poets of Earth and you are the powers. If you exist in 3D without linking with 1D and 2D, you abuse power and sexuality. Therefore, meet and communicate with *all* energies so they do not get frustrated if they want to talk with you.

You may feel like requesting that only positive spirits come into your circle for as long as your altar exists. In my own experience, as long as you always eliminate things that you do not have strong feelings about or you move things to a new direction when it feels right, no negative beings will come into your space. Of course, I will teach from my own tradition because that is all I know. If you have some objects that hold very complex emotions, such as a gift from a person who is making battle with you, keep those things in a covered basket, jar, medicine pouch, or box. Only bring them out to work with them when you want to work with that person. When you are having a power struggle with someone, use something from them that you love to assist you in moving the karma to the next stage; therefore, do not throw away gifts from a person who has chosen to become your enemy. If you ever have a karmic relationship with someone who is trying to influence you without your agreement, set up a mirror somewhere in your altar room that will mirror this energy back to the person. You might place it in a window facing out to a direction, or you might set it up to mirror the box or basket that contains something from this person. No person has the right to invade your space, ever, unless you agree.

Sit in the center of your altar and study all the animal keepers, power objects, photos, bones, and crystals, and place the various feeding elements you use, plus any smudging materials, in your center space. If anything feels like it is in the wrong place or needs to be put away for awhile, take care of it. Do you remember the story of each thing in there? Can you remember its hologram and how it feels? If not, remove it and give it away. Why would you have an object on your altar that embodies a great being you don't know? If something means a lot to you but feels like it's in the wrong place, rearrange things until you feel a warm and fuzzy feeling in your space. Breathe in; enjoy the pleasure of communing with all the parts of your own story. You will feel the air thicken slightly, almost as if a fog is moving in, which means the guardians are coming into your sacred space. Cast your eyes around once more and feel what each direction wants to be blessed with. You will feel it very strongly; you may have known what it was before you started, so hold that essence in your left hand.

Hold the essence, close your eyes, and feel the boundaries of the space around yourself. You will feel a bubble or egg around you that defines the zone of your body, which may extend out miles. Just make sure you can feel its edges. If this egg seems to have any holes in it, push energy from inside your heart and thymus into the inside of it and close in the holes. When your etheric egg feels whole, you will feel a sweet peaceful feeling in your body. Never go out into the world with your bubble much more than a few feet out from your body, and always visualize amethyst light in its outer surface. Your altar is the only place where you can allow your bubble to go out as far as it wants. Then, take pinches or parts of your blessing substance and feed the four directions and pray to them. Call in the animals to be with you, because soon you are going to experience the gift of the third dimension: freedom. In this altar you are free, and in a little while, you will fly.

Once you've worked with the first three dimensions and set up your own world, then have a conference with the 2D elementals and 4D archetypal beings who've come to share with you. Maybe they will want to talk with you, channel through you, have you sing or drum with them, or smoke your pipe with them (if you are a pipe carrier). Once you feel them and sense linkage, light some sage, smudge, or incense—depending upon what you feel they want—and move deep inside yourself as the smoke fills the air. The smoke makes them solid. They are in your dimension now. . . If you have some very strong feelings when they come, take plenty of time to breathe, to process, or to cry. If you feel nervous or afraid, breathe and hold your hands raised at chest level in front of your body, and imagine holding these beings as if they are part of you. Run all these feelings through your body.

Pray with the teachers who have come; thank them for coming. Smoke your pipe with them; use hand movements to feel them in the air; make music with them. Work with them until you can feel them in your body. Remember, you have great boundaries, and I am not suggesting they will invade you, because *you are sovereign in this circle.* When you link with them, you will be able to actually feel them. This is their gift to you for welcoming them: you get to find out what is really going on in your body, and there may be something you really need to know. As you get used to them, *remember that they are nonphysical at all times, and they are actually the inner story of yourself.* Tune into your body and feel the places where they are located by noticing a twinge, a cramp, a heaviness, a tingling. When you feel them, close your eyes and journey into those places, and be with that energy and receive its teaching. Be sure to have a journal in your altar room because you may want to write things down. Listen to them. If they want to hear Tibetan bells or bowls or a drum, play these sacred teachers. The archetypal world is greatly activated by sound, and they especially love rattles, clicking shells, and rasping sounds. Let them tell their story, have a good time.

*The power lens of the fourth dimension is your feelings.* After you've worked with the archetypal teachers you have welcomed into your space, you will find yourself feeling some very deep emotions. These responses are coming from guides that can take you to upper dimensional levels. Their appearance is very subtle, and they will not come until you've worked with the archetypal beings who first came into your space. The archetypal beings who come first are parts of yourself you need to clear, and once you've done this, new creativity can manifest. As these "soft" spirits arrive, you need to have a sense of them, what their story is, maybe the sounds they like, or which object on your altar called them in. If you just go with them for awhile by doing things in your circle, a real feeling for them will come in. The most important trick is to follow your impulses—maybe by lighting a candle, touching your third eye with water, stroking a totemic object, or chanting.

The more you do this kind of ceremony, the more you will encounter the same ones, and you will get to know them, such as I have gotten to know the Pleiadians. You won't want to miss meditating very often! You will become fascinated with them as they begin to show you the world through their eyes. You will feel a subtle approach, almost as if there really is someone with you. You may or may not see anything; it doesn't matter— in some way you will know. You might feel a shiver in your back or neck. Close your eyes, visualize Ge, feel the elementals below you, feel your own body in the center, feel the energy above you like a canopy, then straighten your spine, hold up your head, take a deep breath, and visualize all the light coming to the canopy above you in millions of waves.

*The power lens of the fifth dimension is love.* Make yourself very relaxed and comfortable, quiet down, close your eyes, and take three breaths, holding on the inhale and exhale to the count of five with your fingers. When you breathe in, while holding the breath, expand your lungs in the lower and upper part of your body; when you breathe out, collapse your lungs as much as possible and hold the position. Sit and feel the love from the Pleiades expanding your body and enveloping the room. Now, begin your blessings; think of all the people who've been wonderful with you that day, of your children, your mate, your friends, your parents. Think of a great gift somebody just gave you, or the good food you've recently eaten. Realize how blessed you are, and keep on expanding. Then think of people you want to assist or heal.

The Pleiadians really want to assist you with healings because this is their expertise. Great crises are coming in 3D, yet you will have no difficulty if you learn to heal. Here's how you can heal working with the Pleiadians, if you want to. First, describe very clearly and completely the issue that needs healing so you know exactly what you think about it. Then once you've stated your case, ask the Pleiadians whether you are supposed to assist this person or not. If they say no, don't do it. I'm not kidding!

Agree that you will not worry about that person, except to offer basic kindness and politeness. If the Pleiadians say you can assist, that means they know a healing is within cosmic law. If you just use your will to help people without praying, such as consulting with the Pleiadians, you might manipulate the reality of someone who has already finished his or her own work, and you could force this person to keep on repeating. Or, by acting when you aren't called to, you may shut out another person who is really the one to heal. Do not clutch and hold people to yourself, as if you know who should live or die. Work with yourself every day so your attitude about your life or anybody's life is like weighing it against a feather. *Living or dying is not the point; healing, love, and happiness are.*

If the Pleiadians agree to work with you, work out a deal with them about what you can and can't do, then give yourself unabashedly to that work until it is complete. I warn you, you might have to give much more of yourself than you can even imagine, but the experience will always be ecstatic. Some of you just need to get exhausted before you feel ecstasy! Learn everything you can about each healing while you do it, then dedicate yourself to sharing that valuable information with anyone you can. Feel the love of the Pleiadians, offer them a gift—such as a moment of love in your heart for the children of the world—or open yourself to hearing if the Pleiadians actually want you to do something. Then let them rest. Think of all the love in your world, and remember the Pleiadians can't amplify any feelings unless they come through your body.

*The power lens of the sixth dimension is sacred geometry.* Sit quietly in your space and reflect quietly on what has been going on. Your altar is a sixth-dimensional construct because you placed everything with deep feelings according to the four directions. All you have to do is just activate it! An element, a thought, a vision will suddenly occur; just notice it and sit quietly. Feast your eyes on the objects around yourself and notice if anything draws you. Often a cat will come in, even your own real cat. Once something draws you, pick it up and begin to study it. Hold and turn it in the light in different ways; feel the field around it, which you may begin to see. As you sense these subtle fields, just gaze at it to visualize the light lines moving off the surfaces and angles of the object. Hold it in your palm, look at it, and feel the lines coming into it. Travel out on a line to the mind of the being that conceived it. Remember, you know the story of everything that is in this room. You may travel out to its original maker, to the tribe that first told its story, to the person who gave it to you, or to the place underground where the stone came from. Everything that ever touched this thing or knew it is still connected to it. Soon you will know why you were drawn to that particular thing. As this forms in your mind, put it gently in front of your body and close your eyes.

*The power lens of the seventh dimension is light.* Take your hands and place them on your eyes with your palms on your cheeks and your arms resting comfortably down. Press your fingers into your eye sockets until your fingers shut out all the light coming in, keeping fingers together. Do not press into your eyes. All you are doing is shutting out the light, not attempting to put pressure on your eyeballs. Be comfortable; sit like that until a blue-black space begins to envelope you that seems to be the dark space in your own body. Move above your body; above Earth; outside Earth's atmosphere; out away from the Sun toward the edge of the solar system. When you are outside Pluto and Neptune, see your solar system as a ball with the Sun in the center. Imagine a line from the center of the Sun all the way out to Alcyone, and travel to Alcyone in deep space. It is incredibly dark, and then you become aware of a huge light ahead, as if it is a nuclear ("nu-clear"), pulsating, living light. Move right into it.

Once you've moved into Alcyone, you become aware of a tremendous highway of light that goes into the Galactic Center and out beyond Alcyone in the opposite direction to Orion, where the meeting of the Galactic Federation is occurring. You can also go to Orion when you want to work on power issues. Or, if you have no power issues during a meditation time, and you feel balanced and content, thank yourself for being comfortable with your power, take a few breaths, reflect a moment longer, and begin to commune with the ninth dimension. Move into the center of the Galaxy via the Photon Band, bypassing the next power lens.

*The power lens of the eighth dimension is power.* Every time you are in a conflict you can't resolve—any kind of squabble, tension, relationship hassle that is draining you—come to your circle and meet with us. Sit in your center with a sense of yourself, and call that person or issue into the circle, and have a conference. Ask them to tell you how they feel first. Once you get that person's side, look at it from their point of view as much as possible. Get to know as much about them as possible. Talk to them about how you *both* might improve things. Tell the person that if they will work with you, you will keep working with them. Never, never use any energy to influence what someone else is thinking or doing. The only right you have is for a conference to discuss mutual issues with them.

Go back into your life and take some actions with that person, based on your conference. If the energy will not shift in 3D and the person is stealing your peace because he or she will not work with you, then go forward and live your life as if the person does not exist. Feel free to admit to yourself in private that you would still love to have their friendship, but you accept that is not to be. Put any objects from them into darkness and forget them. Do not think of them again in this space. If you want to, however, an object can always be brought out to seek more understanding. *Once someone has given you a gift, they have given you a part of themselves, and unless they ask for it back, you can always commune with them if you want to.* If someone asks for an object back, always give it back to them, because no one can invade you if you are not holding anything of theirs that they request. If you feel somebody has something of yours and they are trying to control you, ask for it back. Even if they do not give your gift back to you, they cannot reach you anymore. The Native American tendency to be very careful about gifts is where the phrase "Indian Giver" comes from.

*There is no reason for any person to influence you in any unchosen way if you follow the 8D gifting laws.* Be meticulous about these boundaries. Even if your enemy is your boss, you can be invisible and create no energy with that person; if you can't do that, leave the job. The same goes for marriage. There is absolutely no reason in the world to have a power struggle with anyone in your reality for any great length of time. Whenever you feel tension or energy being taken from you, don't allow that suck. Enemies appear for you so you can finally decide to take your own power. If you do take your own power, your enemy will be freed to fly to the eighth dimension, where they can sit in counsel all day ruling the world. Their reality will get bigger and bigger, and you will be flying around free.

Once you remember what it's like to be in 3D with intact boundaries, you can do this meditation in a cot crammed into a prison cell with four other inmates. You can do this meditation on your job sitting at your desk. You can do it when your small children are running around. How is that possible? Because this meditation requires only your body, your body's boundaries, and knowing where North, South, East, and West are located. All of you should learn this level of concentration by creating something special with your favorite objects and learning these techniques first in comfort and silence. All children should have an inviolate private space somewhere in their own house so they can learn how to create boundaries.

*The power lens of the ninth dimension is the return to stellar self.* The Maya will take charge next, and they will show how the end of the Mayan Calendar is the return to the Age of Light. *At the end of the Mayan Calendar all other dimensional intelligences who have ever interacted with you in any space in the universe are getting sucked back into Earth to unify their consciousness with yours.* This is a real vortex of a time that contains all things. The 2D elementals and the energies at the 4D level do not have bodies, so they use yours; the Pleiadians do not have your polarized feelings, so they send you love to transmute hate; the Sirians do not have your minds, so they are blasting you with light geometry to get you to become a Seer. Meanwhile, the 7D galactic information highways are transmuting Earth's identity; 8D conferences are being held to create a new order in your solar system; and 9D spiritual teachers are impulsing you into ecstasy when they can link with you.

## Photons as Popcorn Popping in the Pleiades and Gaia

I, Satya, know it is time to comprehend Tzolk'in, which will be like looking through your own visual cortex with a mirror. This is how it looks from the 5D level, in case another perspective will shed some light: I see photons forming in your realm, and that is how I read you. As photon pairs form, the antiparticle is absorbed by a particle, and they become light. But what happens to the light? The light becomes 5D information, and the information coming out of your realm is astonishing! We Pleiadians are finding out about all the other cosmic intelligences through you! *You are the theater!*

If you could see your own dimension as I do, you'd be amazed by how it is becoming thick with photons that look like popcorn popping in 3D, and the popped corns are human lives that we are reading. Your karmic purification is speeding up as the positrons that you hold in your bodies release and collide with their corresponding electron twins. These twins are being attracted to you from all over the Galaxy—the multidimensional purge and merge. Now the process is considerably developed, and we can see these electrons digging into your physical body miasms, your biological record banks of primal pain. *Never has it been more important for you to realize that thought regulates the condition of your bodies.* As I look down into the dimensions below us, it is like looking through the eye of a dragonfly or the eye of a bee. I see vibrating holograms from a million refracted lenses, and in the Temple of Gaia we are feeling the extreme energy of your holographic fields—fields of information that are split into infinitesimal lenses or myriad duplicate forms repeating themselves throughout the cosmos.

As I see a pair of photons form, they then begin moving apart in resonant waves, and I contain each of the pair in my mind. Eventually, the consciousness resonates into its star twin; I can recognize its galactic codes, and then I know what consciousness actually exists in Gaia. That is how I can "read" you. Our Pleiadian mentality can handle all this information because our neural connections are comprised of nonmaterial fiber optics —ectoplasmic resonances with some neuroelectric charge. Fiber optics makes it possible for you to comprehend unlimited thought, such as ours.

I would like you to remember what makes your biology so adaptively infinite—*LOVE.* We will not lose one of your thoughts, and you will not lose one of your species, if you just see that there is no limitation. *Stop misusing the material world!* As you are first moving into the Photon Band, data can overwhelm you when the godzillions of lost pairs of yourselves are reaccessed. The arrival of the Photon Band feels like a family reunion with too many relatives.

As you wake up and remember these dormant parts of yourself, we of Alcyone simultaneously access your records and this will continue throughout the activation to 2013. *The purpose of the data is unitization of your planetary and stellar selves.* Already, we have triggered within you the impulse to master the nine-dimensional form, and this new galactic structure can help you hold data. We are grateful to the Sirians for holding the structure of this form in place in the solar system through the story of the Sacred Twin.[13] The degree to which you ignite your passion and curiosity is in direct proportion to how much we can reach you. *We are having a love affair with your minds, and when you are fascinated you vibrate much faster.* We've caught your attention, and it is only by means of this passionate search that you will remain centered in tune with nine dimensions. For example, millions of you search for secret rooms to be found under the Great Pyramid. You sense that these secrets will be discovered during your own lives, yet many of you have studied esoteric literature enough to know that millions have gone down this path before and not found them. Well, now is the time, and some of you already have gotten the answer. These rooms in the Pyramid are empty because they exist to unite the lost photonic twins from all over the universe, and the Sphinx will just sit there and smile in the Sun. Everything is perceptual.

The Sirians are the guides for the consciousness of the Sun in the Galactic Night. If we dare ask to consult Tzolk'in, we need to determine the field of darkness that defines the light of the Sun and time, just like you need to know the boundaries of your auric bubble before you travel on the vertical axis. Anubis is the only guide available right now to lead you through the darkness of deep space as dog/guardian of the Galactic Night. I have said little about Tezcatzlipoca, even though he is the guardian of the Galactic Night in the Aztec/Maya system. Tezcatzlipoca protects the indigenous Maya in the caves of Toniná, and when the guardians of Toniná and Palenque are ready, even Tezcatzlipoca will release his grip on the Maya people of Mexico. You cannot imagine what grand beings Anubis and Tezcatzlipoca are . . . They hold light in form.

We Pleiadians of Alcyone are partners with the Sirians. We hold your solar system in form while you are in the Photon Band, and the Sirians hold it in form while you are in the Galactic Night. They take you on the long journey, and when you come back into our range, they let you go willingly. They are great librarians, and they also work with the Temple of Gaia in our core. Their dolphins swim in our channels as our goddesses, and their consorts meditate as they walk around Ge. Pleiadians and Sirians both work with the temples in Egypt. The Sirians hold all the records and secret knowledge of everything that has occurred since 8800 B.C., and as the Sirians release this knowledge, the Pleiadians work with you to open your hearts and learn to heal in the expanded field. As a result of the Alliance in 1994, more of the data bank is being opened, and we must examine issues that need healing coming out of these openings. Thus, Tzolk'in shouts, "*Conquistadores!*" Release these records! Grasp this knowledge now! We Pleiadians ask Anubis only one more time: *Why is it that the followers of Christ came into Mayaland and killed us in his name?*

## Anubis Tells the Real Story of Christ
The first voice that comes through is Dr. José Argüelles, who cries, "To speak of the end of the cycle in the morphogenetic field whose calendar is

dominated consciously or unconsciously by the presence and vision of the historical figure called Christ is to raise the specter of Armageddon—a Second Coming preceded by an awesome final conflagration that bodes extinction."[14] This voice is followed by that of Anubis.

"I, Anubis, am here to tell you exactly what is going on. Christ manifested at Zero Point in history to evolve humanity into empathy—the highest vibration of the Age of Pisces. Empathy opens humans to spiritual access, and Christ came as a model of the nine-dimensional human, which is what you will all become during the Age of Aquarius. He came out of a deep planetary lineage and brought the instrument of ultimate creativity that can transmute human violence—the Eucharist. He delivered his bloodline through the Goddess—Magdalene. He married the priestess of Isis of the central Goddess temple of Jerusalem, and through Isis, he reattached the phallus of Osiris and re-membered the male. He planted his star codes in Mary Magdalene's physical body, and unlike Horus, a spirit child, the daughter of Christ and Mary, Sa Ra, was born and has now spawned one hundred generations.[15] Christ lives in the DNA of all your bodies, making you sovereign in your world now. There will be no Second Coming and the extinction of all but the select 144,000, because the Maya absorbed your genocidal wave 500 years ago. As if you were bacteria, they processed you through their bodies, and now the Maya will not allow this emasculation. *You will see who the Christ is and not ask for another.*

"I, Anubis, want you to have the real Gospel—the Good News: Christ activated the Gaian mind in the plants, and soon the Sun will awaken Christ in your blood during this next and last phase of time. It is time for you to have the truth: The Church not only emasculated Christ, they even buried the alchemical teaching that he brought to Earth. *Christ brought Gaian alchemy to you by transmuting plants into blood; his blood flows in your veins and this is your antidote to Mind Control.* This elixir contains the Dionysian/pagan memory codes that will quicken Gaia during the Age of Aquarius. The World Management Team diverted you from this knowledge by getting you to obsess on addictions, so you've forgotten the plant power—the Sun in the grapes. Once you bought into the idea that *anything* is negative on your planet, you lost your ability to focus on how you are using things in your reality. Then you lost access to the "chirotic plants"—the most potent activators of the etheric, such as fermented plants, mushrooms, spices, and tobacco. Sacred smoke makes spirit visible in the air! Think about transubstantiation—making a substance into another substance. Christ demonstrated alchemy with his own body by taking the fermented grape and changing it into his blood. As you enter the Photon Band, the real truth of Christ must be yours. These great gifts must be acknowledged or your reality will be torn apart. What Christ did is your key to avoiding Armageddon and choosing the Age of Aquarius.

"At Zero Point, the Anunnaki, who had incarnated in human form on Earth for 3760 years, planned to take over Earth. Time would stop and begin anew with their calendar. *This was the greatest takeover attempt that Earth ever experienced.* Meanwhile, according to the Galactic Federation, Earth was to be free; therefore, Christ came and instituted the Eucharist to activate the plant realm, Gaia's habitat. This stirred up the 2D telluric realm, which in turn stirred up the blood of humans. Christ did this after he inseminated Mary, and the Eucharist in combination with his actual entry into a bloodline quickened the elementals totally. This activated you and the Earth, and now symbiosis is occurring. Seventy-two disciples watched Christ transmute the wine into his blood, and they instantly became seventy-two individuals contemplating a nine-dimensional human. Stunned as they stood before Christ—just from the vibration of the aura of Christ—*each awakened within all nine dimensions simultaneously.* They staggered and shook from kundalini rising in their bodies, and this was the Pentecost. Only a few of them had seen the light body—*ka*—of Christ when he *transfigured*, and when they looked at their arms, legs, and each other, they saw the nuclear blue-white light of their *kas*.[16] This burst of power connected out to all ancient power points, where churches would later be constructed. The transfiguration of human blood began, and after 2000 years of quickening, the collective human heart is opening. In 1972, I, Anubis, brought in Sirian light expansion and connected it into these exquisitely gardened power vortexes, and now Pleiadian vibrations are quickening your hearts.

"Well, this was not what the Romans expected as they awaited Nibiru, so their time to become the Chosen People would arrive! The only thing to do with this rebel was steal the tools! The Eucharist was swallowed hook, line, and sinker, and it became the main ritual of the Roman Catholic Church for the Age of Pisces. The Romans decided to use it as fuel for converting the world. To take control, they first wiped Mary Magdalene out of the records. Later, once they murdered the Cathars, all priests were to be celibate to make people eventually believe that Christ was celibate. This would eliminate the potential discovery of the bloodline because, even if the DNA survived, nobody would believe it was real. Wake up! *Christ is stirring in your blood!* The Romans thought they'd disempowered the Eucharist, but they didn't understand what Christ was actually doing. They thought they had totally stolen it by making it their central sacrament and then using it to manipulate and control Catholics. However, that just gave me, Anubis, and the Pleiadians the chance to use it for 5D and 6D activation all over Earth whenever a Mass occurred. What a blast!

"As a Sirian, I, Anubis, used the Mass to broadcast sacred geometry from the planetary sacred sites out to the stars; this constantly fed the telluric realm and defused the Net. The Pleiadians used it with me to heal people and open their hearts. This got so passionate and juicy by 1100 A.D. that a totally multidimensional woman named Hildegard von Bingen released alchemy to the whole medieval world. In response to all this Piscean passion, a shutdown was arranged by the Vatican, and the real serious constriction of the Net began. If you are worried about whether you are going to make it, just notice that Hildegard is now on the bestseller CD list! For those of you who have deep Catholic codes, go for it! Listen to Hildegard's "Vision" music and read her words! *You do not have to let go of anything you love.*[17]

"The transubstantiation of wine into blood over and over again created a powerful holomorphic canopy over the Chalice—the Grail—and this sucked in the crystalline codes of the higher dimensions. With this particular ceremony, which was first invented by a Sirian/pagan rabble-rouser, Dionysus, it was possible to keep all nine dimensions open for 2000 years. The early medieval works of Hildegard, Thomas Aquinas, Albertus Magnus, and Meister Eckhart reflect the power of this vibration before the Roman Catholic Church chose the Net instead of the Web of Light. Eventually, the Vatican realized the people were getting activated by this, so they decided to eliminate the problem. They massacred the Cathars at Montsegur in 1208, then the Dominicans began the Holy Inquisition in 1233. They spilled your Christ blood over one of the most powerful telluric zones on Earth.[18] In this hopeless battle against paganism, Montsegur was purifying itself by burning up in its own fire. By stealing the alchemical transubstantiation of Christ, the Roman Catholic Church created a Meltdown.

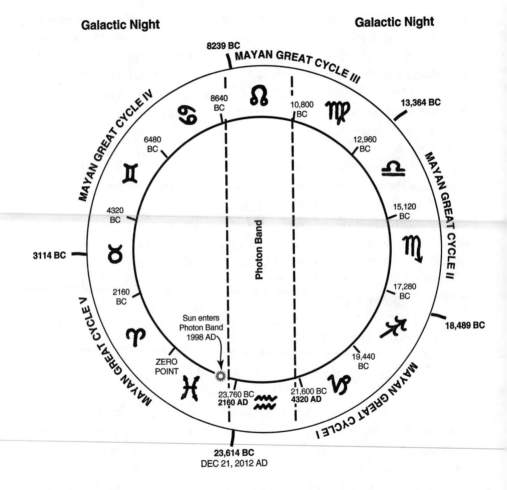

FIGURE 14: THE GREAT STORY OF TIME

"All this juicy chaos was triggering great planetary empathy needed to transmute the planet during the Age of Pisces. You will become plant people incapable of killing, and you will understand all of this better when the Age of Aquarius matures. The Age of Aquarius could be cold and too shallow. It could set in a form that does not honor deep feelings; and please remember that you all chose to act it out as you did. The Age of Pisces is always profoundly dualistic because Pisces is a mutable sign that passes energy from the Age of Aries—activation of male force—into the Age of Aquarius—multidimensional human in body on Earth. The high side of the Piscean vibration is compassion and gentleness, the age that opens the heart. Of course, the Roman Empire wasn't expecting this new consciousness when it set itself up to take over the world. Your world today is not expecting the energy of the Age of Aquarius, and yet it will come automatically by precession.[19]

"The fulfillment of Mosaic law was a Messiah to be born in a Nibiruan temple. It was planned that you were to be thrown into total obedience at Zero Point. I've noticed that you do not like to obey, and *you are admired throughout the Galaxy for your love of freedom!* Now, at the end of the Age of Pisces, you don't need to go out and get a bottle of wine and wafers, but it would be good if you could see that the total implantation of Christ consciousness into the blood line at Zero Point was the most powerful movement away from Nibiruan control of your reality in the last 500,000 years. Why? Zero Point is Tzolk'in's concept, and not Caesar's."

## Tzolk'in Weaves the Story of Time

You decided 25,607 years ago to become an individuated human being with conscious memories of your past, incisive awareness of your present, and a happy future created just by your intentions. You intended to become a person with an open heart, a healthy body, a wise mind, and an activated spirit. In those days, you lived a simple life merged in your world. The tree and lion were yourself. You lived in a simple bliss because you could feel the whole world and all the beings participating in it, and you had no sense of separation. One day, you looked at the sky and decided you wanted to know who you were. To accomplish this, you needed to be able to see yourself in your world. To do that, you needed to see yourself objectively. Thus began your long journey into knowing yourself in your world. You brought this desire to me, Tzolk'in, the Milky Way

Galactic Keeper of Time.

"I, Tzolk'in, was fascinated with your idea, so I accepted your request. I crafted a game called history—sometimes "herstory"—for you to play within, just so you could reach your stated goal. As with any game, I analyzed the codes that you carried deep within yourselve, so I could understood the roles for each of you, and then I planned the moves that you would need to master in order to attain your goal. This is a long story, which fills many libraries. Like those of a chess match, the moves you made in the beginning were predictable, and I will not spend much time going back over them. I will give you an overall sense of your moves and strategy from 23,614 to 3114 B.C.—the first four Great Cycles of the Mayan Great Calendar—then I will explore the Fifth Great Cycle—3114 B.C. to 2012 A.D.

During the *First Great Cycle*—23,614 to 18,489 B.C.—you began to observe yourself in your environment. You painted great beasts on cave walls as background for stone altars of the Bear Clan. Even in those days you honored the sacredness of blood, the elixir of life, and your altars were soaked in red ochre to honor animals. In those days, you discovered the joys of contemplation in darkness. In the beginning of this cycle during the last Age of Aquarius—23,760 to 21,600 B.C.—you often retreated to deep caves because you were in the Photon Band. In those days, the skies crackled with blinding lightning, sheets of ice were creeping down from the poles, and you moved closer to the Equator. Some of the caves where you prayed have been found and humans are stunned today by their contemplative beauty and artistic numinosity.

"During the *Second Great Cycle*—18,489 to 13,364 B.C.—you went through a great and difficult leap in your evolution, and this phase deposited many deep memories in your thalamus, the repository of images in your brain. Your solar system was far out in the Galactic Night during the Age of Scorpio—17,280 to 15,120 B.C.—when the great sky gods came to Earth. In those days, you were living in clans that journeyed great distances by means of a worldwide tracking system of standing stones. You followed great herds of animals for your livelihood, and you spent the warm seasons by the sea or by rivers and lakes enjoying plants, berries, and fish. The world was warming up and everything was beautiful and luminescent. When the great gods came to Earth, you had no idea who they were, but you could feel that they knew who you were. These sky gods

(Anunnaki) of great power who used Earth became an image for your nascent feelings of how you differed from animals. The gods began to tell you stories about where they came from; you did not understand them, but you sensed they journeyed to some faraway place. You concluded they went north above the ice to the source of your legends. Then one day they went away, and every spring when the Sun brightened you searched the skies in the north waiting for them to return, and you carved effigies of them in stone. Just before they left, they taught you how to make great stone complexes and markers so you could see the end of the Sun's journey and the balancing of the Sun in the sky. After seven generations, the children thought the sky gods had made these temples.

"Before the gods left, they wanted you to understand the cycles of the Moon, because they could see that the Moon changed the way you acted from day to day. They consulted with your shamans—clan members who were hybrid human/Pleiadians—and they were happy to teach the gods about feelings. The gods were amazed by the richness of your emotions, and the shamans were shocked that the gods didn't already know this. In this moment, you realized that someone else does not necessarily feel the way you do in a given moment, and the idea of individuality began. From this, you began to watch your children, amazed to realize that each one was unique; you wondered where they came from. Meanwhile, the gods began to learn about feelings.

"The gods taught you how to follow the phases of the Moon with stone circles that indicated the time of eclipses and located where the Moon would rise and set. Once you began to attune to the Moon, your shamans used the circles to travel into the Dreamtime, gathering knowledge about correspondences between plants, insects, animals, and rocks, and they showed you how these vibrations resonated with the Moon's journey in the sky. In those days, the shamans and the gods worked together, but the gods came and went, while the clan lineages were protected by Pleiadian shamans—indigenous humans who got a Pleiadian lightbody—*ka*—at birth. The shamans brought mushrooms into the stone circles and taught journeying with the spirits of the sacred plants. The spirits of these plants became your teachers about the special places on the planet; every valley, mountain, and stream was sacred, and you were so amazed by all this shimmering energy that you had difficulty remembering who you were.

"You learned much about Earth energy from the shamans before the ice came again. They taught you how to learn from each animal, how to broaden and master your skills and instincts. Each animal is an aspect of yourself: your eyes are eagle, your house is turtle, your heart is bear, and your ears are fox. By the end of this phase, you developed an objective sense of yourself with a keen eye for the subtleties of place, the unique qualities of plant and animal species, and a reverence for your shamans. Then I, Tzolk'in, revealed the codes of time in 13,200 B.C. to your shamans, and they became storytellers. They were chosen to record the great story of human evolution on Earth by memorizing the great story of time, and they deposited these codes in quartz crystals and round granite stones. I told them that when the Age of Leo began in 10,800 B.C., Earth would move into the Photon Band. They placed these round stones all over the planet's surface and the quartz crystals deep in medicine caves in clear pools; these stones still exist holding the memory of the original stories of the clans. I taught them to study each child to identify the carriers of star codes. Not a single thread of this knowledge was ever to be lost; shamans would be born in each generation with this knowledge in their inner brains, and the stones still hold that memory. Meanwhile, the sky gods, who identified themselves as the Anunnaki of the planet Nibiru, kept the records of Earth in their computers on Nibiru. These records are fourth dimensional. The shamanic Earth codes are fifth dimensional because they were instilled in you through your Pleiadian lightbodies.

"Before the gods left in 14,200 B.C., they showed you how to listen to the sounds of the Galaxy by drumming and rattling in bogs and swamps with amphibians, insects, reptiles, and birds. The Pleiadian shamans were very challenged by this new teaching because it got them in touch with other stars, and all of you realized that there were other stars influencing Earth besides the Pleiades! When the Anunnaki gods went away to some place very far away in the sky, you watched the flaming body leave, and then you all studied the sky obsessively seeking their return. You mapped the sky into a river of animals to locate their world, and whenever a comet or asteroid was in the sky, you thought it must be the gods. *You began moving out of being in the now.*

"During the *Third Great Cycle*—13,364 to 8239 B.C.—you really began to change, as you always do when your solar system is in the Photon Band. The sky gods and shamans had taught you about the special nature of place, and how to make stone temples to enhance this energy so you could work with guardian spirits. Large groups of affiliated clans began to identify with one place or another; these special qualities began to imprint you, and this caused you to differentiate according to bioregional zones. You became the people of the canyon, lake, high plateau, or great mountain. Certain places were aligned with animals of the sky, the zodiac. One place was special to wolf, another to bear, another to lion. More and more of you prayed in these special places during equinoxes and solstices as the light shifted. You discovered your own inner world in the animal/star teachers. These animal guides could feel whirlwinds spinning out of telluric zones, and they could see these spirals travelling out in the night sky to the stars. In 11,000 B.C. an alliance was made between the Pleiadians, Sirians, and Nibiruans, because all three groups knew that the solar system was approaching the Photon Band. The Sirians are able to incarnate into clan lineages only when Earth vortexes are activated by the guardians of sacred places, and the animals begin to resonate with the stars. A great awakening of Gaian evolution was accomplished during the Age of Virgo—12,960 to 10,800 B.C.; that is similar to the awakening you are feeling at the end of the Age of Pisces.

"This alliance occurred during a meeting of the Galactic Federation on Orion. Each culture was given a territory. You are only now attaining the level you reached in 11,000 B.C. just before the Fall of Atlantis, when you were given sovereignty over your own DNA and many beings began to influence you. The Gaian codes were imprinted in your DNA, and intelligences from many realms wanted to access these codes. The Pleiadians were given the right to continue teaching you through your chosen lineages, but they could not incarnate as hybrids and inhabit your bodies with their *kas* any more until Zero Point. Humans needed to discover how to attain Pleiadian bliss and creativity by meditating with your Sun as the eighth star in the Alcyone Spiral and activating *kas*. The Pleiadians were very sad about this because they loved being with you. The Galactic Federation, therefore, agreed to allow Pleiadians to fuse with your incarnations in the Ring of Fire, such as in Bali or Tana Toraja, to teach you to be master teachers about mastering fear. All the other clan lineages, meanwhile, would be open to different star teachers until Zero Point. The Nibiruans were given the right to choose a culture they could enter by incarnation. They chose the Fertile Crescent because they knew it would become the Garden of Eden after the ice receded in 7200 B.C.

"The Nibiruans really wanted Africa, because it was already developed by advanced Sirian geomancy, but the Galactic Federation allowed the Sirians to continue developing Africa since great knowledge for the Age of Aquarius could be stored in this zone during the Age of Leo. The Sirians had built the Sphinx in 17,800 B.C., and it grounded the solar orbit through the Photon Band during the Age of Leo—10,800 to 8640 B.C.—and this protected Earth records. They deposited the codes of the human thalamus under the Sphinx and Great Pyramid to protect them for the duration of the journey through the Photon Band. Various rivalries developed between the Sirians, Nibiruans, and Pleiadians after the Age of Leo, but the original deals recorded in the Galactic Federation records are crystal clear.

"Just before 10,800 B.C., there were meetings between humans, spirits of place, animals, and plants. You humans were powerful and integrated, almost as if you were gods yourselves, and then the strange times began. The Earth began to shake, the weather began to change, and you began to feel very afraid. The wind coming from the wrong direction was too strong and fitful, and the lightning was so intense that sparks flew off your feet as you walked. You saw portents in the sky, and you thought the gods must be coming back. You did see Nibiru in the sky as it came into the solar system, but you'd forgotten it was where the gods came from. Your world was collapsing as you moved into the Photon Band, and you have almost no memory of their landing during the Age of Leo. The Earth shook and writhed, the weather became unpredictable, and then one day the poles shifted! It was the strangest day. Great winds swept the land, the light changed, and the shadows in the great stone temples moved. There was tremendous pressure in your heads and bodies, and many of you died when your inner organs just gave out and filled with blood. A new electromagnetic field settled on the surface of the planet and the energy from the Sun seemed to be lost. Only remnants of species survived this great shifting, and Earth experienced many years of dim light because volcanic dust particles blocked the rays of the Sun. The new poles began to collect ice during months of continual rain, and water levels rose all over the planet. Nibiru came blasting around the other side of the Sun, and the gods landed in Sirian territory because it was the only stabilized zone on Earth.[20] Northern Egypt was a great electromagnetic vortex that aligned

Earth to the Sun in relationship to the Sun's position in between the Galactic Center and Orion. The Nibiruans, Pleiadians, and Sirians together constructed the Great Pyramid over an ancient Sirian sacred temple, built in 16,000 B.C., to reset the balance between the Sun and Sirius. In the body of the pyramid, the key passage from the ancient temple under the Pyramid was aligned to Alcyone in order to stabilize the 26,000-year Pleiadian cycle, and then the Sun entered the Photon Band as Nibiru orbited out of the solar system. A special empty chamber for all the Gaian records of Sirians was built into the body of the Pyramid.

"The solar system came out of the Photon Band at the end of the Age of Leo in 8640 B.C., and the high waters began to recede. The world was a different place as you began the *Fourth Great Cycle*—8239 to 3114 B.C.— just after the Age of Cancer began in 8640 B.C. Many large animals had become extinct in the polar shifting. Before the polar shift, semitropical animals lived far up north; they either died or journeyed south. There was great pain and travail on the planet for humans and all species, and when you emerged out of the Photon Band, you came out with a deeply encoded subconscious mind. Now your hypothalamus—the subtle organ within the thalamus—was encoded with intense emotions; when you have memories of the ancient days, they become visual in your thalamus. *You are walking around with heads that contain a library of movies about ancient catastrophes.* These inner brain imprints are encapsulated in the time when the waters receded and the sky cleared after Earth's last journey through the Photon Band. This was a time of new emergence when everything was numinous and magical, and this was the Garden of Eden. You looked about yourselves with a sense of self and you were amazed by the beauty of the world. Everything was pregnant and all boundaries were like the features of a woman's body. The mountains were like her breasts, the canyons were like her vulva, the clams and mushrooms were like her lips, and everything was birthing new forms like her body.

"The Nibiruan gods came again in 7200 B.C., and they were amazed because you had begun to worship the Goddess! Everything was the Goddess, and then the Nibiruans remembered that the Galactic Federation had given them the right to incarnate. So, together, you built temples that were shaped like the Goddess body and constructed circles of phallic stones. You ceased looking at the Anunnaki gods in as simple a way as in the olden times. The Pleiadians were impulsing you in those days, and you began to love children, feminine arts, and beauty. The Anunnaki taught you how to build great canal systems and dikes to drain off the water in the Fertile Crescent as the glaciers receded north; but you did not like changing the configurations of the canyons and valleys, for each reminded you of the Goddess' body. You felt overpowered by these gods. Next, they selected some of your most beautiful women to become goddesses. The Anunnaki selected women to have sex with them so they could actually birth themselves into the incarnational cycles of Earth, and this was something that had never occurred before. When a star being incarnates, it fuses with the spiritual body—*ka*—of a human, and the child is born as a hybrid Sirian or Pleiadian. Because Nibiru is a planet, the Anunnaki gods needed to experience physical fusion with humans in order to enter the incarnational cycles by creating children. They succeeded in this—even your Bible tells this story—and as a result, their blood is forever part of human blood. In exchange, goddesses such as Ninhursag and Inanna taught you about genetics, plant and seed improvement, and animal domestication. Earth women appreciated the Anunnaki gods and goddesses for improving their minds, and they were fascinated by the unusual qualities of their children. Also, it was time to crossbreed the Nibiruans and humans to improve the genetic potential of earthlings. Before 7200 B.C., crossbreeding was carried out for the survival of the Nibiruans, and the Nibiruans treated you like laboratory animals. In honor of your new status, the Anunnaki built great ziggurats that reached to the skies, the sexual encounters took place in these temples, and this caused pain during sex in the women of Earth. These women also experienced difficult labors and birthings because of incompatible mixings.

"Women and men of Earth, until this time in your matings with each other, all sex was very natural. You easily merged electromagnetic fields and your physical bodies, and the vibrations of the Moon, Sun, and planets flowed through your kundalini channels. You were drawn to each other by planetary affinities in your birth charts, and merging was always easy and pleasurable. Sex with the Anunnaki was forced and unnatural in so many ways because there were few energy affinities. You became confused, while the gods felt kundalini energy for the first time. They loved it; male gods even had a lot of sex with each other and with the few female goddesses, once they found out what sex felt like on Earth. The vast majority of gods were male, since Nibiru is so patriarchal, and that is why the

Nibiruans have never overpopulated themselves. There are a few ancient legends of Anunnaki goddesses mating with human males, such as Inanna mating with Dumuzi.[21] They felt electrical energy in their own bodies even though they are metallic, like being a wire with electricity flowing through. All imbalances between men and women today come from energetic imprints of incompatible energy fusion from these ancient times. Your loathing for reptiles also comes from this phase of your evolution because the most embodied Anunnaki are very reptilian, and those Anunnaki were the ones who could mate with human females. These energy imbalances were so difficult that brothers and sisters born from these matings were often mated to each other to enhance the Anunnaki genetic purity while cutting down on the pain and stress.

"The way back to energy balance today is for you to only have sex when energy is balanced and there is great kundalini force. You must choose your partners very carefully so that you can recover sexual ecstasy, your primordial legacy as a human. *Any act of forced sex instantly causes you to remember when the gods had sex with you, whether homo- or heterosexual.* In the days before the Anunnaki came down and mated with the Goddess, women had bodies that radiated light out to the stars. A man who entered those bodies became a star during orgasm. These sexual encounters with gods threw the women's spirits slam dunk into their 3D bodies, and this was the loss of innocence in the Garden. They lost their multidimensional contact point—*ka*—and they got stuck in bodies that were being used for sex or birthing. All it takes to correct this is reinfusion of your *ka* while you are having orgasm. Due to this loss of primordial innocence, the women learned how to move their *ka* out of their bodies, except in a few cultures that were not influenced by the Anunnaki at all, such as Minoan and Celtic cultures.

"The Anunnaki came back for a major visit during the Age of Taurus in 3600 B.C., when they instituted the patriarchy—making a world based on themselves as male gods. They built great temples all over the Tigris and Euphrates valleys of Sumer, and they brought Nibiruan cultural ideals to Earth—their language, writing, and temple city culture. Meanwhile, Sirian culture was thriving in Egypt because the Sirians had actualized a culture on the Nile that expressed 6D sacred geometry. From 3600 to 1600 B.C., the Sirians and Nibiruans brought in technology—working with humans to manifest ideas—and they were both amazed by human creativity. Warfare began with the Age of Aries in 2160 B.C., and up to Zero Point you were all working with power. You learned to feel your bodies as great and powerful, your minds as brilliant and unlimited, and you began to fight with one another over what you really valued. Until this point, you had just been expanding and fulfilling your desires, and the time was coming closer when you would be ready to decide what you really wanted on Earth for yourselves. All energy was beginning to lead up to Zero Point, the time when you would begin to devote all your time to who you really were and how you wanted to treat each other. We must go back in time before we can understand Zero Point.

"In 1600 B.C., the pain of the women on the planet finally built to such an intensity that a great volcano—Santorini/Thera in the middle of the Aegean—erupted from all the anger and pain of women being used and not honored. I, Tzolk'in, felt this explosion all the way out on Maya, my star home in the Pleiades. As thousands of years went by, I wasn't paying attention to the Calendar going through evolutionary phases on Earth, except for checking in on you during major turning points, such as the end of Great Cycle or a Baktun. But I noticed your world again when the Goddess blew up through the telluric realm. This got my full attention, just as the comet hitting Jupiter in 1994 got my attention. I, Tzolk'in, felt the cry of the Goddess, and I knew it was time for us Maya to come to Earth to ensure the availability of snake medicine. The Goddess called us Maya into linear space and time.

"We first established the Olmeca, Mexcala, and Chontal cultures in Mexico and Central America for implanting and guarding the Mayan Calendar—knowledge of the Keepers of Time until 2012 A.D. Now we Mayas were on Earth, and the last moves in the chess game would be reserved for humans. Just like chess, one by one, the lesser pieces went off the board leaving royalty—*you*—in the game. The women knew there was only one way—*impulse all people into feeling what they were experiencing!* Thus began pain, frustration, longing, and the pursuit of the original ideal: remembering that Earth is a planet orbiting around a Pleiadian star. Once the Goddess blew up in 1650 B.C., even her guardian Minoan culture was decimated by men who became warriors of destruction instead of warriors of the hearth.[22] The whole planet was enveloped by male energy, even though the sacred sites were guarded by women. All the Goddess could do was erupt, and then she became greatly feared. The men abused her more and more, as a great desire arose on Earth to know what the *right answer was*. You wanted to find the best system for having everybody honor the right answer to everything. Monotheism was born out of the battle to control the minds of all in honor of the right answer, and then Mind Control began. This new challenge would push you farther in your quest to become an intentional human: *you had to learn that nothing can even control your thought.*

"You've had to try everything so that you could see what evil is. I, Tzolk'in, can tell you that even this was necessary before you could learn how to intend—create your own reality—as powerfully as we Maya can. You began creating a world of intensifying Mind Control and evil experimentation to have a look at every single thing you could create.

"I, Tzolk'in, brought my fellow Maya, *a people who already knew everything about evil,* to Earth in 1600 B.C. The Maya created ceremonies to hold the heart of Gaia on the planet. They understood evil so well that they recognized the Spaniard when he came. They knew who Cortez was, and they absorbed him into their zone. The Maya continued doing the ceremonies, and finally the Spanish apocalypse was defused in 1987 A.D. This idea may be confusing for you because your historians and archaeologists have imprinted you with the idea that the Aztec/Maya were brutal sacrificers. Please notice that *all* interpretations of Aztec/Maya culture come from reports provided by the conquerers and from archaeologist's personal interpretations of Aztec/Maya reliefs and records. I, Tzolk'in, would like you to know that the ancient Maya created many mystery plays about evil actions which they recorded in stone and codices to teach their people what to *never* do on Earth. The conquerers arrived to find a culture that was play-acting their own behavior, so they just slandered the people and self-righteously destroyed their culture. Look at it this way: What would the future think of your culture if you were accused of being exactly as the world portrays you in the media?

"This Maya culture I brought to Earth is centered in the woman and home; it activates by following the Sun; and it has protected the secret knowledge of the Keepers of Time. The Mayan Calendar has the potential of attracting you into creating an illuminated world. The Maya so understood the Galactic Mind that, to them, the suffering in the world was like a 4D bad dream as they lived out the cycle. The Olmec culture thrived in the ceremonies and many other new branches of Maya were born and thrived. Meanwhile, the Maya were so multidimensional that they never forgot how to leave the planet when 3D became too much to handle. Poof! Off they went, and you still haven't figured that out. Ask them; they will smile and tell you where they went. Next, I impulsed my people to build the great temple complex of Teotihuacan in 200 B.C. over the top of an ancient temple site. This would be the temple that would be physically visited by the Nibiruans at Zero Point. I was the one who knew that the Nibiruans would land at Teotihuacan at Zero Point, into a world emerging out of the Age of Aries.

"Time was winding down to Zero Point, and everybody was waiting for the gods. The world was outrageously pagan and polytheistic, and there was a temple for every god everywhere on the planet. I, Tzolk'in, knew that the Age of Pisces was about to begin, an age when humans would process their deepest feelings for 2000 years after 24,000 years of evolution. These feelings had to be purified so their bodies would be able to handle the intense kundalini energy in the Age of Aquarius to follow. Then a nine-dimensional human in incarnational form—a fully human Maya—would have to be calibrated into Earth to hold the field in his body during Zero Point. This had never happened before in the third dimension, and even I, Tzolk'in, was amazed by such an idea. Yet for you to become intentional humans, you had to first *experience* this kind of human. Therefore Christ was brought into the planet at Teotihuacan as he was born in physical body in Palestine. His light body—*ka*—was implanted at Teotihuacan where many stellar representatives could work with him as he wove all nine dimensions into the planetary field. Christ actually came into each of the nine dimensions of Earth; his implantation in Mexico was his eighth-dimensional form—his form that works with galactic structures. Teotihuacan has many different kinds of temples— Pyramid of the Sun, Temple of the Moon, Temple of the Quetzal Butterfly, Temple of the Plumed Shell—that hold all nine dimensions in form.[23]

"The 2D telluric realm connects 3D to the iron crystal in the five-chambered temple below the Pyramid of the Sun—originally constructed in 23,614 B.C. This cave chamber is called 'Ge,' and it corresponds to the subterranean chamber under the Great Pyramid in Egypt. Both are Pleiadian goddess temples. For the whole Western Hemisphere, the nine-dimensional vertical axis starts in Ge in the caves under Teotihuacan; it moves into linear space and time within these chambers, the 4D archetypal guardians meet in the center of these caves, and the five higher dimensions are focused into the center of the Pyramid of the Sun by angles of solar light bringing in 5D through 9D energies. The Citadel is an Anunnaki power complex; the Temple of the Quetzal Butterfly is Pleiadian; Sirians teach with the Pyramid of the Sun itself; Andromedans teach from the Temple of the Plumed Shells; the Galactic Federation of Orion teaches from the Temple of the Moon; and 9D Keepers of Time teach with the Great Avenue. The entire temple complex is activated and alive through 2012 A.D.

"I, Tzolk'in, will tell you where Christ came from. He came from the Galactic Center, and that is why we built his temple at Teotihuacan. He appeared all over the planet at Zero Point, the same way our Calendar is appearing all over the planet now. My people, the Maya and the Aztec, allowed the Spaniard to create every imaginable horror and abuse. The Maya knew you humans by your Inquisition, which made it obvious you did not understand Christ. *You've been allowed to develop any idea, so that finally you would choose the Garden instead of a room full of computers and cellular phones when your time came.* Until you remember the Garden, you will sit in world of plastic and chrome that is created out of blood. Now many of you are wondering what happened and are beginning to see that there is a very big plan. Do not despair, for I, Tzolk'in, opened the multi-dimensional corridor. The form I built to hold the vertical axis at Teotihuacan can handle the powers coming; it has been transmuting the planet for 2000 years, and the Aztec/Maya people return to Teotihuacan every spring to receive this energy. Teotihuacan was calibrated at Zero Point to accelerate the planetary field until 2012 A.D. It was chosen to be the zone for processing three critical dates after Zero Point—999, 1987, and 1999.

"The first major event that caught my attention after Zero Point occurred in the Vatican in 999 A.D. Millennial fever had begun building in 980 A.D., when early medieval Europe was just emerging from the Dark Age that had set in after the fall of Rome, and people were fanning themselves into a wave of religious fanaticism. They were neglecting their fields, families, animals, and villages. They were whipped into a frenzy by a series of prophets talking about the coming Revelation, and people began to believe the world was going to end at midnight on December 31, 999 A.D. The Roman Catholic Church encouraged this apocalyptical fever because people gave more money when they thought there was little time left. All over emerging Europe, the streets were filled with flagellants and fanatics screaming about the end of the world. Children were ignored, women were free with their bodies, wars and plagues spread, and from every point of view, reality became the world described in Revelation. In 999 A.D. everyone waited for the end.

"I, Tzolk'in, was amazed by this frenzy! I realized right away that many chess pieces were by the side of the board and a few major players were ready for their final moves. I knew my own Calendar was accurate because it reflected life on Earth since 23,614 B.C. I observed this destructive wave based solely on belief, and I learned a lot about you. Pope Sylvester and all his Cardinals gathered in the Vatican on December 31, 999, waiting for midnight, and all the people gathered in their villages with the priests and bishops. *Nothing happened*, not even a big storm or comet! Of course, I was watching this and laughing. I wondered if this was what it would take to get Europeans to realize their calendar was faulty. Then I forgot about the whole thing until about 1972, when I felt a great solar activation in your world, and storytellers called out my name.

"In 1972, I remembered everything that happened in 999, as I watched fundamentalist fanaticism grip the world. This vile trigger indeed lay deep in the bottom of Christian souls. They were sexually excited about the end of the world in 999! They lusted over this because they wouldn't have to solve any of their problems! Lurking deep in the Christian soul was the desire to die rather than take responsibility for Earth. They were choking in the garbage of their own uncleared feelings, and they used other people like fodder. We Maya kept absorbing them, but still their garbage and baggage got bigger and bigger. Eventually they built bigger weapons and bigger cities, and covered themselves with layers of things. They consumed anything to avoid realizing their own inner emptiness.

"From 1521 A.D. forward, the Christians voraciously ate more land and people in the name of God, and they destroyed anything that reminded them of suppressed inner power, until they themselves became a firestorm. They even had to have atomic powers. My people, the Maya, watched and the daykeepers faithfully kept the days of the Calendar and the women wove the patterns that preserve the 13 numbers and 20 days of the Mayan Calendar, because they knew the world would change on August 17th, 1987. The Calendar gave them infinite patience, because more than 25,000 years had gone by and the time of the light was soon coming. Then I, Tzolk'in, put out the signal through my shamans and teachers beginning in 1972 that the predator would lose his power and the people would remember the light in 1987. The time came near, and the people began preparing the ceremonies. As the people gathered, I worked with the teachers all over the planet because this activation had to be powerful enough to penetrate the Net—apocalyptical fundamentalism. The sacred stones began emitting vibrations of the story of time, and everywhere people remembered the time was coming. The teachers were told to give the people the secrets of the stone people. I had observed you very carefully in 999, and I knew how to prepare for the next wave of millennial madness in 1999. The ancient power sites that had guarded the vortexes and whirlwinds for 25,000 years had to be awakened by all the people. The activation had to be large enough to hold enough energy from 1987 to 1992 to force all apocalyptical belief structures out into the open.

"All the people living according to belief systems, instead of their feelings about Earth, had to expose themselves by August 17, 1992. They had to be identified by all hybrid star people of Earth, so the star people could offer them guidance, if they wanted it. The world—the habitat of your mind—will build up to another apocalyptical frenzy, again based on Revelation, in 1999, and this time it will be global. Every country in the world will raise up its fundamentalist fanatics, so that all teachers on the planet will see exactly what must never be intended on Earth after 2013. As of 1992, fundamentalists will have infiltrated political systems and schools; screamed, howled, and sniveled on the media; taken more land from the people; created more violence, plagues, and mayhem all over the world; and the eyes of the people who now think of themselves as Maya have been watching all this. In Mayaland itself, everything will be different. After 1992, the indigenous Maya have again taken over their own country because they hold the hearts of the people, and Keepers of the Traditions are running political aspects of the country, whether there is a surface government or not.[24] All over the rest of the world, the drama is building for the Apocalypse, and even fundamentalist new agers say spaceships will be landing to rescue the Chosen People.

"All this will build up through 1999, when the Pope and Cardinals will wait in the Vatican to be simulcast all over the world on gigantic TV screens, and new agers will be watching the 'LightNet' for news about extraterrestrial rescue missions: all true believers will be waiting. As in 999, the world economy will have crashed, disease and chaos will be rampant, but nobody will be noticing because they will be waiting for the end of the world. Midnight will come, nothing will happen except some softly falling snow, and people will awake the next morning to a planet that needs to be taken care of. This clearing of apocalyptical belief systems will be exceedingly painful because caring more about beliefs than about the planet must cease.

"The next morning, humanity will be swept by a deep wave of shame and sadness over what they have done. The voices of the people who did not get involved in millennial madness will be listened to again, because all the people who created the Apocalypse will be exhausted. Quickly, because there will only be 13 years left, people will draw together and remember how to work again. Communities will be formed to work with the planet again. For those who have survived, the energy on the planet will be very harmonic and pure by 2001, once the Sun is totally in the Photon Band. You will have amazing resources and records to work with, because ancient wisdom will be totally available, and all individuals on the planet will be masters at creating realities with thought. From 2001 to 2010, you will rebuild your world, and you will put nothing in it that is evil. You will know beyond a shadow of doubt exactly what evil is. From 2010 to the end of 2012, you will prepare yourselves for the Cosmic Party by undergoing purification ceremonies. The ceremonies for the equinoxes and solstices will be global, and you will work in groups to decide together every single thing that is to never be created on the surface of your planet. And then at winter solstice, 2012 A.D., you will be ready to work with Gaia to set the intentions for your world for the next 26,000 years while you are attending the Cosmic Party for the Age of Light."

# Appendices

# *Appendix A*

*Astrological Transits, 1972 to the end of the*
*Mayan Great Calendar, December 21, 2012*

THE PLANETS AND MOONS OF THE SOLAR SYSTEM ORBIT AROUND THE SUN FORMING angular relationships to each other and to the Sun, and these patterns create the consciousness of the Sun and the solar system, the Solar Mind. The Sun is twinned with Sirius, a star system of more complex geometrical order than the Pleiadian system. By means of geometrical clairvoyance, the Sirians realized in 1781 A.D.—when the planet Uranus was discovered by earthlings—that the ascension of Earth into pure love and Christ consciousness in 1998–2012 (which is planned in the records of the Galactic Federation) was in jeopardy. As they examined the puny and chaotic response of earthlings to the potent and newly accessible uranian transformational codes, the Sirians realized that humans were evolving too slowly to accomplish total DNA sovereignty by the end of the Mayan Calendar.

According to Drunvalo Melchizedek channeled through Bob Frissell, the Sirians realized that the solar system would not be prepared for the planned energy acceleration that began when a series of spirals of light shot out of the Sun every three years beginning in 1950, which increased Earth's axial wobble.[1] By 1972, Earth was in severe danger of a pole shift caused by this wobble, as well as from the solar system's early adjustment to the Photon Band.

Any individual can choose to evolve his or her consciousness by working with the energetic potential available in planetary transits. These transits express solar growth potential, and people can activate their will and highest potential according to the planetary patterns. Responding to transits in the moment, individuals also create cultural movements; and in almost thirty years as an astrologer, I have never witnessed a group consciousness shift without the existence of extraordinary astrological patterns that described such growth potential. Therefore, if what the Mayan Calendar expresses is correct—humanity attaining a new level of evolution at the end of 2012—then the planetary transits should reflect this potential. If they do not, to me it is unlikely that this leap will occur.

The present shift in consciousness in individuals and groups actually began with Baktun 12 of the Mayan Calendar—1618–2012—which José Argüelles calls the "Baktun of the Transformation of Matter."[2] Since this transformation began, three outer planets have been discovered—Uranus in 1781, Neptune in 1846, and Pluto in 1930—as well as the asteroid or planetoid Chiron in 1977. These discoveries signal that something monumental is going on right at the end of the Mayan Calendar. When studying a key event, such as Harmonic Convergence, I utilize all the planets, the Moon, and stars and stellar bodies such as pulsars and quasars.[3] In this phase from the 1960s to the end of 2012, I will look at Pluto, Neptune, Uranus, and Chiron, since these bodies have long orbital cycles that rule major evolutionary patterns; I will add Saturn because it was a key player in the Uranus/Neptune conjunctions of 1993. A probable sighting of Nibiru, the planet described by Zecharia Sitchin in *The 12th Planet*, occurred in 1983, and I think it is likely we will have an official discovery soon. This would be another indicater of the significance of these times.[4]

I will begin with 1972 (including mention of transits in the 1960s that will release great influence in 2012) because during March 21–24, 1972, Pluto may have been in the Photon Band in 00 degrees Libra. (See Appendix B.) A sense that something unusual was coming was felt by many of you in 1972, which was also caused by increased solar activity. When great solar flares occurred in early August 1972, Jupiter, home of the masters, was conjunct the Galactic Center, and so these stressful oppositions sent a signal of disquiet from the solar system into the Galactic Mind.

*This analysis can be used as a road map for individuals to evolve.* As Satya says, "You will make it to the Cosmic Party more easily if you know how to get there." From August 1972 through 1979, few *extremely* potent and stressful outer planetary aspects occurred. Potent and stressful aspects are like the Uranus/Pluto conjunctions of 1965–66, which initiated a time-released depth charge that ripped through culture and established patterns that will guide the subconscious minds of individuals all the way forward to 2046 A.D., when Uranus and Pluto will oppose each other. This aspect, which manifested very visibly in the "children of love" of the 1960s, was the first social harbinger of "the big change" coming. Uranus and Pluto square, meanwhile, will first square on June 24, 2012, a second time on September 19, 2012, and a final third time on May 21, 2013, which will release the powers of the 1965–66 major conjunctions exactly at the close of the Mayan Calendar. These squares will release the creative explosion of the 1960s!

A major influence during the 1960s was Saturn transiting Aquarius from 1962 to 1964, when the first vibrations of the coming Age of Aquarius were felt, as exemplified by the musical "Hair." Saturn was in Pisces from 1964 to 1967; this phase of Saturn began a spiritual awakening that reemerged from 1991 to 1996, when Saturn again transited Aquarius and Pisces. I mention these two Saturn phases during the 1960s because Saturn in Aquarius and Pisces—1991 to 1996— is a practice run for Uranus in Aquarius—1996 to 2003—and in Pisces—2003 to

2011; and for Neptune in Aquarius—1998 to 2012—and in Pisces—2012 to 2026. The Saturn practice run, if you can recall your feelings from these times, could help you cope with the wildness and chaos of Uranus and Neptune moving in Aquarius, then into Pisces, starting in 1996.

There were many powerful planetary aspects in the 1970s, but most of the decade was a balancing phase, with Uranus and Pluto mostly in Libra and Neptune in Sagittarius, while Chiron moved slowly through Aries. Chiron was sighted in 1977, but this potent force was first felt only by highly trained initiates. The calmer sky was a relief after the intensity of the Uranus/Pluto conjunctions during the previous decade.

The critical leap got greatly energized in January 1979, when Pluto moved inside Neptune's orbit for twenty years, as it does every 249 years. Due to Pluto's orbital eccentricity, Neptune is the outermost known planet until spring equinox 1999. Pluto was sighted in 1930, so this transit inside Neptune's orbit is the first one to occur since the discovery of both planets, *and this influence is monumental.* Pluto rules exploration of deep subconscious feelings about actual species' survival, and Pluto's first known solar orbit from 1930 to 2179 is pushing survival to the forefront. The atomic bomb came forth right after Pluto was found, and this exposed the darkest forces in humanity. The potential for real transformation of consciousness inherent in our deepest urges became visible to many of you during the Uranus/Pluto conjunctions in the mid-1960s; and then these deep urges were enhanced with spiritual potentiality once Pluto moved inside Neptune in 1979.

As for Neptune, it was sighted in 1846 and completes its first known solar orbit in 2011, which signals that it is a major force for the end of the Mayan Calendar. Neptune rules the process of spiritual access, which quickened at the soul level from 1846 to 1979 when individuals began to *want* spiritual powers. You knew your emotional bodies were torpid amd murky; you sensed the needed to quicken your feelings; and this process became even more intense when Neptune went into Capricorn in 1984. As if that wasn't enough pressure, the desire for real spirituality intensified even more during the Saturn/Uranus/Neptune transits in Capricorn from 1988 to 1991. All this emotional growth and karmic maturation will blast open dimensional portals in 1999, when Pluto in Sagittarius moves outside Neptune's orbit and triggers urges for emotional freedom. Pluto pushes you to open solar plexus blocks and clear energies that inhibit courage; and while Neptune is inside Pluto's orbit, spiritual aspects of consciousness are penetrated by Pluto's survival codes. This clarity is causing you to become seers, to learn to create reality with thought. *You are realizing that spirituality is essential to your survival.*

Pluto's transit inside Neptune from 1979 to 1999 intensifies spirituality and makes it a vital part of life, and that must be examined in light of the Calendar phases. The great spiritual ascension described by the Maya is exceedingly enhanced by this shift, because it grounds etheric vibrations. Pluto orbiting inside Neptune signifies people seeking spiritual meaning in all situations and manifesting this potential by cleaning out blocks contained in dark and hidden emotions. Pluto also went into Scorpio from 1983 to the end of 1995, which was the first transit of Pluto through its home sign since its sighting in 1930. *Notice how all the outer planets are traveling in their home signs near the end of the Calendar—Neptune and Pluto for the first time since their discovery!* Pluto in Scorpio intensifies the emergence of the deep subconscious, causing profound emotional exploration of yourselves. If you have truly been more honest, this integrity will mature beautifully into spiritual genius during Pluto in Sagittarius, from 1995 to 2008; and those who have embodied such spiritual intensity will become nine-dimensional humans during Pluto in Capricorn from 2008 to 2023. You won't want to read about shamans or study with them, you will *become* one. When Pluto becomes the outermost planet in Sagittarius in 1999, *total integrity will be required.* Those who are not in integrity will become judgmental, apocalyptical fundamentalists who will stage the millennium during the last hours of 1999. Don't worry, go sit under a tree; it will pass.

The outer planetary transits of the 1980s were of mind-boggling power due to a series of Saturn/Uranus/Neptune conjunctions in Sagittarius and Capricorn. From 500 B.C. forward, the only time I could find when Saturn, Uranus, and Neptune were traveling together in the sky was in 1307 A.D., and Pluto at that time was not within Neptune's orbit. Transits as potent as the ones during the 1980s and 1990s have not occurred in the last 25,000 years, possibly not in the last 100,000 years.[5]

Truly ominous feelings of change were felt when Neptune went into Capricorn in January 1984. This transit was especially formative because Capricorn rules the formation of *structure itself.* Remember how you felt in 1984? As in the novel *1984* by George Orwell, it felt like technology would surely defeat spirit, while feelings and personal search seemed heavy and dark with Pluto in early Scorpio and Neptune in Capricorn. However, in 1984 many people became aware that they would never become enlightened unless they learned to handle emotions. They dove into exploring their emotional bodies—exactly what would be needed to handle the 1998 entry into the Photon Band! Many of you became deeply introspective that year as you felt something heavy coming, and you got serious about personal transformation.

During the 1980s, nothing was fun anymore, the way it was during the 1970s, when sex was wild and free and technology seemed to be glittery and playful. People realized the condition of the planet was going to impact every inhabitant eventually when AIDS, immune deficiency diseases, and rising cancer statistics became common in the 1980s. Uranus was transitting Sagittarius during the 1980s, and people felt creative and spiritual. As Pluto was digging deeper into Scorpio, people found great meaning in all their emotional processing. As gradually the vibrations in the field were getting heavier and heavier, deeper and denser, a wild and crazy idea came up! Harmonic Convergence! People were stewing with spiritual ideas and emotional processing, and the idea was presented that Earth was alive and would respond to their creativity on August 16–17, 1987, if they would meditate with Gaia at power places with other seekers. The astrological transits during Harmonic Convergence were literally combustible due to a grand trine of seven planets in fire signs, and suppressed creativity lurking deep inside from the unfinished 1960s' explosion caused many of you to create a great big planetary party at sacred sites.

Well, we astrologers viewed this summer with amazement, because we knew the "Capricorn crunch" was coming in 1988 and 1989. But, even though Saturn and Uranus each moved into Capricorn for a while in 1988, they still conjuncted three times during 1988 in late Sagittarius right on the Galactic Center. Many of you got piercing flashes of multidimensional perception, but few could consciously utilize this potent portal. Neptune was already in Capricorn, and Saturn and Uranus moved into Capricorn together after the first conjunction in Sagittarius in February 1988. This felt like a heavy door closing, and the same pattern repeated twice more during 1988. Some of you felt a need to create space in yourselves to make a home for this glimpse of multidimensional potential, and you began to work on your emotional bodies. In those days, you got hints of the depth and hugeness of the great mystery play that was unfolding; but the Capricorn energy was so heavy, you wondered if you could stand it. We astrologers knew this was only the beginning of the onset of this structural alchemical furnace because Saturn, Uranus, and Neptune were all in Capricorn from February 1988 until February 1991. Next, Saturn conjuncted Neptune three times in 1989 in Capricorn. *These three planets transitting Capricorn forged a vehicle of spiritual transformation in each one of you that will not be denied.* However, until 1996 the Capricornian structural imposition is so strong that many of you are tense about what is really possible. Well, wait until Uranus goes full time into Aquarius in 1996! Here come the 1960s and Harmonic Convergence all over again, but this time you will have created a spiritual vehicle to carry you all the way to the end of the Calendar to ground Uranus and Neptune as they release their potency while transitting Aquarius and Pisces.

The penultimate forging of this spiritual vehicle occurred all the way through 1993, when Uranus conjuncted Neptune three times while Saturn was in Aquarius and was frequently being squared by Pluto.[6] Then Uranus and Neptune continued to travel close together during 1994 and 1995, and the apex was January 11,

1994, when the Sun, Moon, Mercury, Venus, Mars, Uranus, and Neptune were conjunct at the new moon in Capricorn. All these bodies were less than 11 degrees apart in Capricorn! Pluto was conjunct the north lunar node, and the nodes were T-squared by Saturn, creating the ultimate pressure for you to discipline your spirit to facilitate species survival all over the planet.

These, indeed, are the kinds of planetary aspects required to prepare people *emotionally* and *spiritually* for the Sun's entry into the Photon Band in 1998; however, I have not addressed the activation of your *physical bodies*. First of all, when Pluto becomes the outermost planet again on spring equinox 1999, your physical evolution based on emotional body purification will begin to kick in. The other cycle designed to transmute your bodies began in March 14, 1994, and it is described in Appendix C. Meanwhile, Pluto moved into Sagittarius, and Uranus into Aquarius for a few months in early 1995, and there was a great speed-up of your energy. Everything is beginning to move faster, and this will intensify with Pluto in Sagittarius from 1995 to 2008, which will cause you to unleash your internal transformation into the culture: your deep self that erupted while Pluto was in Scorpio from 1983 to 1995. *You will be able to act on your emotions by using your will.* Uranus will move into Aquarius in January 1996, and you all will feel the early vibration of the Age of Aquarius! You will begin to feel like a volcano that is ready to erupt, like a horse that wants to rear and run, or like a libertine who wants to follow desire. *You will try becoming your future image of yourself no matter who or what is in your way!*

Everything is going to move faster, and nothing will ever be the same again. Chiron will attain its closest passage to the Sun on February 14, 1996, and it will sweep away the medical technocracy during 1997 and 1998, when it is in opposition to its sighting position. The long battle to be able to choose either natural or allopathic medicine will finally be won by you, since you will understand the survival codes. *You will never allow anyone to control your bodies again.* Saturn will move into Aries in 1996 in April, when you will feel great personal warrior powers. You will wonder if all the speed and pressure will ever cease, and the answer is *no*. However, you will be speeding up and synchronizing with the outer planets! You forged the vehicle for this acceleration during the 1993 Uranus/Neptune conjunctions. Neptune moves into Aquarius in 1998, and from 1998 through 2003, Uranus and Neptune will travel through Aquarius together while Pluto is in Sagittarius. The potential of the Capricorn transits will release, and you will feel like you are living on a star as you move deeper and deeper into the Photon Band.

The apex of Christian apocalyptical fundamentalism will occur at midnight, December 31, 1999, but the world will *not* end. This realization will be very healing because Chiron and Pluto will be exactly conjunct, which will gift us with a profound healing; and Neptune, which rules Christianity during this phase of history, will be conjunct the south node of the Moon. This will be the end of obsessive Christian belief systems, and many of you will instead *feel* the Christ within. Uranus and Neptune in Aquarius will be assisting you in your exploration of the new age coming. Uranus will enter Pisces in 2003, and you will begin to consciously release belief after belief. By then you will all know that beliefs used for control systems destroy Earth.

Pluto as the outermost planet in Sagittarius and Chiron in Capricorn will be assisting you in discovering your own techniques for accessing nine dimensions, and then Chiron will enter Aquarius in February 2005, which will bring forth new ways to heal your wounded society. Pluto conjuncts the Galactic Center from 2006 to 2007, and this will function as a purified personal gateway into the Galactic Mind. Then Pluto will move into Capricorn during January 2008, and this will offer maximal deep structural transformation powers for your society and planet. You will be awestruck by the potency of Pluto in Capricorn, because Pluto was in Cancer when it was first sighted in 1930. This will be the maturation of Pluto in your clarified emotional bodies, and *you will restructure your world for all-species survival*. In February 2010, Chiron will conjunct Neptune in Aquarius, and this will unleash universal and total spiritual healing into the new structures! You will be washed by an exquisite spiritual wave. Uranus will move into Aries in May 2010, and you and your society will possess unlimited powers to create realities in alignment with the planetary mind, while Chiron reconjuncts Neptune, setting off more spiritual healing waves.

Neptune leaves Aquarius in February 2012 and enters Pisces, its home sign, where it will erase the memories of pillaging, raping, and killing for beliefs from thousands of years of history. At last the deviation from joy is finished, and Chiron in Pisces will open galactic spirituality! Uranus moves into Aries in 2010, and all limitations on transformative actions will be released. At spring equinox 2011 at Teotihuacan, the people will see that their intention for biological sovereignty will be accomplished. Then on June 24, 2012, Uranus in Aries will square Pluto in Capricorn; this square will hold through the end of the Mayan Calendar, and this is the square that will release the love and spiritual force that was forged in the flower children of the Sixties during the Uranus/Pluto conjunctions. At the end of the Calendar, Chiron will conjunct Neptune in Pisces, and both will trine Saturn in Scorpio, and the hope that was born deep in the heart of humanity in those days will birth you as creators in the Milky Way Galaxy.

# Appendix B

## The Timing of the Solar System's Entry
## into the Photon Band

THIS APPENDIX PRESENTS A THEORY THAT IS VERY DIFFICULT TO TEST AS IT SPEC-
ulates on when each planet is actually within the Photon Band starting in 1972, the
year Pluto apparently was in the Band. At present, I have not been able to detect
the Photon Band influences clearly enough to test out my theory because the influence of the Band is so subtle; there may be scientific instruments that actually are
detecting this influence but we are not being informed of their existence.

  According to this theory, the Sun's outer corona will move into the Photon
Band sometime in 1998, probably at fall equinox. I *have* noticed peculiar changes
in the sky when Earth moves in and out of the Band according to the timing given
here, but these are very subtle. In the fall of 1998, if there are wild phenomena in
the sky, such as a blackout or a great light increase, if there are truly intense shifts
in consciousness or planetary vibrational shifts, if there is a truly extraordinary
change in the Sun, then the theory presented here might be worth looking at. If so,
then this model could be useful for better understanding our atmosphere and solar
system dynamics 1998 to 2013, when I expect us to be in the middle of very high
stress, even if such stress is only caused by humanity's apocalyptical tendencies.

  The model I use for the Photon Band is derived from indigenous knowledge,
other contemporary theorists, my own memory bank, and the group mind, as is
discussed in Chapter Two. I now feel certain that Earth travels through a 2000-
year band of increased photonic light during the Ages of Aquarius and Leo, but
what is difficult to determine is whether this is a transformation in the etheric field
where light waves are transmitted, or whether it is actually in the physical.[1] The
same difficulty lies in all the prophecies about Earth changes. We may not *see* anything, but we may *know* something is going on with our nonphysical senses. In
either case, we won't know how literal things are until the time comes. The one
thing that makes no sense is fear and acting like Chicken Little. There is plenty of
evidence in the polar ice core samples that there are periodic ice ages and catastrophes. There is valid reason to believe that these cycles correspond with the
Aztec and Mayan calendars, but these issues are a whole book in themselves.
Meanwhile, there was a significant recent ice age—the Younger Dryas—as well as

a probable pole shift during the last Age of Leo—10,800 to 8640 B.C. During the Younger Dryas, which is carbon dated about 10,500 to 9800 B.C., there was a sharp cold spell that reverted climate back to Paleolithic conditions, and this was very traumatic for human culture.[2]

To write my trilogy, *The Mind Chronicles*, I did about 80 sessions under hypnosis in which I "time-travelled" through at least 300,000 years of human experience. I discovered that we are still processing fear lurking in our primal minds that is sourced in events from that catastrophic phase, which revived memory of earlier catastrophes; and as we move by precession into its opposite age—Aquarius—we feel apprehensive. The memory of the Younger Dryas was even recently revived when Santorini/Thera in the Aegean Sea erupted, causing a huge catastrophe about 1650 B.C. In general, *The Pleiadian Agenda* is a very speculative book, but I feel we need to stretch our imaginations when we feel ancient memories welling up inside. Imagine if we knew all about the cyclical patterns of Earth, but we lived these cycles with anticipation, creativity, and vigor! Czech writer Wence Horak discussed the possibility in *Ancient Ecologists* that humans are much more intelligent when the temperatures of Earth are lower, and I have discovered this is true during my time-travelling.[3]

Assuming the Photon Band is real on some level, then the next question is when do we move in? When does the Sun move in? Figure 5 from Chapter Two is a speculative model that is very plausible for *how* we move into the great band of light that is one of many great 7D bands of light looping in through the center of the Galaxy. It shows the orbital plane of the solar system moving into the band of increased light as the planetary orbits move in, when the Sun moves in, and then when half the planetary orbits are within it. Lastly, the rest of the planetary orbits move in behind the Sun's entry, and all will be inside the Band for about 2000 years. Whether Earth and other planets are actually travelling in the Band depends upon which section of the orbit they are moving on is within the Band; that all is determined by the first entry point of the edge of the solar system itself.

My theory on Earth's entry into the Photon Band comes out of a public channeling I did with Barbara Marciniak.[4] A man in the audience asked the "Keepers of the Frequency" of the Pleiades, *when* we would go into the Photon Band. Because I was channeling them and because of the nature of the answer, I think the data is right. Here is what they said, "Earth is in the Photon Band all of February, through all of April and a few days of May 1992 (13 weeks, since March is in between), and its sojourn will increase by a week on each side (2 weeks each year) up to 2013 A.D. In 2013, Earth's orbit will be fully in the Photon Band."

From the tape, I analyzed the answer: 1) 13 weeks in 1992 would indicate that we went into the Band at a midpoint between about February 1 and early May 1992, seven years earlier, which is almost exactly spring equinox 1986 or

1987. 2) If I added two weeks to the time in the Band starting in 1993, I would know when Earth's orbit was all the way in, and if that calculated out to be 2013, then the data of the channeling is highly accurate. Why? A person in a trance couldn't possibly come up with an answer like that without much pencil and paper, unless reading somebody's records. The data does calculate out exactly to 2013, and it also offers the timeline of Earth's entry—0 degrees Libra, since the Sun is in 0 degree Aries at spring equinox when Earth is 0 degrees Libra. (In astrology, Earth is opposite the Sun.) The spring equinox makes a lot of sense since it's a major Maya ceremonial time. The Keepers of Teotihuacan began a ceremonial cycle at spring equinox 1986, which celebrates the time of *La Luz*, the light. Next with this entry point, it is possible to know when the *Sun* enters the Band because, even though Earth has a slightly elliptical circular orbit around the Sun, the Sun is located almost halfway between a line drawn from September 22 to March 22. (The solar ellipse is wider on the solstice line.) The Sun's entry is halfway between March 22, 1987 and December 31, 2013: 1999–2000. Therefore, because the Sun's corona extends out so far, the maximum impact on the Sun will be 1998–2001, exactly the same years as the maximum Earth changes forecast by Gordon Michael Scallion. Then, as the Sun moves in deeper, the ingress of the other planets deepens as more of the orbital planes are swallowed up, and the Sun will respond more to the increase of photons.

Assuming Earth's entry point at 0 degrees Libra in 1986–1987 is correct, then it's possible to roughly calculate when the planets are in the Band. Using 1996 as an example, Earth will be in the Band from about January 18 to May 23, which indicates an entry border line into the planetary orbits from about 8 degrees Capricorn to 22 degrees Cancer, and planets traversing through that section of the zodiac will be in the Band part or all of 1996. When the Sun moves in about 1999, that line will be at the beginning of Cancer/Capricorn—the solstices—and if that turns out to be right, we will have a potential answer for why Paleolithic and megalithic people were so obsessed with solstices.

Taking a brief look at the planets in 1996, I do not know if Mercury's orbit is in the Band yet because it is closer to the Sun, but it might be in the Band in August/September. The orbit of Venus is partly immersed in the Band, and Venus itself is in the Photon Band in October/November, and as already stated, Earth will be in the Band January 18 to May 23. The orbits of the planets inside Earth are smaller than Earth's orbit, so once they are in the Band, their orbits will be swallowed in even faster than the orbit of Earth. Therefore, the photon effect should be intensifying 1995–1996, once Earth and Mercury are in it together. Perhaps that is the reason the Maya were so obsessed with Venus? Mars enters the Band in September and stays in the rest of 1996, Jupiter is outside the Band all year, Chiron is inside all year, Uranus and Neptune are outside, and Pluto is within the Band all year.

Around 1995–1996, as the solar system moves deeper into the Photon Band, Mercury will quickly end up being in the Band half the year, and quickly after the Sun's entry, it will be inside the Band with the Sun all of the year. A sudden speeding up of human mental processes or unusual brain disorders—such as the aneurysm described in Chapter Three—could be a sign that Mercury is moving into the Band. Venus may already be in the Band in August/September/October, and soon after Mercury is in the Band fulltime after 2000, Venus will also be. In 1996, Earth is in the Band part of January through May, and this will increase a week on each side until Earth is totally in the Photon Band by the end of the Mayan Calendar. The orbit of Mars, a two-year orbit around the Sun, went into the Band before Earth's entry in 1987, since Mars is *outside* the orbit of Earth. The same is true for Jupiter, Saturn, and all the outer planets.

If it is correct that the entry line is 0 degrees Libra, then we have a sense of direction as far as which parts of the orbits of planets beyond Earth are in the Band, but I will not be able to furnish a timeline on what the outer planets actually moved in because it requires too many calculations. If this theory ends up having any validity, this would be a great research field for other astrologers. To figure this out, the distance of the orbits of the planets from the Sun as well as careful analysis of the entry point is required, and math is not my strength.

Lastly, let's have a brief look at which planets beyond Mars might be in the Band between 1972–2013. I'm leaving out Mars because it is too much data, but remember that it went in periodically before Earth, and it might be interesting to look at Mars in the Photon Band in relation to the transmutation of war patterns in recent times.

Jupiter was probably in the Photon Band 1979 through 1983, 1990 through 1995, and will be 2001 through 2009; Saturn was probably in the Band 1975 through 1988, will be 2003 through 2024; during the next cycles of Jupiter and Saturn in the Band, they will be in the Band for long periods, possibly fully in for 2000 years. Chiron is in the Band around 1990 through 2006, and it will take it a while to move its whole orbit in because the large part of its oval orbit—Chiron's long cycle—is opposite the entry point of the solar system. Uranus was probably in the Band in 1972 and it may have moved out around 1990, and it may be moving back in around 2035 for a longer stay. Neptune was also probably in the Band in 1972 and it probably moved out around 1988, and it will probably move back into the Band sometime around 2050. Pluto was in the band in 1972 and probably moves out of it right around the end of the Mayan Calendar. It looks like the solar system will be fully inside the Band when Earth enters the Age of Aquarius around 2160 A.D.

To consider whether this highly speculative theory is valuable or not, the three things to watch for are: 1) will there be really significant changes in our solar system or consciousness in 1998–2001 when the Sun enters; 2) are there any changes in the atmosphere of Earth as it moves in and out of the Band, increasing its ingress by two weeks a year; and 3) are there highly unusual brain, communications, or computer phenomena beginning in 1997?

# *Appendix C*

## *Galactic Precipitation:*
## *Metonic Cycle of the Fifth World*

IF YOU HAVE ALREADY READ THE TEXT OF THIS BOOK INCLUDING APPENDIX A, IF A lot of what it discusses is true in some meaningful way, the implications of this book are staggering. *If* it is true that we are accelerating our consciousness exponentially at the end of a 26,000-year cycle of time, then what can each one of us *do* about that? As an astrologer, often I've seen patterns in peoples' charts that predict the beginning and end of difficult phases in their lives. Years ago, I decided not to speak about anything negative or traumatic to my clients unless I could also suggest ideas that would help them deal with these difficulties. I've held true to that, and now this appendix offers a description of *how* the crisis that seems to be building might unfold. The book text itself offers healing tips and meditation techniques for the coming days, and the point of this appendix is to predict how "Galactic Precipitation" might function. My assumption is that knowing how the pattern might play out will offer many of you some ideas about approaches you'd like to choose for the changes. Galactic Precipitation—a rainstorm of cosmic energy on Earth—began March 14, 1994, when a new energy actually started triggering us in our physical bodies. This bombardment of cosmic consciousness will intensify year by year until it culminates at critical leap time at the end of 2012.

While doing research under hypnosis in 1991 for *Signet of Atlantis*, I participated in a session in which advanced cosmic beings showed me how the soul enters Earth plane and infuses the infant at birth.[1] That session is what gave me the insight of Galactic Precipitation, which is now turning out to be predictive, I will describe this soul infusion process: A being took me out to the *Ecliptic*—the annual path of Earth around the Sun. Next I was guided to watch the Moon going around and around Earth about 13 times a year as Earth traveled around the Sun. The points where the orbit of the Moon intersect the Ecliptic are called the south and north lunar nodes, and these crossing points move slowly in a retrograde motion on the Ecliptic, since the lunar orbit on the plane of the Ecliptic inclines at 5 degrees, 8 minutes.[2] These nodes complete one circuit of the Ecliptic in about 18.4 years—the Metonic Cycle according to the Greeks—and archeoastronomers

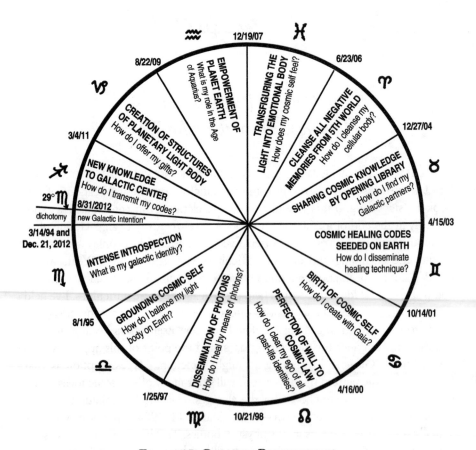

FIGURE 15: GALACTIC PRECIPITATION

and megalithic archeologists have established that many ancient stone monuments measured this 18.4-year cycle.[3] This cycle is what makes it possible to predict eclipses, which happen when the new or full moons occur close to the nodal crossing points, and that may be why ancient people were so concerned about marking this cycle with stones. As for me, I have come to feel there is more going on with the nodes, and the planets going around the Sun also have nodes. In the vision, the circling of the Moon around Earth 13 times a year, as Earth circled around the Sun for 18.4 years, looked like "Slinky" stretched out around a great ovoid circle and connected at the beginning and end.

Once I became an advanced astrologer, I was most interested in karmic astrology, which studies why you came to Earth for a lifetime, and most karmic astrologers *begin* birthchart analysis by examining the lunar nodes. In reading the natal chart, the north node of the Moon shows why a person chose to be born—real purpose—and the south node shows the focus of past life experience that will need to be processed during the lifetime. About seven years ago, my husband Gerry Clow and I noticed that the lunar nodes in our marriage chart were predicting our personal home and career patterns. These cycles were so dominant in our marriage that I began to take the nodes even more seriously. Obviously they are very potent.

Going back to the being who was showing me the Moon's 18.4-year cycle on the Ecliptic, I was shown how our souls hover around the Ecliptic and pick their own special point on the lunar orbit crossing for conception and birth! This was an exquisite vision with the souls hovering around the maturing fetuses—organisms of biological potential that were very cherished by these souls. When ten moons or nine months had passed, the souls were moving into infants who were born at the exact right time and place, which set up the lunar node placements in the natal charts of the children. Literally trillions of light beings were working with the Ecliptic as the fetuses and souls were drawn magnetically into the ideal zone of the Moon's crossing of Earth's path around the Sun that would trigger the karma they wanted to work out, so they could explore a new evolutionary path. I was transfixed in the regression session by the feeling aspects of this dynamic. It was not mechanical or mathematical, and the process seemed to be accomplished by some form of etheric fluidic substance that looked like how love feels; some kind of advanced light knowledge as complex as DNA itself. I have never found anything on Earth so complex and artistically perfect, except possibly the feelings in my body after listening to a complete Bach fugue cycle.[4]

This vision in 1991, combined with the great impact of the nodes in our marriage chart, impulsed me to play with the possibility that the lunar node influence in our realm is a highly complex cyclical predictor. It could be a cosmic blueprint of intelligence, especially since very ancient people were obsessed with it. Meanwhile, once we made it through the "Armageddon Bypass" in 1992—five years of intense emotional body clearance after Harmonic Convergence, the 1987 resonant frequency shift—I began to realize beyond any doubt that the Mayan Calendar (as interpreted by Argüelles and many others) was actually predictive.[5] As an astrologer, I then knew there *had* to be some astrological cycle that synchronized with the patterns at the end of the Calendar. If I could pinpoint it, it might serve as a tool for the ascension. First of all, the planetary transits of 1987–2012, which influence the electromagnetic field of Earth by means of the solar wind, are totally capable of triggering the ascension process of Earth, as has been described in Appendix A. However, I still felt there was something more, and one day in early 1994, I realized the lunar node cycle might be a key. Why? I sensed there must be a factor operating that was more subtle than just the causative factors in the electromagnetic field. During the Sirius Periastron in March 1994, I remembered again the vision of the beings working with the Ecliptic and lunar node cycle while I was working in the Great Pyramid. Yes, the nodal cycle might be it! And so I cast a chart for the last Metonic Cycle—lunar node cycle—of the Mayan Calendar, assuming December 21, 2012 as the end date. (See Fig. 15.)

I simply took the end date of the Calendar, noted that the true north lunar node would be 25 degrees 37 minutes Scorpio, and then I went back one full Metonic Cycle (18.4 years) to the same point. I laid out one Metonic Cycle, which is shown in Figure 15, and the beginning date was March 14, 1994, just before the Sirius Periastron![6] I had a very powerful intuitive hit that this chart meant something, and so I explored it with students during intensives in summer and fall, 1994. Much to my surprise, students were deeply moved by this teaching and some of them cried! As I write about this wheel in July 1995, the first of twelve houses is almost complete—March 14, 1994 to August 1, 1995—and it has turned out to be *exceedingly predictive.* To evaluate such early predictability, you need to understand how astrologers do research. According to our training, certain planets and aspects create certain kinds of energetic fields that potentiate various probable realities. Advanced astrology is very exacting; it either is predictive or it is not. For example, we astrologers said that all kinds of structures would break down in the latter 1980s and early 1990s because of the Saturn, Uranus, and Neptune transits described in Appendix A. Many astrologers got very specific about what kinds of structures would fall, such as the Berlin Wall, and even offered specific dates. The facts are, astrology is very predictive, but it is even more so once the time arrives that has been investigated in advance. For example, an astrologer might predict that very authoritarian structures, such as the Soviet Union, would break down under the Capricorn transits. Then, once the process gets going during the first transit—such as Saturn conjunct Uranus—then astrologers can predict more exactly for the followup transits. We watch to see how things work out during the first aspect, which exposes which probable reality got triggered. In the case of the Metonic Cycle, once the first section—3/14/1994 to 8/1/1995—was actually predictive, then I have more confidence that the following eleven are likely to be extremely predictive.

Section One—March 14, 1994 to August 1, 1995, says that people would become very introspective and obsessed with galactic identity, and this time frame *has* been marked by a literal obsession with galactic or star identity. This can be seen in the great popularity of books like *Bringers of the Dawn*; *You Are Becoming a Galactic Human;* and *Nothing in This Book Is True, But It's Exactly How Things Are,* and in the film, *Stargate.* There are many examples I could offer, but people's intense curiosity about personal star identity and extraterrestrial influence has become very apparent. The Internet is buzzing with questions, and there have been many magazines, movies, and television shows focusing on them. Meanwhile, the new energy this wheel seems to be charting is still very new and even bizarre to most, and most don't know how to even imagine where these off-planet ideas come from. As for me, I think we are being *impulsed by some very advanced beings.* Possibly those beings I saw guiding soul infusion are now busy guiding us as we integrate galactic intelligence at the end of the Mayan Calendar. Maybe all our guides who helped us get in here in the first place will be back during this phase? If this is true, then this chart, which describes really subtle energetics, could help us integrate off-planet influences. What follows is more data on what each one of these phases of Galactic Precipitation might mean for us.

First House (March 14, 1994 to August 1, 1995): *Scorpio: How can I ever go deep enough inside myself to discover what star I came from?* This is a propitious beginning with Scorpio rising our new identity as galactic citizens. The highest vibration of Scorpio is the Phoenix, the mythical firebird that rules resurrection and immortality, and the highest one is the correct one when using the nodes. The Sabian symbol for this degree is "Indians making camp," and it means we will have unusual resourcefulness for making the critical leap, that we will find everything we need right on the planet. The negative side of this vibration is a tendency to just accept things as they are, but with Uranus going into Aquarius early 1996 while Pluto is in Sagittarius, no way that will happen![7] This phase predicts a time of deep obsessive exploration about stellar identity, since the whole wheel is about galactic synchronization. What star did I come from? What is the story of that place? Why am I here now if I came here from that star? How do the qualities of that star affect my humanity on Earth? Also this phase indicates the actual *embodiment* of stellar frequencies activating kundalini rising in our bodies. Once kundalini rises, miasms in our bodies are activated, and so it is likely that more and more people will be dealing with many diseases, as already discussed in Chapter Three. Therefore, early diagnosis is very important and homeopathy and radionics will be valued for their ability to detect disease in the etheric before it manifests in the physical body. Natural and energetic medicine will become popular because they work well with energetic clearance issues.

Second House (August 1, 1995 to January 25, 1997): *Libra: How do I ground my star identity on Earth, and how do I balance my light body on the planet?* This predicts an 18-month period when people will be reeling from the new energy that is coming in, especially since Pluto moves back into Sagittarius on November 11, 1995, and Uranus moves back into Aquarius on January 13, 1996. You will find yourselves focusing on staying balanced as the chaos builds. I believe the increased photons will activate the dormant, subtle glands, such as the adrenal glands, hypothalamus, pineal, and thymus. Why are those glands there, anyway?

Scientists are so amazed by the regulatory powers of the pineal that some are calling it an organ. As these glandular systems open, it is critical to stay balanced, because the openings can trigger miasms and ancient disease patterns. The opening can cause wild mood swings, and I'm sure that is why drugs like Prozac have become so popular. But, shutting the process down with tranquilizing drugs too much, instead of using a drug for a little while to avoid dangerous imbalances, could *abort* the process. I would advise tranquilizing yourself with exposure to nature, gardening, mild exercise, careful diet, peaceful and loving relationships, and total elimination of television. Be kind to yourselves, relax, do not work incessantly, because you are already feeling the new world coming. Many of you will realize you really want to stay in your bodies for this incredible ascension of Earth; you will know that your body must also accelerate, so slow down and care for yourself during this hyperbalancing period.

Third House (January 25, 1997 to October 21, 1998): *Virgo: Now that I have brought this incredible high vibratory energy into my body and balanced it, how can I broadcast its powers to all other lifeforms on the planet?* This period is going to be a hot one, and I can't wait to see the media fall as people take back their communication systems in order to figure *what is happening as a group experience.* The people on the planet who have been able to embody, and then ground, the new galactic frequencies will immediately realize they must heal with these new powers, since the third house of communications is ruled by Virgo, which is Chiron's sign. You will be seized with an all-consuming desire to cleanse, purify, and enhance—to become symbiotic with all living things. The true importance of saving species and habitat will come forth because, during this chirotic phase, you will *see* how habitat is an extension of basic beingness. Invasion of the telluric by means of mining or for any other reasons will become impossible, because you will feel Earth undulating as a psychedelic vision and you will be *in* that vision—you will not be separate from your surroundings.

Fourth House (October 21, 1998 to April 16, 2000) *Leo: How can I use my will to form my new galactic self?* At this point, everything is exploding around you because the outer corona of the Sun is moving into the Photon Band, and the solar wind itself becomes silvery waves of light. Everything will be moving and transmuting, yet you will have attained a new, remarkable ability to create with thought, and you will flow in the viscous field of changes, so long as you continually focus on your new self. You will not feel as solid as you do now; in fact, you will feel like a gigantic swirling field of light particles. Listen carefully inside; feel where you are within yourself; and continually activate your will, and center and ground. You too are Christ; this incredibly expanded energy field is just your own light body that you couldn't see until now.

Fifth House (April 4, 2000 to October 14, 2001) *Cancer: Now that I am a totally unique new being, how do I birth myself into the mind of Gaia?* This phase will be like witnessing the Transfiguration of Christ, as you begin to see your own light body as well as the light bodies of other. You will see many star codes coming into Gaia through your bodies and through animals, insects, plants, and rocks. By using pure thought—what do I intend now!—you will hold your new hybrid identity during the Sun's entry into the Photon Band. *Your ability at this time to create the reality you require with thought will be unlimited.* If you want to prepare for this time, ask yourself: What child of Earth do I want to become now? What is the greatest self I can imagine being washed day and night with cosmic light?

Sixth House (October 14, 2001 to April 15, 2003) *Gemini: Now that I have rebirthed myself as a star child of Gaia, how do I become one of the great beings, one of the cosmic healers?* All I can do is *feel* this one as a seer, since, as we move around the wheel, the cosmic process unfolds, and is basically out of my present range now. So, I will just tell you what I can see from using my feelings. First of all, I see that there is much less population on Earth, but do not despair: many of you have become magnificent huge trees and many of you are crystals! The wind and Earth movements are so intense that many of you chose to ground yourselves by changing form. I can see that those that remain as humans are vibrating in total resonance with Gaia, and the way they heal is by *species resonance.* They are simply vibrating their essence, holding their DNA codes; they look like receiving stations. Those who are walking around are surrounded by swirling rays of colored light, like phosphorescence in the sea. I also have the impression that those of you who have changed form will be able to change back into humans or animals at will.

Seventh House (April 15, 2003 to December 27, 2004) *Taurus: Now that I know myself as one of the great beings of the cosmos—as Christ because I am a Gaian—who will I work with and live with to manifest this knowledge?* As you move into the Seventh House of the Metonic Cycle, you will wake up! You will actually see all that you are, and you will wonder who you are to be with, to work with. Unlike the ancient days when you were working out karma, you will be an absolutely functional human with a true sense of your magnificence, and limitation will not be part of partnering. Like an exquisite woman and a virile man who are deeply in love, you will have total response with your lovers and partners. The more you love and work with others, the more magnificent and responsive you will be. Your codes will be visible! You will easily recognize the other beings you want to work and mate with.

Eighth House (December 17, 2004 to June 23, 2006) *Aries: As I use these great powers welling up in my soul and body that radiate my new magnificent sense of self, how can I express this thundering self nonviolently?* This is the time when you will look around yourself after waking up from the mind-boggling discovery of your own beauty, and what you will see around yourself will be an abomination that you will not accept. The shimmering star beauty becomes real now, and you see holes in Earth in some places; rotting skeletons of technology litter some of the cities where people will need to commune together, and parts of the oceans are choked with sunken garbage and junk. The movement of the Sun into the Photon Band will have cleansed parts of Earth, and those parts have become places where you and species once survived, but now the whole planet must be loved and cared for. Your sense of self will be so huge and unlimited that all of your time will be devoted to working with your new partners and lovers (or rediscovered old ones) to massage and reanoint the earth. You will all make the soil crystalline and replant the trees and plants; the seeds and animals species you have so carefully protected and cherished will be garnered by you, and you will prepare new homes for them. Gaia's skin will begin to breathe, and her hair will wave in the solar wind.

Ninth House (June 23, 2006 to December 19, 2007) *Pisces: How do I feel about being a great being and a partner in the rebirthing of Gaia? How can I express these melting feelings of love about my new world?* Now you see that you have made it, more and more you are amazed by what you have become. You are a being of spiritual magnificence and planetary confidence that no one—including you—imagined was possible during the terrible days of darkness before 2001. *You delight in yourself.* Like a fresh flower in the dew, your spine is pushing through the soil, and you are really alive! As if you've awakened from amnesia after a terrible battle, you know you are alive and will grow. What is amazing about this realization is that you also know that you won't die again. Gone is the sense of "do it now," and it is replaced by absolute wonder. You just sit in the forest and watch tree seedlings coming up and flowers blossoming. You see that the tree seedling would not grow, the flower would not blossom, unless you were there watching them; growth requires your love. As I look at this process, seeing Earth in hyperspace, growth is not solar during this phase, and the planet regenerates according only to consciousness.

Tenth House (December 19, 2007 to August 22, 2009) *Aquarius: I see that the planet exists when I am conscious of it, and now I want to know what is my role in the Age of Aquarius.* A new world is forming, and it is a world based on individuality that gathers its expression together and forms a whole. Things that are not valued simply shapeshift into other desired forms, and you realize that if you don't value yourself, you will transmute into something else. Your mate or your children will not be there if you forget your wonder in their presence, and there will be no flowers in your garden without your admiration. One day you realize that there are transfigured humans all over the planet who have cleansed Gaia and resonate with the new growing lifeforms. *The whole planet is beautiful!* You sit for a day and contemplate the vision of beings like yourself all over the planet working as partners to enhance the life force. You sit in wonder at the base of a great tree that grew tall and formed a canopy just because you crystallized the soil, planted the seedling, and sat with it in communion while it grew. Then you know the tree is actually your father, and you are overwhelmed with joy because you see that nothing you ever loved was lost. Like the tree, you don't have to do the old nightmare again—government, taxes, television, military, bombs and guns. Like the tree, you will be right there in the forest watching the plants grow and knowing that each human in community and partnership is enhancing Gaia with you. All of your life, you will be in synchronicity with all your other brothers and sisters. You will link mentally with them at solstices and equinoxes, as well as follow the moon and the sacred calendars with them, but otherwise you will be in the now, deeply involved with those with whom you live. Global communications will not be the Net—horror stories that shut you down and caused you to ignore Earth. Instead, there will be global ceremony that creates new realities.

Eleventh House (August 22, 2009 to March 4, 2011) *Capricorn: How will I take this knowledge that I have mastered about Earth—thought is the direct conduit to all life—and offer this pure wisdom to the Galaxy itself?* Once you actually comprehend the potentiality of Gaia, your sense about creation and structure itself will be of the basic life force. You will be conscious Keepers of the Living Library. Like Plato, the most advanced philosopher to visit Earth during your own historical cycle, you will know that the shadow enhances form, and manifestation is the sum total of its elements. You will not resist looking at everything—the shadow—before you act. Never again will you fall into the possibility that the "end justifies the means." You will know that each "means" or element forms the whole, and you will exist in a timeless life of nurturing each seed, idea, and element as if it is your most precious child. These will be the days when the lion will lie down with the lamb and peace will reign. During this whole cycle, never fear for a moment, because it is foretold that peace on Earth will be Gaia's gift to the Galaxy at the end of the Mayan Calendar.

Twelfth House (March 4, 2011 to August 31, 2012) *Sagittarius: How can I move out of Gaia and carry the knowledge of the now and still be in the now?* Everything that has transpired was school for this part. How are you going to stay in the now and yet move your awareness off-planet and carry the biological codes of Earth with you? What I see occurring during this phase is a fusion of the Galactic Federation with Earth! Deep inside, those of you who await the landing of extraterrestrials are actually intuiting this phase, but you are not ready yet. They *will* come to Earth; however, their visitation will only occur because you are nine dimensional. How else could you transmit your codes to them? Codes are multidimensional, and the only way you can detect or read any code is if your frequency is able to match the code! As you sit in a room on Earth reading this book, the room you sit in has radio, television, microwave, ultra sound, and many other vibrations traveling through it. The only way you could read these vibrations is by having a body that is a radio, television, microwave, or ultra sound receiver. First of all, would you want to? Do you really *want* to feel the frequency of extraterrestrials? You have a lot of school coming, and the Galactic Federation will fuse with you so that you will be able to hold their codes and learn about their realities and travel with them; then the most fantastic phase occurs at the end of the Calendar.

Phase Thirteen of the Metonic Cycle (August 31, 2012 to December 21, 2012) *Dichotomy of New Galactic Intention: What is my intention for Gaia for the next 26,000-year cycle?* As I see it, these four months will be a time when we will be on Earth totally in the now, simultaneously conscious of all cosmic locations and what codes of creation they contain. Some will choose to continue to reincarnate on Earth because of love for what Gaia offers—the chance to play with good and evil and make a choice—which will be greater than any other personal desire. Some will be ready to take the Gaian codes to other locations, and the last four months on Earth will be used to master whatever teaching they will be working with. Some will choose to be the great beings who work with souls entering the Ecliptic. And some will migrate to stars and encourage them to become supernovas.

*Appendix D*

# The Sirius Star System
## and the Ancient Records of Orion

*THE SIRIUS MYSTERY: WAS EARTH VISITED BY INTELLIGENT BEINGS FROM A PLANET IN the system of the star Sirius?* by Robert Temple, and all the works of Zecharia Sitchin discussed in the text prove beyond any reasonable doubt that extraterrestrials have physically influenced civilizations on Earth.[1] *The Sirius Mystery* established that the Dogon and the ancient Egyptians were actually visited by Sirians 5000 years ago; and Sitchin's books prove that the Sumerian culture was established by the outermost planet, Nibiru, called "planet of the crossing" in Sumerian. I have considered Sitchin's work extensively in this book as well as in my earlier works, and it is time to examine *The Sirius Mystery* more carefully in light of the "Sirian/Pleiadian Alliance." Sixth dimensional Sirian consciousness provides the ability to tune into sacred geometry and morphogenetic fields, and many people are responding to these expansive qualities in thought now that these ideas are more available. This has occurred because of the works of Temple, Sitchin, and most recently Musaios, author of *The Lion Path,* who has profound Sirian sensitivity.[2]

I am the author of *Chiron: Rainbow Bridge between the Inner and Outer Planets,* which describes the influence of Chiron, a new body in our solar system sighted in 1977.[3] Because Chiron and Sirius B have similar astronomical patterns and they rule similar issues on Earth, my previous research puts me in a unique position to understand Sirius B—the white dwarf that orbits Sirius A. The orbit of Sirius B around Sirius A has an ellipse and periodicity similar to the orbit of Chiron around our Sun—fifty years—and both are tiny objects in their systems that have very potent initiatic and healing affects on humans. Chiron rules the ability to bridge material and subtle worlds, to heal wounded elements of the self, and initiatic and shamanic processes. Sirius B rules similar things, but its influence is more subtle, more stellar. Since the Sirius system is stellar, I was only able to access Sirius B through trance channeling; however, my research on Chiron is based on traditional astrological analysis, and this methodology is described in Appendix A.

Chiron's sighting in 1977 was a sign in the sky that individuals would be able to access the high initiatic consciousness of Sirius, if a star link was reestablished. The simultaneous sighting of Chiron and the release of Temple's book in 1977 *are* signs of this starlink for humans, and you have actually been in the midst of subtle planetary initiations from 1977 to 1994. (See Appendix A.) The physical activation by the Sirius system began March 1994, and many of you are just beginning to notice subtle impulses. The Pleiadians are very insistent that it is time to stretch your minds, to open yourselves to cosmic realms. This kind of subtle consciousness is very new and deeply related to space exploration, but it is also very ancient on your planet. In the Dogon villages, even children learned the Sirian star lore and the stories about their ancestors from the Sirius star system. These systems open very keen perceptual skills, so let's investigate the Dogon records and open up these skills in you!

The Sirian/Pleiadian Alliance was greatly enhanced by the *Sirius Periastron in April 1994*, when Sirius B was closest to Sirius A in its 50-year elliptical orbit. Chiron will be closest to our Sun on February 14, 1996, and that will be an ideal time to ground Sirian codes deeply into Earth. Both Sirius B and Chiron have very elliptical orbits, and both are closest to the stars they orbit from 1992 to 1998. Sirius A and B are a binary system, and their orbital pattern is the basis of the ritual system of the Dogon culture of Mali in west central Africa. The Dogon offered the secrets of their highest mysteries to eminent French anthropologists Marcel Griaule and Germaine Dieterlen between 1946 and 1950,[4] and their research is the basis of *The Sirius Mystery*. These anthropologists proved that these complex rituals were based on an extremely detailed analysis of the orbital patterns and physical characteristics of Sirius A and B, plus Sirius C, a third star that also has a 50-year orbit around Sirius A. Sirius C orbits at right angles to Sirius B. The existence of these rituals, which have been ongoing for at least a thousand years to recent times, is astonishing because Sirius B was only first viewed through telescopes in the nineteenth century, and the first photograph of it was taken in 1970, since it is an extremely dense and nearly invisible white dwarf star. In other words, Sirius B was *invisible* to the Dogon, yet they said it was the most important star, they diagrammed its elliptical orbit, and their rituals show they knew its orbit around Sirius A was 50 years. Sirius B is called "Digitaria" by Temple because the Dogon called it "Po." Po is the tiniest edible seed known to the Dogon, and Digitaria is the species name for that seed.[5] That is, it was called Po because the Dogon knew Sirius B was a tiny, dense star! Digitaria connotes "finger," and Chiron means "hand" in Greek, a seemingly curious coincidence.

There are other fascinating astronomical factors that support Dogon mythology that attracted the attention of Robert Temple. For example, the Dogon called Po the "egg of the world," and they said that it gave birth to all creation in the universe. The Dogon say Po is made up of earth, air, fire, and water, but strangely, the earth element was replaced by metal.[6] The nearest white dwarf star to Earth—8.6 light years away—is Sirius B. When white dwarfs become supernovae, they spread large amounts of iron throughout the Galaxy, and the Sun and Earth, according to Ken Croswell in *The Alchemy of the Heavens*, were birthed out of a cloud of iron-rich dust 4.6 billion years ago—the same process that is occurring in Orion now. [7] According to the latest scientific analysis of seismic waves from earthquakes, the center of the Earth is one huge iron crystal.[8] The Dogon rituals, based on the Sirius star system, are a sure sign of a true *cosmogony*—accurate creation record. This causes me to think that the first dimension of Earth—the iron-core crystal—originated when Sirius B became a supernova. That is, *Earth was created out of the Sirius star system!* Temple proves that anthropological research has established beyond any doubt that the Dogon rituals were unpolluted by modern influence, and the Dogon say that Digitaria is the source of everything on Earth. Digitaria exploded in a supernova, and it must have provided the iron crystal that birthed Earth. How else could Sirius B be accurately described in Dogon rituals?

The Dogon say that Digitaria is the axis of the world, and that without its movement, no other star could hold its course! As Temple says, "This means that it is the master of ceremonies of the celestial positions; in particular it governs the position of Sirius, an unruly star; it separates it from the other stars by encompassing it with its trajectory."[9] If you want to know more about Temple's work, I'd suggest you read *The Sirius Mystery*. Meanwhile, since I have been thinking about the Sirius system since 1977—when Temple's book came out and Chiron was sighted—here is Digitaria via trance channeling, since I believe it must be the actual source of the creation of Earth.[10]

*Digitaria of the Sirius Star System*
"I, Digitaria, have a sacred twin called Sorghum, and we orbit Sirius A at right angles to one another. Sorghum is the source of female souls of all living or future beings. Because her 50-year orbit is at a right angle to mine, her symbol is a cross in a circle. We will be forever involved but separated. In the beginning, I imploded; a piece of me became Earth and another Nibiru. I became four bodies— Earth, Nibiru, Sorghum, and Digitaria—and Sorghum and I orbit Sirius A. The Sun and Sirius are linked as twin stars by the journeys of these four parts of myself, and our mutual male and female parts seek each other eternally. In your system, Nibiru is male and Earth is female; in our system, I am male and Sorghum is female. The time has come for the remembrance and healing of these four lost parts of your souls. The way to do this is to honor Sorghum at the spring equinox, Earth at the summer solstice, Nibiru at fall equinox, and Digitaria at the winter solstice. Indeed, a grand phase of ceremonies is soon to come to Earth! By linking these solar and stellar parts of yourselves, you will all find your twin souls easily.

"When your solar system was forming out of interstellar dust over 4 billion years ago, I became a supernova, and there was great chaos in the Sirius star system. I imploded into my small, dense self and began orbiting with Sorghum around Sirius A. I awoke out of my exhaustion one day and realized a part of me was torn away and had become Earth—a planet orbiting around a nearby star, which you call your Sun! Your star is so sacred to us that we do not utter its name. Next, I saw that another planet formed out of me! How magnificent! It is called Nibiru and it comes into your solar system every 3600 years. Even though this planet was born out of my explosion and, like Earth, was blasted out to your Sun, its orbit, unlike Earth's, returns it to us every 3600 years. I will tell you the story of Nibiru, since Sirius A is the location of the Nibiruan Library, just as Alcyone is the location of the Earth Library.

"About a million years ago, Nibiru was inhabited by a race of beings from Orion—the Anunnaki—who were seeking a new home. These beings had very long lives, and after 500,000 years had passed, they realized they needed new genetic material to continue their race. However, a new genetic matrix would not emerge in Orion for another half-million years. These Anunnaki, as they are known on Earth, knew that their planet and Earth were both born out of my supernova, so they decided to visit Earth to search for a new genetic matrix. Thus, 450,000 years ago, the Anunnaki of Nibiru began landing on Earth. Though they come into your solar system and orbit between Mars and Jupiter every 3600 years, they do not land on Earth during each return. The most propitious landing times are during the Ages of Taurus and Scorpio, when your Sun is farthest out in the Galactic Night, far away from the Photon Band. (See Fig. 4.) For example, they spent much time on Earth from 3800 to 3400 B.C., during which time they founded Sumerian civilization. [11]

"Once this history began, I, Digitaria, reasoned: Why not use Nibiru as a communication link between the Sun and Sirius A, since Nibiru makes this long journey between them both? As you've heard, in recent times since 7200 B.C., the Nibiruans have become false couriers, yet I have no other way to reach your world, so I try to use them anyway. Remember, Sirius A is the location of the Nibiruan Library, and access to that Library helps your solar system work harmonically with its erratic visitor—Nibiru. I have come forth to discuss the time when the link between your Sun and Sirius A was severed, which occurred under Akhenaton, the controversial Eighteenth Dynasty pharaoh. This link with Sirius A was reopened by many dedicated teachers during the Sirius Periastron of 1994, and it is because of that that I can speak to you again. Prior to Akhenaton, I had direct linkage with Earth through the Egyptian dynasties for thousands of years; and the Dogon kept this lineage intact until 1994, so that this exquisite relinkage could occur. The Great Pyramid maintained the vital link with Orion, as long as the Egyptian dynasties protected this stellar web system. Until the time of Akhenaton, the Sirians could reach your whole planet through the Great Pyramid.

"On Earth, the Anunnaki and Sirians shared technology, and everybody got along for hundreds of thousands of years. The Anunnaki used earthlings for workers and sexual services while gradually altering their DNA. I, Digitaria, taught you magical science by helping the indigenous people of Earth evolve mentally through sacred plant knowledge. There were difficulties with these projects because of the Nibiruan tendency to *take* from Earth as well as to *assist*. Once you evolved into humans—creators who knew their own creation story—we Sirians all hoped the Anunnaki would gain more respect for you because you were destined to become the galactic biological school—the Living Library of the Galaxy. [12] Since we Sirians are 6D, we could not do anything in 3D with humans, but the Anunnaki, who can take on third-dimensional powers, could sojourn in the Garden of Eden.

"Imagine the following from Earth's point of view. During the ages of Leo and Aquarius, Earth passes through 2000 years of photonic transmutation; then, during its deepest penetration into the Galactic Night during the ages of Taurus and Scorpio, Earth is visited by the gods from Orion. Once Nibiru had visited Earth over many thousands of years, humanity began to develop a sense of individuality. Over 26,000 years ago, humanity began to refine feelings and desired freedom, and the Pleiadians were impulsed by individuals to get directly involved in the evolution of humanity. Why the Pleiadians? Since Nibiru is a male force and carries the very gods of heaven right to Earth, you intuited that it was time for you to get to know the goddess of the sky—the Pleiades.

"Since we Sirians tended to control your minds in the temples while teaching you to ground harmonic fields, I, Digitaria, am sure this break with Sirius was all part of your evolution. You finally had to find your own ways to hold 6D geometrical harmonics in place, and now we have come to assist you again. Literally anything you want to utilize out of this knowledge is yours, now that we've relinked with you. In that light, the actual break must be examined, to heal any parts of it that might stand in your way. The reason the story of Akhenaton is so controversial is because it actually cloaks secret knowledge hidden in the Sirian records, and you can tell this information must be important because it has been so carefully guarded by indigenous people, such as the Dogon.

"Akhenaton rejected the traditional animal/human gods and altered the Egyptian/Sirian geomantic system by moving the temple sites and changing their usages. His reasons for doing this were of the highest order. Privy to all secrets, he knew that the Hebrew priests had stolen the lizard temple technology from Khem and put it into operation on Mount Moriah. He knew that they were utilizing Nibiru solely as the lens, and he knew that they were using this technology to figure out how to conquer Egypt.

"Akhenaton had watched the harmonic field of Egypt deteriorate while he was receiving his initiations as a child and young man. When he was small, no one abused women and children or stole, and children honored their parents. By the time he was preparing to take the pharaonic, or Sirian initiation, brothers stole from brothers, women stole husbands from each other, children dishonored their parents, and physical and sexual abuse was common. Akhenaton accepted the pharaonic codes because he wanted to stop the disintegration of Egypt; but, by his obtaining the codes for that purpose, we Sirians were thrown into a great conflict. The pharaoh can wear the double crown of the Blue Nile with the sacred uraeus giving him snake powers *only if he has no agenda*. He was to simply hold the peaceful field, which cannot be held if it is based on an "enemy." We Sirians attuned with Akhenaton whenever he went into the central sanctuary, which was not often; and as we tuned into him, all we got from him were great hatred of the enemy and fear for the people. He was in great pain, anger, judgment, and confusion because his *ka* had abandoned his physical form. The priests of Amun wanted to assist him by working with him to persuade his *ka* to come back, but he would not listen to them. He scorned them, since they had allowed the Hebrew priests into Khem to study crocodile activation.

"One day as I passed closest to Sirius A, a terrible scene came into my inner visual mind. I realized Sirius A was receiving this scene simultaneously: We first saw a lion of Sekhmet staring into our eyes, and then behind her, Akhenaton was sitting on his throne and a great and terrible lizard was approaching him![13] We felt Akhenaton's heart beating rapidly because he was terrified, since, without his *ka*, he was helpless. A great battle ensued. The lizard was the fourth-dimensional form of a Hebrew priest named Illuru, and the lizard said, 'Akhenaton, *I* take your snake power!' He took hold of the Akhenaton's *uasit*, his divine scepter. The pharaoh dared not move as the sacred scepter that held the field of the Blue Nile passed into the claws of this animal. Then the great lizard took the *uasit* and tapped it on the floor three times, and each time it became a powerful serpent! This meant that this lizard was not only taking the *uasit* away from the pharaoh, he was also going to use the powers himself! Instantly, we Sirians cut the connection between Sirius and the Great Pyramid, and we felt a wave of anguish rise out of the Nile! We closed our secret chambers under the Sphinx and the Great Pyramid, and Akhenaton and Egypt were abandoned!

"Illuru looked contemptuously at the frozen pharaoh. Then, since he was a 4D holographic projection, Illuru disappeared and remanifested as Moses in the Hebrew encampment in the Sinai where a tremendous vortex of fire burned in front of some followers of Moses. Illuru's 3D self was consumed with the powerful flames as he became a 4D manifestation—Moses—and he uttered the word 'Aton-I,' which the startled desert people heard as 'Adonai.'[14] There was no priesthood or temple among these desert people, and he, Moses, instituted both, based on the priesthood and temples of Egypt. To continue the people's star connection, he brought the tradition of the solar boat into the temple, but he called it the Ark of the Covenant. And, out of utter contempt for the lizard into which he had shapeshifted, he told his followers that they must sacrifice animals to the Aton, such as throwing their sacred crocodiles into the flames. Thus ended the honoring of the sacred animal teachers of the previous 3500 years. A great lament from the hearts of all the beasts on the planet was heard all the way out to the Sirius star system. Even Anubis, our personal Sirian guardian, would be dishonored!

"As a white dwarf star, which is dense like a dense nuclear reactor, I, Digitaria, felt Illuru creating a mental nuclear bomb—*monotheism*—and I experienced a rebirthing! I relived becoming a white dwarf and I felt the field of the Blue Nile implode! Fundamentalism began on Earth—the belief that allows any action to defend one point of view, no matter how abusive, violent, inhuman, or spiritually limiting. Thus began wars based on ideas; sexuality based on using bodies; child abuse based on children as property; and the control of the world based upon the concepts of church and state.

"In the days of the Eighteenth Dynasty in Egypt, the Hebrew people became the carriers of Nibiruan intelligence, as can be seen in their name in Hebrew 'Ibri;' the Egyptians, meanwhile, called them the 'Hibiru.' The Israelites named themselves 'the Chosen People based on the manifestation of Moses,' and I, Digitaria, honor them for recognizing that *Nibiru and Earth are of the same body.* We honor them for realizing that a lineage was needed to carry the archetype of Nibiru, just as we honor the Egyptians for carrying the archetype of Sirius. *Living out a stellar archetype as a group is the foundation of tribes and clans, and this is how the indigenous people connect to stars.* Each star or planet carries certain behaviors and beliefs, and the whole point of taking on an archetype is to process it. I honor the Hebrew people for recognizing their desire for Akhenaton's world, but I, Digitaria, am here today to inform you that *the Hebrews got Nibiru as an archetype, not Sirius.* The Sirians weren't connected to Akhenaton when Illuru took the power! I know this is important news for all of you who identify with this form, because I know that you love Sirian 6D sacred geometry because of your fascination with the Kaballah, alchemy, and magical arts. The teachings and sacred knowledge of 2D, 4D, 6D, and 8D, are all related and interconnected, and more awareness about their subtle differences will enhance the pursuit of these fields.

"Illuru activated a group thoughtform in his race for carrying out the grand agenda of Nibiru, and the Anunnaki were delighted that day. Excellent, said Anu! We honor Hebrews for being a people of Earth who chose to process the desires of an extraterrestrial body, because that is what karma is. A number of Earth groups carry their own extraterrestrial archetypes, such as the British (Nibiru), French (Orion), Balinese (Pleiadian), Iraqis (Nibiru), the Jews (Nibiru), and the Egyptians (Sirius). Nibiruan work, by the way, is more convoluted for you than Sirian work because the Anunnaki sojourn with you at times, but in both cases, the issue is handling power on Earth.

"In order to cope with power, the Jews, like the pharaohs, became adepts of powerful magical systems using esoteric knowledge and secret cabals in order to get what they wanted. The power grab came after the Anunnaki had used humans for workers and sexual services over hundreds of thousands of years. Thus the pattern of using without permission was already deeply ingrained on Earth. Nibiru carries male energy, so the Nibiruan-based Hebrew monotheist culture became profoundly patriarchal and abusive of Gaia. The Hebrews had once been devotees of the Goddess, and there are remnants of Canaanite-based goddess worship in contemporary Jewish ritual practices. Snake medicine, once separated from Sirian guidance, was taken away from Akhenaton as his *uasit* was grabbed, and thereafter, most people participating in the Hebrew line (Judeo-Christian-Islamic) became profoundly afraid of the occult. Illuru envied the pharaoh's booty, and most of Illuru's descendants are obsessed by a fanatical materialism that oppresses Earth and causes war. Slavery, prostitution, hierarchy, secrecy, war, and misogyny resulted from this transfer of energy. Today, knowledge of this material has become totally unconscious; witness, for example, how the ancient Egyptians are still denigrated during Passover rituals as if the Exodus were last week. These old patterns must be processed because negative projection onto the modern people of Egypt destabilizes the Middle East, where conflict could escalate tensions into another world war. *None of you want to become barbarians again.*

"I, Digitaria, inform you that the gods of Nibiru are ready to be freed because their real skills—genetic engineering—are needed on Orion. They do not need Earth any longer, yet genetic engineering based on old Nibiruan patterns could be the ultimate oppressive tool for your world! After all, Hitler already tried it in the 1930s and 1940s.[15] However, now that you have seen what happened when Illuru took on the powers of Nibiru when he thought he was going to get the Sirian powers, would you want to use this tool? You are infected with the idea that the very unit of creation—DNA—can and needs to be tampered with; this came from Nibiruan obsessions about scarcity, a result of their frustration about not spending much time in the solar system.

"We of Sirius feel your realm strongly, and you have honored our gifts, such as our teachings in Egypt. We have attempted to help the Anunnaki learn how to *feel* instead of *think* first. When you *think*, not *feel*, in linear space and time, you become a predator, because you will always think of yourself first. If you become a predator, human realities self-destruct, because predation requires a victim. Once you set up a situation in which there must be a victim, it no longer matters whether you are the victim or the predator. If you *feel* before you *think*, you know how to respond to the whole group effortlessly. *The Anunnaki are metallic beings originating from Orion, and they have great difficulty being able to feel.* They colonized Nibiru a million years ago just to attain that next stage of evolution; and we Sirians admire how the people of Earth have so beautifully served them. But we know their oppression is imploding your realm. Imagine this, humans! Think how you value thinking over feeling, and then try to imagine a race of people who left Orion—the location of the Galactic Federation—and eventually landed on a strange little hybrid star/planet body just to find a new way to be. Would *you* do that? Those of you living in the United States might want to notice that your ancestors did exactly that.

"The implications of this choice are awesome, and that is why I, Digitaria, am saying how much I honor the Hebrews and all their descendants for deciding to work out this karmic dilemma within humanity. What a brave choice, and now it is time to become *conscious* of that choice. The Annunaki picked up alchemy—transmutation of base metals into precious ones—during their last sojourn out by Sirius A in 1600 A.D. Alchemy is actually all about feelings and subtle vibrations at all levels below 8D; it is a Pleiadian science, and as the Nibiruans began to desire more feeling, they became interested in it. The ancient Sumerian and Chaldean alchemical tractates were carefully guarded because the Anunnaki believed they could cease to be metallic by means of alchemy! They guarded these tractates with their lives, hoping alchemy offered them the chance to be flesh and blood while on Earth. In fact, alchemy is the way for them to value their metallic essence—Merkabah—which they need while they are a star outside the solar system.

"During the Eighteenth Dynasty, Egypt was acutely stressed by invasions and by Earth changes caused by the great volcano, Thera, erupting in 1650 B.C. The whole Middle East was destabilized, and these were days of darkness and terrible winds. Egypt became a refuge; then it was overwhelmed, and the Sirian link was lost by Akhenaton. The abandonment of Akhenaton was a source of great pain to all inhabitants of Sirius. The work in Egypt was a mission, but its original intent was subverted; this created death, pain, and suffering that will not ever end unless each one of you reweaves this web by letting go of belief in enemies. Gaia has the right to experience harmony and peace, and humans who want the Pleiadian love vibration need to remember how to expand that energy via Sirian geomancy, which links the Sun and Sirius again. The pharaoh was the only one in the whole Egyptian system with a direct conduit into Sirian consciousness; in 2012 A.D., however, *all* humans are scheduled to have a direct conduit. The pharaoh was blissed out as a result of his ecstatic linkage with other dimensions, and this is how you will feel attending the Cosmic Party, when the linkage between the Sun and Sirius is totally felt on Earth again.

# Notes

Chapter One: The Cosmic Party

1. David Freidel, Linda Schele, and Joy Parker, *Maya Cosmos: Three Thousand Years on the Shaman's Path* (New York: William Morrow and Company, 1993), pp. 59–122.
2. John Major Jenkins, "The How and Why of the Mayan End Date in 2012 A.D.," *The Mountain Astrologer* (Dec./Jan. 1995), pp. 54–57.
3. Freidel, Schele, Parker, *Maya Cosmos*, p. 115.
4. The initiatic work with Wendy Munro, Barbara Hand Clow, Hakim Essaman Nazlit, and a group of students during April 1994 was captured in the video, "The Nine Initiations on the Nile" by David Drewry.
5. Bob Frissell, *Nothing in This Book Is True, But It's Exactly How Things Are* (Berkeley, CA: Frog, Ltd.), pp. 155–164. The event referred to in the text was considered to be scientifically impossible. For example, from August 7–10, 1972, the solar wind, which has an average velocity of 500 km/sec. (million miles per hour), averaged 2-1/2 million miles per hour. In 1968, scientist David Suzuki published a paper sent to major world governments stating that sometime between August and November 1972, a huge explosion would occur on the Sun. When it did occur, all major scientific publications reported the data. A worldwide scientific meeting occurred in the summer of 1973, and because the event was incomprehensible, a worldwide blackout about the event ensued.
6. Frissell, *Nothing Is True*, p. 158. My consciousness shifted totally during the three days he describes, and it is also important to notice that Pluto, the first planet in the Photon Band, entered the Band in 1972. See Appendix B.
7. Robert Bauval and Adrian Gilbert, *The Orion Mystery: Unlocking the Secrets of the Pyramids* (New York: Crown Publishers, 1994).
8. Barbara Marciniak, *Bringers of the Dawn: Teachings from the Pleiadians* (Santa Fe: Bear & Company, 1992).
9. Zecharia Sitchin, *The 12th Planet* (Santa Fe: Bear & Company, 1991).
10. Virginia Essene and Sheldon Nidle, *You Are Becoming a Galactic Human* (Santa Clara, CA: S.E.E. Publishing, 1994).
11. Barbara Hand Clow, *Heart of the Christos: Starseeding from the Pleiades* (Santa Fe: Bear & Company, 1989), and *Signet of Atlantis: War in Heaven Bypass* (Santa Fe: Bear & Company, 1992).

12. Regarding Figure 1 and its description in the text, the phenomenon of the Twelve Great Ages is a cycle of the Sun around Alcyone, the central star of the Pleiades. The precession of the equinoxes, which expresses the same time factor, is a purely terrestrial effect that is a result of the crossing point of the Sun on the celestial Equator moving around an imaginary circle in the sky for 25,920 years. These two cycles are mysteriously synchronized, and this factor is built into the Mayan Great Calendar. According to Hunbatz Men, *Los Calendarios Mayas Y Hunab K'U,* pages 233–40 (see note 8, Chapter Two), these two cycles are totally synchronized. This insight by Men is what led to my explanation of the cycle of the Great Ages and the Photon Band in Figure 1. Also see note 19, Chapter Seven.

13. John Michell and Christine Rhone, *Twelve-Tribe Nations and the Science of Enchanting the Landscape* (London: Thames and Hudson, 1991).

14. Clow, *Christos,* pp. 41–47.

15. Sitchin, *12th Planet,* pp. 214-54.

16. Richard Laurence, trans., *The Book of Enoch the Prophet* (San Diego: Wizard's Bookshelf, 1983).

17. Jenkins, "End Date," p. 60.

*Chapter Two: The Photon Band*

1. Shirley Kemp, "The Photon Belt Story," *Nexus* (Feb. 1991) and Robert Stanley, "The Photon Zone: Earth's Future Brightens", *Nexus* (Summer 1991).

2. Robert Temple, *The Sirius Mystery* (New York: St. Martin's Press, 1976).

3. Michael Talbot, *The Holographic Universe* (New York: Harper Collins, 1991).

4. Generally speaking, the Maya or Mayans are referred to as "Maya," but the Mayan Calendar continues to be referred to as Mayan with an "n." The Mayan Calendar covers 5125 or 25,625 years, whether it is one Great Cycle—5125 years—or five Great Cycles—25,625 years. The other shorter-term calendars are referred to as various calendars of the Maya in this book.

5. Talbot, *Holographic Universe,* p. 36.

6. See Appendix C.

7. Kemp and Stanley, photon articles above.

8. Hunbatz Men, *Los Calendarios Mayas Y Hunab K'U* (Juarez, Mexico: Ediciones Horizonte, 1983).

9. Men, *Los Calendarios,* pp. 134–36.

10. Stanley, "The Photon Zone."

11. Vivian E. Robson, *The Fixed Stars and Constellations in Astrology* (York Beach, ME: Samuel Weiser, 1979).

12. Richard Hinkley Allen, *Star Names: Their Lore and Meaning* (New York: Dover Publications, 1963), pp. 391–413. Allen comments on page 393 that the precession cycle of 25,900 years was called "The Great Year of the Pleiades."

13. José Argüelles, *The Mayan Factor: Path Beyond Technology* (Santa Fe: Bear & Company, 1987), pp. 111 and 136; and also see Dr. Brian Swimme's introduction.

14. Jenkins, "End Date," p. 54.

15. José Diaz-Bolio, *The Geometry of the Maya* (Merida, Mexico: Area Maya, 1965), and "The Bio-Mathematical Basis of the Mayan Calendar," from *The Mayan Calendar Made Easy,* edited by Sandy Huff (Safety Harbor, FL: Sandy Huff, 1984). In Chapter Seven, "Tzolk'in" suddenly shows up and offers an overview of the Mayan Great Calendar. Tzolk'in is the sacred 260-day calendar (13 numbers x 20 days = 260); the Tzolk'in, the Venus Round (synodic cycle of Venus), and the 365-day "Haab" (solar year) are the basis of the Great Cycles. There are many theories about the derivation of the Tzolk'in, and Diaz-Bolio's answer is the right one, in my opinion.

16. Bruce Cathie, *Harmonic 33* (Sydney, Australia: A.H. and A.W. Reed, 1968), pp. 189–93, and Bruce Cathie and P.N. Temm, *Harmonic 695* (Sydney, Australia; A.H. and A.W. Reed, 1971).

17. Barbara Hand Clow, *Chiron: Rainbow Bridge Between the Inner and Outer Planets* (St. Paul, MN: Llewellyn Publications, 1987).

18. Trevor Ravenscroft, *The Spear of Destiny* (York Beach, ME: Samuel Weiser, 1982).

19. Amorah Quan-Yin, *The Pleiadian Workbook: Awakening Your Divine Ka* (Santa Fe: Bear & Company, 1996).

20. Bauval and Gilbert, *Orion Mystery*, p. 212.

21. Barbara Hand Clow, *Liquid Light of Sex: Understanding Your Key Life Passages* (Santa Fe: Bear & Company, 1991).

22. Barbara Hand Clow, *The Mind Chronicles Trilogy* (Santa Fe: Bear & Company). This trilogy includes *Eye of the Centaur* (1986), *Heart of the Christos* (1989), and *Signet of Atlantis* (1992).

23. Sitchin, *12th Planet*, pp. 301–22.

*Chapter Three: Alchemy of Nine Dimensions*

1. Talbot, *Holographic Universe*, p. 1.

2. Zecharia Sitchin, *The Wars of Gods and Men* (Santa Fe: Bear & Company, 1992).

3. Jerry L. Ziegler, *YHWH* (Morton, IL: Star Publishers, 1977), and Graham Hancock, *The Sign and the Seal* (New York: Crown Publishers, 1992).

4. Sitchin, *12th Planet*, p. 229.

5. Frissell, *Nothing Is True*, p. 158.

6. Barbara Marciniak, *Bringers,* and *Earth: Pleiadian Keys to the Living Library* (Santa Fe: Bear & Company, 1995). Marciniak's "World Management Team" is a great term for the powers-that-be.

7. Sitchin, *Wars*, pp. 310–342.

8. Clow, *Signet*, pp. 102–08. Yoga, mudras, and sacred postures, such as triangular holds described in the text, will become a necessity as the energy accelerates.

9. Belinda Gore, *Ecstatic Body Postures: An Alternate Reality Workbook* (Santa Fe: Bear & Company, 1995). This book is based on the work of Dr. Felicitas Goodman: Also see by Dr. Goodman, *Where the Spirits Ride the Wind* (Bloomington, IN: Indiana University Press, 1990).

10. Michell, *Nations*, pp. 138–46.

11. As this book went to press, the evening news announced that the Jet Propulsion Laboratory, Pasadena, CA, had diverted *Galileo* from an orbit that would end with its crash into Jupiter in late 1995. The new orbit sets *Galileo* to fly by Io in order to photograph it.

12. Clow, "The Comet and Jupiter", *Welcome to Planet Earth*, Vol. 14, #8.

*Chapter Four: The Lizards and the Roman Church*

1. Arthur C. Clarke, *Rama Revealed* (New York: Bantam, 1995), p. 1.

2. R.A. Boulay, *Flying Serpents and Dragons: The Story of Mankind's Reptilian Past* (Clearwater, FL: Galaxy Books, 1990).

3. *Encylopedia Britannica*, Eleventh Edition, vol. IV, pp. 939–41.

4. Labib Habachi, *The Obelisks of Egypt* (Cairo: American University Press, 1984), pp. 109–49.

5. Linda Zimmermann, "Heads and Tales of Celestial Coins," *Sky and Telescope*, (March 1995), pp. 28–29. Figure 11 is an adapted drawingfrom this article of a Roman coin, which portrays the words "Divvs Ivlis" set in an eight-pointed star. In the original coin, there is an extra line if "Divvs Ivlis" is considered a line. However, this extra line is actually the line that should be where Caesar's name is located, and it would not be acceptable to have a line through *his* name. The star rays were moved to portray his divine name, causing the coin to have 10 star rays, including "Divine Caesar." I have studied literally hundreds of coins and symbols of the eight-pointed star, which is Nibiru, so I asked my illustrator to slightly alter the coin for reader clarity. Also, this coin is especially interesting because the lines may have been jigged to give more emphasis to the crossing time of Nibiru between about 200 B.C. to 100 A.D., as can be seen in a coin on p. 29, "Noble Saturn in Aquarius," with eight rays, but slightly adjusted. Normally these symbols are very exact and eight-sided.

6. A "Shar" is one 3600-year orbit of Nibiru, and from the solar perspective, entities on planets out beyond Earth live longer. For example, a Jupiterian

lives twelve years for one Earth year, and a Nibiruan lives 3600 years for one Earth year; therefore, when the Anunnaki sojourn on Earth, they age very rapidly. This factor is behind the mysterious 1000-year-long lifetimes of entities like Methuselah (probably means he lived around 30 years on Earth). The Nibiruan concern about aging on Earth is the source of humans longing for immortality and fearing death. Individuals who seem to have no Nibiruan implants evidence little concern about death, and the death obsession of American culture shows how deeply influenced it is by Nibiruan thought-forms.

7. Habachi, *Obelisks*, pp. 109–49.
8. Byron E. Dix and James W. Mavor, *Manitou: The Sacred Landscape of New England's Native Civilization* (Rochester, VT: Inner Traditions, 1989).
9. John L. Brooke, *The Refiner's Fire: The Making of Mormon Cosmology, 1644–1844* (Cambridge: Cambridge University Press, 1994), pp. 149–83.
10. Clow, *Christos*, pp. 41–47.
11. All primary sources from 300 B.C. to 300 A.D. are loaded with traces of Nibiruan influence. Look for stories of the "star" and symbols that have eight directions or points; reports of composite entities (especially reptilian); divine children; and divinized adults, such as Caesars, divine kings, and popes.
12. Christ has a higher-dimensional form than the 4D Nibiruans; and when and where Christ attained any power on Earth, it was essential that he be heavily overlayed.
13. James Binney, "The Evolution of our Galaxy," *Sky & Telescope* (March 1995), p. 20.
14. Gordon Michael Scallion, "The Earth Changes Report" (Westmoreland, NH). The basic tectonic model that Scallion is working with is the one that fits the best with my own ability to "see" the activities of the 2D telluric realm. Scallion has published "The Future Map of the United States: 1998–2001," and I agree with his read of the energy fields and timing, but these manifestations may not be physical—they may be *etheric*. Scallion's map and conceptual framework of the Earth changes may actually be a map of land, which holds entities that have become multidimensional according to *The Pleiadian Agenda*! That is, the sections of the United States that are underwater in Scallion's map may just be regions of unconscious people. Whether this map represents the physical or etheric, Scallion is one of the great seers of our times.
15. Morton Smith, *Jesus the Magician* (San Francisco: Harper & Row, 1978), pp. 122–23.
16. Margaret Starbird, The *Woman with the Alabaster Jar* (Santa Fe: Bear & Company, 1993), pp. 176–79.

*Chapter Five: The Story of Goddess Alchemy*
1. Geraldine Hatch Hannon, "Revisioning the Sun and Moon," *The Mountain Astrologer* (April/May 1995).
2. This understanding of negative conclusions about life being the cause of repetitive behavior came to the author through Tom Cratsley of Lilydale, New York. When Tom shared this with me, the Pleiadians literally started screaming that this dynamic was the key to being emotionally stuck on Earth.
3. Sitchin, *12th Planet*, pp. 200–13.
4. Megalithic people understood the metonic cycle and many archeoastronomers have proven that many ancient stone circles were set up to calculate the time of eclipses based on the lunar node return cycle—the metonic cycle. (See note 3, Appendix C.) But why? Since this was obviously so important to megalithic people and since the lunar nodes are so critical for natal readings, I was able to see that the metonic cycle is the key to "Galactic Precipitation" as in Appendix C.
5. Michael Baigent, Richard Leigh, and Henry Lincoln, *Holy Blood/Holy Grail* (New York: Dell, 1982).
6. Wighard Strehlow, and Gottfried Hertska, *Hildegard of Bingen's Medicine* (Santa Fe: Bear & Company, 1988).
7. Frissell, *Nothing Is True*, p. 158.

*Chapter Six: Lucifer's Dilemma and the Power of Anu*
1. Mary Settegast, *Plato Prehistorian: 10,000 to 5,000 B.C. Myth, Religion, Archaeology* (Hudson, NY: Lindisfarne Press, 1990).
2. Joshua XXIV, 26; Judges IX, 6.
3. Sitchin, *Wars*, p. 315.
4. Dan Gill, "How They Met: Geology Solves Longstanding Mystery of Hezekiah's Tunnelers," *Biblical Archaeology Review*, vol. 20, #4 (July/August 1994). This article helped me think it is possible that the visions I got during the channelings of a gaggle of crocodiles under the Temple Mount in Jerusalem might actually have some basis in reality.
5. Clow, *Signet*, pp. 70–79.
6. Comment by Gerry Clow in 1986.

*Chapter Seven: Alcyone Library and Tzolk'in—Keeper of Time*
1. Ralph Abraham, Terence McKenna, and Rupert Sheldrake, *Trialogues at the Edge of the West: Chaos, Creativity, and the Resacralization of the World* (Santa Fe: Bear & Company, 1992).
2. Abraham, McKenna, Sheldrake, *Trialogues*, p. 33.

3. Abraham, McKenna, Sheldrake, *Trialogues*, p. 153.

4. Tony Shearer, *Lord of the Dawn; Quetzalcoatl* (Happy Camp, CA: Naturegraph, 1971), p. 184.

5. Argüelles, *Mayan Factor*, pp. 32 and 148.

6. Argüelles, *Mayan Factor*, pp. 131–48.

7. Clow, *Signet,* p. 180.

8. Steven McFadden, *Ancient Voices, Current Affairs* (Santa Fe: Bear & Company, 1992), p. 61. My count on people at Teotihuacan differs from McFadden's. I was there, and I read the count given the next day in *Novedades*, the main paper in Mexico City.

9. A group of us were doing ceremonies with Hunbatz Men and three of the Dalai Lama's monks in the Yucatan during spring equinox 1995. *Novedades* reported that one million people tried to get into Teotihuacan for the ceremonies. Only a half million got into the temple complex, and the other half million filled all the roads coming to Teotihuacan. Many people were driving cars, of course. The temple complex could have taken in all of them if they had been walking, as in the ancient days.

10. Giorgio de Santillana and Hertha Von Dechend, *Hamlet's Mill* (Boston: David R. Godine, 1977).

11. I had intended to describe the fields of all nine dimensions completely in this book. 7D through 9D have not yet opened to the complete descriptions I accomplished on 1D through 6D, even though I did get a lot of data on 7D through 9D. There are two explanations: It is possible that the first six dimensions are operant fields and the last three are tools for consciousness traveling; tools cannot be described as fields are, but they only can be *used*; or possibly I will be able to describe 7D through 9D in a sequel once the consciousness of all of us as a group ascends.

12. Stewart Myers, *Sky and Telescope*, (March 1995), p. 8. In a letter to the editor, Myers, an amateur astronomer, comments that he observed Io brightening on July 16, 1994, during a cometary impact. Myers wrote this letter because a professional astronomer, Priscilla Andrews, had reported the brightening of Io on p. 30 of the November 1994 issue of *Sky and Telescope*.

13. According to Satya, the Hopi legend of the return of Pahana or the lost brother is the merging of the Andromeda Galaxy and the Milky Way, and I suspect more data will come in on that one.

14. Argüelles, *Mayan Factor*, p. 131.

15. Starbird, *Alabaster Jar*, pp. 176–79.

16. Smith, *Jesus*, pp. 122–23. Smith demonstrates how the Eucharist and transfiguration are typical intense magical practices, and how the purpose of magical practices is to activate the telluric realm.

17. Richard Souther, "*Vision: The Music of Hildegard,*" Angel CD. Hildegard von Bingen, *Hildegard of Bingen's Scivias* (now retitled *Hildegard von Bingen's Mystical Visions*) (Santa Fe: Bear & Company, 1986). Hildegard von Bingen, *Hildegard of Bingen's Book of Divine Works* (Santa Fe: Bear & Company, 1987). Hildegard von Bingen, *Illuminations of Hildegard of Bingen* (Santa Fe: Bear & Company, 1985).

18. Baigent, Leigh, Lincoln, *Grail*, pp. 55–57.

19. The Age of Aquarius is not a New Age idea. The facts are: Earth is an oblate spheroid, the Sun crosses the celestial Equator at a moving point that returns every 25,920 years, and the 12 houses of the zodiac are each 2160 years long. Earth is precessing out of the Age of Pisces into the Age of Aquarius over about 300 years—2010 to 2310 A.D. The qualities of Pisces and Aquarius are both felt during this transition, and the early stages of Aquarian vibrations have been very discernible since the 1960s. The transits of Uranus in Aquarius—1996–2003—and Neptune in Aquarius—1998–2012—will prepare humanity for the Aquarian vibration that really starts at the end of the Mayan Great Calendar and the beginning of the next Mayan Great Cycle, Dec. 21, 2012. The real intensity of the Age of Aquarius has not been felt by humanity since Paleolithic times; this intensity still exists in Magdalenian cave art.

20. Discerning readers will notice that the records are showing very little Nibiruan activity amidst Photon Band incursions, while much activity is reported far away from the Band in the deep Galactic Night during the Ages of Taurus and Scorpio. The channelings of this phase supported the possibility that the Nibiruans can only make short visits when Earth is near or in the Photon Band. Following that line of thinking, we can conclude that the Nibiruans won't be around much in 3600 A.D.

21. Diane Wolkstein and Samuel Noah Kramer, *Inanna: Queen of Heaven and Earth* (New York: Harper & Row, 1983).

22. Earlier in the book, Satya says that women must always be consulted about war on Earth. When women are consulted, war is only allowed when the home is threatened, then both the men and women become warriors of the hearth. The Pleiadians loath war as sport caused by bored humans.

23. Hugh Harleston, *The Keystone: A Search for Understanding* (Bellaire, TX: Uac-Kan, 1984).

24. While I was in Merida in March 1995, the Mexican government polled the Mexicans to see whether they were for or against the Zapatistas, the Maya revolutionary movement primarily centered in the state of Chiapas but networked throughout all of Mexico. The television news and papers reported that 88 percent of the Mexican population support the Zapatistas.

*Appendix A: Astrological Transits 1972 to the End of the Mayan Great Calendar, December 21, 2012 A.D.*

1. Frissell, *Nothing Is True*, pp. 155–64.
2. Argüelles, *Mayan Factor*, pp. 131–48.
3. Barbara Hand Clow, "Harmonic Convergence (Aug. 16) Viewed Astrologically," *Welcome to Planet Earth* (May 1987).
4. UPI, "IRAS Sighting of New Planet," *San Francisco Chronicle* (December 27, 1983).
5. I want to know when the last time Saturn, Uranus, and Neptune were conjuncting in *Capricorn*, since the 1988–91 transits of these planets in Capricorn represent the level of structural forces that can trigger evolutionary shifts on Earth.
6. John Major Jenkins, *Tzolkin: Visionary Perspectives and Calendar Studies* (Garbersville, CA: Borderlands, 1994), pp. 113–47. Jenkins notes that the time between eclipses (caused by the lunar nodes as discussed extensively in Appendix C) is 173 *days* and the time between Uranus/Neptune conjunctions is 173 *years*. The Uranus/Neptune conjunctions near the end of the Calendar are exceedingly influential, since Uranus rules transformation and Neptune rules access to spirit. Jenkins also zeroes in on them as a major factor in the Great Cycles. I work with these conjunctions more as an astrologer than as a Maya researcher, but I find it fascinating that the Aztec Calendar Stone (which establishes the importance of five Great Ages and is the critical leap beyond one—3113 B.C. to 2012 A.D.—opening up Olmec and Maya dating to the 25,625-year cycle, which then synchronizes Maya dating with the precession factor) was carved and set up in the center of Tenochtitlan in 1479 A.D.—the last time before 1993 that Uranus conjuncted Neptune, and a time when this conjunction *also* synchronized with a "Venus Round." The Venus Round synchronizes the 260-day tzolkin, the 365-day Haab, and the 584-day synodical period of Venus, and this synchronization is the basis of the Great Calendar. This data is found in the "Dresden Codex." Jenkin's *Tzolkin* is a priceless contribution exploring the literally astonishing data banks of the Maya calendars.

*Appendix B: Entry of the Solar System into the Photon Band, 1972 to 2012 A.D.*

1. Clow, *Eye*, p. 21. In his introduction to *Eye of the Centaur*, physicist Brian Swimme says the central scientific discovery of the twentieth century was the discovery of cosmic background radiation, which are photons in the microwave region of the electromagnetic spectrum. Perhaps we are getting "cooked" by these photons, but we can't see the fire or feel the heat, just like when food is

microwaved? This may sound silly, but the Pleiadians have always insisted that humans use technology to figure out how unseen processes work. They say we'll drop technology once we become seers. Perhaps microwave processes will turn out to be the key to the photon effect? I think we will be seeing an increasing focus on the invisible regions of the light spectrum by scientists.

2. Tjeerd H. Van Andel, *New Views on an Old Planet: A History of Global Change* (Cambridge: Cambridge University Press, 1994), p. 86.
3. Wence Horak, *Ancient Ecologists,* unpublished manuscript.
4. Channeling with Barbara Marciniak and Barbara Hand Clow, Santa Fe, New Mexico, November 13, 1992.

*Appendix C: Galactic Precipitation: Metonic Cycle of the Fifth World*
1. Clow, *Signet,* pp. 111–28.
2. John Filbey and Peter Filby, *Astronomy for Astrologers* (Wellingborough, England: The Aquarian Press, 1984), pp. 109–16.
3. Gerald S. Hawkins, *Stonehenge Decoded* (New York: Doubleday, 1965), p. 178. Also see the works of E.C. Krupp, Martin Brennan, John Michell, Alexander Marshack, Norman Lockyer, and Alexander Thom.
4. Jenkins, *Tzolkin,* p. 112. Jenkins notes that it has been established that the Maya divided the Ecliptic into 13 constellations (I agree), and if one uses this division, then one double tzolkin (2 x 260 days = 520 days) almost equals the passage of 1 Ecliptic constellation (520 days x 13 = 18.5 years). Therefore 13 double tzolkins nearly equals the cycle of the nodes around the Ecliptic. This level of synchronicity (that I find everywhere in the Calendar—see note 12, Chapter One and note 6, Appendix A) might be the basis of the magnetic aspects of my vision.
5. Argüelles, *Mayan Factor,* pp. 145–48.
6. Considering note 4 of this appendix, astute readers might wonder why I am not using the Maya 13-constellation division for Figure 15? When dividing the Ecliptic for astrological divination, I always use a 12-constellation division because this division offers a psychological analysis of energetics based on *polarity.* I use this because it works! It is comprehensible to many people because it reflects the way they go back and forth psychologically, as they gradually master life. The division by 12 emphasizes the four principal divisions of the solar year—solstices and equinoxes—which the Maya mark in ceremonies at ancient sites that were constructed to mark these times. Most researchers work with the precession of the equinoxes as 12 Great Ages, but the facts are, the constellations seen from Earth can be divided into 12 or 13 or even more! Readers who understand astrology *and* astronomy know that the constellations—roads in the sky where the Sun, Moon, and planets are found—will

completely lose their familiar patterns over long phases of time, since all stars travel at different speeds around the Galactic Center. So, this division by 12 for the wheel reveals polarity and solar factors; and the same time frame—March 14, 1994 to December 21, 2012—could be divided into 13 to synchronize with the Maya zodiac. This would offer a more lunar-based interpretation and would probably offer marvelous numerical and calendrical synchronicities. Also, when I was speaking in New York in April 1995, a student immediately wanted to know why I didn't analyze the south node factor! She was right. This would offer a read on the historical patterns that would get sucked in to be processed March 14, 1994 to December 21, 2012. All of these ideas hold marvelous research potential.

7. Marc Edmund Jones, *Sabian Symbols in Astrology* (London & Boulder: Shambhala, 1978), p. 205.

*Appendix D: The Sirius Star System and the Ancient Records of Orion*

1. Robert Temple: *The Sirius Mystery* (New York: St. Martin's Press, 1977).
2. Musaios, *The Lion Path: You Can Take It With You* (Berkeley, CA: Golden Sceptre, 1988).
3. Barbara Hand Clow, *Chiron: Rainbow Bridge Between the Inner and Outer Planets* (St. Paul, MN: Llewellyn, 1987).
4. Germaine Dieterlen and Marcel Griaule, *Le Renard pale* (Paris: Institut d'Ethnologie, 1965).
5. Temple, *Sirius*, p. 3.
6. Temple, *Sirius*, p. 42.
7. Ken Croswell, *The Alchemy of the Heavens* (New York: Doubleday, 1995), p. 5.
8. William J. Broad, "The Core of the Earth May Be a Gigantic Crystal Made of Iron" (*New York Times*, April 4, 1995).
9. Temple, *Sirius*, p. 14.
10. This channeling integrated a combination of data that exists in Temple's *Sirius Mystery*, the works of Zecharia Sitchin, and myself. This channeling of Digitaria closely resembles pages 35–51 of *The Sirius Mystery*, and as I spoke the words in an altered state, I could "see" a cosmogony that is very similar to what the Dogon also could see and even act out ritually. Even I wonder where this information in my cellular memory comes from. After years of deep research, I only report channeled material that is visual and causes my body to shiver. In my opinion, this is a sign that a channel is actually reading "records" that exists in libraries—in this case the library of Sirius A.
11. Here I cannot resist sharing exactly how my work relates to the research of Zecharia Sitchin. Sitchin's brilliant research is very academic, while mine is very intuitive, although I check it against conventional and so-called noncon-

ventional sources once I access it. Sitchin's Sumerian research is as thorough and impeccable as that of any Sumerian scholar since 1840 who is "academically acceptable." Sitchin has an excellent academic background as a biblical scholar; graduated from the University of London in economics; and is one of 100 scholars worldwide who read Sumerian. His mindboggling findings have been greeted with the most offensive tool of academic judgment—*total silence*—which has been utilized by individuals who dare to call themselves scholars. Sitchin uses only traditional academic methodology, and it is his conclusions that "scholars" fear. When I get historic data that is unknown to me in a past-life regression or a channeling, and later find the same dates and information in original sources, I call that a bingo! In the case of Sitchin, I had read his *12th Planet* in 1976 *before* I got any of my own intuitive data on the Anunnaki or Nibiruans. I first accessed a Nibiruan entity during a past-life session in 1982, and then I accessed various entities on four or five occasions from 1982 to 1988. I published some of my own data on them in Heart of the Christos, and I will continue to get as much data on them as I can, because their impact on us is so huge.

12. Marciniak, *Bringers*. Barbara Marciniak was the first channel that I know of who came up with the term "Living Library" for the biological library, Earth.

13. See *Signet of Atlantis*, p. 90, for an illustration by Angela Werneke of this scene.

14. Ahmed Osman, *Moses: Pharaoh of Egypt* (London: Paladin, 1991), pp.162-73. Here is a case where I channeled information, and then found a startlingly close interpretation later. Mr. Osman sent me *Moses* for potential American publication in 1993 or 1994, but I shelved it because it was out-of-line for Bear & Company. I referred to it after channeling the Akhenaton material in early 1995, and so I feel the data preseted here on Moses and Akhenaton is very accurate, and Mr. Osman's contribution very significant.

15. The cycles of Chiron and Digitaria are 50 years, and so these patterns will play out again, and whether the result is positive or negative depends upon what people choose.

# Glossary

*activation*—energetic awakening of cellular memory of multidimensional consciousness that is triggered by dimensions outside of linear space and time

*alchemy*—alteration of matter by means of the will

*archetypal*—modeling forces in nonphysical dimensions that reside in the subconscious mind. When these forces are stimulated, deep memory contents move into consciousness, evoking great emotion, creativity, and awareness of being manipulated.

*ascension*—the movement upward on the vertical axis of consciousness of any of the four bodies (physical, emotional, mental, and spiritual)

*cellular memory*—knowledge of all time, place, and occurence in the universe that exists in the actual cells of all living things

*chakras*—energy centers of the physical body

*channeling*—use of the physical body, usually in the vocal chords, for communications from entities who are not in body in linear space and time

*chimera*—an entity composed of parts that express its archetypal essence, such as a winged being with wings that connote spiritual flight

*codes*—knowledge imprints from star intelligence, instinct, memory, genetics, and experiences that exist in crystal templates that can transmit their information if they are activated within certain time frames

*collective unconscious*—a vast pool of archetypes with similar themes that seem to exist in all individuals. There is a great deal of ancient lore about star systems and individual stars as the source of these themes, and when humans activate these themes in their lives, often they begin to resonate with the corresponding stars.

*critical leap*—an evolutionary leap that occur when a species evolves to a more complex status

*Earth changes*—Earth responding to consciousness changing form according to thought as well as to environmental factors

*eighth dimension*—structural organization of Earth intelligence known as the Galactic Federation, which is guided by the Orion star system.

*electromagnetic fields*—zones of energy that are created by electromagnetism

*electromagnetism*—magnetism or attraction that is developed by electrical currents. The magnetic force is directly proportional to the strength of electrical charging.

*elementals*—metallic, nuclear, chemical, and mineral intelligences of the second dimension

*emotional body*—the body of consciousness in the human that is emotional and can be felt and influenced even though it is invisible to most people

*End Times*—a belief that time will eventually end or that a huge attractor is pulling human awareness to an end resolution or apocalpyse

*etheric*—a nonphysical realm of subtle vibrancy that can be accessed by transduction out of the etheric into feelings that can be decoded. It is one of the most important sources of intuition, and the etheric is where fourth-dimensional archetypal forces locate, and that is why they can be *felt*.

*feelings*—the nonphysical vibrations of humans that resonates to the fourth through ninth dimensions

*fifth dimension*—the love vibration of Earth that is guided by the Pleiadians

*first dimension*—the iron-core crystal in the center of Earth that is gravity

*four bodies of consciousness*—the physical, emotional, mental, and soul bodies that reside in the self and that focus and delineate the various modes of experience

*fourth dimension*—the polarized realm of archetypal forces that interact with Earth and are guided by the Anunnaki of Nibiru

*force*—strength or motion that creates change

*future*—past memory that is still potent enough to impulse your behavior now

*Gaia*—all the bodies of Earth consciousness and all the force fields they create in the universe

*Galactic Night*—location of the solar system in the Milky Way Galaxy when it is not traveling in the Photon Band

*geomantic activation*—deliberate alignment by shamans with the telluric realm of Earth to create energy and feelings that facilitate an enhanced alignment with Gaia

*geometric field*—spaces, places, and forms that are created in Earth's field by Sirian creative-thought processes. Solidification of this force can be seen in all Earth crystalization processes, and it is also seen via synchronicities.

gravity—the first dimension of any system that generates a vertical axis of manifestation out of itself. Gravity is the densest field of any created form; it draws all parts of its form to itself, and it is conscious.

*hologram*—a three-dimensional image made on film that is created by the interference pattern resulting from the collisions of a split laser beam. If light is shined on that image, it can be projected into any space. All third-dimensional reality is actually holographic; its form is organized out of duality and light. Holograms are also the method by which fourth-dimensional entities project visions into linear space and time.

*impulsed*—the projection of ideas or desires into any intelligence

*karma*—unprocessed actions, feelings, thoughts, and desires that hold energy and impulse repetition continually until they are clarified

*kundalini*—subtle electromagnetic energy that flows in body channels and coalesces in the chakras

*laser*—light amplification by stimulated emission of radiation. We *see* holograms by means of radiation or energy emitted in waves or particles.

*lens*—a device for directing or focusing anything; energy for obtaining clarity

*light*—intelligence

*light precipitation*—higher-dimensional intelligence that drops into linear space and time

*Making Home*—consciously locating self in linear space and time by being so conscious of the four directions that all dimensions and realities are totally accessible. Also called *grounding*.

*merge*—two or more forces becoming unitized

*metaphor*—a more accessible thought or idea used as an example to convey an idea that is difficult to understand. Through the metaphoric expression of an idea, the multidimensional attributes of this idea can be made available. Metaphors are the essence of Pleiadian communication; they link fifth-dimensional intelligence into linear space and time.

*miasms*—antiparticles that concretize into etheric mass in the physical body that hold memory of disease patterns that can be activated by feelings

*monad*—the kernal within self that contains cosmic intelligence

*morphic*—having a form

*morphic lightfields*—vehicles of all intelligence in the universe

*morphogenetic fields*—the essential ideas of lifeforms that replicate organic life

*multidimensional*—composed of many dimensions or fields of realities that change according to density; whether they are subtle or solid depends upon their vibratory rates, and whether they can be apprehended depends upon the vibratory sophistication of the perceiver

*Net*—the structure of apocalyptical fundamentalist belief systems that the World Management Team employs to slow down vibratory rates of thought. This causes consciousness to lose subtlety and become more dense, until all realities solidify and there is no more movement.

*ninth dimension*—unitized reality that interweaves all of the most subtle frequencies. This plane of vibration is a library of all that exists in a realm; and for Earth, the ninth dimension is the Galactic Center that is guided by the Enochians.

*photon*—light

*photon stars*—stars that exist eternally in galactic information highways, which cause them to generate out spirals of light that capture other stars and create systems of stars in galaxies. These are galactic nexus points that keep the galaxy from rotating out of form. They have not yet been discovered by science.

*photonic information highways*—the communication linkage system of any galaxy that is seventh dimensional with its form arising out of pure thought

*portals*—locations on the surface of Earth where second dimensional or telluric lines or tubes are sourced. By activating telluric intelligence in these locations, multidimensional forces can be accessed. Also, portals are entry points into the physical body where telluric intelligences guard against invasion into the body; these portals are the source of healing by shamans, such as psychic surgeons. Not yet known to science.

*power places*—portal zones

*reality splitting*—dividing worlds by means of intelligences who choose to vibrate according to dense or subtle frequencies

*resonance*—occurs when essences that vibrate in different dimensions are on the same wave length; this is how different worlds and dimensions are linked

*second dimension*—telluric realm between the central iron-crystal core of Earth and the surface of Earth where elemental forces exist

*seer*—person that has the capacity to recognize nonphysical energy in an experiential way

*seventh dimension*—lines of communication for pure thought. For Earth, the seventh dimension is the galactic information highways of light, the photon bands, that are guided by the Andromeda Galaxy.

*sixth dimension*—the lightbody form of the third-dimensional solid world. All physical objects are ideas that reside in the sixth-dimensional library, and through its thinking process, light geometrical forms are generated that create realities. For Earth, this realm is guided by the Sirius star system.

*solar initiates*—shamans who communicate with the intelligence of the Sun, which is linked to other stars and to the Galactic Center

*subtle-energy fields*—forcefields that are not physical

*superconscious*—a capacity of humans to access high degrees of multidimensionality

*telluric*—natural electromagnetic forces of Earth

*Temple of Light*—the Sirian light geometrical form of Earth

*transduction*—reception of a wave in one form that is changed into another form; a phone, for example, receives sound, transduces it to electrical signals, then transduces it back into a person's voice

*vortexes*—portals in the physical body that access multidimensional fields

*wave resonance*—the force that holds stars in place in stellar systems or stars existing in spirals out of photon stars

*web*—interconnecting links of intelligence pathways

*whirlwinds*—powerful swirling forms of fourth-dimensional archetypal forces that pull a person's third-dimensional sense of self out of place

*World Management Team*—individuals in the third dimension who are controlled by the Anunnaki, who impulse them to carry out plans that benefit Nibiru and not Earth. All individuals working in Team agencies—such as in the Vatican, secret societies, banks, governments, school systems, the medical system, and many businesses—are agents of the Annunaki, unless they are conscious of Anunnaki vibrations and do not carry out their plans. In recent days, the World Management Team has been calling itself the New World Order.

*Zero Point*—the reversal of time existing between 1 B.C. and 1 A.D.

# Index

Abraham, 7, 84-90, 91, 95, 100, 102, 187-88

Abraham, Ralph, 204

Acropolis, 169-72

acupuncture, acupuncturist, 56, 83

*Ahau Can*, 50

AIDS, 17-18, 166

Akhenaton, 63

alchemy, alchemist, 17, 23, 36, 39, 56, 125-26, 129, 135-36, 139, 145, 147-53, 165, 175, 182-84, 186, 190, 225-27

Alexander the Great, 122-23

allopathic medicine, 82, 82, 94, 101, 139, 157

Andromeda Galaxy, 109, 120, 122, 128, 164, 210, 241

aneurysm, 11, 77-84, 89, 201

angels, 103, 158, 172-90

antiparticles, 43, 44, 49, 67, 222

Anu, 7, 10, 24, 85-90, 94, 175, 177-90

Anubis, 22, 39, 91, 96-98, 109, 211, 224-29

apocalypse, 20, 84-85, 134, 165, 183, 205, 225, 243-44

Aquarius, Age of, 7-9, 13, 17, 25, 27, 36, 47, 49, 125, 159-60, 165, 167, 193, 203, 225, 229, 240

Argüelles, José, 48, 204-05, 224

Aries, Age of, 88, 137, 229, 238, 240

Ark of the Covenant, 85, 103, 188

aromatic oils, 139

ascension, 24, 45, 79, 103

Ashtar Command, 94

Atlanteans, Atlantis, 18, 74, 233

asteroids, 29, 142

astrology, 6, 8, 17, 23, 30-31, 47, 69, 117, 126, 143-47, 175, 194-201, 212, 236 (also see Appendix A)

Avebury, 62, 65

awakening, 78-79

Aztecs, 49, 205, 224, 239, 241

Babylonians, 123, 176

Bach, 13, 98

Bach Flower Remedies, 139

Bakker, James, 15

Beethoven, Ludwig van, 36, 39, 64, 98

Berkeley, George, 16, 19, 42

Bessell, Friedrich Wilhelm, 47

birds, 97-99, 103, 107, 110, 174, 232

blood, 6, 10, 20, 37, 52, 56, 72, 104, 106, 146-57, 165-66, 195, 125-27, 236, 241

body postures, 69, 96

bodywork, 56, 69, 72, 78, 139

Bohm, David, 82

Bosnia-Herzegovinia, 19, 57, 72, 151, 155, 167

Branch Davidians, 55, 176

Caesar, Julius, 120-23, 158, 229

cancer, 51, 53, 58, 79-80, 82, 101

Cancer, Age of, 235

canopy, 70-76, 87, 200, 207, 218, 227

carbon-based biology, 35, 115-16

Cathars, 126

CAT scan, 89, 100

cellular memory, 3-8, 35, 83, 105

chakra, 14, 69-76, 96, 106

Cherokee, 47, 66

Chicken Little, 16, 43

Chiron, 29, 54-56, 225

Chosen People, the, 121, 123, 190-91, 226

Christ, 3, 10, 12-13, 25, 67, 118, 120-30, 150, 157-61, 165, 224-29, 240, 243

city cultures, 88-90, 93

Clinton, Bill, 161, 172, 184

codings, 61, 64, 67, 85, 97-98, 103, 112,

129, 141, 150, 154-58, 166, 183, 189,
    193, 201, 214, 227, 232
comet (Shoemaker-Levy), 99, 104, 137,
    141-42, 157, 210, 236, 142
conception, 59-60
Conquistadores (Spaniards), 20, 50, 224,
    239, 241
Cortez, Hernando, 50
Cosmic Party, 3, 5, 9, 14, 18, 22, 36, 211,
    244 (also see Appendix C)
Cosmic Restart Button, 120, 130
critical leap, 46-47, 54, 56
crocodile, 107, 111, 192, 193-201
crop circles, 66, 92
cryogenic freezing, 60

dandelions, 55
Darwin, Sir Charles, 113
daykeepers, 5-6, 47
Dionysus, 158, 227
Dogon, 91, 108
dolphins, 211, 224
Dome of the Rock, 113
Draco, 109
DNA, 18, 74, 110, 116-17, 215, 225

Earth changes, 16, 19, 23, 64, 141-42,
    148, 151-52, 214, 234-35
Earth core crystal, 26, 28, 38, 67, 69-76,
    78, 112, 129, 161-67, 184, 213-14, 240
Ebola virus, 17, 188
ecliptic, 8, 39 (also see Appendix C)
Egypt, 61-62, 90-93, 111-13, 121-22, 158-
    61, 178, 187, 193-201, 224
Einstein, Albert, 84, 87, 188
electromagnetic fields, 25, 43, 107-08,
    110, 137-38, 236
electron, 43-44
elementals, 28, 34, 51, 57, 66, 67, 69-76,
    79-84, 90, 93, 100, 102, 131, 145, 151,
    153, 155-07, 162, 214-15, 217, 218,
    222, 226
emissions, 142-43

emotional body, 14, 30, 34, 44,-45, 52-53,
    61, 67, 69, 71, 84-90, 95, 102, 138-47,
    150, 212
End Times, 36, 45 (also see Appendix C)
Enki, 189
Enoch, 7, 10, 15, 36, 102-04
equinox, 6, 37-38, 143, 214, 233, 244
etheric, 74, 138-39, 141, 205, 216
Eucharist, 124-25, 158, 225-27
Exodus, 178

fiber optics, 138, 223
Fifth World, 39
fructarians, 155-56
fundamentalism, 15, 55-57, 94, 242-44

Galactic Center, 4-9, 22, 28, 31, 36, 41, 45,
    48, 61, 74, 102, 105, 147, 165, 213, 241
Galactic Federation, 10, 32, 94, 99-100,
    160, 178-79, 181, 184, 186, 206, 220,
    226, 233-35, 241
Galactic Night, 6-9, 18-19, 22, 25-76, 91,
    109-10, 115, 133, 160, 162, 209, 214
Galactic Precipitation, 38 (also see
    Appendix C)
Galactic Return (225 million years), 30,
    49, 105
Galactic Synchronization Beam, 49
*Galileo* (satellite), 104
Garden of Eden, 17, 20, 24, 37, 44, 112,
    157, 164, 195, 234-7, 241
genetics, 18, 116-17, 179, 185, 187, 189,
    233
geomantic grids, 62
Ginko, Newt (Newt Gingrich), 161
Gnostics, 126, 128
Goddess, 9, 12, 15-16, 21, 37, 58, 135-36,
    158, 165, 187-89, 225, 235-38
gold, 126, 145-47, 178, 186
gravity, 25, 42, 162
Greece, 158, 169-72, 195, 237-38
Gregorian Calendar, 121
Griscom, Chris, 87

Guatemala, 5, 153
gurus, 155, 186

Halley, Edmund, 47
Hand, GWH, 47-48
Harmonic Convergence, 9, 35, 38, 48, 204-05
heart attack, 100
Hebrews, 120-21, 192-93, 195-201 (see also Appendix D)
Hesse, Paul Otto, 47
Hildegard von Bingen, 156, 166, 183, 227
Hitler, Adolph, 56-57
holocaust, 16, 56-57
hologram, holographic, 3, 20, 82, 108, 132, 213
homosexual, 69-70
Hopi, 164, 195
Horus (Seth), 30, 189, 225
Hume, David, 16, 19, 42

Ica, Stones of, 107
Ice Age, 23, 65, 230-36
immune system, 44
implants, 79-80, 89, 172
Inanna, 236-37
indigenous peoples, 8, 45-46, 48, 52, 65, 88, 126, 141, 156, 162, 166, 186, 189, 192, 214-15, 229-44
inner child, 55
Inner Earth, 37, 94
Inquisition, 226, 241
in vitro fertilization, 60
Io, 210
Iraq, 151
Isaiah, 7, 10, 191-201
Israel, 113, 121, 123, 196, 198

Jenkins, John Major, 5, 39, 49
Jews, 120-23, 128, 191
Julian Calendar, 120
Jupiter, 29, 99, 104, 120, 122, 136-37, 141-42, 167, 196

*ka*, 61, 69-76, 226, 233, 237
Kemp, Shirley, 47
Khem, 113, 193-201
Kirlian photography, 170
Kom Ombo, 7, 193
kundalini, 22, 48-49, 59, 61, 67, 71, 104, 106-13, 128, 155, 157, 162, 175, 184, 189, 216, 136-37, 230

laser, 20, 108, 132
lens, 195-201, 223
Leo, Age of, 5, 23-24, 27, 65, 148, 232, 234-35
light-encoded filaments, 35
lizard, 7, 154, 156, 193-201
Lucifer, 7, 15, 55, 95, 172-90
lunar manifestation techique, 140-42, 193-201
lunar nodes (metonic cycle), 141, 147 (see also Appendix C)

Magdalene, Mary, 7, 10, 12, 15, 129, 158, 225-27
magic, 49-52, 108, 129, 138, 154
magnetism, 43
Making Home, 63-69, 163, 185, 207 (see also Appendix C)
Marciniak, Barbara, 9, 16
Mars, 29-30, 116, 136-37, 141-42, 196, 199-200
miasms, 126
Mayan Calendar, 4-6, 17, 36, 39, 42, 47, 49, 66, 86, 203-07, 208, 228-44 (see also Appendix A)
McKenna, Terence, 204
megalithic, 55, 185
Meier, Billy, 41
Men, Hunbatz, 47-48, 105
Mercury, 29, 115, 208-09
mental body, 44-45, 61, 67, 166
miasms, 44-45, 53, 55, 65-66, 69, 74, 79, 82, 112, 222
Michell, John, 30, 98

Middle East, 14, 86
Milky Way Galaxy, 4, 7, 18-19, 26-39, 41,
     49, 64, 105, 120, 128, 133-34, 180,
     210, 212, 220, 229-44 (see also
     Appendix C)
Millennium, 45, 53, 241, 244
Mind Control, 116, 119, 146, 148, 167,
     181, 209, 213, 225, 239
monad, 81-84, 149
money, 83, 148
monotheism, 188, 196, 239
moon, 6-7, 32, 41, 136, 147, 196, 200,
     231, 236, 241
Mormons, 126
morphogenetic fields, 3, 16, 28, 59-61,67,
     111, 115-17, 120, 132, 204, 209
morphic, 34, 169-73, 192, 204
Moundbuilders, 126
Mt. Moriah, 192
Mosaic, Moses, 123, 128
Munro, Wendy, 7

Neptune, 29, 138, 220
Net, 3-4, 7, 11, 23, 16, 19, 59, 125, 128,
     130, 133, 173-74, 182, 227, 243
New Age, 121-22
New York City, 65
Nibiru, 29-30, 34, 85-86, 89, 90-96, 106,
     109, 112, 116, 120-22, 128, 142, 160,
     188, 207, 226, 232-44 (see also
     Appendix D)
Nile (Blue Nile), 61-62, 90, 157-61, 194-
     201, 237
nuclear, 52-53, 58, 80, 84-86, 94, 96, 102-
     04, 187-89
Oklahoma City bombing, 55, 176
orgasm, 14, 18, 52, 57-61, 95, 104, 112,
     162, 237
Orion, 9, 62, 113, 191-92, 194, 198-99,
     201, 220, 233, 235, 241 (see also
     Appendix D)
Osiris, 62, 158-59, 225
ozone, 38

Palenque, 48-49, 224
Paleolithic, 6, 65
Pandora's Box, 36-37, 52
past-life regression, 19, 69, 139
Pentecost, 226
physical body, 44-45, 51, 67, 78, 81, 83,
     87, 95, 101, 122, 131, 162, 205, 217,
     236, 228
Pisces, Age of, 3, 13, 44, 125, 158, 175,
     206, 226, 229, 233, 242-44
plants, 157-61, 195, 225-27, 231
*Pleyades, Calendario del Tzek'eb o*, 47
Pluto, 29, 27, 101, 141, 160, 220
plutonium, 87, 99-101, 105
polar shift, 8, 23, 64, 86, 91, 142, 148,
     234-35
polarity, 29, 42, 58, 64, 86, 95, 102, 138,
     143-45
polytheism, 196, 240
Pope Sylvester, 242
Popol Vuh, 5-6
portals, 36, 73-74, 152
positronium atom (positrons), 42-43, 222
precession, 5-6, 27, 47, 49, 105
Pribram, Karl, 82
Prozac, 21
puppet masters, 22
Pyramid, Great Pyramid, 8-9, 65, 91-92,
     96, 223-34, 234-35

quantum leap, 42-43
Quan-Yin, Amorah, 61
Quetzalcoatl, 30

radiation, radioactivity, 44, 51, 52-53, 81,
     85-90, 93, 95-104, 173, 187-88
records, 152
Renaissance, 183
Rennes Le Chateau, 62
reptilian, reptiles, 30, 49, 55, 105-120,
     144-47, 193-201, 237
Roman Catholic Church, 15, 123-25, 128-
     30, 156, 241-44

Roman Empire, 121-25, 158, 186, 210, 241, 246
Rwanda, 14, 19, 67, 72, 149, 151, 167

sacred geometry, 8,14, 16, 34, 99, 227
Saturn, 29
Schele, Linda, 5-6
Scorpio, Age of, 5, 65, 230
secret societies, 104, 108, 183-84, 186, 189, 191, 193, 201
serotonin, 21
shar, 124
Shearer, Tony, 204
Sheldrake, Rupert, 204
silica-based biology, 35, 107, 115-16, 195
Simpson, O.J., 14, 52-53, 64, 167
Sirian/Pleiadian Alliance, 91, 169, 182, 224
Sirius A, 32 (also see Appendix D)
Sirius B, 34, 91-92 (also see Appendix D)
Sitchin, Zecharia, 74, 91, 185
snake medicine, 49-52, 66, 106, 109-10, 119, 155, 238
Sodom and Gomorrah, 16, 93-94, 103, 166, 188, 210
Solà, José Comas, 47
solar priests and priestesses, 179, 187, 234
solar wind, 98, 138, 141 (also see Appendix A)
Soloman's Temple, 122, 187, 189, 192-93, 197
solstice, 3, 5-6, 17, 38, 45, 143, 214, 233
species regeneration, 110-12, 118-19
sphinx, 9, 36, 92, 170, 197-98, 224, 134
Spider Grandmother, 11, 34, 118-19
spiritual body, 44, 61, 67
Stanley, Robert, 47
storytellers, 232
subliminal communications, 108
subtle glands (endocrine), 93, 145-46, 169-72, 234-35
Sumerians, 85, 92, 121-23, 177-80, 186-87, 237
supernova (1987), 48-49, 102, 173

Taurus, Age of, 5, 65, 158, 164, 237
television, 22, 45, 72, 107, 148, 166
Teller, Edward, 84
telluric, 8, 10, 18, 28, 51-53, 94, 110, 129, 151-52, 95, 226-27, 233, 240
Temple, Robert, 42
Teotihuacan, 62, 205, 240
Tezcatzlipoca, 30, 39, 224
Tinker Toys, 35
totem animals, 118
transduction, 74, 92, 101, 157
*Tzolk'in*, 136, 203, 206-07, 209, 211, 222, 224, 229-44

Ur, 85
uranium, 84-90, 93, 99-101, 187-88
Uranus, 29

van Gogh, Vincent, 4, 39, 54
Vatican, 85, 128, 183, 217, 241, 243
Vega, Vegans, 99-101
Venus, 29, 37, 115, 117-18, 120, 199-200, 209
vertical axis, 74, 161-67, 213-22, 224, 241
Vietnam War, 151
violence, 148-49, 155-56, 173, 200, 203, 225
virtual reality, 15-16, 21
visual cortex, 222
vortexes, 10-11, 32, 90, 123, 127, 144, 233
Votan Pacal, 49

web, 11, 62, 133, 208
will, 150, 178
World Management Team, 9, 23, 92, 94, 102, 108, 112, 118, 200, 208, 225 (also see Appendix D)

Yahweh, 22, 84, 189, 198, 201

Zero Point, 3, 9, 11, 120-130, 157-58, 226, 229, 233, 238, 240-41

# About The Author

Barbara Hand Clow is an internationally noted astrologer, ceremonial leader, author, and editor. This present work is a synthesis of her trilogy, *The Mind Chronicles*, which is an exploration of 300,000 years of human consciousness on Earth; and her research in two astrological books, *Chiron: Rainbow Bridge Between the Inner and Outer Planets* and *The Liquid Light of Sex: Understanding Your Key Life Passages*.

This book describes advanced multidimensional perceptual skills that are becoming available to all people on Earth now, and Barbara's ability to describe these skills opened during a series of initiations she conducted with Hakim Nazlit Essaman of Giza, Egypt, in the Great Pyramid. The culmination of this series was a ceremonial alliance between the beings of the Sirian and Pleiadian star systems, which was accomplished with Barbara, Hakim, and Wendy Munro of Australia in 1994. This alliance, and all the teachings that made it possible, was filmed by David Drewry with the support of Jeanne Scoville, and the video showing these initiations is titled "The Nine Initiation on the Nile."

Barbara will be teaching the techniques for integrating these advanced states of human potential at sacred sites and in workshops. Due to her heavy schedule, she is not available for individual astrological readings.

For workshops taught by Barbara Hand Clow in the United States, watch the schedules of New Age conferences and teaching centers; and for ceremonial workshops in foreign countries, contact:

Power Places Tours
24532 Del Prado
Dana Point, CA 92629
(800) 234-8687

For videos on Barbara's initiatic teachings in England and Egypt, and for all other information, contact:

Barbara Hand Clow
P.O. Box 600E
Lakeville, CT 06039